Eco-Warriors, Nihilistic Terrorists, and the Environment

Eco-Warriors, Nihilistic Terrorists, and the Environment

LAWRENCE E. LIKAR

Praeger Security International

 PRAEGER

AN IMPRINT OF ABC-CLIO, LLC
Santa Barbara, California • Denver, Colorado • Oxford, England

Library of Congress Cataloging-in-Publication Data

Likar, Lawrence E.
   Eco-warriors, nihilistic terrorists, and the environment / Lawrence E. Likar.
     p. cm. — (Praeger security international)
   Includes bibliographical references and index.
   ISBN 978-0-313-39236-8 (alk. paper) — ISBN 978-0-313-39237-5 (ebook)
1. Ecoterrorism. 2. Environmentalism. 3. Environmental policy. 4. Green movement. I. Title.
  GE197.L55 2011
  363.325'93337—dc22   2010052071

ISBN: 978-0-313-39236-8
EISBN: 978-0-313-39237-5

15 14 13 12 11   1 2 3 4 5

This book is also available on the World Wide Web as an eBook.
Visit www.abc-clio.com for details.

Praeger
An Imprint of ABC-CLIO, LLC

ABC-CLIO, LLC
130 Cremona Drive, P.O. Box 1911
Santa Barbara, California 93116-1911

This book is printed on acid-free paper ∞

Manufactured in the United States of America

Contents

Preface   vii

Acknowledgments   xi

1   Introduction   1

2   The Environmental Nexus to Terrorism   8

3   The Basic Concepts of Terrorism   33

4   The Terrorist Mindset   56

5   The Radical Environmental Movement: Eco-Warriors
    or Terrorists?   75

6   Nihilistic Terrorists: Fanatical Cells, Lone Wolves,
    and Hybrid Groups   107

7   The Risk of Terrorism   137

8   Security Planning for Environmentally Linked Terrorism   165

9   Conclusion   194

Appendix A: Attack Tree: Destruction of Urban Fixed Facility   199

Appendix B: Maps   201

Notes   207

Bibliography   245

Index   265

Preface

Today, the natural environment is threatened by many forces, the most powerful of which is mankind. We are aggressively destroying this essential part of our own existence. The wounded state of the environment is now apparent in many regions of the world and has attracted the attention of individuals and organizations who either want to protect it or further exploit it for personal advantage. Terrorists, loosely defined as individuals or groups who use violent acts to achieve various social or political goals, now have a nexus with the natural environment.

This book deals with this dangerous nexus and the security methods that can protect individuals and organizations from the actions of those terrorists who perceive the natural environment as a motivational cause, vulnerable target, or powerful weapon. The natural environment, human violence, and security are subjects that have engaged my interest for most of my adult life. These interests led to and were enhanced by my choice of careers. First, an early career in the U.S. Army's Special Forces, where training and operations in wild regions of the world developed my appreciation of the importance of wilderness to human existence. Then, a lengthy career in the Federal Bureau of Investigation (FBI) taught me more about the human capacity for violence and our ability to commit and then justify horrific crimes than all my years of formal education. My current career as an associate professor of justice, law, and security at La Roche College in Pittsburgh, Pennsylvania, has given me the opportunity to study and advance my knowledge in the areas of violent crime, terrorism, and security. This book is the culmination of individual experience and academic study.

PURPOSE AND SCOPE

To accomplish my purpose in this work, the subjects of climate change and resource scarcity, environmentally linked terrorism, and the disciplines of risk assessment and security planning were integrated with the goal of achieving a synthesis of the subject matter.

The research approach was predominately qualitative. It encompassed literature reviews, legal and policy analyses, analyses of various media accounts and online sources of information, and historical research to develop a genetic interpretation of environmentally linked terrorism. Some quantitative research was conducted through a secondary analysis and application of data concerning terrorism. The data was drawn from the following repositories of terrorism data: the American Terrorism Study, the Worldwide Incidents Tracking System maintained by the National Counterterrorism Center, the National Consortium for the Study of Terrorism and Responses to Terrorism (START), and the FBI's series of reports— *Terrorism in the United States, Terrorism 2000/2001,* and *Terrorism 2002–2005.*

Judgments made and hypotheses offered are based on my belief in their validity. The issue of the validity of judgments made in the field of terrorism studies is somewhat controversial. The social sciences have become heavily oriented toward a quantitative methodology in the belief that truth about social phenomena can only be discovered through mathematical analysis of empirical data that is objective and scientific. From the historical and legal perspective, probable truth can also be determined without statistical evidence. Some researchers can accomplish this through studying qualitative data and judging its validity. This judgment is based not upon a guess or hunch, but on "the common grounds derived from life: general truths, personal and vicarious experience (which includes a knowledge of previous history), and any other kind of special or particular knowledge that may be relevant."[1] Admittedly, this approach has a strong subjective element and lacks the desired objectivity of a more science-based approach. However, I have some doubts about the degree of validity of a scientific approach to understanding human beings and their various cultures. Both qualitative and quantitative approaches offer their own insights and have their own limits to understanding. Of course, in regard to my presentation of the environmental crisis, I relied on the best scientific evidence available in formulating my beliefs and to support my offered conclusions.

The eclectic approach adopted for this book, which was designed to be as appealing to a general audience as to scholars and security practitioners, is used to advance the following proposition: the nexus between the increasingly vulnerable environment and the tactic of terrorism threatens our national security, the security of other nations, and the security of multinational corporations operating throughout the world. Those institutions and individuals responsible for the security of the nation's people and infrastructure should prepare for this threat, whose attacks are difficult to predict yet will certainly occur and may result in terrible consequences for human beings and the environment that gives us life.

CHAPTER MAP

The book focuses on three main subjects: the natural environment, terrorism, and a behavioral science-based approach to security. Chapter 1 is an overview of the book. In chapter 2, the current environmental crisis is described. Chapters 3, 4, 5, and 6 cover the basic concepts of terrorism, examine the terrorist mindset and analyze those specific terrorists who perceive the environment as a motivational cause, powerful weapon, or target to be destroyed. Chapters 7 and 8 discuss the methods and problems of risk assessment as applied to terrorism and explain a strategic approach to security planning that emphasizes external environmental scanning techniques and detection-based countermeasures to prevent terrorist attacks.

Acknowledgments

This book would not have been written without the assistance and encouragement of several special individuals to whom I offer my heartfelt thanks.

The genesis of this book began when a literary agent, Brian Romer, contacted me about my possible interest in writing a book about environmental terrorism. His encouragement and assistance led me to submit my book proposal to Steve Catalano, senior editor for Praeger Security International, who liked my proposal and then motivated and guided me throughout the writing process.

The idea of the book became a reality when Barbara Bencsics, my friend and faculty secretary, agreed to be my administrative assistant for the project. She handled every task with professionalism and aplomb while motivating me with her own enthusiasm for the project.

My colleagues at La Roche College were always encouraging and excused my distracted manner and absences from meetings and college functions. I am particularly indebted to the following colleagues: La Verne Collins, library administrator, whose ability as a researcher and whose rapid response to my requests was amazing; subject matter experts Barbara Herrington, psychology, and Gail Rowe, biology, who reviewed the substantive content of several chapters and furnished valuable editorial suggestions; Chris Abbott, director of La Roche College's Writing Center, who edited several chapters of the book and significantly improved its clarity; and Josh Bellin, Paul LeBlanc, and Ed Stankowski, all published authors, who offered encouragement, advice on writing a book, and editorial suggestions throughout the writing process.

I also requested advice and critiques on the substance of the book from top professionals in the fields of environmental and wildlife preservation, municipal policing, and security planning. These experts, through a strange coincidence, were also my oldest, closest friends. John Toppenberg, the director of the Alaska Wildlife Alliance, has always influenced my thinking about wild animals and the importance of their survival to our own. In this case, he also offered a unique perspective, as an environmental activist, on the mindset of activists who become radicalized to the degree that they commit acts of terrorism. Joseph Hoffman, chief of police in a suburban Pittsburgh community, former federal agent, and fellow judoka, furnished a municipal police perspective on terrorism. David Mahon and Frank Coffey, both retired FBI special agents and current high-level security planners for private industry, reviewed the risk assessment and security planning chapters of my book. As former fellow SWAT team members and sailing buddies, they had no problem critiquing my efforts, and I have always trusted their judgment.

My greatest resource during this project has been my wife, Georgiana, whom I thank for allowing me to write this book and for her assistance in typing, fact-checking, and finding reference material for me during the entire process.

Finally, I thank my dog, Danny, for his constant companionship and for encouraging me to get out of the house and take a walk in the woods with him.

CHAPTER 1

Introduction

Night and day he [the revolutionary] must have but one thought, one aim—merciless destruction.

—Sergey Nechaev

Thus using fire to aid an attack is enlightened, using water to assist an attack is powerful.

—Sun Tzu

If Sergey Nechaev and Sun Tzu were resurrected, they would understand the ideas expressed in this book. Nechaev's *Catechism of the Revolutionist*, written in 1869, captured the radicalization process that can turn social activists into nihilistic terrorists.[1] Sun Tzu's classic, *The Art of War*, written in the fifth century B.C.E. during China's warring states period, recognized the importance of strategic planning and understood that the natural environment could be used as a weapon of attack.[2] This book explores the dangerous nexus of terrorism and the deteriorating natural environment and presents a strategic approach to security planning that detects and prevents environmentally linked terrorist attacks.

THE ENVIRONMENTAL CRISIS

The world is in the prodromal stage of an environmental crisis.[3] This crisis has been described by the Pulitzer Prize–winning journalist Thomas Friedman as "the world . . . is getting *hot, flat,* and *crowded*. That is, global warming, the stunning rise of middle classes all over the world, and rapid population growth have converged in a way that could make our planet dangerously unstable."[4] In analyzing the linkage of the environmental crisis to terrorism, there are four critical terms: *environment, ecosystem, greenhouse gases*, and *environmental threats*.

Environment, the broadest term, refers to the sum of all external factors, both biotic (living) and abiotic (nonliving), to which an organism is exposed.[5] The environment includes the *built environment*, which refers to those areas and structures affected or built by human beings, such as dams and buildings,[6] and the environment's *natural resources*, which refers to those living and nonliving objects that are "found in or arising from nature, as opposed to being produced by human labor."[7]

The term *ecosystem* refers to "the organisms and physical factors in a specific location that are interrelated through the flow of energy and chemicals to form a characteristic trophic structure."[8] Ecosystems are dynamic and interdependent. If human actions or natural events damage or destroy one resource in such a system, cascading effects can occur and may result in resource scarcity in other areas of the ecosystem. For example, a forest is a dynamic and interdependent system. If too many trees are removed from a forest for economic reasons, the results can include loss of soil, destruction of the diverse plant and animal life that is part of the forest ecosystem, and a decrease in the forest's contribution to the reduction of global warming.[9]

As dynamic systems, ecosystems have a constant flow of energy and chemicals. This includes *greenhouse gases* (GHG), which are positive climate forcings—things that are imposed externally—that warm the climate. GHGs derive from both human and natural sources. They include carbon dioxide (CO_2), methane (CH_4), nitrous oxide (N_2O), ozone, halocarbons, and water vapor. Water vapor does not force the climate but is considered a feedback process that amplifies the warming forced by the other GHGs. Increases in carbon dioxide, which are strongly contributed to by human actions, are the largest climate forcing contributing to global warming.[10] The excessive amount of anthropogenic GHGs is possibly the largest threat to the global environment, but it is not the only one.

A review of the relevant literature concerning *environmental threats* consistently identifies the most serious threats as climate change, destruction or loss of natural resources, toxic pollution, and human consumption and impact. These environmental threats are linked together, which increases their danger and makes them difficult to ameliorate. Currently, climate change has generated the most emphasis, and it is the current focus of numerous efforts to foster a combined international response to stop or mitigate it.[11]

Unfortunately, the nations of the world have not acted effectively as this ecological crisis progresses. Abundant evidence exists for the proposition that some components of this crisis have already reached either the acute stage (e.g., deforestation and wetlands destruction) or the chronic stage (e.g., air pollution with toxic chemicals and pesticides).[12] This failure to be productive derives from a lethal combination of individual indifference, business resistance, and political venality. Powerful business interests, such as the coal and oil companies, have and will continue to work against environmental legislation that could reduce corporate profits. Their lobbyists, which far outnumber lobbyists for alternative energy use, have the power to kill, weaken, or delay needed regulations.[13] An example of this process is the ongoing congressional resistance to enhanced air pollution controls. This occurs despite the fact that "deaths in the U.S. from air pollution alone are conservatively estimated at 130,000 per year."[14] Further, in 2007, the United Nations released the Intergovernmental Panel on Climate Change (IPCC) report that concluded the planet is becoming warmer, which could have deleterious effects on our climate. The conclusions of the IPCC have been undergoing heavy criticism from conservative talk radio and cable news commentators; business groups, like the U.S. Chamber of Commerce; and some members of the U.S. Congress. This resistance and criticism may obstruct governmental efforts to pass legislation that could ameliorate the negative effects of climate change.[15]

While elected officials procrastinate, there is some awareness and concern among the general U.S. populace concerning climate change and environmental fragility. Nevertheless, the acrimonious debate between environmental activists and climate change naysayers will continue. The IPCC's finding that anthropogenic warming could cause abrupt changes in our environment that may be irreversible should, but may not, cause increased concern on the part of the general public.[16] Awareness is growing in many sectors of the world's populace, however, that the natural environment is endangered and that all facets of our current existence may change for the worse. Comprehensively examined in chapter 2, the critical societal issue of this century will be environmental change and national and world government's corresponding response to it. Such change, if not effectively addressed, will serve as both a protective motivation for environmental activists and a catalyst for terrorist activity.

Historically, terrorism has always been linked to actual or perceived societal problems. These problems sometimes act as powerful forces that engender fanatical behavior in those individuals who are predisposed to extremism. The radicalized individuals whose motivations are either the defense of the environment or the use of the environment as a weapon or target of attack are today's ecoterrorists and nihilistic terrorists, respectively.[17]

THE TERRORISTS

On September 8, 2009, Daniel Andreas San Diego—animal rights activist, fugitive from justice, and alleged terrorist—was portrayed on FOX TV's *America's Most Wanted* program as the first domestic terrorist to be placed on the FBI's Most Wanted Terrorists list. Unlike Osama bin Laden, also on the FBI's list, San Diego is not wanted for murder but for the 2003 bombing of the offices of two companies he believed were connected with live animal testing. San Diego's alleged actions did not conform to the standard "no harm to human or animal life" tactics of U.S. ecoterrorist groups, as one of the bombs placed by San Diego incorporated nails that upon detonation became potentially deadly, 100-mph projectiles. In addition, an e-mail posted by "The Revolutionary Cells—Liberation Brigade," who claimed credit for the attack, threatened harm to the families of company employees. *America's Most Wanted* also displayed photographs of San Diego's ominous tattoos, which portray buildings, a foliaged valley, and a lone tree—all in flames.[18]

When a writer deals with the subject of terrorism, the definition of the term is always an issue, and environmentally linked terrorism is particularly problematic. The term *terrorism* does not have a universally accepted definition.[19] Historically, the general concept of the tactic or strategic approach that today we call terrorism (the subject of chapters 3–6) involved the intentional commission of violent acts for the purpose of engendering fear in an identified target that may or may not have been the physical victim of the attack.[20]

The tactic was first named during the French Revolution, when the Jacobins would refer to their intimidation and execution of suspected counterrevolutionaries as "the terror." British statesman and writer Edmund Burke brought the term into English when he referred to the French revolutionaries as terrorists.[21]

Today, *terrorism* has varied definitions, but most official and scholarly ones contain the following elements: (1) the use of violence, (2) political objectives, and (3) the intention of sowing fear in a target population.[22] Given these elements, terrorism may occur in multiple manifestations, and this book focuses on two types that, although environmentally linked, are distinctly different. The first, *ecoterrorism*, has been defined by the FBI as "the use or threatened use of violence of a criminal nature against innocent victims or property by an environmentally oriented subnational group for an environmental-political reason, or aimed at an audience beyond the target often of a symbolic nature."[23]

The second, *environmental terrorism*, can refer to either an attack against persons or property using an element of the natural environment (e.g., water or fire) as a weapon or an attack directly against a natural resource (e.g., forest or ocean reef) for the purpose of instilling fear in a human target.[24]

San Diego represents a bridge between two antithetical types of terrorists whose actions have a nexus with the environment. The decentralized cells and individuals who claim credit for terrorist attacks under the banners of various environmentally linked groups, such as the Earth Liberation Front (ELF) and the Animal Liberation Front (ALF), are part of the radical environmental movement (REM), which champions the protection of the natural environment, including wild and imprisoned animals.[25] Other groups and individuals adhere to Nechaev's edict and recognize no moral limits in regard to tactics and targets. For these groups and lone individuals, the environment, because of its increasingly recognized value and fragility, can serve as a justification for murder, a target to attack and a weapon for destruction.[26] Based upon motivational and ideological factors, these two types are characterized in this book as ecoterrorists, who often identify themselves as eco-warriors, and nihilistic terrorists, respectively. Although normally distinct types dissected in separate chapters of this book, it is possible for individual members or cells of ecoterrorists, who regard themselves as principled eco-warriors that do not intentionally harm human or animal life, to evolve into pure ecoterrorists who engage in serious acts of property destruction and violent crimes against persons. Some ecoterrorist groups and individuals have the potential to develop the nihilistic ideology of "merciless destruction" as advocated by Nechaev. If this were to occur, it would result in the use of tactics that include the intentional and incidental taking of human life. San Diego and the group who claimed credit for the bombing could be harbingers of a more violent type of ecoterrorism that justifies using violent acts against persons as a tactic to meet what it perceives as an enhanced threat to the survival of natural ecosystems.

Although the FBI and its Joint Terrorism Task Forces have recently had great success in preventing, arresting, and convicting both ecoterrorists and nihilistic terrorists,[27] it is extremely unlikely there will be an end to such terrorism. As law enforcement increases pressure on these terrorists, the groups will only further decentralize and shrink in size. Some individuals will leave these groups but will continue to commit terrorist acts alone—as "lone wolves." Lone wolf terrorists have always existed on the fringes of extremist social movements. These types of terrorists are prone to a nihilistic ideology that needs to "cleanse the world by destroying it" and that believes a better world will be constructed with their ideology.[28]

The law enforcement and intelligence agencies of the government and the private security forces of organizations and multinational corporations will increasingly face the challenge of environmentally linked terrorism. Part of the response to such terrorism should be the use of a comprehensive security planning methodology that incorporates the natural and built environments into both the risk assessment and strategic planning processes.

SECURITY PLANNING

In most areas of the world, terrorist attacks are characterized as low probability but high criticality events. The risk of such attacks is difficult to reliably quantify because of their random and rare nature.[29] On a macro level (state and national government), the possibility of extreme consequences resulting from a successful attack is a sufficient impetus for comprehensive planning. Such planning should include the deployment of an extensive array of physical countermeasures and intelligence initiatives. This book takes both a macro-level and micro-level (nongovernment organizations and multinational corporations) perspective on security planning. Its standpoint is that of an organization's security planners. The macro-level planning process is based on a public-private cooperative partnership. The risk assessment and security planning chapters examine the use of external environmental scanning as a necessary component of the strategic planning process. This scanning process includes the identification of certain regions of the world that are dangerous because of their vulnerable environment and the presence of terrorists. Terrorist threat analysis and detection-oriented countermeasures are emphasized as cornerstones of security planning for environmentally linked terrorism.

The book's approach to planning methodology and countermeasures is tempered by the author's experience-based belief that defensive security measures will defeat only a limited percentage of terrorist attacks. Any argument to the contrary should first consider the 1996 Atlanta Summer Olympics' Centennial Olympic Park bombing, which was committed by Eric Rudolph, a lone wolf, antiabortion terrorist who is currently undergoing life imprisonment in the federal maximum-security prison in Florence, Colorado.

Knowing that the Olympics are always a possible target for terrorists, the Atlanta security planning team utilized the following assets and practical exercises, at a total cost of $117 million: 30,000 police and security experts, more than 2,000 explosive experts, 40 bomb-sniffing dogs, 1,000 video cameras, 200,000 ID badges, a computerized command center (consisting of 100 computers), and practical exercises for a release of sarin gas, a massive bomb attack, and a plane hijacking.[30]

In his attack, Rudolph utilized only three large pipe bombs wrapped with nails and stuffed inside a military field pack. He intended to funnel the blast with a metal plate that he also inserted in the pack. Rudolph penetrated the security net and placed the timer-controlled explosive pack under a bench. Fortunately, the pack was accidentally knocked over, and at detonation the full force of the explosion was diverted. The explosion caused two deaths and over 100 injuries. Rudolph had left the scene before the explosion and was not arrested for the bombing and resultant murders until 2003.[31]

Relying solely on a defensive security plan when faced with potential attacks by adaptable threats like terrorists is a mistake. This book's intelligence-based planning methodology incorporates a behavioral science approach to security that focuses on the terrorist adversary's beliefs and pre-attack actions in order to detect planned attacks and make them impossible to implement.

Terrorists, even lone wolves and small cells, can be rational actors. As such, they can often be deterred by security countermeasures that are based upon an analysis of behavioral characteristics of specific terrorist types, and are selected to increase the risk and/or effort to conduct a successful attack. This rational appraisal of risk and effort was demonstrated by terrorist cell leader Mohamed Shnewer, who was recently sentenced to life imprisonment for his involvement in a plot to murder soldiers stationed at Fort Dix, New Jersey. Results of an FBI investigation revealed that Shnewer, after he had conducted surveillance, rejected plotting a similar attack on Dover Air Force Base in Delaware. He believed the security at the base made an attack too difficult.[32]

The security professional responsible for protecting an organization's personnel and property from a terrorist attack must not rely solely on a defensive strategy. The security planning process should integrate both detection and defensive countermeasures in order to stop attacks by terrorists who regard the natural environment as a cause, target, or weapon for an attack. In planning that security, remember the following advice from Sun Tzu: "Thus it is said that one who knows the enemy and knows himself will not be endangered in a hundred engagements."[33] The information contained in this book and the principles set forth help the security planner both understand enemy terrorists and know how to defeat them.

CHAPTER 2

The Environmental Nexus to Terrorism

The life of all of mankind is in danger because of the global warming resulting to a large degree from the emissions of the factories of the major corporations.

—Osama bin Laden

The use of terrorism across historical periods usually occurs in conjunction with a perceived political, cultural, or religious problem or conflict. The endangered status of the natural environment may be the most important issue facing our world today. Worldwide, individuals and organizations who perceive environmental degradation as threatening the survival of themselves, their families, or their nation will take action, and such actions can take a variety of forms. The most threatening form of action is terrorism, and it is probable that life-altering changes to the natural environment will cause it to increasingly serve as a nexus to terrorism, both domestically and internationally.[1]

Our modern perspective on the environment as endangered has gone through several stages. Concerns about the detrimental effects of environmental pollution and the rapid growth of the human population were expressed initially by a small activist segment of the population in the 1960s. In the 1970s, public concern for the environment increased in response to high-profile tragedies, such as Lake Erie being declared dead because of industrial contamination and the discovery of toxic dumping at Love Canal in Niagara Falls. The 1970s saw the creation of the Environmental Protection Agency and the first Earth Day in the United States. While the 1980s were a time of decreased environmental initiatives by the Reagan administration (1981–89), they were also a time of increased research into various at-risk environmental components, as well as growth in grassroots activism. The increase in concerned activism was justified by scientific studies and created a renewed interest in the environment in the 1990s that culminated in an organized, worldwide movement to combat climate change in the 21st century.[2] Today, climate change, environmental degradation, and the disastrous effects of human actions on the environment are prominent social issues, but they are also a source of controversy among disparate segments of the world's populace.

CLIMATE CHANGE

The main factor driving the current interest in the environment is a consistent message from prominent scientific organizations that climate change is already affecting ecosystems, freshwater supplies, and human health, and although the most severe impacts of climate change can still be mitigated, the time available for such action is rapidly running out.[3] The current focus on climate change began with a scientific discovery that revealed the fragile nature of our atmosphere's protective cover.

In 1985, scientists discovered a hole in the ozone layer over the Antarctic. The stratospheric ozone layer protects us from the effects of harmful UVB radiation, and its depletion was caused by man-made chemicals called chlorofluorocarbons (CFCs), which were used in refrigeration systems. This discovery catalyzed interest and reinvigorated research on the effects of human-initiated environmental change on the atmosphere, and both national and international organizations significantly accelerated research on environmental influences on our planet's wavering health.[4]

The United Nations Environment Program (UNEP) and the World Meteorological Organization (WMO) were prominent among international organizations, and, in 1988, these organizations joined to establish the IPCC. The IPCC was tasked with examining the state of scientific knowledge concerning climate change, determining the impact such change was having on the world, and formulating appropriate response strategies. The first IPCC report was issued in 1990 and confirmed a scientific basis for the negative effects of greenhouse gases on the Earth's climate. IPCC research led to the subsequent adoption of the United Nations Framework Convention on Climate Change (UNFCCC) in May 1992, and the numerous signatory countries, including the United States, agreed to decrease their nations' GHG emissions according to the steps specifically stated in binding protocols. In 1994, the convention's protocols entered into force, and today, 165 nations have signed and ratified the convention. The Conference of Parties (COP) is the convention's ultimate authority. The IPCC issued a second assessment report in 1995, and the COP held its second session in July 1996, with a third session in December 1997, all for the purpose of signing the Kyoto Protocol, which set new emission-reduction targets for signatory nations. In 2001, the IPCC issued the third assessment report (TAR), and the fourth, and current, assessment report on climate change was made public in 2007. The fourth IPCC report (AR4) is today regarded as the gold standard in regard to climate change and has published the following definitive and vital conclusions:

- "Warming of the climate system is unequivocal" based upon observed increases in global air and ocean temperature averages, widespread melting of snow and ice, and rising global average sea levels.[5]
- In observing the effects of climate change, the IPCC had "high confidence that natural systems related to snow, ice, and frozen ground are affected." One empirical example of the effects of global warming is evident in ground instability in permafrost regions of the world.[6]
- Human activities since 1750 have caused a marked increase in global CO_2 concentrations, dramatically exceeding pre–industrial age levels going back thousands of years. Between 1970 and 2004, concentration levels of CO_2 increased a striking 70 percent, and "there is a very high confidence that the global average net effect of human activities since 1750 has been one of warming."[7]
- Anthropogenic warming over the last 30 years has "likely" influenced the observed changes in global ecosystems.[8]
- On a regional basis, "non-climate factors (such as land use change, pollution, and invasive species) are influential."[9]
- "Anthropogenic warming could lead to some impacts that are abrupt or irreversible, depending upon their rate and magnitude of the climate change."[10]

Scientific opinion is virtually unanimous that our societies need to adapt to and mitigate the effects of climate change. While Arctic temperatures have increased much more than in other regions, it is clear the planet's landscape and unique ecosystems are rapidly changing. What's more, our current global level of CO_2, the highest level in 650,000 years, continues to rise. The scientific consensus is that our world has been hotter during the last three decades than at any other time period since 1600 C.E. Undoubtedly, human lifestyles are changing the climate. The primary indicator of change is the continuing increase in atmospheric levels of CO_2 and other GHGs over the past 100 years. Before the Industrial Revolution, there was a crucial balance between the naturally produced CO_2 emitted into the atmosphere and the amount the Earth's plants and other "sinks" absorbed. The burning of fossil fuels over the past century, however, has released additional CO_2 into the atmosphere. Today, roughly half of the anthropogenic excess is still capable of being absorbed by oceans, plants, and trees; the rest continues to accumulate in the atmosphere.[11]

Despite the litany of changes, the major concern of climate scientists is the possibility of abrupt climate changes at the regional level. For climate scientists, abrupt is defined as within a decade. The Dustbowl in the U.S.

heartland during the 1930s was an example of such abrupt change, and it displaced hundreds of thousands of people living in the Great Plains. It is difficult for humans and ecosystems to adjust to any change, even more so when it is abrupt. It is clear that reducing GHG emissions is central to preventing abrupt climate change, and such reductions demand formidable national and international political will, innovative and costly technology, and deeply committed human effort.[12]

Ecosystem Damage

The Earth's warming is exacerbating disruptions in the world's ecosystems. The starting point throughout the world for measuring temperatures by thermometer was 1850. Since that year, the average temperature on the surface of the planet has risen 1.3°F. Along with this rise in temperature, sea levels have also risen, and the water cycles of supply and demand are out of balance. Our oceans are acidifying as they absorb more CO_2, and the carbonic acid formed by CO_2 and seawater harms marine life, including corals. Climate change has also instigated weather extremes, such as drought and flooding, that affect our ability to grow food crops reliably, and, with the exception of water, nothing is more important to our survival than food.[13]

When changes to global ecosystems affect our food supply and initiate other environmental problems, there is cause for concern about our world's political stability. The rise in the world population of humans and the concurrent increase in their overall standards of living have led to greater demand for resources that are already declining because of environmental degradation. Deforestation and field desertification have led to crop shortages and to populations shifting toward coastlines. Increased reliance on fishing as a food source, however, has caused the collapse of some important fisheries, such as the Great Banks cod and North Sea herring industries.[14]

Additionally, our current system of agriculture inflicts extraordinary ecological costs because of its overemphasis on livestock and the creation and maintenance of the habitats necessary for their survival. In fact, this overemphasis on livestock habitat is one important cause of the deforestation of large areas, and deforestation, an ongoing process in many regions of the world, is believed to have been a key factor in the decline of several past societies. This emphasis on livestock habitat also causes water pollution, and the excessive use of grain to feed livestock results in scarcities for humans. This agricultural system also affects climate through animal emissions of CO_2, methane, and nitrous oxide.[15]

Clearly, the world also has chronic pollution problems, for human-generated pollution is causing grave damage to our ecosystems. Plastics, toxic chemicals, pesticides, caustic substances, and smoke cause increased societal ills, such as cancer, birth defects, and reproductive illnesses.[16]

CONTRARIAN ARGUMENTS

Despite the overwhelming evidence of climate change, ecosystem disruption, and the overall degradation of our environment, the extent and cause of such damage remain a source of political and social controversy. For example, in a 2010 issue of *U.S. News and World Report,* Republican senator James Inhofe, a member of the Senate Committee on Environment and Public Works that issued a minority staff report accusing climate scientists who believe global warming is affected by human-generated GHGs of acting with a political agenda, dismisses the findings of the IPCC as flawed. Inhofe goes on to state that in regard to the scientific consensus concerning global warming, "there is no consensus—except agreement that there are significant gaps in what scientists know about the climate system."[17] In one of his 2009 *Newsweek* magazine columns, George Will, a conservative political and social commentator, expounded on his belief that the whole idea of global warming is based on computer modeling that could be flawed because of false assumptions.[18]

However, this controversy should not be unexpected. In the 1960s, for example, Rachel Carson's work on the harmful effects of pesticides, popularized through her book *Silent Spring,* led the chemical industry and its political supporters to accuse her of being a hysterical radical, possibly even a communist, whose ideas would destroy America's farms and the U.S. system of agriculture.[19] Today, affected industries and their political supporters have concentrated on both climate change and the human contributions to such change. Sadly, however, climate change deniers often have political and economic incentives to deny that the Earth's climate is changing in any manner except, of course, the normal cyclical variations that have always existed in global temperatures. Climate change deniers also assert that it has never been proven that human intervention is a major factor in global warming. Moreover, an array of their final arguments maintain that the severity of global warming's effects are unknown, will be less severe than predicted, or will occur far in the future, and that the way to prevent these effects (if they do occur) will be through technological inventions. It seems the goal of all climate change deniers is to discredit any political or social movement that would restrict the usage of carbon-based resources, even government-initiated restrictions.[20]

The energy industry has been particularly concerned about any type of aggressive governmental program designed to reduce carbon pollution. The power of this industry to influence legislation is demonstrated by the 2,810 Washington, D.C.–based lobbyists working daily to influence climate change legislation. Of those nearly 3,000 lobbyists, only 138 are advocates for alternative energy sources. The energy companies who employ the majority of these lobbyists also fund research studies dedicated to supporting the still-unsubstantiated arguments that today's climate change is nothing more than the normal temperature variation that has always occurred on the planet and that passing laws that cap emissions will destroy the economy. In fact, the 2009 goal for energy industry lobbyists was to stop Congress from passing legislation that would impose significant restrictions on carbon pollution before the start of the international climate summit at Copenhagen in December 2009. The lobbyists won. Cap and trade legislation was not enacted into law, and the international summit failed to produce a treaty. At Cancun, Mexico in December 2010, the United Nations climate change conference achieved, by most accounts, modest success, but again failed to produce a treaty. The Cancun Agreement was an improvement over the Copenhagen Accord and allowed the participating nations another year to decide if they would extend the 1997 Kyoto Protocol.[21]

The United States has the largest per capita influence on worldwide climate change, an influence that would seem to demand a concomitant responsibility. Unfortunately, some corporations with a powerful economic interest in carbon-based energy have used their influence to sway the public and its elected representatives. Their goal is to delay or stop any governmental action that would affect the current standard for GHG emissions significantly. This objective was demonstrated at the Copenhagen conference, where the president of the United States and members of his administration attempted to reach an agreement on climate change with other nations. While the president was acting to reduce the problem of climate change, four Republican members of the House of Representatives were also in Copenhagen with the expressed purpose of countering the administration's argument in regard to climate change.[22] Unfortunately, climate change deniers, supported by industry money, have had great success in manipulating those portions of the U.S. population who have neither the time nor the inclination to actually study the volumes of scientific reports that support the reality of human-influenced climate change.

PUBLIC OPINION POLLS

Between 2007 and 2008, Gallup polls in 128 countries showed that 24 percent of the world population had never heard of global warming, while 61 percent knew about the problem. In the United States, where 97 percent of the population is aware of climate change, only 63 percent of that 97 percent believed global warming was a serious personal threat. (These results were similar to a poll taken in April 2006 wherein only one-third of Americans predicted global warming would pose a serious threat in their lifetimes.) Only 49 percent of Americans believed rising temperatures were the result of global warming. The only other first-world nation with this degree of disbelief in how global warming affects rising temperatures was Great Britain. Remarkably, another Gallup poll shows that nearly half of all Americans (41%) believe the seriousness of global warming is exaggerated.[23]

Although Americans are not highly concerned about global warming, they are worried about water pollution, air pollution, and toxic waste. In the 2009 Gallup environment survey of American opinions on the importance of eight environmental problems, global warming was number eight while water pollution and toxic waste were the biggest concerns. In addition, the poll revealed that only 37 percent of Americans were greatly concerned about the extinction of plant and animal species. The overall trend in concern for the eight environmental issues, except for a slight increase in concern for drinking water quality, has actually declined since 2000.[24]

Despite political and public controversies over the environment, there has been a growing movement among academics, military officials, and civilian members of the U.S. national security establishment to examine the link between environmental problems and conflicts around the world. This movement is part of our national security strategic planning and policy formulation.[25]

CONFLICT AND THE ENVIRONMENT

Historically, the natural environment has always been involved in human conflicts, from disputes over fences all the way to war and terrorism. In the classical world, armies looked to and relied upon elements of the natural environment, such as fire, earth, and water, as sources for the production of weaponry and other methods of defense. For example, earth was used to form embankments, water was used for moats and to flood opposing warriors, and fire was a component of siege weapons. Thucydides's *History of the Peloponnesian War,* for instance, recounts the Athenians' defeat at Aegitium, where the victorious Aleutians killed many escaping Athenians by burning the woods down around them. The Athenians also used the elements by destroying water systems that furnished drinking water to cities under siege.[26]

The Bible itself is rife with scenes of conflict involving environmental weapons and targets. For example, Moses parted the Red Sea to escape, and then he destroyed the pursing enemy by closing the sea and drowning the Egyptian army.[27] Similarly, the legendary Chinese general Sun Tzu recommended fire as a weapon to burn trees and brush. He also viewed water as a good attack weapon, advising that water be diverted to flood opposing military forces.[28] In the sixth century B.C.E, Sennacherib, the ruler of Assyria, attacked the Babylonians and flooded their city by diverting water from its canals. One hundred years later, the Assyrians seized water wells as a tactic of their war strategy against Arabia. They also poisoned water wells with human and animal bodies to induce epidemics.[29]

Closer to home, during America's Indian wars of the 19th century, our national and state governments seem to have encouraged soldiers and settlers to attack the environmental resources of various Indian nations. Indeed, this tactic may have been an implicit part of national and state strategies to eliminate the Indians from desirable territory. For example, the Cherokee nation was destroyed because their land and the resources it contained were valuable and desired by non-Indian settlers in Georgia. Later, during the Indian wars on the western frontier, the U.S. Army destroyed entire buffalo herds to gain victory over those Indians who resisted incursions into their territories. The Indians relied upon the buffalo not only for food, but also for many other functions integral to Indian culture. The destruction of the buffalo helped crush the will of the western Indians, leading to their eventual surrender.[30]

In the modern era, our ability and willingness to harm the environment as a military tactic or strategy has become much greater and more dangerous to our existence. For example, during the Vietnam War, the United States targeted heavily foliaged areas with chemical attacks to destroy a natural resource used by the Vietnamese to avoid detection. The harm these attacks caused to the natural environment and to human beings, including American soldiers, is still not fully tabulated. This use of defoliant chemicals in Southeast Asia led, in 1977, to the United Nations Convention on the Prohibition of Military or Any Other Hostile Use of Environmental Modification Techniques.[31]

The UN's prohibition on destroying the environment had its first test in 1991 during the first Gulf War. Iraq's military forces, while retreating from Kuwait under fire, released enormous amounts of oil into the Gulf and blew up hundreds of Kuwait's oil wells, blackening the sky with toxic smoke. Prior to the attack, Iraq's dictator, Saddam Hussein, had said he would destroy the oil wells if the allied forces invaded.[32] According to Daniel Schwartz in a 1988 article, the destruction of the oil wells was the genesis for the use of the term *environmental terrorism*. President George H. W. Bush's administration began referring to Iraq's actions as environmental terrorism and Hussein as an environmental terrorist. The term was rapidly adopted by the media, was analyzed by political and legal scholars, and soon entered society's lexicon of terms that are widely used but whose exact meanings are not clearly delineated. Schwartz defined the term as the threatened or actual use of force against an environmental target with the objective of instilling fear of harm to the environment in a primary target (generally, the civilian population or governmental forces). The goal was to coerce the primary targets to accede to the demands of the terrorist group or individual.[33]

Another form of environmental terrorism occurs when environmental assets are manipulated or destroyed as a means of attacking a primary target to instill fear in the target for the purpose of coercing the target or secondary targets to accede to the goals of the terrorist group or individual. In this situation, the environment is used as a tool or weapon. An example is an attack with a biological toxin or agent.[34]

In both forms of environmental terrorism, the primary target is not the environment, but the terrorist group has decided that destruction of the environment is a viable tactic. It is also possible for the two forms of environmental terrorism to be combined. The best example would be a "fire weapon" using the biomass of a forest. This tactic could destroy humans but could also cause secondary targets to fear not only the loss of human life but also the loss of the forest.[35]

The development of the environmental terrorism concept was integrated into and aided the development of the environmental security concept. Thus, in the United States, President Clinton created the position of deputy under secretary of defense for environmental security, and the first appointee to that position soon perceived environmental terrorism as a threat falling within his purview.[36] Terrorism with a nexus to the environment has become one of the forms of conflict that threaten environmental security on both a national and international basis. Thus, the two forms of environmental terrorism join ecoterrorism, which has as its goal the protection of the environment (discussed in chapter 1), as the representative forms of terrorism that interact with the environment. The role of the environment as a nexus with terrorism will be examined from four perspectives: (1) as an environmental security component of our national security strategy, (2) as a weapon or tool of terrorism,[37] (3) as a symbolic target of terrorism for the purpose of engendering fear of its destruction, and (4) as a valuable, threatened resource to protect by committing acts of terrorism or to use as a justification for terrorist attacks against the U.S. government and multinational corporations.

ENVIRONMENTAL SECURITY

Today, there is an increasing awareness that the environment is vulnerable to being manipulated in violent conflicts that can affect the national security of any nation state. This strategic national security view of how the environment can be used to support violent conflicts, including terrorism, looks at the issue from both a domestic and international standpoint, recognizing that one nation's environmental problems can quickly spread beyond its borders to other nations. This viewpoint acknowledges the increasing importance of the environment's increasingly anarchic global commons (i.e., the components of the environment that are not under the control of any nation) because of their potential impact on national security.[38]

The United States's environmental security movement is grounded in the environmental activism of the 1960s, an era of increased social consciousness initiated both by the civil rights movement and the Vietnam War. Rachel Carson's book *The Silent Spring* raised environmental awareness, which engendered concern and popular support for protecting the environment. The importance of oil to the welfare of the United States, the increasing influence of the Organization of Petroleum Exporting Countries

(OPEC), and the 1973 oil crisis made Western nations aware that their life-styles could now be dramatically affected by resources withheld by other nations. In 1980, President Carter and his national security advisors recognized oil, a natural and finite resource, as vital to our nation's security. The United States could not supply all its oil needs and feared losing access to Middle Eastern oil. This vulnerability influenced our strategic approach to the Middle East, causing President Carter to issue what has become known as the Carter Doctrine—a warning that the United States would go to war over oil, even if that valuable resource was in the possession of another country.[39]

In 1986, with the meltdown at the Chernobyl nuclear facility, the ongoing use of nuclear power as an energy resource came under scrutiny as a new threat to human existence. The meltdown caused widespread harm to a wide swath of territory in the former Union of Soviet Socialist Republics (USSR) and widespread anxiety to nations with nuclear power plants. It also demonstrated how one nation's actions could affect the welfare of all living organisms.[40] In the late 1980s and through the 1990s, academic researchers published articles linking the environment to national security. Jessica Tuchman-Mathews's seminal article "Redefining Security" was both influential and prophetic in regard to our current posture toward using the environment to improve or weaken national security. For Tuchman-Mathews, unaddressed environmental decline ultimately leads to conflict; thus, national security forces must be alert to the impact environmental shifts and shortages can have on a nation's economic health. Environmental decline can function as a trigger for a pervasive poverty that leads to instability in governmental institutions. From local police and fire services to national infrastructures, such as social security and defense, structural breakdowns often result in conflict. Tuchman-Mathews called for a broadening of our concept of national security to include the natural environment, its resources, and human influences on their respective health.[41]

The nonacademically oriented members of the U.S. government and the more literate members of the general public were made aware of environmental security issues with the publication of journalist Robert Kaplan's 1994 article "The Coming Anarchy." Drawing upon the chaotic social conditions in West Africa, Kaplan posited that environmental degradation, combined with poverty, weak governments, and access to cheap weapons, could lead to anarchic conditions and violent conflicts in many regions of the world.[42]

The environmental security concept has engendered many academic debates. One thread of the controversy involves assessing the adequacy of current research methodologies used to determine the validity and strength of the links between environmental shifts and national conflicts, especially as those links compare to other conflict-related variables. The degree of likelihood that an environmental factor could be a direct cause of conflict rather than a dependent variable was also debated in academic journals.[43] Although academic arguments reflected some disagreement over the exact impact of (and on) the environment in relation to violent conflict, the United States and other world governments began to link the two—the environment and potential conflict—as issues involving national security.[44]

This nascent environmental security movement can be seen in the U.S. national political structure, beginning in 1991 with President George H. W. Bush, who made the environmental threat part of national security planning.[45] The subsequent Clinton presidency, particularly Vice President Al Gore, incorporated several environmental issues into foreign affairs policies, culminating in the administration's support for the IPCC by signing the UNFCCC, commonly referred to as the climate treaty. The vice president also actively supported the Kyoto Protocol. Without congressional support, however, the U.S. weakness in fostering international environmental initiatives became obvious, and though Vice President Gore signed the Kyoto agreement on climate change, it was never brought before the Republican Congress so certain was the administration that it would not be approved.[46]

The position taken by the United States in the 1990s on the natural environment's importance to national security was influenced by dominant academic theories proposing a causal relationship between damage to the environment and violent conflict. The work of Peter Gleick, for example, explores the historical and present-day relationship between violence and access to fresh water.[47] Homer-Dixon and the Toronto group developed extensive case studies on environmental resource scarcity and its impact on intrastate stability. According to Homer-Dixon, the research and case studies he relied upon show that when environmental stress worsens, there is an increased likelihood of environmentally linked conflicts. For Homer-Dixon, the key independent variable that affects conflict will not be environmental degradation but a lack of "renewable resources." However, this scarcity of resources is unlikely to be a direct cause of conflict or "resource wars"; instead, it is a variable that could interact with other independent variables to cause conflict, both subnational and diffuse.[48]

Currently, the academic position on linkages between the environment and conflict are still emerging. There is consensus, however, that climate change and the probability of its negative influence on the environment leading to conflict cannot be assessed without factoring in other intervening political and economic variables. Although nations not experiencing conflict can still lack security, the academic literature views conflict as the key factor in determining the status of a nation's security. The issue of conflict and its complex linkage to the environment has seized the interest of all affected parties.

From the standpoint of national security professionals, the environment—specifically climate change and the availability and health of natural resources—can precipitate armed conflict, and thus they are linked. These professionals believe climate change is important for its potential effect on valuable natural resources.[49] According to UNEP, since 1990, 18 violent conflicts have been fueled by the exploitation of natural resources. In addition, at least 40 percent of the world's interstate conflicts occurring over the last 60 years have been linked to quarrels over natural resources. What's more, UN professionals believe there is a high probability of additional conflicts developing because of natural resource issues, as the probable consequences of accelerating climate change, such as water scarcity, could aggravate existing societal stressors, thus causing these new conflicts.[50]

National security and environmentally focused organizations, both governmental and private, have asserted that environmental concerns should be integrated immediately into security planning.[51] These organizations identify non-state entities, such as terrorists, as among the potential actors expected to engage in environmentally charged conflict. Terrorists will seek out unstable, war-torn, and weak countries to be used as recruiting grounds and safe havens. It should be noted that other diverse, non-environmental causes of national and communal insecurity, such as religious, racial, and ethnic discrimination, have increased in the third world. To these varied threats, we can now add environmental degradation as a contributing factor to social instability and conflict. In a sense, environmental vulnerability multiplies the effects of existing social problems, increasing the possibility that social problems will engender forms of armed conflict that threaten a nation's security.[52]

U.S. National Security Strategy

To study national security connections to both the environment and terrorism, the best window is the U.S. government's published National Security Strategy (NSS). The NSS is the president's statement outlining the priorities and goals of the executive branch of government, the various threats faced by the United States, and the administration's plan both to promote the goals and counteract the threats. In 1986, congressional legislation required, for the first time, that the president of the United States state publicly the administration's strategies both to protect the security of the United States from foreign and domestic threats and to foster the nation's vital interests at home and abroad. Since then, each president has been required to submit to Congress an annual report on the administration's NSS.[53]

The nation's first NSS was issued by President George H. W. Bush in 1991. President Bush first made protection of the environment part of our national security plan by placing the following statement in the NSS: "The environmental depredations of Saddam Hussein have underscored that protecting the global ecology is a top priority on the agenda of international cooperation—from extinguishing oil fires in Kuwait to preserving the rain forests to solving water disputes to assessing climate change."[54] NSS 1991 also had a separate subsection titled "The Environment," which stated that environmental problems are often international and are already "contributing to political conflict."[55] NSS 1991 was a revolutionary document in its recognition of the symbiotic relationship between a healthy natural environment and a strong national security policy. Almost 20 years later, the decline in the health of the world's natural environment was one of the critical issues facing the Obama administration.

President Barack Obama issued his administration's first NSS in May 2010, 17 months after taking office. In the first paragraph of his introduction to the NSS, he identifies the dangers America faces as international terrorism, deadly technologies, economic upheaval, and climate change. He then presents as one of the steps to advance his NSS the development of energy sources that will not damage our planet and that can fuel our industries while eliminating our need for foreign oil. He explicitly lists what he views as the challenges of our times: violent extremism, nuclear weapons proliferation and the existence of unsecured nuclear materials, and climate change.[56]

In his personal introduction, President Obama clearly states the importance with which he views the overriding environmental issue of climate change. This is instructive because the body of the NSS, as a document prepared by the president's National Security Council, represents a consensus viewpoint on the many security challenges facing our nation. The 2010 NSS was written by policy realists, not idealists, with a focus on America's national interests as the primary driver of America's national security strategy. The drafters begin their overview of the NSS with the words: "To succeed, we must face the world as it is."[57] This statement announces the realistic perspective of the planners. Political realism versus idealism has been described by former national security advisor Brent Scowcroft as follows:

To me, realism is a recognition of the limits of what can be achieved. It's not what your goals are, but what you can realistically do. The idealist starts from the other end—What do we want to be? What do we want to achieve?—and may neglect how feasible it is to try to get there and whether, in trying to get there, you do things which destroy your ability to get there and sacrifice the very ideals you were pursuing.[58]

President Obama and his National Security Council team, originally under the leadership of General James Jones, believe the most exigent threat facing America is the combined threats of weapons of mass destruction, particularly nuclear weapons, and violent extremists, who are trying to obtain these weapons. Thus, the first objective of our Security Strategy is the physical safety and security of our nation's inhabitants. The second objective of our security strategy is to increase our economic power. The third objective is to shape a new international order that is capable of combating the worst problems of our time. The NSS links the new international order to "a global effort to combat climate change."[59]

In the 2010 NSS's section 2—"Strategic Approach"—the description of our strategic environment incorporates two natural environmental issues: pollution and climate change.[60]

In section 3—"Advancing our Interests"—the objective termed "Enhance Science, Technology, and Innovation" includes an extensive exposition on the linkage between a strong environment and America's ability to become more innovative. In this subsection, the NSS planners issue a warning to America's citizens that if the United States does not take the "lead in the development of clean energy technology . . . the United States will fall behind and increasingly become an importer of these new energy technologies."[61]

The 2010 NSS's subsection titled "Sustain Broad Cooperation on Key Global Challenges" states definitive positions on critical environmental issues:

- The danger from climate change is described as "real, urgent, and severe." It is linked to conflicts, natural disasters, and worldwide land degradation.[62]
- A planned reduction in GHG emissions is listed as "in the range of 17 percent by 2020 and more than 80 percent by 2050"[63] if regulatory legislation and implementation of those regulations can be accomplished.
- The administration will take action on a global basis to implement and improve the Copenhagen Accord with the proviso that "any approach draws upon each nation taking responsibility for its own actions."[64]
- It recognizes the importance of safeguarding the global commons and defines them as the "shared sea, air, and space domains." Those domains are described as "the connective tissue around our globe upon which all nations' security and prosperity depend."[65]

The NSS states that we are an Arctic nation with "interests" in the region, including the protection of the environment.[66]

Finally, in the conclusion of the NSS, the planners emphasize that the 2010 NSS reflects a "broad conception of what constitutes our national security."[67] The 2010 NSS is truly an inclusive approach that takes the long view of protecting America's security. Securing the viability of America's environment is part of that approach, and the NSS clearly explains our national interest in also protecting the global environment.

The United Nation's Position

Darfur, Sudan, could be called the poster boy for environmentally linked conflict. This region, termed the Sahel, has experienced over "300,000 deaths and the displacement of more than two million people since 2003."[68] Uncovering causations for the violent conflicts in this region, particularly the role of environmental scarcities, leads to two opposing viewpoints. On one side stands spokesperson Ban Ki-moon, secretary-general of the UN, who locates the conflict's beginning in a scarcity of food and water brought on by a long drought partially caused by human-generated global warming. The other side considers the primary cause of the Darfur conflict as rooted in Sudan's long-standing governmental policies that discriminate against black farmers in favor of Arab herdsmen. This second argument at least acknowledges the exacerbating role played by climate change in causing water and food shortages. Both sides agree that long-lasting peace in the region will only be achieved with the development of effective adaptation strategies designed to ameliorate the competition among different ethnic groups over necessities like water and fertile land.[69]

In September 2009, the UN secretary-general issued a report titled *Climate Change and Its Possible Security Implications*. This report summarized the secretary-general's view on the security implications of climate change as being largely untested; however, the costs of preventing such change are outweighed by the possible future costs of unmitigated climate change. The report reviews recent literature and takes the position that certain impacts addressed by the IPCC may be occurring faster or on a grander scale than reflected within the report. The report also linked national security to individual and community security, terming them interdependent. The secretary-general's report is in agreement with the UNEP's position that climate change acts as a threat multiplier, and the report expands its position by explaining how climate change functions to worsen current problems through five existing channels: (1) most vulnerable communities, (2) economic development, (3) local populations' lack of adaptability, (4) weak nation states, and (5) lack of natural resource availability or access causing competition and disputes between countries.[70]

In terms of terrorism, the secretary-general's report takes the position that in weak states climate change can overwhelm adaption strategies and, in combination with other variables, could cause political instability and the radicalization of vulnerable members of the population. The density of that population may be another strongly predictive factor for armed conflict. Although the report specifically states that empirical evidence linking climate change and conflict is limited, it still forecasts that Africa will be severely affected by climate change due to environmental and demographic issues and an inadequate ability to adjust to climate-induced changes. The high percentage of youths in Africa's population base, its accelerating urbanization, and rapid population increases are examples of societal problems that climate change can worsen.[71]

In addition to Africa, the secretary-general's report identified four other hot spots that are expected to become critical problems the world will have to address in the near future: (1) the melting of the Himalayan glaciers, which supply much of the water for India, Pakistan, and China; (2) the eventual statelessness of small, low-lying countries, such as the Maldives, Papua New Guinea, and the Carteret Islands; (3) the depletion of the Indus River system, shared by India and Pakistan under the terms of a 1960 treaty, which is being threatened by a decreasing amount of available water due to the Himalayan glacier melting; and (4) the Arctic, because the sea ice is melting and the resultant access to the region could lead to competition over its natural resources.[72]

Undoubtedly, the environment is a variable to consider when trying to understand the various causes of conflict. The environment almost certainly will degrade in the coming decade without significant societal cooperation and coordination to stop or reduce such degradation. Unfortunately, it seems doubtful the poorer nations of the world will be successful in mitigating increases in global warming. Thus, environmental changes will occur, and, with climate change acting as a driver, conflicts will increase to include acts of terrorism and the development of terrorist organizations in economically and politically weak areas of the world. This has already occurred once and could occur again in the failed state of Afghanistan. Other weak or failed states—such as Yemen, Pakistan, and several African states—are probable targets for terrorist organizations. These organizations will regard the degradation of a state's environment as an exploitable weakness in its national security structure that will act as a force multiplier for acts of terrorism.

ENVIRONMENTAL WEAPONS

The environmental weapons that have had historical success and are the most probable weapons for today's terrorists to utilize are fire, water, and contaminated resources, such as food and water. Some natural weapons can be augmented by and combined with human-engineered biological agents and toxins that can harm human beings and are often categorized as weapons of mass destruction (WMD). Although some terrorist groups are believed to be actively working on chemical and biological weapons, their limited and relative lack of success provides evidence of the difficulty these weapons present to terrorist organizations.[73] In contrast, natural environmental weapons, such as fire and water, require little expertise to deploy.

The Fire Weapon

Fire has been used historically as a weapon in a variety of applications. Intentionally set wildfires are an obvious weapon choice that has been employed successfully by known terrorist organizations in the Middle East. Specifically, terrorist groups in conflict with Israel, such as Hamas and Hezbollah, have relied upon arson to destroy Israeli forests. Arson was used during the first intifada in the late 1980s, for example, when terrorists burned the forests in Israel as a method to inflict both economic and psychic damage on the citizens of Israel.[74]

The strategy of economic jihad has been openly promulgated by terrorist groups such as Hamas, Hezbollah, and al Qaeda. Along with Israel, the other logical target for these groups is the United States because of their support for Israel. Hezbollah is a revolutionary Iranian-backed political organization that uses terrorism as a tactic and strategic approach to achieve the goal of an Islamic state. During the 2006 war with Israel, Hezbollah used "katyusha" rockets to attack Israel. The rockets ignited forests in the Galilee area of Israel. While the forests were clearly a target, the wildfires were also used as a diversionary weapon to draw Israeli resources away from the battleground in south Lebanon. In addition, Hezbollah used the fires to demoralize the people of Israel. This objective was part of a strategic approach based upon their knowledge that Israelis revere their limited forests and would be psychologically devastated by their destruction. Hezbollah has psychological and economic objectives as part of its war-fighting strategy, and the burning of a valuable resource is a tactical component of both strategic objectives.[75]

Climate change increases fire risks to the dry segments of forests. In many areas of the world, the built environment, in the form of personal residences and commercial structures built by the hospitality industry, is juxtaposed with wildlands that often include extensive forests.[76] In 2009, both the United States and Australia suffered extensive damage to forests and the built environment because of intentional fires. Although it has not been proven that terrorist organizations were responsible for these fires, the possibility that terrorist groups could accomplish such tasks has become a subject of concern for both the United States and Australian governments.[77]

To date, there has been no definitive evidence that al Qaeda or similar jihadi groups operating outside the Middle East have ever used forest fires as a weapon.[78] Terrorist organizations are aware of this tactic, however, and such attacks could also be initiated by nihilistic terrorists operating as lone wolves or autonomous cells that recognize such a tactic as being within their capability. The real threat to the United States, as to Australia, is that once such nihilistic individuals or small groups become aware of the magnitude of damage that has been caused by negligent persons or criminal arsonists, they will begin to focus on implementing such attacks themselves.

An example of a lone wolf arson attack on wildlands occurred on June 27, 1998, near Espanola, New Mexico. The attack resulted in the destruction of 5,185 forested acres of the Santa Fe National Forest and Santa Clara Pueblo lands. A letter sent to the *Albuquerque Journal* claimed responsibility for the act in the name of a militia group called the Minutemen. The letter stated that the fire, termed the Oso Complex Fire, was set as a statement against the killing of gray wolves. On February 24, 2003, the FBI arrested Raymond Anthony Sandoval for setting the fire. He subsequently pled guilty and was sentenced to 84 months of incarceration.[79]

As a tactic, wildfire arson is a simple and potentially effective way for terrorists, whether lone individuals or small autonomous cells, to conduct terrorist actions that have little risk of detection.

The Water Weapon

Water may be the oldest environmental weapon. In great quantities, water can become a tactical weapon of great destructive power. Diverting watercourses or destroying dams uses the power of water to flood and destroy both people and property. The building of dams to generate much-needed hydroelectric power is dramatically increasing in the developing world. Using dammed-up water as a potential weapon has been identified as a risk and is already a major national security problem in several of the world's hot spots. For example, water contained by the Hwanggang Dam in North Korea has been recognized by South Korea as a potential weapon of terror. In 2009, without any warning, North Korea released 40 million cubic meters of water from the dam, causing a tidal wave on one of South Korea's rivers that resulted in the drowning of six individuals. Although North Korea apologized for the incident, South Koreans are now certain that dammed water can be used as a weapon during any conflict with the North.[80] Also in 2009, the Tamil Tigers terrorist organization used explosives to penetrate the walls of the Kalmadukulam Reservoir as a tactic to stop the advancing Sri Lankan military during its battle with the government's forces.[81] In 2008, although they did not carry through on their threat, Taliban insurgents issued a warning that they would blow up Pakistan's Warsak Dam, which would have destroyed the main source of water for the city of Peshawar in Pakistan. The Taliban threat was issued as a response to a Pakistan army offensive in the Peshawar region targeting the Taliban.[82]

Water also has the property of incorporating other agents into itself. Water can thus be used to transport and spread both poisons and disease-causing organisms. When water is poisoned stealthily to kill members of a target population, then water is being used as a weapon. Because water also dilutes and lessens the effectiveness of many substances, such attacks are not easy to successfully accomplish and may require scientific and technical knowledge on the part of terrorists.[83]

Contaminated Resources

In addition to the air we breathe, food and water are the most important resources for continued human existence. Food production worldwide is generally concentrated in rural areas, which are not generally well-secured locations. Food, both animal and crop sources, can easily be contaminated with toxins for the purpose of infecting and terrifying urban populations who rely upon rural food sources. The strategic goal for terrorist organizations is to foster the kind of panic in a population that leads to a loss of trust in governmental effectiveness. There are several diseases, as well as various poisons, that could contaminate agricultural sources without public knowledge, which could drastically affect urban populations.[84]

The most probable biological toxin to be used by terrorists is botulinum toxin, produced by the bacterium *Clostridium botulinum*, the most toxic of known biological food contaminants. Others, less potent but still potentially deadly, are *Escherichia coli (E-coli)* O157:117, *Shigella dysenteriae*, and *Salmonella enterica* (serovar Typhi). The food chain is most easily attacked at its origination points, and there have been numerous instances of unintentional contamination causing loss of life and lack of public confidence in food supplies.[85] For example, botulism poisoning, which occurs periodically in the United States, has a mortality rate of 30 percent if the disease is not caught rapidly and treated effectively. Cases are treated as public health emergencies because a high percentage of victims who recover will sustain long-term medical problems. Botulism symptoms can include respiratory failure, which requires a respirator to keep victims alive.[86]

In 1984, *Salmonella*, a toxin milder than botulinum, was used to intentionally poison customers at several different restaurants in The Dalles, Oregon. The perpetrators were members of a religious cult known as the Rajneeshees, who practiced vegetarianism and believe in free love. Perhaps because of their advocacy of free love, the cult attracted many members and sought to increase its political power in its county of residence. To sway election results, the cult's leadership decided to poison prospective opposing voters. Although no one died from the poisoning, hundreds became ill from *Salmonella typhimurium*. This was the first large-scale use of a biological weapon to attack food sources in the United States.[87]

Although not nearly as deadly, in terms of the number of possible victims, as biological agents, such as smallpox and plague (which fortunately are not transmitted by food), foodborne toxins hitchhike their way along the food chain and into our bodies with relative ease. Outbreaks of public poisoning always cause some degree of public concern. Intentional poisoning could result in a public panic.[88]

ENVIRONMENTAL TARGETS

Intentional destruction of the natural environment that results in a scarcity of renewable resources (e.g., cropland) can exacerbate existing societal problems, such as poverty, and help stimulate the social disruption of a country that is the primary target of a terrorist organization.[89] Attacking the environment can also multiply the effects of a bomb or arson attack, for the environment's natural resources are a soft and valuable target for terrorist attacks.

Bombs and arson are the respective weapons of choice for nihilistic terrorists and some ecoterrorists, and there is a long-standing history of the successful use of these weapons. Relatively simple, highly adaptable, and deadly, these weapons have the greatest potential for effective results when terrorists decide to attack an environmental target. Terrorists have also experimented with the use of biological, chemical, and radiological weapons, and they are believed to be intent on acquiring nuclear weapons.[90] To plan an attack, terrorists not only choose a weapon, but they also estimate the value of the physical target to the psychological vulnerabilities of their perceived enemies, the probability that security forces will detect or prevent the attack, and the amount of effort needed to accomplish the attack. When one assumes a terrorist's perspective to analyze the environment as a physical target, it becomes apparent that the natural environment provides terrorists with five logical and potentially devastating strike areas: (1) air and food supplies, (2) wildlands-built environment junctions, (3) natural ecosystems, (4) water resources, and (5) built environments (e.g., mining sites and energy infrastructures).

Air and Food Supplies

Although chemical and bacteriological weapons, normally classified as WMD, present difficulties for terrorists, they are potential weapons that could be used to poison the air we breathe and the food and water we consume. For example, the biological agents *Bacillus anthracis* and *Salmonella* have been used successfully in attacks in the United States. The 2001 anthrax attacks involved the transmission of *Bacillus anthracis* spores in five letters mailed to persons in New York City, the District of Columbia, and Boca Raton, Florida. These acts resulted in five deaths from inhalation anthrax (inhaling anthrax spores) and 17 injured survivors who suffered inhalation or cutaneous anthrax. The FBI's seven-year Amerithrax investigation ended with the identification of the perpetrator, Dr. Bruce Ivins, a government-employed anthrax researcher who committed suicide by drug overdose shortly before charges could be filed accusing him of the crime.[91]

The Amerithrax case demonstrated how the use of a biological weapon—even in a restricted manner with limited numbers of potential victims—could instill fear in the public and disrupt normal social operations (e.g., new postal restrictions and posting security police at post offices for a while). To function as a true WMD, weaponized anthrax must be dispersed through an aerosol spray system or by expulsion from a plane in order to use wind currents for widespread dissemination. The fact that this bacterium produces endospores (spores) that can persist in the environment and endure adverse conditions (heat, cold, dryness, etc.) for decades makes it well suited for such dispersal.[92]

While *Salmonella*, the weapon of choice of the Rajneeshees in their 1984 poison attack in The Dalles, Oregon, did not kill anyone, it sickened over 700 individuals.[93] Using *Salmonella* to attack our food supply would be particularly effective if directed against restaurant chains. The results could be grave: fear, sickness, possible deaths, and economic loss.

The first chemical agent used to poison the air by a non-state actor was sarin gas employed in 1994 and 1995 by the Aum Shinrikyo cult. Cult members first disseminated the gas through an apartment building in Matsumoto, Japan, which caused 7 deaths and injured 200 individuals. The cult's next attack was on the Tokyo subway system in 1995, and it caused 12 deaths and injured over 1,000 persons.[94]

Chemical and bacteriological weapons are a threat to human beings because they can be used to poison the environment. However, these weapons do not possess the ease of material acquisition and use of bombs and arson devices. Terrorists also know that with a force multiplier, such as the environment, bombs and arson may approximate the physical and psychological effects of a WMD.

Wildlands-Built Environment Junction

Because of increased deforestation in many regions throughout the world, wildlands have become an increasingly valuable resource. In developing areas of the world, for instance, survival often requires burning wildland trees and brushland for cooking fuel and subsistence farming. Additionally, the incidence of wildfires has increased over several decades due to more frequent lightning strikes caused by warmer climates, which increase both the air's warmth and the number of incendiary fires.[95]

In the United States, human activity is still the greatest cause of wildland fires—seven times greater than lightning strikes. Our forests are important to our economy, which uses and produces more industrial wood than any other country.[96] In fact, our wildlands are a perfect "soft" target for terrorists. The frequency of human-initiated fires demonstrates how easy it is to start a wildfire without being detected. Terrorists are undoubtedly aware of the difficulty faced by security personnel charged with protecting wildlands from arson attacks.

The most vulnerable area for terrorist attacks is the intersection of wildlands with the built environment, especially considering the magnitude of the built environment's growing encroachment into wildland areas. In the West, 38 percent of new home construction occurs in the junctions between the wildlands and built environments. The potential for arson-caused loss of lives, property, and valuable natural resources is significant. From 1985 to 1994, wildfires in the western United States destroyed over 9,000 homes. In 1991, for example, a single fire in the wildlands–built environment juncture in the East Bay Hills of Oakland, California, resulted in 25 human deaths and the destruction of 3,000 structures. In Florida, during the summer of 1998, 500,000 acres and hundreds of structures were destroyed by fire, with a cost to Floridians of $620 to $890 million.[97] Once a wildfire gains momentum, it is difficult for firefighters to control, let alone extinguish.

Four problem areas arise for firefighting organizations when they are faced with fires in the wildlands–built environment junction. First, the water necessary to fight such fires may be insufficient due to lack of access to a municipal water supply. Second, jurisdictional and control problems could develop if multiple agencies are involved. Third, access problems could arise if transportation structures in the junction area are inadequate; for instance, the existing roads and bridges may not be able to support heavy firefighting equipment. Fourth, the training of responding fire companies may be insufficient to accomplish their mission. Fighting wildfires is significantly different from battling structure fires, and most departments are not trained in both methodologies. Once initiated by arson, these fires are extremely difficult to stop, which makes the interface between wildlands and built environments a perfect target for a terrorist arson attack.[98]

Natural Ecosystems

By attacking an ecosystem, terrorists can affect the human beings who are uniquely situated within that system. Ecosystems are absolutely essential to the continued existence of our species, yet various ecosystems today are imperiled by human activity, both accidentally and intentionally destructive. Many of the world's ecosystems have become weak and vulnerable to selective human attacks by (1) killing the ecosystem's animal species with firearms, explosives, or poisons; and (2) inserting invasive foreign species into the ecosystem to disrupt it and eventually destroy its capability to support life.

Killing Other Species

Our ability and predilection to kill the animals living in specific ecosystems is an obvious threat to those systems. For example, the mountain gorillas in the Virunga Mountains region of Africa were essentially used as hostages in the late 1990s by Rwandan Hutu militias who used the area for base camps while attacking the Rwandan government's forces and facilities. More recently, the mountain gorillas have been killed by rebel soldiers who still control areas of the gorilla's habitat. In 2007, Congolese Mai Mai rebels attacked three park ranger stations in the Democratic Republic of the Congo's Virunga National Park before fleeing into the park's gorilla habitat and issuing a threat that they would kill the gorillas if the park's wildlife rangers tried to come after them. Just a year before this attack, the Mai Mai had killed hundreds of hippopotamuses in order to achieve recognition for their movement. In 2008, Rwanda, Uganda, and the Democratic Republic of the Congo signed a 10-year agreement whose sole objective is to preserve mountain gorillas and their habitat.[99]

Invasive Species

Inserting invasive species into an ecosystem could be economically devastating. In 2009, fish and wildlife officials had to dump poison into the
Chicago Sanitary and Ship Canal to kill the Asian carp invading U.S. waters and currently threatening to invade Lake Michigan. With a total lack
of predators, the Asian carp will take the food supply from other fish, and
it could even destroy the freshwater ecosystem of the Great Lakes, severely
damaging the lakes' fishing and recreation industry, valued at seven billion dollars. Ironically, our own government brought the Asian carp to Ar-
kansas in 1963 to control aquatic weeds. However, they escaped, spread
north up the Mississippi River, and now dominate many river systems.[100]

The latest examples of intentionally or accidentally released invasive
species are the Burmese and African rock pythons now making their home
in Florida's Everglades and potentially moving into other southeastern
states. Again, with no natural predator, these snakes could overpopulate
the Everglades, destroying the bird population and severely damaging the
ecosystem. Its only rivals are the crocodile and the American alligator, and
so far these species have not been capable of curtailing the population increases of these two snakes.[101]

The ruining of our ecosystems with invasive species has already begun
with people who accidentally or intentionally release foreign species into
the wild. If terrorists intended to harm an ecosystem by deliberately using
invasive species, the results could be much worse.

Poisoning Water Resources

We have already discussed the historical use of water resource poisoning as a military tactic, and it is still being used today. Several instances of
labor disputes in France have escalated into threats to poison rivers, and,
in one instance, strikers actually poisoned a river. The most recent occurrence involved French haulage-firm strikers in 2009 threatening to pour
fuel additives and oil into a tributary of the Seine River. Thankfully, the
threat was never carried out, as a deal was struck between the companies
and the employees. In referring to this poison threat, Antoine Faucher,
campaign director of Greenpeace France, stated the incident was "significant because today, perhaps unlike previous years, the environment is
recognized in itself as a resource. . . . To take it hostage may be of greater
value now than it was before."[102] The French labor movement has a history of threatening rivers as a negotiation strategy. In the one instance of
river poisoning, workers whose factory had been closed first threatened
and then actually did dump 5,000 liters of red-dyed sulphuric acid into the
Fender Channel, which leads to the Meuse River, located in France's Ar-
dennes region. Ecological disaster was prevented by French firemen using
sandbags to block the entry of most of the polluted channel water into the

Meuse. The workers had used this tactic to force the French government to pay them for their loss of employment.[103]

Modern terrorists are well aware of the powerful tactic of poisoning water sources. In fact, according to the Middle East Media Research Institute, in August 2008 a member of the Islamist forum Al-Boraq advised forum members that "poisoning the water systems of major European cities is just one of many options."[104]

The Built Environment

Logical targets for both ecoterrorists and nihilistic terrorists are the numerous facilities and supporting infrastructures connected to a myriad of business activities. When these structures and supporting infrastructure are within or intersect the natural environment, they are a valuable, soft target. Mining facilities, oil and gas drilling facilities, transportation infrastructures, and fresh-water containment sites have often been the targets of terrorists.

Mining Facilities

Mining for coal and minerals entails an extensive supporting infrastructure with storage areas for chemicals and explosives, as well as containment ponds for liquid by-products of the mining process. Bomb or arson attacks would not only cause economic and possible personnel losses but also damage to the natural environment, specifically wildlands and freshwater lakes and streams. These types of attacks could also easily be accomplished, for while these locations often have security, the predicted threats are usually thieves and vandals, not terrorists. Because it may be possible to limit the effects of attacks on the built environment to property damage, these targets appeal to those groups and individuals whose ideology justifies harm to property but not to humans. This broadens the scope of potential attackers.[105]

Oil and Gas Facilities

Oil and natural gas drilling sites, as well as their transportation infrastructures, are also valuable targets. Conventional and irregular armed forces historically have targeted energy production sites, and attacks on these sites can include intent to also inflict damage to the surrounding environment. This is an example of using the environment as a force multiplier for traditional weapons—bombs and arson.[106]

Oil pipelines are targets with the longest history of successful terrorist attacks. Leftist guerrillas—such as the National Liberation Army (ELN) and Revolutionary Armed Forces of Colombia (FARC)—used to routinely bomb pipelines owned by Columbian and U.S. oil companies. The sabotage of oil pipelines has also occurred in the United States and Canada. In January 2010, police in Canada arrested Wiebo Ludwig, an evangelical preacher and environmental activist, for allegedly blowing up six natural gas installations in Northern Canada. (Although arrested, Ludwig was released the next day without charges being filed.) One of the installations was a pipeline owned by EnCana, one of Canada's largest natural gas companies.[107]

Water Containment Sites

Freshwater containment sites, such as dams, reservoirs, and hydroelectric plants, are a potential target of both nihilistic terrorists and ecoterrorists. Edward Abbey's fictional group of saboteurs in *The Monkey Wrench Gang* dreamed of dynamiting the Glen Canyon Dam to save the environment. Nihilistic terrorists perceive freshwater resources as valuable secondary targets that can have multiple effects on the primary target: the civilian populace. These effects include not only the destruction of the population's supply of drinking water, but also the loss of any existent hydroelectric power, damage to related buildings, and death and injury to the people caught in the resultant flood.[108]

In this century, we are experiencing the confluence of an environmental crisis with an increased threat of terrorism conducted by individuals and groups with various environmentally linked motivations. America's National Security Strategy, with the formulation of the 2010 NSS, now integrates environmental security into its overarching security framework. Unfortunately, the environment's weakened status is increasingly apparent, and individuals and groups, like sharks circling a wounded seal, will regard it as prey. In following chapters, these human predators—along with those ecoterrorists that misguidedly want to use violent acts of property destruction to protect the environment—will be dissected in order to understand their history, mindset, organization, strategy, and tactics.

CHAPTER 3

The Basic Concepts of Terrorism

> Anarchy is a crime against the whole human race; and all mankind should
> band against the anarchist. His crime should be made an offense against the
> law of nations, like piracy and that form of man-stealing known as the slave
> trade, for it is of far blacker infamy than either.
> —Theodore Roosevelt, First Annual Message to Congress, 1901

On November 5, 2009, at Fort Hood, Texas, U.S. Army major Nidal Malik
Hasan, a 39-year-old psychiatrist, walked into the base processing center
and began firing a handgun at any visible human targets. During the attack, Hasan, a Palestinian American, shouted *"Allah Akbar"* ("God is great"
in Arabic). Stopped only by two base police officers whose bullets wounded
and disabled him, Hasan succeeded in murdering 13 individuals and
wounding 29. Arrested by military authorities, Hasan has been charged
under the Uniform Code of Military Justice with 13 specifications (the military justice system equivalent of counts) of premeditated murder and 32
specifications of attempted murder. Hasan is currently awaiting trial, which
will be before a general court-martial.[1]

The Hasan case raises several questions: Was Hasan's crime an act of
terrorism? Does the finding by investigators that Hasan acted alone negate
a terrorism determination? If Hasan's motive was only hatred of the U.S.
military, does that negate a terrorism determination? These are difficult
questions to answer without first understanding the basic concepts of terrorism: its definitions, types, organizational structures, strategies, and tactics. This chapter explores these concepts.

DEFINING TERRORISM

The use of violent actions to inflict fear in other people is an ancient form of human conflict. Long before the advent of the organized violence known as war, individuals and small groups used fear as a weapon to "achieve limited goals—to overthrow existing leaders, to ward off potential rivals, or to frighten opposing groups from lands they wished to claim for themselves."[2] Then, when man advanced to formal warfare, armies sometimes used violent acts to physically harm and frighten innocent noncombatants as a tactic to weaken their support for their own military forces. This tactic was known by several names. For instance, the Romans used the term *destructive war* to refer to attacks on both warriors and noncombatants, including women and children, as both a punishment for resisting Roman armies and to break their enemies' spirit.[3]

Today, some scholars believe the term *terrorism* is "simply the contemporary name given to the modern permutation of destructive war deliberately waged against civilians with the purpose of destroying their will to support either leaders or policies that the agents of such violence find objectionable."[4]

The first use of the word *terror* in the context of violent political conflict originated during the French Revolution. It referred to the revolutionary government's use of violence to induce fear in its citizens in order to control them. During the period in 1793 and 1794 known as the Great Terror, thousands of French citizens were executed by the revolutionary government, including King Louis the 16th and Queen Marie Antoinette, both of whom were guillotined in 1793. The use of terror to control the upper classes and other political dissidents who were considered a threat to the new French republic entailed the execution of approximately 27,000 French citizens whom Maximilien Robespierre and his Jacobin political party had decided were traitors. Robespierre justified the extreme violence as necessary and believed the use of terror would lead to virtue and from virtue would come a good society.[5]

In the 19th century, using terror as a tactic or strategy against national governments became part of an overall revolutionary strategy. As Nikolai Morozov—a member of the 19th-century Russian revolutionary group Narodnaya Volya (People's Will), which had assassinated Czar Nicholas in 1881—stated in a pamphlet titled "The Terrorist Struggle," "Before November 19 no one would have believed that the conspirators could penetrate to the tsar's castle. But terroristic struggle has exactly this advantage—that it can act unexpectedly and find means and ways which no one anticipates."[6]

In the post–World War II world, insurgent movements occurred in places such as Aden, Cyprus, Algeria, and Indonesia. The goal was national liberation, and the battles against the Western nations that controlled the various colonies involved both guerrilla warfare and acts of what Western

governments called terrorism. The insurgents denied they were terrorists because their goal was liberation, and thus they were freedom fighters, not terrorists. The Western nations disagreed with this assessment
and uniformly stated that the insurgents' tactics involved terrorism and
that the insurgents were terrorists. The debate between the Western nations and the Soviet bloc states occurred at the United Nations and in
the world press. Government leaders, statesmen, UN officials, and respected scholars with international reputations tried unsuccessfully to
reach agreement on the parameters of the tactic of terrorism. The debate
continues today, although with less heated rhetoric.[7] The debate is cen-
tered on three questions: What is the scope of the term *terrorism*? Should
the definition of the term include a "just cause," or "ends," component or
should it be restricted to include only the use of violence against civilians,
or a "means" approach? Should the definition of terrorism be restricted to
organizational entities or should this definition include individuals acting on their own without any organizational support (i.e., the lone wolf
terrorist)?

Academics take varied positions in response to these questions. For
example, Bruce Hoffman believes that "to qualify as terrorism, violence
must be perpetrated by some organizational entity . . . beyond a single individual acting on his or her own."[8] Alternately, Jeffrey Addicott, a legal
scholar at the Center for Terrorism Law, believes that "individual terrorism can be committed by persons seeking personal rather than political
gain, or even by individuals who are mentally ill."[9] Regarding the ends-
versus-means argument from Richard Falk's perspective, violent acts that
have "moral and legal justification" should not be considered terrorism.[10]
Addicott focuses on a limited definitional approach, concentrating "on
the act and not the . . . causes which motivate the act."[11] Lastly, Mark
Juergensmeyer, in his work *Terror in the Mind of God*, finds current usage
of the word *terrorism* problematic and overly broad. For Juergensmeyer,
concentrating on the means (the violent act) without considering a motivational component is simplistic and inherently biased or subjective. He
justifies his position by arguing that "a violent act is 'terrorism' technically
only in the eyes of the court, or publicly in the eyes of the media, and ultimately only in the eyes of the beholder."[12]

Terrorism may always remain a slippery term. There has never been a
universal consensus on a precise definition of terrorism. The type of behavior the general public refers to as terrorism probably includes the planned
use of illegal threats or violence against a victim to coerce the victim or a
secondary target to accede to a perpetrator's demands. Certainly, there
would be scholarly objections to this definition because of its lack of a political motivation. In the academic arena, there are disagreements over the
types of goals, victims, and tactics that should be included in a comprehensive definition of terrorism. For example, the REM's Earth Liberation
Front and Animal Liberation Front have published guidelines that limit

direct actions to attacks on property. Does this restriction of the choice of tactics mean that these groups are vandals but not terrorists?[13]

In the professional world of the detective, special agent, prosecutor, and judge, the definition of terrorism has legal ramifications, despite the fact it still suffers from a lack of consistency. Recognizing that the term *terrorism* is inherently vague because no consensus has been reached on proposed universal definitions, the law enforcement community has attempted to bypass the definitional problem by concentrating on the specific criminal acts that must be committed and on the specific targets that must be protected.[14]

STATUTORY DEFINITIONS

The FBI is the U.S. agency with primary responsibility for the investigation of terrorism, and it is instructive to analyze the definitional problem as seen through this agency. In a landmark 1972 decision, the U.S. Supreme Court, in *United States v. Keith,* set down constitutionally based restrictions that would be imposed upon terrorism investigations conducted by the FBI within the United States. The "Keith decision" requires that the FBI ensure its investigative procedures do not violate civil liberties.[15] The FBI was thus forced to separate its investigations into three types: criminal, domestic terrorism, and international terrorism. The FBI's first step was to adopt a nonstatutory definition of domestic terrorism to guide investigations: "Domestic terrorism is the unlawful use, or threatened use, of force or violence by a group or individual based and operating entirely within the United States or Puerto Rico without foreign direction committed against persons or property to intimidate or coerce a government, the civilian population, or any segment thereof in furtherance of political or social objectives."[16]

In the area of international security, the FBI did not adopt a definition, but, in 1978, Congress passed the Foreign Intelligence Surveillance Act (FISA), which included the following definition of international terrorism:

(c) "International terrorism" means activities that—

(1) involve violent acts or acts dangerous to human life that are a violation of the criminal laws of the United States or of any State, or that would be a criminal violation if committed within the jurisdiction of the United States or any State;

(2) appear to be intended—

    (A) to intimidate or coerce a civilian population;

    (B) to influence the policy of a government by intimidation or coercion; or

    (C) to affect the conduct of a government by assassination or kidnapping; and

(3) occur totally outside the United States, or transcend national boundaries in terms of the means by which they are accomplished, the persons they appear intended to coerce or intimidate, or the locale in which their perpetrators operate or seek asylum[17]

The FISA definition was the first statutory definition of international terrorism. It remains the same today and is used as the basis for other definitions of international terrorism subsequently adopted by the federal government. The most significant change in FBI terrorism definitions occurred in 2001 with the passage of the Patriot Act, which significantly changed the FBI's definition of domestic terrorism:

(5) the term "domestic terrorism" means activities that—

    (A) involve violent acts dangerous to human life that are a violation of the criminal laws of the United States or of any state;

    (B) appear to be intended—

        (i) to intimidate or coerce a civilian population;

        (ii) to influence the policy of a government by intimidation or coercion; or

        (iii) to affect the conduct of a government by mass destruction, assassination, or kidnapping; and

    (C) occur primarily within the territorial jurisdiction of the United States.[18]

Although included in Title 18, which includes all federal crimes of the *U.S. Code,* the new statute is only a definitional statute, not a criminal statute that includes a penalty provision. It changes the FBI's prior definition by eliminating the social-political cause aspect and broadening the definition of domestic to include acts that could have some relationship to a terrorist group's planning or post-operational activities outside the territorial jurisdiction of the United States.[19] The Patriot Act also modified the Title 18 definition of international terrorism that had been in place since 1992, which was based primarily upon FISA. These Title 18, section 2331 definitions of terrorism are not a specific element of any criminal law offense. However, because of their incorporation into other statutes and regulations, they are a key part of federal terror law.[20]

Defining terrorism is not the only problem in dealing with the subject. Indeed, the "what is it" question may be answered, but answering this question leads only to a new inquiry: Who are the terrorists? Answering this question necessitates another difficult journey—this time into the realm of terrorist typology.

TYPOLOGY

While there is scholarly consensus on certain types of terrorism, academics and counterterrorism experts often differ as to the nomenclature and standards for the inclusion of some individuals and groups. Some forms of terrorism take their nomenclature from insurgent movements; other forms are sui generis, and differing nomenclatures may refer to the same type of terrorism. One debatable type of terrorism—terror from above, or "state terror," which refers to a state using fear to control its populace—certainly exists today, as all terrorism scholars will agree. They disagree, however, about incorporating state terror into a typology of terrorism. Some scholars feel this typology should only include terror from below or terror against both the state and weaker or equally powerful groups.[21] This position recognizes the difficulty in determining when a state is using terror to control its populace. For this reason, state terror should be assumed to exist but will not be part of the typology discussed in this book.

Terrorism typologies, of which there are many, are often developed from an historical perspective, which can extend as far back as written works exist and often expands the definition of terrorism to include the actions of individuals or smalls groups who use assassination as a tactic to eliminate tyrannical rulers. Aristotle's *Politics* discusses tyranny by examining the motives, such as hatred and contempt, that men have for killing tyrants. The Roman Senate's assassination of Julius Caesar, who they considered a tyrant, is often used as an example of tyrannicide.[22] Although tyrannicide should be considered a political crime and possibly an act of terrorism, it may not include today's generally accepted, fundamental elements of an act of terrorism. These historical examples from Greece and Rome did not entail systematic efforts by a group to use violence as a strategic tool to engender fear in a target audience. Based on current definitions of terrorism, however, there is general agreement that the first uses of terrorism as a strategy involved the religions of Judaism and Islam in the Roman (1st century C.E.) and medieval (11th to 13th century C.E.) historical epochs, respectively.[23]

The Jewish Sicarii sect operated in the Roman-controlled province of Judea from 66 to 73 C.E., often engaging in acts of banditry and extortion but also as part of the Zealot insurgency against Roman rule. The second religious-based terrorism group, the Assassins, was a fanatical branch of the Shiite Ismaili sect. The Assassins operated from the 11th to the 13th century, sometimes striking at the occupying Christian crusaders; but mainly attacking Sunni Muslim leaders in the regions of Persia and Syria. Both groups, the Sicarii and the Assassins, used the dagger as their weapon of choice, and both were prepared to die as a result of their assassination missions. The Sicarii were eliminated by the Romans at Masada in 74 C.E., and the Mongols eliminated the Assassin sect in the 13th century.[24] With the elimination of these groups, systematic political terrorism from below died out and did not reappear until the middle of the 19th century.

Anarchist-Terrorism

Some of the political processes that formed what today is considered modern terrorism emerged in mid-19th-century Europe as revolutionary activities by workers, peasants, some merchants, and others were directed against absolute monarchies and defenders of the status quo. In the year 1848, there were uprisings in major capitals in Europe. But with the failure of the varied revolutions and the ability of the monarchies to reassert their primacy in Europe, many radical democrats who participated in the 1848 revolution were driven into exile or underground. Various socialist and anarchist perspectives flourished in this milieu, along with a widely held view that violence was necessary to destroy a corrupt society so it could be reborn to allow rule by the people. Within this context there arose a current that can be termed *anarchist-terrorists*.[25] The ideology of these anarchist-terrorists was influenced by a variety of radical theorists. Some of these—such as Karl Marx and Pierre-Joseph Proudhon—adhered to non-terrorist strategies. It is also the case that some variants of anarchism (for example, that associated with Leo Tolstoy) have been committed to the philosophy and tactics of nonviolence. But others, such as the Russian revolutionaries Mikhail Bakunin and Sergey Nechaev and the German American Johann Most, inclined toward the following principles and beliefs: (1) there is no absolute morality, (2) all states are inherently evil and cannot be reformed but must be destroyed by violent means, and (3) law is only the instrument of those in power.[26] Their tactics laid the groundwork for a justification of individual terrorism against what they considered to be symbols of tyranny.

Variants of this orientation spread throughout some portions of the working classes in Russia, Europe, and Great Britain from 1880 until 1920, and in the late 19th century it arrived in the United States. The major tactic of anarchist-terrorism was assassination by the use of gun and bomb. Like all terrorism, it was a response to major events and causes of the time: the industrial revolution, the repression of unions, labor unrest, and the ideological struggles between socialism and capitalism. The anarchist movement was responsible for the assassination of leaders in many countries. In the United States, an anarchist, Leon Czolgosz, assassinated President William McKinley. The new president, Theodore Roosevelt, wanted to expel all anarchists to their countries of origin and advocated a worldwide attack on anarchist-terrorism. In fact, the successes of anarchist-terrorism led to operational changes in law enforcement organizations and demonstrated to an international populace how easy it was for a terrorist organization to force governments to overreact and curtail civil liberties.[27]

For example, in 1919, a number of package bombs were sent to prominent persons across the country. These bombings were believed to have been the acts of anarchists and led President Wilson and Attorney General A. Mitchell Palmer, himself a bomb recipient, to order the arrests of suspected radicals in over 30 U.S. cities. In a massive raid on the night of January 2, 1920, thousands of alleged radicals were arrested, but most were eventually released. Some Russian anarchists and innocent Russian immigrants were deported back to the Soviet Union. These Red Scare raids were criticized for violations of civil liberties, but the attorney general remained firm in his belief that the actions of the Department of Justice were necessary to stop an extreme threat to American society. Subsequently, on September 16, 1920, in what is believed to have been revenge for the Red Scare raids, a large bomb was set off in front of J.P. Morgan's banking house on Wall Street, resulting in the deaths of 34 persons and injuries to 200. This case was never solved.[28] Today, the Wall Street bombing marks the winding down of anarchist-terrorists activities in the United States. Yet the historical example and ideas of this ideological current are capable of inspiring new disaffected elements, particularly with the resurgence of anarchist perspectives.

Nationalist-Terrorism

As the anarchist movement dissipated in the early years of the 20th century without achieving its goals, nationalist-terrorism became the predominant form of terrorism operating in the world. In reality, nationalist-terrorism had been occurring in certain areas of the world at the same time as anarchist-terrorism, but it did not have the international reputation, or notoriety, of anarchism. Because each campaign of nationalist-terrorism was limited to a specific country, as opposed to the international scope of anarchism, there was no international campaign directed against it. Then, in 1914, came the most famous assassination in history—"the shot heard around the world"—the death of Austrian archduke Franz Ferdinand and his wife at Sarajevo. This murder, perpetrated by a Bosnian Serb, Gavrilo Princip, was considered the spark for World War I. Princip was a member of Young Bosnia, a nationalist-terrorist group, and may have received assistance from a radical faction of the Serbian Nationalist Society called the Crna ruka, or Black Hand.[29]

Nationalist-terrorism expanded after World War I, and it was waged predominantly in countries occupied by the British. The seminal example of nationalist-terrorism occurred during World War I with the revolt of Irish radicals against the British that occurred in 1916 on Easter Monday in Dublin. Also, before and during World War II, several Jewish nationalist-terrorist organizations operating in Palestine were engaged in both suppressing Arab resistance and trying to expel Great Britain from the disputed territory. By 1948, their combined efforts had succeeded in accomplishing both objectives. Before and after World War II, varied insurgent movements whose goal was an end to colonialism resulted in the expulsion of European powers from their regions of control in Africa and the Middle East. Nationalistic terrorists referred to themselves as freedom fighters, believing that the perceived justice of their cause negated the tactics they used.[30] The goal driving nationalist-terrorism is independence from an occupying power or the territorial separation and independence from a country in which the terrorist group is an ethnic, cultural, racial, or religious minority. Unlike anarchists, who want freedom from governmental control as a general principle, nationalistic terrorists base their concept of freedom on physical separation.

Irish nationalism was the political goal that drove the development of modern history's longest-lasting insurgency. Irish terrorism grew in the 19th century with the Irish Republican Brotherhood's use of bombings and assassinations. These criminal acts were directed against both the Protestant Irish who wanted Ireland to stay part of Great Britain and the occupying British military forces. The failure of the British government to grant home rule to Ireland led to the Irish Volunteers' Easter rebellion against the British in 1916. The failure of the rebellion led to the formation of the Irish Republican Army (IRA).[31]

Under the leadership of Michael Collins, the IRA developed a strategy of selective terrorism that combined the anarchist tactics of bombing and assassination with a military-like organizational structure. Collins ultimately forced the British to agree to the formation of the Irish Free State in southern Ireland in 1921; however, other leaders in the IRA did not agree to the separation of Ireland and continued their campaign of violence, including the murder of their former leader, Michael Collins. The IRA went on to become the archetype for modern terrorist groups. Their struggle began with nationalism and developed into a religious, cultural, and economic campaign of terror that has culminated today into a confusing mix of criminal, anarchic, retributive, and reactionary terrorism that incorporates actions conducted by both the IRA and the Protestant, Unionist-based groups who oppose it.[32]

After World War II, ideas of nationalism were also greatly influenced by the ideology of communism. In a series of revolts, insurgents utilized guerrilla warfare as the predominant strategy to overturn colonial orders, and new countries emerged. Terrorism, specifically urban terrorism, was also a strategy used by some insurgents. The anticolonialism movement and its opposition to Western occupiers revealed an ideological battle between Western capitalism and communism as propagated by the former USSR and China. Nationalistic insurgencies and their strategy of terrorism even influenced countries that were not physically occupied by colonial powers but whose governments were influenced and, in some cases, controlled by Western powers. Perceived social inequities became the basis for revolutionary activities against the existing government. Unlike anarchists with a limited range of tactics, these revolutionaries used tactics that were based on military principles and incorporated a greater use of military armament. The definitive revolutionary movement of the 20th century was the successful Cuban revolution (1956–58) led by Fidel Castro and Che Guevara. Moreover, throughout the 1960s and 1970s, Cuban fighters tactically and ideologically influenced ongoing struggles in Africa and Latin America.[33]

Revolutionary-Terrorism

In the 1960s, motivated by political, economic, and cultural movements—such as the Vietnam War, the Cuban revolution, and Israel's 1967
successful six-day war with Arab forces—revolutionary terrorist groups
began operating in Western Europe, Latin America, the Middle East, and
the United States. Their goal was to change or replace existing governments. Their left-wing ideology was based on Marxism or Maoism and
advocated an anticapitalist, anti-imperialist, multinational campaign of
urban-based terrorism. There were a variety of revolutionary groups (e.g.,
Uruguay's Tupamaros, the Palestine Liberation Organization, and Italy's
Red Brigades), and these revolutionaries were opposed not only by
their respective governments but sometimes by other domestic terrorist
groups.[34] These opposing terrorist groups arose as a reaction to the possibility that the revolutionary group would succeed and change the government.

Reactionary-Terrorism

Reactionary terrorist groups normally support the government in power
and, in some cases, are themselves an underground arm of the governmental forces. They commit attacks not only against revolutionary terrorist organizations but also against the public for the general purpose of
discrediting the revolutionary insurgency. Reactionary terrorism is often
supported, or in some cases initiated, by the government. When these
groups are autonomous, they may commit actions against the government
if they believe the government is not supporting the interests of the state.
Reactionary terrorists often target members of religious, ethnic, or racial
groups that the terrorists regard as a threat to their state. This can occur
even if the targeted persons are neither part of an insurgency nor engaged
in terrorist activity. In the United States, the Ku Klux Klan has a history
of terrorist violence committed to maintain political systems controlled
by white persons. In Northern Ireland, the Ulster Defense Association
has carried out terrorist actions with the goal of maintaining a state connected to Great Britain and separate from the Republic of Ireland and later
tried to carry out a political strategy that entailed separation from Great
Britain.[35]

In the 1980s in the United States, groups like the Aryan Nations incorporated religion as part of their reactionary ideology. Fundamentalist in
tone and with irrational doctrines that support the group's ideas about
society, various religions have been structured to support the reactionary group's political objectives.[36] Whereas religion was just one of several
motivations of Western reactionary-terrorist organizations, other groups
developed in the Middle East and Asia that were motivated entirely by
religious beliefs.

Religious-Terrorism

Religious belief as a motivation for acts of terrorism is at the forefront of today's terrorist threats. Historically, religion has often been linked with violence and the urge for power over property, land, and the souls of men.[37] Today, the most powerful source of religion-based terrorism is a fundamentalist version of Islam that condones an armed struggle (i.e., jihad) against designated enemies of Islam. It is referred to by various titles (e.g., Jihadism and Caliphism), but the basic ideology is anti-Western, anti-Israel, and has the long-range goal of establishing an Islamic state based on Sharia law. The prototype of a transnational religious-terror organization is al Qaeda.[38] Unlike al Qaeda, terrorist groups that espouse a distorted view of Christianity are generally domestic but have some links to groups with similar beliefs in other countries.[39] These groups desire a revolution that will replace a government they believe is controlled by a demonic force with one based on principles of Christian patriotism.[40]

Single-Issue Terrorism

Along with the rebirth of religious terrorism in the 1980s came the development of what the FBI has termed single-issue terrorist groups. These groups focus on what they perceive as a specific religious, political, or social problem. Unlike other terrorist organizations that respond to more broadly based religious, social, or political movements, these groups have a limited focus. Although limited in focus and scope to one particular cause, single-issue groups display all the characteristics of other terrorist groups. For these single-issue groups, contrasting political ideologies exist on both the right and left political wings. In the United States, the Army of God (antiabortion) and the Earth Liberation Front (environmental protection) are examples of single-issue groups with respective right- and left-wing ideologies who both "use violence to compel society to change its attitudes about specific causes."[41]

Criminal-Terrorism

There are two additional types of terrorists that transcend the traditional types: (1) small cells or single individuals acting for egoistic reasons who espouse a variety of ideologies and goals and engage in terrorism as disaffected angry individuals acting without direct control by any organization (nihilistic), and (2) groups that engage in both organized crime and terrorism (hybrid).

Nihilistic individuals and groups are prone to conspiratorial beliefs, often possess a millenarian perspective, and have identified a demonized enemy whose murder at their hands will validate their existence. The groups often function as domestic terror cells with little connection to international groups. They embrace both a "leaderless resistance" organizational structure and a cause, such as jihadism or white supremacy, that allows the release of anger toward some perceived demonic enemy. Nihilistic terrorists advocate individual acts of violence with great destructive power. Examples of such terrorists are Timothy McVeigh, who killed 163 people by bombing the Federal Building in Oklahoma City in 1995, and Theodore Kaczynski, also known as the Unabomber, who committed 16 bombings, 3 of which resulted in the death of a person.[42]

Hybrid groups have a criminal orientation with limited political motivation for their actions. They can begin as either terrorist or (in rare cases) criminal organizations, and they metamorphose into hybrid organizations through two different processes that depend on their initial identification. Examples of hybrids that began as insurgent groups are the Revolutionary Armed Forces of Colombia and today's Irish Republican Army or one of its progeny.[43] Both these terrorist organizations began criminal operations to raise funds for terrorist activities, but the profit from their activities caused them to change their orientation from political revolution to monetary profit. In contrast, criminal groups can begin utilizing terrorism as a tactic when their parasitic existence is threatened by the host state. If they have sufficient power, like the Sicilian Mafia in the 1990s, they use terrorism directed at the state to force the state into an accord.[44] Hybrid groups are covered in more detail in chapter 6.

In launching a terrorist campaign, two things are necessary: a goal, such as political power or social change, that unites and motivates the members and an organizational structure that enables attacks to be planned and carried out while allowing the group to survive governmental campaigns of counterterrorism.

ORGANIZATIONAL STRUCTURES

Small Cells

Historically, as noted earlier, the first terrorist organization of long duration was the radical sect of Ismaili Shiites known as Assassins. The suicide attacks the acolytes committed were justified by a religious ideology that engendered fanatical loyalty toward the Ismaili sect. Their goal was to disrupt and destroy the Sunni Muslim religious order that controlled the regions of what today would be considered Syria and Iran and that considered the Shiites heretics. Their religious beliefs alone, however, would not have been sufficient for the Assassins to endure for two centuries as an organization that practiced assassination directed at members of the powerful Seljuq Empire. They also needed organizational skills. Assassins first developed secure bases in remote regions of Persia and Syria, the most famous of which was Alamut Castle. This castle sheltered the sect's 12th-century leader, Hasan-i Sabbah, whose organizational structure had a security system based on secrecy. The underground campaign of assassination was supported by an aboveground political and religious organization. This organization's activities engendered needed logistical support and gathered intelligence concerning the group's enemies—predominantly the more numerous members and militarily powerful leaders of the Sunni Islam–practicing Seljuq state. The sect's operational units were one or a few assassins armed with knives—a small cell engaged in asymmetrical warfare.[45]

An historical and often-cited work that deals with organizing a terrorist group titled *Catechism of the Revolutionist* was written by Russian revolutionary theorist Sergey Nechaev in 1869. Nechaev believed that revolutionary groups should meet to discuss and agree on potential operational plans, but, when carrying out the plan, each group was to act individually without interaction with other groups unless absolutely necessary. The recruitment and utilization of the group's members was specified. The most interesting prescription was that prospective members be required to commit "deeds" before being admitted into full membership. Nechaev presaged the 20th century's concept of leaderless resistance, discussed later in this chapter.[46]

In the 1880s, Narodnaya Volya, a Russian revolutionary terrorist group, also emphasized small groups, strict conditions of secrecy, and the use of assassination as a tactic that was restricted to government officials and members of the ruling class as primary targets.[47] From 1900 to 1917, the Russian Socialist Revolutionary Party's organization of its Combat Organization (CO) as an underground terrorist cell that was allowed to select its own tactics and members made the CO difficult to penetrate and allowed it to carry out long-lasting, coordinated campaigns.[48]

For 19th-century European and Russian anarchists, decentralization, secrecy concerns, and the total operational autonomy of small cells and lone individuals made communication and organization within the anarchist movement difficult. These small groups and lone individuals had some degree of effectiveness by using "propaganda by deed," usually in the form of assassination. They were, however, incapable of mounting extended campaigns involving fortified targets or even assassinations on a broader scale. Their organizational strengths and weaknesses were similar to the lone wolf terrorist of today.[49]

Column and Cell

The next significant development in terrorist group organizational methods occurred in the 20th century with the formation of the IRA. The IRA was essentially a combination of a guerrilla force and a terrorist group. The IRA was part of an insurgency with an aboveground front organization. The IRA was structured on military principles with modifications to ensure needed secrecy. The IRA used a column and independent cell structure controlled by a central command called the Supreme Council. The IRA also used military terms for its various components. To control the system, the autonomous operational cells were regulated by disciplinary units that were internal but separate from the remainder of the organization. The problem with this column and cell organizational structure, however, is the inevitable disputes that arise among components of the organization. Because of the emphasis on secrecy and the decentralization of the cells and columns, the organization will have difficulty conducting combined operations. The unity of command principle is violated, opposing leaders often develop, and large terrorist organizations are prone to split into groups. These organizations are harder for governments to penetrate by developing knowledgeable informants, but the operational effectiveness of the organization suffers. The IRA has suffered from these deficiencies during its history of terrorist activity.[50]

The reason a unified control element is often necessary to support a terrorist campaign is that the organization has important non-attack roles, such as training, logistics, and intelligence, as well as general support roles, such as manufacturing documents, obtaining safe houses, and acquiring weapons, food, and medical supplies. In some cases, if the group uses the tactic of kidnapping, staffed underground prisons may even be necessary. Terrorists, unlike most criminal groups, must be trained to carry out most operational activities and will need facilities and instructors. Moreover, large terrorist organizations that plan and execute complex attacks will need some degree of bureaucracy in their organizational structure.

The organizational structure problems for today's terrorists have improved. Terrorists still use small cells as a foundation and develop a network of such cells as the organization grows. The leadership element maintains a link with the cells through use of the Internet, laptop computers, software programs, and encryption systems. However, the central command required to direct these cells is still a problem. The presence of a central command makes it possible for government forces to roll up a cell network if they are able to infiltrate the central command.

Leaderless Resistance

In 1983, Louis Beam, a former Texas Ku Klux Klan leader and participant in the white supremacy movement, wrote an article titled "Leaderless Resistance" in which he postulated that a resistance movement could dispense with a central command. Beam believed that small individual cells needed only to know the mission in order to carry out terrorist actions and that the mission could be transmitted to the cells through a variety of mediums without revealing the other components of the organization. The leaderless-resistance concept has become the favored form of organizing for both single-interest terrorist groups and loosely affiliated terrorist groups with religious and nihilistic ideologies.[51]

The global communication systems readily available today to most terrorist organizations afford a mechanism for leadership and motivational guidance from a central control group. This central control may be able to communicate strategy, goals, and tactical advice to cell leadership links without the links having any knowledge of the central control's current identity or location. Of course, this makes these organizations difficult to penetrate, limiting the effectiveness of a successful penetration of an individual cell by informants or undercover agents. This organizational structure, however, may be detected through the use of electronic surveillance techniques. Individual cells, self-generated without any central control and operating without any linkage to other terrorist cells, are the hardest groups to penetrate. Their high degree of security, however, is matched by their lack of capability in carrying out a strategy to achieve their ultimate goals.

STRATEGY

The strategy of all terrorists, both organizations and individuals, begins with an intention to use violence to induce fear in human targets to obtain an ideologically driven goal. The decision to utilize terrorism as a strategy has been embraced by various political insurgencies. In regard to insurgent movements, terrorism is often one component of an overall strategy to obtain the insurgent organization's ultimate goal, which usually includes one or more of the following changes and controls: "regime change, territorial change, policy change, social control, and status quo maintenance."[52]

The strategic use of terrorism will focus on short-term, intermediate, and long-term objectives designed to culminate in one or more of the aforementioned ultimate goals, which, historically, have rarely been achieved. When the terrorist strategy is the main or only insurgent strategy, the goal, if it is to be successfully achieved, must be very limited. For example, the German Red Army Faction (RAF), a left-wing revolutionary group operating in the 1970s and 1980s, had a strategic goal of replacing Western Germany's democratic government with a Marxist regime. The RAF was small, 30 or fewer members, and the actions they took seemed sensational to the public, yet they were limited in both scope and operational effectiveness. The RAF was never close to achieving its strategic goal and was eventually eliminated as a viable organization by the German authorities.[53]

To achieve operational success in using terrorism as a strategy requires a realistic acknowledgment that most conventional military tactics, when used by a terrorist group, will rarely be effective against the armed forces of a government. To accomplish their goal, terrorists must utilize specialized tools and asymmetrical tactics to offset the power of the opposition.[54] The most important objective for terrorist tactics is to have a psychological impact on the targeted human audience. To achieve this objective, competent terrorists follow a set of ideas or principles that guide their actions.

Propaganda by Deed

The term "propaganda by deed" was first used by 19th-century anarchists. The concept, however, was probably first utilized in the first century c.e. by the Sicarii during the Zealot insurgency against Rome. The phrase means that the physical act of violence is the preferred way to publicize an insurgency's cause and that it is superior to other forms of propaganda. The Sicarii, for example, engaged in public assassinations of Roman soldiers and fellow Jews who were collaborating with the Roman occupiers. Images of daggers wrenching flesh were meant to intimidate members of the public, both Roman and Jewish, and served to publicize the existence of the Sicarii and demonstrate their power.[55]

When terrorists strike, the real target of the violent act can be either the physically affected target, usually human, or a symbolic target that represents the true enemy. Anarchist terrorists in the 19th and early 20th centuries generally restricted their acts to human targets who symbolized the government. This sort of restriction is contrary to the idea of indiscriminate attacks on civilians without symbolic meaning, entailing large numbers of casualties, that are utilized by other groups, most prominently the jihadist and nihilistic terrorists.[56]

Provocation

Provocation is another principle used during insurgencies, and it is often implemented through the use of terrorism. Carlos Marighella, a Brazilian urban terrorist and theoretician, stated in his 1969 *Minimanual of the Urban Guerrilla* that one key principle of terrorism is to provoke the target in order to obtain a reaction from the civilian population favorable to the terrorist movement.[57] Provocation as a principle of insurgency was also successfully used by the Front de Libération Nationale (FLN) in Algeria during its 1954 to 1962 campaign to win independence from France. The FLN, during their terrorist operations in the city of Algiers, conducted shootings, bombings, and raids directed against the French security forces for the purpose of provoking a reaction from those forces that would necessarily entail a repression of the civil rights of the civilian population.[58]

Intimidation

The principle of intimidation is used to spread fear in a population that has a significant group of citizens who are neutral observers to a particular conflict. To implement this principle, selected members of the population essential to the efficient operation of its system of government become targets. Once the effective operation of the government has been severely damaged, the objective is for those once-neutral members of society to become disgruntled with the government and become supporters of the terrorist movement.[59]

Chaos

Terrorist groups create chaos by committing enough violent acts of a random, horrific nature that the civilian population loses faith in the government's ability to protect it. The objective is to disrupt the necessary functions of civilian society. This principle is one that can be employed by numerically small terrorist movements and can be implemented by the use of assassination on a random, widespread basis.[60]

Attrition

Attrition, as a strategic principle, forms the major impetus for any terrorist campaign being waged by small independent terrorist groups that lack substantial resources. These terrorist groups operate from a long-war perspective, believing their actions, although limited in effect, are not insignificant. They count on wearing out the enemy through periodic attacks over a significant period of time. For effective use of the attrition principle, the terrorist group has to stay hidden; secrecy is paramount, and high degrees of violence are not necessary. What is important, however, is that attacks continue to happen so the terrorist group gains publicity and the public is aware the group is still in existence and carrying out successful attacks against the government.[61]

According to Professor Gregory Raymond, although the strategic approaches of terrorist groups are usually similar in regard to their intermediate range objectives, they usually have different ultimate goals. The strategic objectives can be classified as organizational, agitational, and coercive. The organizational objective encompasses the enlargement and strengthening of a group. Forging group unity and identity and acquiring resources are additional parts of this objective. Terrorist acts that help attain agitational and coercive objectives, such as bank robbery, extortion, and kidnapping, are criminal actions on the surface, but they are carried out to strengthen the ideological movement. Generally, groups will take action against soft targets to ensure their success and to build confidence among the group's membership, thereby helping them bond. Forcing members to participate in violent actions also lowers defections from the group and reinforces their cohesiveness.[62]

According to Martha Crenshaw, a pioneer in the field of terrorism studies, terrorism is embraced by varied, ideologically motivated groups, but achieving the strategic goals of any terrorist campaign will require the group to commit violent acts. These violent actions may vary according to the group's capabilities and desires, but these groups all have one or more common objectives. According to Crenshaw, these common objectives include the following: (1) publicity, (2) discrediting the government, (3) creating sympathy in support groups, (4) ensuring organizational control, and (5) demonstrating power.[63] To successfully achieve their strategic objectives and ultimate goals through the use of violent actions, terrorists must utilize tactics that are within their capability and that will inflict harm to individuals and property in order to influence their ultimate audience.

TACTICS

Terrorist organizations, because of their generally small numbers, have always used tactics appropriate for a very small group or single individual. According to Brian Jenkins, a highly experienced terrorism analyst, "six basic terrorist tactics comprise 95 percent of all terrorist incidents: bombings, assassinations, armed assaults, kidnappings, barricade and hostage situations, and hijackings."[64] The tactic of choice over the longest period of time has been assassination of a government's officials or civilian supporters. Initially, the main weapon of assassination was the knife or dagger, and even with the development of firearms, the knife has remained an important weapon, resurfacing in a modified form with the 9/11 hijackers who used knives and box cutters to assist in their airplane takeovers.[65]

Firearms were first used by terrorists in the 19th century, and they continue to be a weapon of choice along with the knife. Most recently, firearms were the principle tool used by the Mumbai terrorists to kill civilians and government agents during their attack on that Indian city. The firearms used by terrorists are normally pistols, submachine guns, and rifles. Larger groups of terrorists may employ their weaponry through the use of firing-team tactics similar to military small-unit tactics. Marighella's minimanual furnishes information concerning this tactic, and he describes the four-or-five-person firing group that carries out armed attacks on its own initiative. He states that the "urban guerrilla's reason for existence; the basic condition in which he acts and survives is to shoot."[66]

Bombings were the next development in terrorist tactics and remain the most venerable and asymmetrical tactic in the terrorist repertoire. Until the mid-19th century, a bomb attack involved a black powder weapon, which could be effective but required large quantities of explosives. In 1866, however, Alfred Nobel invented dynamite, a combination of nitroglycerin and diatomaceous earth, for use by the mining and railroad industries. The ease of portability and the power of dynamite revolutionized terrorist tactics, and the bomb supplanted the firearm as the most effective weapon. The bomb could be used to kill, and, if murder was not the objective, it could be used to destroy property and symbolic structures of the government without destroying human life.[67]

In 1881, Johann Most, a German anarchist and terrorist theoretician living in the United States, wrote a pamphlet titled "The Science of Revolutionary Warfare: Handbook of Instruction Regarding the Use and Manufacture of Nitroglycerin, Dynamite, Gun-Cotton, Fulminating Mercury, Bombs, Arson, Poisons, etc." Most's pamphlet had wide distribution in social revolutionary circles, and its most cogent recommendation was that readers should try to obtain explosives through commercial sources and not make them at home because of the difficulty and danger.[68]

The dangers of bomb making have been known since World War I, when the militaries of most nations raced to develop more effective explosives. Although TNT (trinitrotoluene) was a standard military explosive that had been used in a variety of ways, World War II led to the development of plastic explosives, of which C4 has become one of the most versatile. Plastic explosives look and can be manipulated like putty, yet they are more powerful than dynamite. Although there have been many technical developments in the area of plastic explosives, one of the most effective weapons developed has been the ANFO bomb, a combination of ammonium nitrate fertilizer and any type of highly explosive liquid fuel. These ingredients are easy to acquire because there are many commercial uses for the components. For terrorists, the ANFO bomb is a very effective weapon that can be constructed and utilized without a great deal of expertise. The ANFO bomb was used in both the 1993 bombing of the World Trade Center (enhanced with nitroglycerine and hydrogen gas) and the bombing of the Murrah Federal Building in Oklahoma City in 1995.[69] Moreover, new technical developments in explosives and ignition devices were on display in 2001, when the shoe bomber, Richard Reed, attempted to detonate a plastic explosive contained in his shoe while traveling on an airplane, and in 2009, when the underwear bomber, Umar Farouk Abdulmutallab, ignited an explosive device contained in his underwear while trying to detonate it on a commercial airplane attempting to land in Detroit, Michigan, on December 25, 2009. Fortunately, both Reed and Abdulmutallab were stopped by a combination of the ineffectiveness of the ignition systems for their explosives and alert passengers who subdued the bombers before they could repair the ignition systems.[70]

The 9/11 al Qaeda attack displayed an asymmetrical use of aircraft that, given their ultimate effect, had been converted into bombs. The use of the bomb by terrorists runs the gamut: from manufactured high-velocity explosives married to sophisticated timers and ignition devices to the "Black Powder" pipe bomb, which is still the most common bomb used in the United States.[71]

The bomb has also been incorporated in packages, letters, and vehicles since the 19th century. The package bomb, for instance, was effectively used in the United States by Theodore Kaczynski, the Unabomber, who from 1978 to 1995 murdered 3 persons and injured 10.[72] Starting in the 1980s, bombs were located on a person or placed in a vehicle driven by suicidal members of both secular and sectarian terrorist organizations. The suicide bomber is today's most effective system of bomb attacks by terrorists.[73]

Vehicle bombs, in addition to being driven by suicidal terrorists, are also used with remote detonation devices. Such remote-control devices have been a favored weapon of organized crime organizations and are currently in wide use by terrorist organizations in many areas of the world.[74]

Bombs have also been smuggled aboard aircraft, and certain devices can be used to detonate bombs when barometric pressure changes. Possibly the most deadly non-nuclear bomb that could be utilized by terrorists is a radiological dispersal bomb, also known as a dirty bomb, which is made by combining high explosives with radioactive material that could contaminate a geographical area upon detonation. No terrorist organization has actually detonated a dirty bomb yet, although one was constructed by Chechen terrorists and placed in a park in Moscow in 1995. The Chechens warned the Russians by calling a television station and describing the device and its location. The device was located and disarmed by Russian police.[75]

There exists sketchy information that al Qaeda has conducted research on radiological weapons and that the construction of such a weapon is within their capabilities. This organization may even have obtained the needed radioactive material, for much of the necessary material has been relatively available for many years through commercial sources. The actual effectiveness of a radioactive dispersal weapon in terms of loss of life is not as great as the public believes, however. It is not a true weapon of mass destruction because it can cause only a limited number of deaths. The immediate deaths would be approximately the same as those caused by the explosion alone. A dispersal weapon, however, could have other devastating effects on human life and would certainly cause a state of panic among a city's population.[76]

Hijacking

The hijacking of airplanes is synonymous with terrorism in the minds of many Westerners. This tactic was the preferred example of "propaganda by deed" for early Middle Eastern terrorist organizations. Taking over a plane whose passengers included citizens of their enemy nation and having the whole scenario portrayed to an international audience via television was a tactic that appealed to terrorist groups in the Middle East, whose actions against Israel were not having the required effect on its government. Their use of the tactic began in 1968 with the hijacking of an El Al flight to Algiers by members of the Popular Front for the Liberation of Palestine (PFLP). Numerous hijackings followed throughout the 1970s until an increase in security measures made the tactic less attractive to terrorists.[77] The tactic never vanished, however, and the culminating use of this tactic was the 9/11 attack, which combined plane hijacking, hostage taking, a suicidal attack, and the use of a WMD (the planes loaded with fuel driven into buildings), with horrific results.

From 2001 to 2008, there were 21 incidents of airline hijacking apart from the 9/11 hijackings. Of these hijackings, only 3 were committed by terrorists. Only 2 of the 3 were suicide attacks, and both showed some similarity to the 9/11 attacks. On August 24, 2004, two Russian commercial planes were hijacked by female Chechen suicide bombers who Russian authorities believe were members of the Islambouli Brigades of al Qaeda. Although the planes exploded in mid-air, forensic analysis of the wreckage revealed the explosive hexogen, which had previously been used by Chechen terrorists in a 1999 Moscow apartment building bombing.[78] Airplane hijacking is the epitome of an asymmetrical attack. However, current security practices on a worldwide basis will make such hijackings difficult to carry out, and future terrorists will probably attempt aircraft bombings that do not require command and control of the aircraft.

Kidnapping

Kidnapping and hostage holding continues to be a widely used tactic of terrorist groups. Hostage holding is used for the following reasons: (1) extortion to obtain funds or exchange prisoners, (2) publicity, and (3) human shields for operations and bases.[79]

Kidnapping individuals is a complex operation and often involves multiple components that may include criminal gangs. This complexity also makes it difficult for a government to conclusively determine if a kidnapping is a terrorist act or a criminal act using terrorism as a subterfuge. Between 2000 and 2007, there were approximately 600 kidnappings attributed to terrorist organizations that took place in a variety of countries and involved victims of various nationalities. These types of kidnapping incidents reached a low point in 2005 with less than 30 incidents and a high point in 2007 with 150 incidents. While such kidnappings occurred in numerous countries, there were exceptionally high numbers in Iraq and Nigeria during this time period.[80]

Arson

Arson is a consistently used terrorist tactic, either alone or in combination with a bombing attack. Unless an arson attack is claimed by a terrorist group, however, it is difficult for law enforcement to determine if a fire was caused by arson. Arson committed by professionals is a difficult crime to detect. In 2007, terrorist arson attacks, either alone or as part of combined attacks, numbered approximately 500 incidents worldwide. These incidents occurred in numerous countries, and the attacks were committed by a variety of terrorist groups. In the United States there were 55 attacks in 2007, almost all of which were committed by ecoterrorist groups that have stated philosophical positions of not harming either human or animal life. From this philosophical position, arson is the best option to obtain a result destructive enough to gain the publicity desired by the terrorist group without actually killing anyone.[81]

Weapons of Mass Destruction

The most feared yet most unlikely terrorist attacks involve WMD. The term WMD is normally considered to include chemical, biological, nuclear, and radiological weapons (CBNR). Classifying this broad range of deadly weapons as WMD assumes that the casualties and property damage resulting from an attack using these weapons would be beyond that which conventional weapons could normally achieve. In analyzing the use of WMD from 2000 to 2007, only 75 terrorist incidents took place, some of which were ambiguous. The first category reviewed—biological—is normally considered the most dangerous, with the exception of a nuclear weapon attack. During 2000–2007, only 14 biological weapon attacks occurred, and, of those 14, no terrorist groups were identified as the perpetrators.[82]

The most serious biological weapon attack was investigated by the FBI in their Amerithrax case. The case involved letters containing powdered anthrax, considered a WMD, that were mailed to a variety of targets in 2001, causing seven fatalities. The case was solved definitively in 2008. The perpetrator—Bruce Ivins, who took his own life by a drug overdose before he could be arrested—was a microbiologist and anthrax researcher at Fort Detrick, the U.S. Army lab in Maryland. Ivins's motivation for the crime is uncertain, but based upon the available information that was developed and released to the public, Ivins obviously had a severe personality disorder that was a factor in his decision to commit the crime.[83]

The other identified biological attacks involved ricin, a highly poisonous powdered derivative of the castor bean. Three ricin incidents occurred in 2003 and 2004, and all three involved letters whose envelopes also contained ricin; the letters were sent through the U.S. mail to the White House, the Department of Transportation, and Senate majority leader Bill Frist, respectively. The letters never reached their targets; the perpetrator has never been identified, and no injuries occurred. Signing the letters "fallen angel," the perpetrator was further identified in the letters as the fleet owner of a trucking company who was obviously angry about pending trucking regulations.[84]

Chemical attacks conducted by terrorist organizations, including ambiguous attacks, were analyzed for the period from 1970 to 2007 on a worldwide basis. During this time period, 212 incidents occurred. The most significant use of a chemical weapon was in 1998, when chemical bombs were used by the Oromo Liberation Front to attack a Kenyan army base in Wajir, Kenya, resulting in 142 deaths. The most widely known, successful chemical attack, however, was the Aum Shinrikyo cult's 1995 sarin gas attack on the Tokyo subway. Although various chemical weapons are widely available, it seems obvious that attacks using such weapons are difficult for terrorist groups to utilize effectively.[85]

In examining WMD attacks involving biological, chemical, and radiological weapons, their history of usage indicates terrorists either do not desire to or cannot employ these weapons as WMD. The amount of actual damage caused by these weapons has not been significant in relation to other types of terrorist attacks. Nevertheless, the potential remains for their usage by nihilistic groups or individuals with apocalyptic visions.[86] The deployment of selected biological agents and small nuclear devices is a threat with a low probability but high potential for mass casualties. The other types of WMD do not present the same degree of risk at this time.

Recently, the implementation of a cyber attack on infrastructure and critical facilities has been described as having the potential of a WMD. It remains to be seen if this type of attack is actually capable of causing large numbers of casualties or an extreme amount of property loss or damage. Catastrophic cyber attacks by terrorists have been feared for over a decade, but as yet none have occurred.[87]

In examining the basic components of terrorism, one element is essential—a violent act. The capability and willingness to commit violent acts is what separates a terrorist from a social or political activist. The next chapter examines the human capacity for committing violent acts and the mindset possessed by those individuals who become members of terrorist organizations or operate as lone wolf terrorists.

CHAPTER 4

The Terrorist Mindset

There are two methods of fighting, one with laws, the other with force: the first one is proper to man, the second to beasts; but because the first one often does not suffice, one has to have recourse to the second.
—Niccolò Machiavelli, *The Prince*

On March 29, 2010, the federal government, represented by the U.S. attorney general, the U.S. attorney for the Eastern District of Michigan, and the special agent in charge of the FBI's Detroit field office, announced a five-count indictment charging nine U.S. citizens, acting as a Lenawee County, Michigan, militia group called the Hutaree, with conspiring "to levy war against the United States."[1]

The indictment alleged that the Hutaree planned to commit a violent act to "draw the attention of law enforcement or government officials" in order to initiate a response by law enforcement. The Hutaree had developed several alternate scenarios, and each involved the murder of a member of law enforcement (one scenario also included the murder of a police officer's family members). Once this initial murder was committed, the Hutaree planned to attack the resultant funeral procession, which the Hutaree believed would include law enforcement officers from throughout the United States. The Hutaree intended to use improvised explosive devices (IED) and explosively formed projectiles (EFP) to carry out their crime.

According to the indictment, the Hutaree believed their actions would initiate a larger battle between themselves and government forces at several fortified, pre-positioned rally points. The Hutaree believed this battle would serve as the catalyst for a revolution against the U.S. government that would be carried out by militia forces throughout America.[2]

In a four-hour detention hearing subsequent to the arrest of the Hutaree members, the prosecutor recounted information gained by an FBI agent who had infiltrated the Hutaree. According to the prosecutor, the Hutaree are a Christian-based militia group that had been actively training for their planned attack on law enforcement for several months. The Hutaree believed they were battling an organization that was trying to rule the world and had already succeeded in gaining control over all law enforcement in the United States. Before their arrest, the group's members were under orders from their alleged leader, referred to as Captain Hutaree, to kill anyone encountered during their training sessions in preparation for their eventual battle with law enforcement.[3]

In his detention hearing statement to the U.S. federal magistrate, the prosecutor recounted that one of the group members had allegedly told another militia member that he had shot his cat to get ready for the planned operation. This individual was quoted by the prosecutor as saying, "I did it to see if I could do it, to see if I could kill something I had a feeling for."[4]

The Hutaree militia members are accused of sedition, and, if the facts alleged in this case are accurate, they clearly possessed a terrorist mindset. The U.S. government alleges its evidence shows the Hutaree's members possess a distinctive belief system characterized by hatred for the government, demonization of its law enforcement representatives, and a disposition to use violence to achieve a revolutionary goal. This mental structure of beliefs and goals, or mindset, is possessed by all terrorists. It is this mindset that, in conjunction with a situational component, makes it possible for humans to initiate an act of terroristic violence.

Fortunately, although individuals and groups are often motivated to affect radical political or social change, their psychological traits along with situational factors often restrict their actions to nonviolent modes of protest and civil disobedience. Even when situational factors are conducive to violent rebellion, most members of an affected society do not possess the ideological beliefs, goal-oriented thinking, and emotional traits required to commit violent acts for the purpose of fomenting political or social changes. These citizens lack the requisite mindset of the terrorist.

The term *mindset* refers to a fixed mental state relating to an individual's cognitive perception of society. A person's mindset includes inherited and environmentally influenced personality traits, group and individual ideologies, and culturally influenced values, beliefs, assumptions, and biases.[5] It has been described as an individual's "internal map of reality" that serves as a navigational guide through society. Unfortunately, an individual's singular map, or mindset, may not accurately describe the reality of the world.[6]

In examining the terrorist mindset, the first question is also the most controversial: do terrorists have a mindset that distinguishes them from other members of our species who do not use violence to achieve political or social goals? To answer this question, this chapter first examines the historical (yet still pertinent) observations of two brilliant political philosophers concerning interpersonal violence in political environments. Next, the human aptitude for violence is examined from an evolutionary, biological, and psychological perspective. The traits of the terrorist mindset are identified with an emphasis on the processes of motivation, justification, and group dynamics. Finally, the radicalization process is discussed as an introduction to the comprehensive treatment of the subject in chapters 5 and 6.

PHILOSOPHICAL OBSERVATIONS ON THE CHOICE TO USE VIOLENCE

Two individuals—Niccolò Machiavelli and Thomas Hobbes, political theorists who wrote in the 16th and 17th centuries, respectively—developed ideas that, although controversial in their lifetimes, remain influential today because of their perceptive insights into political violence and human nature.

Machiavelli's political environment was Italy from 1498 to 1532. During this period, Italy was a loose confederation of city-states characterized by competing political and religious dynasties, fear of the military forces of France and Spain, violent coups, and battles between mercenary armies of the competing Italian city-states. Machiavelli was both an observer and a political participant in these events. His actual political career culminated in his selection as a foreign affairs and military official of the republican city-state of Florence. His political career ended in 1512 when Spain sent an invading force to Italy that resulted in the surrender of Florence, the dissolution of the republic, and the return to power of the powerful Medici family. An ensuing dispute with the Medici family resulted in Machiavelli's removal from his position, imprisonment, and torture. Released as part of a general amnesty in honor of the election of Giovanni de' Medici as the new pope (Leo X), Machiavelli went into seclusion, where he wrote his seminal work, *The Prince*. Although written in 1513, *The Prince* was not published until 1531, four years after Machiavelli's death.[7]

The Prince was dedicated to instructing a ruler how to gain and maintain power. As part of this instruction, Machiavelli recognized the necessity for the use of instrumental violence in some political situations. His observations on human nature may have been validated by subsequent historical events, but they have also been widely criticized for advocating unscrupulous and immoral behavior. Machiavelli's experience with politics, men, and power caused him to discount the importance of morality to a leader who wished to gain political power and rule over men. *The Prince* was meant to offer guidance for those who desired to rule others. Machiavelli described the charismatic mindset a leader needed to develop in the realm of power and politics. In doing so, Machiavelli formulated the following prescient ideas about human nature that he believed should guide individuals who seek political power:

- Men are naturally wicked.
- Self-interest motivates men and is a trait that can be managed by a leader to achieve a successful result—a strong state.
- Men will respond to both love and fear, but fear is a more effective tool to gain obedience.
- Power is more important than moral values.
- The end, political power, is more important than the often-violent means used to achieve it.[8]

Insurgent movements and terrorist organizations have leaders who obtain political change by utilizing violence and who are accused by victims, both individuals and nations, of being cruel and irrational. In *The Prince,* these leaders find a rationale and a justification for the use of violence to obtain political power.

In the 17th century, Machiavelli's ideas on leadership and power were expanded upon by Thomas Hobbes, a political philosopher who was fascinated with the regulation of interpersonal violence. Hobbes lived from 1588 to 1679, spending his adult years in both England and Europe. His life progressed from student at Oxford, employment as a tutor to the sons of British nobility, recognition as a scholar and controversial political writer, and culmination in a life of scholarly reflection.

Hobbes, like Machiavelli, lived during a time of political and religious strife. In the year 1605, while Hobbes was a student at Oxford, Catholic extremists tried to blow up King James I, along with the members of Parliament. The revolutionary group had managed to obtain a large quantity of gunpowder that, fortunately for the prospective victims, was too damp to successfully ignite. This "gunpowder plot of 1605" was prevented by the arrest of the group's explosives expert, Guy Fawkes, in the cellar below Parliament while he attempted to light the fuse to 36 barrels of gunpowder. This extremist group bears some striking similarities to today's homegrown terrorist cells. The revolutionary cell members were Catholics who felt oppressed by the Protestant government of England. There was, in fact, discrimination against Catholics at the time. The group saw themselves as brave warriors fighting for a holy cause. Guy Fawkes, the actual trigger puller, attempted mass murder for a religious and political cause. Fawkes had been a mercenary and had fought for Catholic Spain's forces against the Protestant Dutch. His military experience furnished his expertise in handling gunpowder, and, upon his return to England, he was recruited into a preexisting Catholic revolutionary cell. After the arrest of the cell members, the government of England used torture to extract confessions from the conspirators, who were all subsequently executed by the government. These executions and their horrific results (all the participants were not only hanged, they were also drawn and quartered) were a highly publicized and controversial issue at the time.

After leaving Oxford, Hobbes became a tutor and companion to the son of a member of England's nobility and resided in France. At this time, England was engaged in the civil war of the 1640s between King Charles I and parliamentary forces under the command of Oliver Cromwell. In this civil war, Hobbes supported the royalists. While Hobbes was still in France, the royalist forces were defeated, and Charles I was beheaded. Hobbes wrote his seminal work—*The Leviathan*—while in France with numerous other royalist exiles. Eventually he returned to Protestant England, with the permission of Oliver Cromwell, because his book had upset France's Catholic government with its criticism of the Catholic Church. Hobbes stayed in England for the rest of his life and was a favorite of Charles II during the Restoration period of England's monarchy.[9]

In *The Leviathan*, Hobbes expressed ideas that were formulated during a long and violent period in England's history. He believed that men were afraid of other men and that this fear prevented the development of a stable society. He believed that interpersonal violence was caused by the passions and self-interest of men and that men lacked altruistic motivations. To Hobbes, fear was the essential condition of man's life, as well as the factor that forced men to curtail their predatory motivations and cooperate with others. Hobbes believed that men had three motivations: "So that in the nature of man, we find three principal causes of quarrel. First competition; secondly, diffidence; thirdly, glory. The first maketh men invade for gain; the second, for safety; and the third, for reputation. The first use violence, to make themselves masters of other men's persons, wives, children, and cattle; the second, to defend them; the third, for trifles, as a word, a smile, a different opinion, and any other signe of undervalue, either direct in their persons or by reflexion in their Kindred, their Friends, their Nation, their Profession, or their Name."[10] For Hobbes, the only way for man to achieve security was to come under the power of government, which to Hobbes was either a monarchy (preferred) or a parliamentary system.[11]

Both Hobbes and Machiavelli developed ideas that remain influential today. Their observations of and axioms about human nature as expressed in the political process have influenced government officials, leaders of organized crime, modern political strategists, and terrorists. The potential of man to choose the use of violence to achieve political, social, or economic goals was, to Machiavelli and Hobbes, an empirically derived fact that neither man ever doubted. They both felt that the security of the individual depended upon the strength of a political leader and believed that security was more important to men than any individual's rights. Their belief that man was driven by selfish motives and not altruism even guided the American founding fathers during their deliberations on the best way to govern their country.[12] Today, the struggle against terrorism furnishes empirical support for a Hobbesian and Machiavellian perspective on human nature.

To Hobbes and Machiavelli, the use of violence was a rational choice. To Machiavelli, men were motivated by self-interest, and violence was an acceptable method to achieve and keep political power. To Hobbes, men use interpersonal violence to gain what other men possess, to prevent the attack of other men, and to achieve glory, which would entail gaining respect from and power over other men. In today's world, individuals engaged in a political or social struggle sometimes choose violent actions to achieve their goals, just as in the eras of Hobbes and Machiavelli. This capacity to choose violence as an acceptable means to achieve political or social change is a component of the terrorist mindset.

THE APTITUDE FOR VIOLENCE

Lone wolf terrorists and selected members of terrorist organizations must be capable of using violence to achieve strategic goals. This aptitude—the ability to use violence in a premeditated, instrumental manner—separates terrorists from a significant portion of their fellow human beings. If violence as a constituent part of a terrorist act means killing another human being, does this ability become the master trait of the terrorist mindset?

Evolutionary and Biological Perspectives

Psychological, anthropological, and biological studies have reached differing conclusions about the human aptitude for violent behavior. According to evolutionary psychologist Stephen Pinker's wide-ranging work on human nature, *The Blank Slate,* individuals differ constitutionally as to their propensity to commit violent acts. Our personalities as a species include certain genetic traits that developed in our hunter-gatherer past. These traits include ethnocentrism, honor codes, moralization, and self-deception. According to Pinker, who also recognizes cultural influences on human aggression, violence "is the near inevitable outcome of the dynamics of self-interested, rational social organizations, the members of which possess these evolutionary traits."[13]

Pinker's evolutionary perspective on human nature is countered by a biological perspective that believes a human being's relation to her environment is influenced by both environmental and cultural influences that are an equal or greater influence on behavior than genes. Paul and Anne Ehrlich are prominent advocates for this perspective and consider culture a component of the environment, positing that our cultural practices and beliefs can override some genetic predispositions. In regard to the trait for aggression, the Ehrlichs believe that unlike those human characteristics that are products exclusively of natural selection, aggression is a trait that has a strong cultural component. This cultural component exercises far greater influence on the human organism's predisposition than behavioral genes.[14]

The Ehrlichs are also skeptical of the theory that humans possess an aggressive disposition as a behavioral trait. They note that intergroup violence is not common among most social mammals and that the chimpanzee studies that have shown predatory intergroup behavior are based on one chimpanzee troupe, which could be an anomaly. According to the Ehrlichs, "work with other primates suggests the environmental flexibility of aggressive behavior."[15]

In regard to human intergroup warfare, the Ehrlichs acknowledge that war occurred frequently among pre-state human groups and prehistorical humans. They have no doubt that humans have the capacity to be aggressive, but they doubt that the trait is determined solely by genetics or culture. According to the Ehrlichs, humans often engage in conflict because of environmental issues such as resource scarcity and population pressures. Thus, decisions to use violence are likely based on situational variables, not evolutionary proclivity.[16]

The Ehrlichs note that even when human beings are organized into armies for warfare, it is often difficult to get most individuals to kill another human being. They point to three great wars—the Civil War, World War I, and World War II—noting the low rate of actual firing among battle participants (information that has been verified through several studies) as an example of humans' disinclination to kill members of their own species. For the Ehrlichs, the Vietnam War was an exception, for by this time in history the human inhibition against killing was known by military trainers, who were able to extinguish this inhibition against killing through the specialized training of soldiers. Their firearms training methods (which used human-like targets) successfully raised the rate of firing and killing in combat during the Vietnam War. Today, these techniques are used by almost all modern armies and civilian police departments, for the disinclination of many individuals to kill others when their own lives are threatened, even on the battlefield, is well-known.[17]

Writing two decades before the Ehrlichs, Irenäus Eibl-Eibesfeldt made claims based on studies of the great apes in his work *The Biology of Peace and War: Men, Animals, and Aggression*. The human capacity for violence probably derived from the evolutionary process, according to Eibl-Eibesfeldt, but humans also inherit inhibitory mechanisms capable of preventing them from murdering other humans during an intragroup conflict, which enables them to live together in social groupings.[18]

According to Eibl-Eibesfeldt, the development of organized warfare (a human form of intergroup conflict) is culturally based. The decision to wage war is not an instinctual drive but a rational choice based on utilitarian calculations that generally involve the forcible appropriation of valuable natural resources. He argues that our ability to kill is culturally based because it is an essential part of intergroup warfare. However, for most individuals to kill another human would be difficult from an emotional perspective. Humans have to suppress their innate aversion to such killing by developing a justification for their act (if one does not actually exist), such as the belief that an identified group of persons is attempting to destroy their country. Because humans' intergroup conflicts often necessitate the killing of other humans, a filter has to be developed to allow such acts. One of these filters is provided by the apparent ability of humans to perceive members of another group as not being fully human and, thus, not members of the human species. The ability to do this, according to Eibl-Eibesfeldt, is a culturally developed mechanism.[19]

The human capacity for violence is complex. The potential for humans to be aggressive has certainly been part of our evolutionary heritage. Unlike other primates, however, our ability to transmit culturally derived traits to other humans makes our use of aggression subject to a greater degree of control and instrumental motivation than is expected in less-evolved primates. Certain terrorists, lone wolves, and selected members of terrorist groups, like Marighella's "firing group," are expected to commit violent acts that may include killing others—even innocent women and children. Most terrorists who are part of an organized group will be able to justify and, thus, participate, in some way, in the killing of selected members of any society. Lone wolf terrorists who possess the capacity to personally kill innocent strangers will, fortunately, always be rare and will usually display evidence of some degree of psychopathology. Terrorist groups, however, use the training and indoctrination of members who may not possess any psychological abnormalities to achieve an overall group capability to plan and execute violent actions. Selected members must have the capability to personally murder innocent human beings without remorse. Such killers have to filter out any murder inhibitions they may have possessed and rely instead upon Hobbes's competition, diffidence, and glory as motivational drivers to foster aggression toward an enemy identified as subhuman.[20]

Psychological Perspective

It is important to note that the term *mindset* is not a synonym for an individual's personality, although certain personality traits undoubtedly influence the development of individual mindsets. Whether a distinct terrorist personality exists is a question that has often been debated among terrorism scholars. The debate concerns two schools of psychology: the psychodynamic school and the psychological trait school.

Psychodynamic Theories

The psychodynamic school of psychology was first developed by Sigmund Freud and is heavily reliant upon various theories of human behavior based on an individual's early childhood experiences. This school of thought is often criticized as not sufficiently scientific, as failing to use experimental research, and as unable to demonstrate causation; indeed, some of its ideas, such as Freud's death instinct, are untestable. The opinion of many researchers in the area of terrorism studies is that psychodynamic theories, which are based upon clinical evaluations rather than measurable, quantitative evaluations, have limited predictive value.[21]

Trait Theory

Currently, trait theory is the primary focus of personality research by psychologists. For many years, psychologists developed personality profiles based on 16 bipolar source traits (e.g., reserved-outgoing) derived by Raymond Cattell. Today, personality profiling is accomplished by evaluating five orthogonal bipolar traits: (1) openness to experience, (2) conscientiousness, (3) extroversion, (4) agreeableness, and (5) neuroticism. These five traits are generally regarded as controlling personality factors that are the source of other, more specific personality characteristics. Trait theory recognizes that the external environment, such as an individual's employment or peer group, affects the way a person behaves—referred to as cross-situational inconsistencies. The behavior-predicting potential of trait theory has many supporters, and its advocates have incorporated an interactionist viewpoint and "see the personality and behavior of the individual at every point in life as the outcome of the interaction between his or her innate temperament and all the experiences he or she has had up to that point."[22]

An ongoing debate among terrorism scholars, related to personality-trait theory, is whether or not the existence of particular personality traits in certain individuals will lead those individuals disproportionately to become terrorists. Jerrold Post furnishes a guarded reply to this question when he states that a high percentage, but not all, of the terrorist population display a damaged self-concept. Those who do, according to Post, resolve feelings of inadequacy by utilizing the psychological mechanisms of externalization, shifting blame to outside forces, and splitting, which entails rejecting the damaged parts of the self-concept and projecting them onto another person or group, who then becomes a target.[23]

Post carefully qualifies his observations by affirming that each terrorist group has a distinct identity that can only be analyzed in the context of its cultural background. In this sense, Post relies upon prior psychological studies of Germany's Red Army, the Basque separatist group Euskadi Ta Askatasuna (ETA, or the Basque Fatherland and Liberty Movement), and Italy's Red Brigade terrorists to support his premise that political violence by some members of terrorist groups is driven by specific psychological characteristics.[24] From a contrasting perspective, John Horgan, in an inclusive review of the literature concerning the predictive ability of trait theory in the realm of individual terrorism, concludes that the theory has limited utility and suffers from "conceptual, theoretical, and methodological problems."[25]

TERRORIST CHARACTERISTICS

If one accepts the premise that there are no definitive psychological traits that distinguish terrorists who commit acts of interpersonal violence from normal individuals, are there physical and psychological characteristics that such individual members *must* possess to operate effectively? For example, the late Eric Hoffer, in his work on political movements, *The True Believer*, states that all religious, revolutionary, and nationalistic mass movements appealed to individuals who shared the same "peculiar characteristics." Hoffer identifies a fervent member of a mass movement as an example of a "true believer: a man of fanatical faith who is ready to sacrifice his life for a holy cause."[26]

For Hoffer, regardless of movement type, "true believers" will possess common characteristics. The most important characteristic is a sense of "frustration," which Hoffer claims generates other identifying traits. Hoffer identifies the following pre-membership traits in those he labels true believers: (1) desire for change, (2) looking to the future, and (3) desire for a new identity tied to a great cause. According to Hoffer, mass movements attract some members from the ranks of the poor and criminal. The group ("collective body") would then develop the other essential traits necessary for members to function effectively and carry out the strategic goals of their organization: (1) self-sacrifice, (2) hatred of the present, (3) hatred and demonization of the enemy, (4) imitation of other members, (5) violence, (6) obedience and submission, and (7) suspicion.[27] Hoffer views violence and fanaticism as conjugates: "The practice of terror serves the true believer not only to cow and crush his opponents but also to invigorate and intensify his own faith."[28] Hoffer's determination that an individual's sense of frustration was the impetus for joining a mass movement leads to the question of causation—what conditions in a society cause some people to become frustrated?

Ted Gurr, in his foundational work, *Why Men Rebel*, focuses on the idea of relative deprivation as an origin of political violence. Gurr defines relative deprivation as "a perceived discrepancy between men's value expectations and their value capabilities"; in other words, what men believe they are going to achieve even though they have abilities that should allow them to achieve much more. He traces the genesis of political violence from the discontent and frustration individuals feel when unable to achieve their desired goals to the externalization of blame onto the existing political system and ending, in some groups, with the commission of violent acts against perceived enemies. Gurr terms this last stage as "actualization."[29] Although relative deprivation leading to frustration may cause some individuals to join political movements, the decision to join a terrorist organization will usually depend upon additional factors.

Bruce Hoffman, in his analysis of the terrorist mindset, identifies a trait trilogy that terrorists tend to share, despite belonging to different organizations: violence, action orientation, and focus on future goals. Hoffman recognizes violence as the master trait of terrorism: "Violence or the threat of violence is thus the *sine qua non* of terrorists."[30] Although violence is a master trait, the ideologies of lone wolf terrorists and varied other terrorist groups affect the degree and target of such violence. For example, revolutionary groups generally focus their violence on members of the government and rarely commit acts that cause harm to innocent members of the population. On the other hand, religious terrorists are more indiscriminate in their application of violence. They are able to justify such violence as a sacred duty.[31] FBI criminal behavior analysts would agree with Hoffman's trait trilogy. The FBI uses a basic axiom for criminal profiling: behavior reflects personality. Individual criminals who resort to violent behavior have a distinct personality profile that includes impulsivity and an orientation for action. It is Hoffman's identification of "future oriented goals" as a terrorist trait that distinguishes most terrorists from most criminals.[32]

Donatella della Porta's research on Italian left-wing terrorism in Italy from 1970 through 1983 includes an analysis of how an aptitude for violence influences both individual motivations for joining terrorist groups and the recruitment process. Della Porta's detailed qualitative data demonstrates how recruitment of individuals is influenced by the existence of "cliques" in which the same individuals interact with one another through participation in a variety of activities. Based on the data, della Porta concludes that the choice by an individual to join a terrorist group is influenced primarily by the individual's social interaction with other like-minded individuals rather than individual motivation to join a terrorist group. Social networks and personal ties were revealed as primary factors in the recruitment process. Italian terrorist groups recruited their members through these networks and looked for militant individuals who had a demonstrated predisposition to commit acts of violence.[33] In considering an individual's capacity for violence, della Porta reached the following conclusion:

People become involved in terrorist activities when they belong to dense political networks and are socialized to accept violence. Previous exposure to violence predisposes individuals to involvement in terrorism. Participation in violence produces a kind of militant for whom political commitment is aligned with physical fights rather than with negotiation or compromise. For these people, the use of physical violence precedes rather than follows entrance into terrorist organizations.[34]

TERRORIST MOTIVATIONS

In any theoretical examination of the terrorist mindset, one problem will present itself to persons who have closely interacted with, or investigated individual members of, a terrorist group. The members of a terrorist group may not have identical mindsets; in fact, their mindsets may be extremely different, and the late Dr. Frederick Hacker was the first scholar-practitioner to fully address this issue. In his examinations of terrorist groups operating in the 1960s and 1970s, Hacker observed that all the groups under study were composed of three types of individual with distinctly different mindsets. Hacker identifies these types as "crusaders, criminals, and crazies."[35]

According to Hacker, the crusader is the prototypical terrorist motivated by an external societal or political cause, one who uses violence as a rational means to achieve a goal that is beneficial, in the eyes of the crusader, to society. The criminal terrorist, on the other hand, is motivated by personal benefit and is not committed to an external cause that does not involve personal profit. Not surprisingly, the crazy terrorist is a rare category. While ranges of mental stability and intellectual capability vary greatly among all individuals, Hacker sees the crazy as "sometimes delusional and unstable, immature, [and] often distractible."[36]

One clear problem with Hacker's "crazy terrorist" category is its overlap with both the criminal and crusader categories. For example, the psychotic individual who displays delusional or extreme paranoiac behavior would not be capable of functioning in a terrorist group, whereas a lesser degree of mental illness or a severe personality disorder, such as psychopathy, might allow an individual to function effectively within a terrorist group structure.[37] This latter group of individuals, however, would probably gravitate toward lone wolf activity or membership in small, disorganized cells, where their self-centered, impulsive behavior would not be detected as readily as it would in a larger, organized terrorist group.

The psychopathic individual is represented in the criminal terrorist population, but the extent of that representation is unknown. According to psychologist Robert Hare, approximately 20 percent of prison inmates are classified as psychopaths, although the exact percentage in the criminal population at large is unknown. In fact, psychopaths have characteristics that make them poor members for a terrorist organization or an organized crime group. For example, their impulsivity, focus on the present, and undependability are characteristics that would make them unreliable and dangerous members of any structured, self-perpetuating organization. Other characteristics, however, would make psychopaths quite valuable, including their capacity for instrumental violence, lack of empathy for victims, and manipulative behavioral skills. As long as a psychopath is conducting successful terrorist actions that showcase her unique skills, participation in group actions will continue and could be valuable to the group.[38]

It is a mistake to discount the possibility that psychopaths are present within terrorist groups and may even have achieved leadership positions. Some would be able to do this because, like crusader terrorists, they may possess the ability to influence and charm prospective followers, as well as the ability to assume a role (imposter) that will, in their own minds, give them a sense of respect and power over others. The key to their success as terrorists would be their ability to cloak their true selves. Referring to this class of psychopaths as subcriminal psychopaths, Hare characterizes them as egocentric, callous, and manipulative yet possessed of intelligence and social skills permitting them to create a facade of normalcy that allows them to achieve success in many careers.[39]

One example of a highly probable psychopathic individual successfully integrating into a terrorist organization occurred in Northern Ireland during the 1970s. The Ulster Volunteer Force (UVF)—an extremely violent Protestant terrorist organization—recruited a group of violent criminals, known as the Shankill Butchers, led by Hugh Leonard Murphy. Murphy murdered, tortured, and robbed for the UVF and his own pleasure. He enjoyed hunting for, and capturing, randomly selected victims on nighttime forays in Belfast. His victims were transported to a Protestant Loyalist social club, and Murphy used butcher's knives and hatchets to torture and kill them. He also never displayed loyalty to his companions; he broke the UVF's rules involving murder and lied to his superiors about his activities in the organization. Murphy operated as a successful criminal terrorist for several years before being killed by members of another terrorist group whose criminal extortion racket Murphy had tried to take over. Murphy is an example of the sort of psychopathic terrorist that some terrorist movements employ because of his skill at murder.[40] To lead a terrorist group, however, the psychopath would have to assume the role of a crusader, a masquerade that would be difficult to maintain for an extended period of time.

Unlike the uncommon psychopathic terrorist, Hacker's crusader is the classical terrorist, one whose motivations predominantly consist of the desire to galvanize social or political change. There are, however, notable variations in the crusader's mindset based both upon the ultimate strategic goal and the tactics used to achieve the goal. Preexisting beliefs and beliefs constructed by the terrorist movement are reconciled and merged, becoming part of the individual's mindset. The mindset's belief structures are linked to the group's tactics, targets, and the logical coherence of the group strategy. This factor is clearly displayed in religious-based terrorist organizations whose strategic goals are linked to religious beliefs. In the United States, individuals or groups that have as strategic goals the achievement of white supremacy or the elimination of a Zionist-controlled government often integrate group goals, however illogical, with individual religious beliefs that validate and justify the violent tactics necessary to achieve the goals.[41]

The major distinction among the three types of terrorists in Hacker's typology is their different motivations. Hacker explicitly states, however, that a pure type of terrorist is rare and that individuals usually have mixed motivations. Also, the motivations of some individuals for engaging in terrorism can change over time; for example, an individual with a crusader orientation could develop a criminal orientation or, in rarer cases, a criminal terrorist could develop a crusader orientation.[42]

Unlike psychopathic terrorists, those terrorists who still possess conscience-driven restrictions on the use of violent behavior generally develop mechanisms to neutralize their inhibitions or justify their violent tactics. These neutralization mechanisms and justifications become part of the terrorist mindset.

JUSTIFICATION AND NEUTRALIZATION

The ideologies of revolutionary movements, particularly religious-based terrorist organizations, include certain standards of behavior and cultural values that the group espouses as part of its appeal to both potential converts and its public base of support. These standards include norms regulating the use of violence.[43] The group's ideology often furnishes members with a justification for the violent acts they are expected to commit as part of the group's strategic plan. The individual member's mindset may include beliefs that serve as neutralization mechanisms. The justification, or neutralization, process takes place during the mental explanation, or "self-talk," that individual members engage in to dispel conscience-driven, moral restraints on prospective acts of violence. For example, this process often entails the use of "slogans invested with recollection of grievance and violence . . . to justify political violence."[44]

The prominent researcher, Albert Bandura, describes this neutralization and justification process, which he terms moral disengagement, as the inhibition of the activation of the self-sanctions that regulate conduct for all socialized people. This process involves mechanisms we use in everyday life to cut off the pangs of conscience when we are about to commit an act that violates our moral standards. Bandura explains moral disengagement as a psychological process involving three components: the act, the results, and the victim. The perpetrator of a violent act must use psychological techniques to justify the act, reinterpret or ignore the results, or demonize the victim.[45]

Using murder as a tactic for carrying out a strategy of terrorism would require most individuals to use the process of moral disengagement. This process involves similar techniques, even though the causes motivating the individual or group are different. For example, an act of murder could be justified as necessary for the defense of the group, or it could be viewed as a religious imperative or as necessary from a utilitarian standpoint. The results could be reinterpreted by using the technique of "advantageous

comparison" based on the historical actions of the state, ethnic group, or religious order the victim symbolizes. For example, it is common to read or
hear jihadi terrorist groups negate the murder of innocent Americans
as insignificant when compared to the many deaths caused by historical
U.S. bombing attacks, such as the World War II use of nuclear weapons
on Japan.[46]

Terrorists, when attacking the military or police forces of the government, routinely use the disengagement technique of demonization. Opposing military and police forces are characterized as cruel and subhuman
by exaggerating their violent acts or publicizing the occurrence of legiti-
mately wrongful actions. In attacking civilians, terrorist groups blame the
victims for not heeding the warnings or for working to support the targeted enemy. Euphemistic language is often used, such as referring to victims as collateral damage.[47]

According to David Rapoport, religious beliefs are particularly powerful ways to sanction terrorist acts. Individuals and groups look to a religious historical past to find a cultural justification for actions taken today.
Rapoport illustrates his point with the historical tale of Phineas, a member
of a Jewish tribe who became a Jewish high priest during the founding period in the Sinai. When Phineas was an ordinary member of the tribe, he
murdered the leader of his tribe and the leader's foreign concubine. Phineas believed the victims had committed the crime of the desecration of a
holy place, and he murdered them without any governmental authority
for his act. The later Zealot-Sicarii insurgency against Roman occupation
used Phineas's act as a justification for their own murder of both Romans
and the Jewish supporters of the Roman government. In the United States
today, Phineas's conduct is used as a justification for the violent acts of religious terrorist groups, and certain lone wolf terrorists have been termed
"Phineas priests."[48]

For some—generally ethical and conscientious individuals—moral disengagement techniques will not easily allow the killing of another human
being. If this individual joins a terrorist group, the group processes will
greatly facilitate the disengagement mechanism.

GROUP DYNAMICS

Group dynamics affect and change the pre-group behavior of prospective members. A terrorist group is actually composed of two opposing
forces: goal-directed behavior (work group) and group-process dynamics (basic group assumptions). For Post, group operations are affected by
three basic assumptions: (1) fight or flight, where the group assumes it has
an outside enemy; (2) dependency, where the basic group desire is for an
omnipotent leader; and (3) pairing, where the group obsesses about the assumed eventual arrival of a savior-like figure. Terrorist groups focus on
one or all three group processes in conjunction with goal-directed behav-

ior, but the dynamics differ in some aspects among the different types of groups.[49]

A collective rationality, or group mind, develops in cohesive groups over time. From a rational-choice perspective on terrorist group decision making, the development of the group mind prevents the "free rider" problem from developing if the individual members regard the group's needs as more important than individual desires. In the development process of the group mind, the psychological identities of the members become submerged in the group. The survival of the group becomes the highest goal, which leads to a disinclination to accept any dissent that could threaten the group. Group members become rigid and obedient, and the group imposes an absolutist ideology on individual members to assist in the justification of violent acts. In effect, each individual ideally shares one morality—the group's.[50]

Because of the emotional pressure caused by the external threat of police and military forces and the group's underground existence, terrorist group members display an exaggerated group mind. The members may develop feelings of invulnerability and become prone to riskier behavior than their former individual predilections would have allowed. They perceive the enemy as an evil force, and plans for violent actions are justified. The group members become more obedient to group-imposed rules, and a core set of shared beliefs develops. Challenges to key beliefs by individual members may result in punishment, expulsion, or possible execution.[51]

The group dynamic makes it easier for individual terrorists to justify violent acts. The group's mindset determines the target and degree of violence used. For example, violence is instrumental for terrorist groups (some individuals may also be satisfying expressive needs), but a jihadi group may use violence more indiscriminately because their mindset regards the use of violence against specified targets as a sacred duty.[52] Belonging to a group also fosters the process of neutralization of morality. The collective nature of actions and decision making allows group members to displace and diffuse responsibility for violent acts.[53]

The size of the group and the personality of the group's leader significantly affect the group mindset. Small groups, the focus of this book, generally have limited effectiveness, but their size makes them difficult to detect, and, more often than large, hierarchically structured groups, small groups often develop an action-supporting ideology that has, at best, a bounded rationality hard for outsiders to understand. Their ideologies are often apocalyptic and millenarian, and they often believe a new world will be constructed based on their ideology. These groups are usually not part of mass social movements or insurgencies, and they do not have a realistic chance of accomplishing a constructive goal. These groups may consist of a small number of autonomous cells with little contact and no combined strategy among the cells. In some cells, the cell mindset justifies extreme violence often exceeding the level of violence set by the groups.[54]

Groups are a powerful influence on individuals who are drawn to them. Certain individuals have mental and physical characteristics that, although not restricted to prospective terrorists, are necessary components of an eventual formation of the terrorist mindset. These traits may also predispose them to recruitment into a radical group and to acceptance of ideologies that could lead to the commission of an act of terror. Today, there is a new emphasis on deciphering exactly how an individual moves from seeming normalcy, although possibly possessing some characteristics common to most terrorists, to the rapid development of radicalization and the eventual commission of an act of terrorism.

RADICALIZATION PROCESS

Since the 9/11 al Qaeda attack on the United States, Western governments—including law enforcement, intelligence agencies, and think tanks—have sought an understanding of the personal transformational process used by terrorist organizations to convert peaceful members of society to individuals who will commit the mass murder of innocent civilians in the name of religion. This process is termed radicalization and, in reference to jihadi terrorism, is defined as "the progression of searching, finding, adopting, nurturing, and developing this extreme belief system to the point where it acts as a catalyst for a terrorist act."[55] One of the factors in this process is the influence of relatives, peers, and social groups.[56]

Initially, the radicalization process was believed to be guided by established terrorist organizations. Organizations, such as al Qaeda, utilized recruiters to seek out potential converts to the organization's cause in a variety of countries, including Iraq. Since the 2004 terrorist attack in Madrid and the 2005 bombing attacks in London, there has been a recognition in the West that individuals without a direct, recruiter-generated link, and possibly without any link, to preexisting terrorist organizations can seemingly self-generate into small jihadi terrorist groups and carry out violent attacks. These individuals—local residents and citizens of a variety of countries including the United States—are now identified as homegrown, self-generating terrorist groups that are not actively recruited or trained by al Qaeda or any other terrorist group. These self-radicalized individuals who use a religion-based ideology as a justification for their violent acts have attacked their own countries. These attacks began in 2004, when Madrid's transportation system was bombed, and include subsequent attacks and attempted attacks in Europe, the United States, and Canada.[57]

The research concerning homegrown terrorist groups is expressed by two types of influential phase models that illustrate the chronology of the process of radicalization: (1) the top-down model and (2) the bottom-up model. The model described by the New York Police Department (NYPD) in their 2007 report on radicalization of homegrown terrorist groups describes radicalization from the bottom-up perspective. The model posits the process as being self-generated by individuals through the facilitation of "radicalization incubators," a concept that includes bookstores, prisons, and the cyber world.[58] The Danish Security and Intelligence Service's 2009 radicalization phase model looks at the process from the top down as generated by an external radicalizer, a person connected to an existing terrorist network.[59]

The current research on the radicalization process is focused on those terrorist organizations that are characterized as Salafi jihadi. Al Qaeda exemplifies a global Salafi jihadi group. Marc Sageman, in his work on Salafi jihadism, defines the term as "a worldwide religious revivalist movement with the goal of reestablishing past Muslim glory in a great Islamist state stretching from Morocco to the Philippines, eliminating present national boundaries."[60] The radicalization process should also apply to other types of terrorist groups that have similar underlying motivations and social networks. Interest in this subject is driven by the realization that unless we develop an understanding of why people join terrorist groups and create mechanisms to deter such behavior, the battle against terrorism is going to be a long war. This issue of radicalization was recognized in Rex Hudson's 1999 governmental report but was essentially dismissed by Hudson as a viable concept in relation to terrorist groups as opposed to guerilla organizations: "The goals of a long-range counter terrorism policy should also include deterring alienated youth from joining a terrorist group in the first place. This may seem an impractical goal, for how does one recognize a potential terrorist, let alone deter him or her from joining a terrorist group?"[61] The question Hudson posed in 1999 has generated possible answers in relation to Salafi jihadi groups. Although the prominent NYPD and PET studies only examined this type of group, it is highly probable that some type of radicalization process applies to all terrorist groups.[62]

The initial interest in Islamist radicalization, on the part of U.S. and European intelligence agencies, focused on Muslims in their native countries. These were Muslims who already possessed a religious orientation and subsequently developed a terrorist mindset as part of the indoctrination process of a terrorist organization such as al Qaeda or Hezbollah. This indoctrination was carried out in most cases by charismatic religious leaders or individuals who claimed this type of mantle. In the 21st century, the focus of the U.S. and European intelligence community has moved to homegrown terrorists because of the realization that a jihadist mindset can develop in some individuals who are not overly active in the Islamic faith, who are not Muslim from birth, and who are, in some cases, well integrated into the law-abiding community.[63]

The top-down process involving contact with and initiation of susceptible individuals by a recruiter from an existing terrorist organization is easily understandable. The bottom-up process, however, where individuals self-generate into a terrorist cell, was initially treated as a new and novel development. Research has revealed, however, that individuals often intersect at various social sites and form peer groups that may facilitate the radicalization process. These social sites, or nodes, consist of informal and formal social settings, such as local gyms, bookstores, mosques, universities, the Internet, and prisons. The way in which these various social nodes foster radicalization in certain individuals has not yet been studied in the United States. However, the prison system and its influence on the radicalization process of certain inmates has been studied extensively and may offer valuable insight into this process.[64]

Marc Sageman's study of terrorist networks led to his theory that homegrown terrorist groups develop from socially alienated "bunches of guys" who join together in a self-radicalizing process that is not initiated by an external guide. Sageman believed, however, that an eventual relationship with a member of the chosen radical movement would be necessary for the self-radicalized group to carry out terrorist actions.[65]

In some areas of the world the pool of potential converts to terrorist groups is quite large. In other areas, including the United States, this does not seem to be the case. Since the 9/11 attacks, there has not been another successful attack by a jihadi terrorist group in the United States. Empirical evidence shows, however, that individuals in the United States and other Western countries are being recruited and radicalized on an individual and group basis. Since 9/11, there have been numerous plots and unsuccessful attempts to commit acts of jihadi terrorism in the United States. The majority of the individuals involved were homegrown terrorists. There have also been several successful attacks by lone wolf terrorists. The threat of single terrorists, operating alone, is hard to address from a security standpoint, and their motivations are not easily understood. Moreover, radicalization is not a 21st-century development but has always been a factor in the development of both terrorist cells and lone wolf terrorists. The anarchist wave of terrorism in the 19th and early 20th centuries consisted of numerous self-radicalized individuals. In the 20th century, self-radicalization was exemplified by Timothy McVeigh's 1996 mass murder in Oklahoma City.[66]

THE NEW THREAT

Self-radicalizing, homegrown terrorists, both lone wolves and small, autonomous cells, have become the newest threat to a civilized society. Chapter 5 explores the ecoterrorists, whose mindset involves a motivation to protect the natural environment but sanctions the infliction of extreme damage to property and the tactic of arson. Chapter 6 examines the nihilistic terrorists, whose mindset is apocalyptic and sanctions the indiscriminate killing of human beings as well as the destruction of our natural environment, and criminal terrorist hybrid groups, whose dual motivations and capabilities are a difficult threat to security organizations in many of the world's most dangerous regions.

CHAPTER 5

The Radical Environmental Movement: Eco-Warriors or Terrorists?

I know violence is morally wrong and non-violence is morally right. But what about results? Non-violent action alone has seldom produced beneficial change on our planet. . . . I compromise by allowing myself violence against property but never against life, human or otherwise.
                   —Paul Watson, *Sea Shepherd: My Fight for Whales and Seals*

[In] cases of the highest importance it is of no consequence whether a man breaks a human law or not.
                   —Henry David Thoreau, "A Plea for Captain John Brown"

On May 5, 2002, 10 days before the Dutch election for prime minister, right-wing candidate Pim Fortuyn was interviewed at a radio station in the Dutch town of Hilversum. Upon leaving the station, he was intercepted by Volkert van der Graaf, a member and cofounder of a small environmental organization called Environment-Offensive. Van der Graaf, carrying a gun wrapped in a plastic bag, shot Fortuyn five times and fled on foot. The ensuing police investigation quickly led to van der Graaf's identification and arrest for the crime of murder.[1]

Fortuyn, already known for his anti-immigration stance, had stated on television before his murder that he would suspend restrictions on animal breeding, including mink farming. He also had written in his book, which serves as the conservative party's political platform, that "it is time we stopped moaning about nature and the environment." Van der Graaf was obsessed with liberating animals from being used for food, clothing, and medical experiments, according to those who knew and worked with him.[2] On April 15, 2003, van der Graaf was sentenced to 18 years in prison for the assassination of Fortuyn.[3]

In the history of the radical environmental movement (beginning in the 1960s), the murder of Pim Fortuyn is the only occasion in which the death of a human being was directly caused by an environmental activist. On the other hand, individuals and groups involved in the REM will point out that they have been responsible for saving thousands of nonhuman lives and have stopped environmental damage caused by industry and government actions that have negatively affected the natural environment of which human beings are a part.[4]

Who are the radical environmentalists? Are they eco-warriors, who fight what they perceive as the evil forces that benefit from their profit-motivated exploitation of the world's ecosystems? Or are they terrorists who, despite their seemingly altruistic desire to protect animals and the natural environment, use illegal acts of violence against property or persons to achieve political or social change? Unlike other individuals or groups defined as terrorists, the radical environmental movement is sui generis.

Many of the individuals and small cells that make up the REM are clearly not terrorists, although they may commit criminal acts of minor degrees and minimal magnitude. Others can be classified as terrorists if the pertinent legal definition of terrorism includes acts of violence directed against property resulting in significant economic loss. Some are clearly terrorists in that they either threaten to commit or do commit acts of violence against people and have a strategic goal of social or political change.[5]

The REM is composed of diverse groups and individuals. To understand this unique movement, it is necessary to examine its philosophical foundation, causal forces, organizational models, and chosen tactics.

PHILOSOPHICAL FOUNDATION

The eco-warrior who is an actual "spear thrower" is usually young and not a philosopher. The predominant belief possessed by most activists in this movement is that action, not ideological debate, must be taken to save the environment.[6] The REM movement, however, as developed or expressed by both its underground terrorist cells and aboveground activist organizations, possesses a philosophical foundation that has developed through the words and actions of environmentalists, philosophers, and activist leaders who have responded to a perceived threatened environment in a reasoned way, including by developing an ideology that justified their actions. Today, the REM's ideology is diverse but possesses the unifying philosophical belief that human beings do not have the right to exercise unrestricted dominion over the natural environment, including the nonhuman species that exist within that environment.[7] This belief can best be understood by examining the thought leaders—those individuals who, for a period of over 150 years, have expressed in deeds and written works the ideas that have resulted in the philosophy of today's REM

Henry David Thoreau (1817–62)

The diminution of the historical belief in the right of human beings to exercise dominion over the earth was first explored by members of the 19th-century transcendentalist movement. Transcendentalism was the first movement that confronted the power of America's growing system of free-market capitalism with the belief that the spiritual nature of the wilderness should be protected against the forces of the market. Although the transcendentalist movement was led by Ralph Waldo Emerson (who wrote a noted work titled *Nature* in 1836), the environmental perspective that influenced today's environmental activists was that of Henry David Thoreau. Unlike Emerson, who appreciated nature but believed man was the master of nature and its products, Thoreau had a perspective on nature that perceived humanity, plants, and animals as equal "animate beings."[8]

Thoreau could be considered the father of the environmental movement, although the term itself and its principles did not exist during his lifetime. In his first work, *A Week on the Concord and Merrimack Rivers*, Thoreau revealed his latent feeling about man's dominion over nature through his reflections on observing an ancient white pine being cut down by human hands.

A pine cut down, a dead pine, is no more a pine than a dead human carcass is a man. Can he who has discovered only some of the values of whalebone and whale oil be said to have discovered the true use of the whale . . . ? I have been into the lumber-yard and the carpenter shop and the tannery . . . but when at length I saw the tops of pines waving and reflecting the light at a distance high over all the rest of the forest, I realized that the former were not the highest uses of the pine. It is not their bone or hide or tallow that I love most. It is the living spirit of the tree. . . . It is as immortal as I am, and perchance will go to as high a heaven, there to tower above me still.[9]

During his trip on the Concord and Merrimack rivers, Thoreau became concerned about a dam on the Concord River and the fact that fish would no longer be able to migrate upstream because of man's manipulation of their environment: "Poor shad! Where is thy redress? . . . Still wandering the sea in thy scaly armor to inquire humbly at the mouths of rivers if man has perchance left them free for thee to enter."[10]

Thoreau actually thought about destroying the dam, a thought that has occupied the minds of today's environmental activists: "Who hears the fishes when they cry? I for one am with thee, and who knows what may avail a crow-bar against that Billerica dam?"[11]

Thoreau is also important as a source for the justification used today by activists who commit acts of resistance. In his reflective essay on laws and obedience, which today is titled *Civil Disobedience*, Thoreau remarked favorably on rebellion against an unjust government: "All men recognize the right of revolution; that is the right to refuse allegiance to, and to resist, the government, when its tyranny or its inefficiency are great and unendurable."[12]

Thoreau, an abolitionist, also advocated physical violence against property and human beings if the situation involved an unjust act, such as enforcing provisions of the fugitive slave law: "I need not say what match I would touch, what system endeavor to blow up; but as I love my life, I would side with the light, and let the dark earth roll from under me, calling my mother and brother to follow."[13]

In his essay "A Plea for Captain John Brown," Thoreau justified the violent actions John Brown had taken in his fight against slavery, including numerous acts of murder. John Brown was found guilty of murder and was hanged for an attack he and his group had made on the federal arsenal at Harpers Ferry in 1859. His actions, however, were considered valorous and noble by Thoreau, because Brown's cause—the abolition of slavery and the freeing of all slaves—was a worthy cause that required violent acts for its success: "It was his peculiar doctrine that a man has a perfect right to interfere by force with the slave-holder, in order to rescue the slave. I agree with him. . . . I do not wish to kill nor to be killed, but I can foresee circumstances in which both of these things would be by me, unavoidable."[14] Thoreau clearly believed that in matters of conscience, a man could break the law. Today, the Web site of the Animal Liberation Front offers a comparison of Thoreau's principles of civil disobedience to an ALF action.[15]

George Perkins Marsh (1801–82)

Although not a philosopher or transcendentalist, George Marsh expressed the first ecological perspective on the environment in his book *Man and Nature* in 1864. Marsh was a Vermont fish commissioner, U.S. congressman, and member of the U.S. Diplomatic Corps. He believed man had an excessive impact on the environment and needed to work with nature in order to restore its resources. Marsh had a utilitarian perspective on wilderness regions and argued that by preserving nature, mankind would benefit both spiritually and economically. Marsh believed the different components of the wilderness were interrelated and that our civilization would decline in economic power if our nation failed to preserve the entire wilderness system.[16]

John Muir (1838–1914)

Bridging the 19th and 20th centuries, John Muir was influenced by Thoreau and the philosophy of transcendentalism. He developed a mystical relationship with the natural environment, referring to it as "God's ca-thedral." His extensive travels through Western wilderness regions were memorialized through his writing. His journals and articles, along with his spoken advocacy, were essential to the eventual establishment of the National Park System. Muir had developed a close relationship with President Theodore Roosevelt, a fellow conservationist, and was able to influence Roosevelt to set aside enormous tracts of land for national forests and parks. The importance of Muir to the radical environmental movement was his stance as a preservationist of the wilderness. Other conservationists, such as Gifford Pinchot, the first head of the National Park Service, believed in conserving the wilderness but using it wisely. This conservationist viewpoint, termed the "wise use school," believed that wilderness resources were valuable but needed to be shared for the benefit of humankind. The "preservationist school," as represented by Muir, viewed the wilderness as a threatened asset that had to be protected from human despoilment. Muir's focus on preservation and a belief in public ownership of wilderness areas led to his successful campaign for the protection of the Sierra region through the creation of Yosemite National Park.[17]

Muir was the first environmental activist and was a founder and first president of the Sierra Club. Muir's most famous environmental battle involved the proposed Hetch Hetchy Valley dam that was being considered for construction in Yosemite National Park. The dam was designed to bring water to San Francisco, which had a severe water shortage, but Muir opposed the dam because it would destroy the valley. Opposing Muir's viewpoint was Gifford Pinchot, who saw the dam as having an environmental value as well as an even greater value to the welfare of human beings in San Francisco. Muir lost the battle, and the dam was built between 1915 and 1920. Muir's battle was emblematic of today's conflict over damming rivers and cutting ancient forests. Muir was a transitional figure to the environmental movement of today, with its emphasis on "quality of life, species preservation, population growth, and the effects of humanity on the natural world."[18]

Aldo Leopold (1887–1948)

Aldo Leopold was a formally trained forester who graduated from the Yale Forestry School in 1909. He began his professional life as an employee of the U.S. Forest Service, where he was an advocate of the preservationist approach to wilderness areas. Leopold worked in the Arizona and New Mexico territories and became known for his ideas on game conservation. Later in life, Leopold became president of the Ecological Society of America. He embraced an ecological perspective that recognized the equality of man and nature. His ideas were expressed in his book, *A Sand Country Almanac*. Published posthumously in 1949, his book is still widely read for its ecological insights.[19]

Edward Abbey (1927–89)

Beginning in 1954 with his first novel, *Jonathan Troy*, Edward Abbey was the midwife to today's radical environmental movement. Abbey's works have been characterized by their themes of anarchism, Luddism, government ineptness, and corporate despoilment of the environment. Abbey defended the American West, and his worst nemesis was the combination of governmental and industrial forces that wanted to construct the Glen Canyon Dam. The Glen Canyon Dam was built and finished in 1962 and stemmed the flow of the once-powerful Colorado River. Abbey's battle over the fate of the Colorado River and Glen Canyon was a repeat of John Muir's battle over the Hetch Hetchy Valley and the O'Shaughnessy Dam. The dam "was a pork barrel project ostensibly built to provide Los Angeles and Phoenix with electric power at low cost; in fact, it was an engineering abomination that destroyed an entire eco-system. Even the dam's conservative godfather—Arizona Republican Senator Barry Goldwater—would eventually admit its construction had been a terrible mistake."[20]

The Glen Canyon Dam was the catalyst for Abbey's 1975 book, *The Monkey Wrench Gang*. Abbey created a cell of anarchists who combated power companies and the logging industry by acts of sabotage directed against the machinery used to destroy the environment. Abbey's book was a blueprint for low-level terrorism, if your definition of terrorism included violent acts against property but no actual physical harm to human beings. The objective of Abbey's group of saboteurs was the destruction of the Glen Canyon Dam.[21]

Abbey's book became the bible for environmentalists who were unhappy with the way mainstream environmental groups were conducting their mission of environmental protection. Abbey became a guru to a new group of radical environmentalists who took the name Earth First! and were inspired by Abbey to practice monkeywrenching (sabotage). In 1981, Earth First! announced their existence by unfurling a black, 100-yard plastic streamer down the face of the Glen Canyon Dam, simulating a fracture in the structure Abbey hated.[22]

Dave Foreman (1947–)

One of the founding members of Earth First!, who helped unfurl the streamer down the Glen Canyon Dam, was a former wilderness society member named Dave Foreman. In 1985, he edited an influential book for environmental activists, titled *Ecodefense: A Field Guide to Monkeywrenching*. This book, still in print and widely read by members of the REM, is a primer on sabotage.[23]

In July 1987, Foreman, as one of the leaders of Earth First!, which in six years had become an iconic environmental organization, set down defining principles for the environmental movement at a rendezvous on the north rim of the Grand Canyon. He explicitly embraced the principle of biocentrism, a philosophy that does not place human beings at the center of the universe and is opposed to our predominantly anthropocentric perspective. To Foreman, all other social concerns were subsidiary to wilderness preservation. He claimed overpopulation and society's overreliance on technology needed to be addressed. To Foreman, the threatened ecosystem is an emergency, and he recommended direct action as an instinctual response to all threats to the environment. Foreman believed that biological credibility, not political or economic criticism, was the core of an environmental movement. He did not believe that a political struggle would be a successful strategy or that the environmental movement should be involved in the workers' movement, as workers are often enemies of the environment. Most importantly, Foreman believed that the strategic goal of monkeywrenching was to protect the wilderness and that Earth First! needed to be a warrior society.[24]

After the Grand Canyon rendezvous, Foreman became embroiled in an FBI undercover operation, codenamed Thermcon, and was arrested in 1989, eventually pleading guilty to conspiracy charges and receiving four years of probation. Today, Foreman has left Earth First! and charges that the organization has become dominated by anarchists, Marxists, social justice, and new leftist anticapitalism forces. Foreman believes there should be three components to today's Earth First! movement: (1) biocentrism, the belief that all organisms are equally important to the environment; (2) monkeywrenching as a means to protect the ecological systems and preserve our wilderness; and (3) direct action to stop and at times confront the businesses, corporation-backed groups, and government agencies that are destroying the wilderness. Foreman believes overpopulation is the keystone problem that needs to be solved for the wilderness to be conserved. Although Foreman is no longer a part of the Earth First! organization, he is still a respected figure in the REM and is still active in wilderness preservation.[25]

Paul Watson (1950–)

Probably the most prominent and successful radical environmentalist is Paul Watson, the founder of the Sea Shepherd Conservation Society (SSCS). Watson was a founding member of Greenpeace at the time when Greenpeace utilized direct actions to further their various environmentally linked causes. Greenpeace was the first environmental organization to be regarded as radical. It utilized a broad array of tactics to protect wildlife. In 1977, however, Greenpeace adopted a policy of not committing actions that destroy property. Watson, who believed destruction of property was a tactic necessary to the success of Greenpeace, left, or was forced out of, the organization and subsequently founded the SSCS. Watson's focus since then has been on protection of the oceans, although he has also been involved in land-based actions against ecological destruction, including the preservation of African elephants.[26]

Today, Watson is most widely known for his activities in the Antarctic region's Southern Ocean, where he has opposed the Japanese whaling fleet's illegal harvesting of whales. Watson, in his battles to protect the maritime environment, has been responsible over the years for damaging several whaling vessels, blockading the Canadian sealing fleet, and destroying the drift net fishing tackle of vessels operating in international waters.[27]

Watson's tenure in the REM stands at more than 40 years. He is decidedly an eco-warrior but not a terrorist. He uses tactics, including violence against property, that have resulted in several arrests over his long career, but he has never been convicted of any felony crime. In explaining why Greenpeace originally decided to protest the killing of seals in Newfoundland, Watson clearly understands the concept of propaganda of the deed: "That decision was made primarily because, in addition to the possibility of saving seals, we could also call attention to the plight of all sea mammals. We saw the seals as a symbol through which we could dramatize the depletion and wholesale mismanagement of entire marine ecosystems."[28]

Watson, in distinguishing between Greenpeace and Sea Shepherd, characterizes Greenpeace as a protest organization and Sea Shepherd as an interventionist organization that will counter, in some cases with physical actions, the illegal killing of marine wildlife and the exploitation of their habitat. Watson grounds his strategic approach to environmental activism on three ecological principles that he believes form the basis for his struggle: "1. all forms of life are interdependent; 2. diversity promotes stability; and 3. all resources are finite."[29]

Deep Ecology Philosophers

Despite the fact that there are a variety of influences, both philosophical and operational, that affect today's REM, it is still accurate to say that an important, if not core, tenant of today's REM is biocentrism—a belief that all life forms have equal value, including nonsentient organisms. Arne Naess, a Norwegian philosopher, developed the principles of biocentrism, which he referred to as deep ecology in a 1973 article "The Shallow and Deep Long-Range Ecology Movement." Naess contrasted a biocentric, or deep, approach to ecology to a shallow ecology, which Naess believed was based on an anthropocentric view of the natural environment. In 1985, American associates of Naess—George Sessions, a philosopher, and Bill Devall, a sociologist—published *Deep Ecology: Living As If Nature Mattered*, incorporating Naess's concept of returning to a prior state of civilization and the re-creation of a wild, primitive environment.[30] The basic principles of deep ecology have been set out by Devall and Sessions:

1. The well-being and flourishing of human and nonhuman Life on Earth have value in themselves (synonyms: intrinsic value, inherent value). These values are independent of the usefulness of the nonhuman world for human purposes.
2. Richness and diversity of life forms contribute to the realization of these values and are also values in themselves.
3. Humans have no right to reduce this richness and diversity except to satisfy vital needs.
4. The flourishing of human life and cultures is compatible with a substantial decrease of the human population. The flourishing of nonhuman life requires such a decrease.
5. Present human interference with the nonhuman world is excessive, and the situation is rapidly worsening.
6. Policies must therefore be changed. These policies affect basic economic, technological, and ideological structures. The resulting state of affairs will be deeply different from the present.
7. The ideological change is mainly that of appreciating life quality (dwelling in situations of inherent value) rather than adhering to an increasingly higher standard of living. There will be a profound awareness of the difference between big and great.
8. Those who subscribe to the forgoing points have an obligation directly or indirectly to try to implement the necessary changes.[31]

Deep ecologists want society to restore civilization to a wilder, less-populated state. To do so, they believe all political decisions must be based on the effects the decision will have on an entire ecosystem and not just the effects on human beings.[32]

To understand the REM, it is essential to understand the effects of a REM activist's absolute belief in the principles of deep ecology. These principles afford a justification for direct actions taken by members of the REM.

CAUSATION PROCESS

To combat ecoterrorism, it is necessary to understand the causation process for the development, within a broader insurgent or political/social movement, of autonomous small, radicalized groups or individuals who utilize terror as a strategy to obtain a variety of goals related to the environment.

Professor Martha Crenshaw formulated a systematic method of examining the causation process from a rational choice perspective. Crenshaw looked at causation by examining the setting, proximate causes, and individual motivations for terrorist acts. In analyzing the setting, or environment, for terrorism, Crenshaw advocated looking at two factors: (1) the preconditions that allow terrorist actions to arise within a specific environment and (2) the precipitants, or immediate catalysts, for acts of terrorism. The Crenshaw process further breaks the preconditions down into permissive and enabling factors.[33] The Crenshaw framework, with the addition of natural environmental factors, furnishes a viable method for examining the development of REM terrorists, both group and individual.

Permissive Conditions

In regard to the REM, it is clear that it is an international movement with some members engaging in terrorist actions that occur in numerous countries. Although the worst overall environments are in developing countries, the most active REM terrorist groups have been in the United States and Europe.[34] That the REM is an international movement shows, in general, that environmental causes are important to a significant element of the general public of several nations, and, to some degree, the REM movement has been tolerated by those nations' democratic governments. Democratic governments, with their increased respect for civil liberties, are inherently permissive political environments that facilitate the organization of radical social movements and terrorist organizations.[35]

Another permissive condition is the increased technological development of Western society. This is a conundrum for the REM because one of their stated goals is a return to a preindustrial society,[36] and yet without the use of the industrial state's technology, specifically the Internet and cellular transmission devices, it would be extremely difficult for the REM to be as effective as it has been.

For example, the Internet allows the REM to furnish a consistent set of guidelines or principles to coordinate a movement that is both national and international. Without the Internet, the structure of REM terrorist groups—small cells or, in some cases, lone individuals, operating without central control—would suffer major problems in the areas of training and operational goal setting. The Internet enables the transmission of information concerning tactics, strategy, ideology, and operational security techniques to any potential or active member of the REM. Web sites that serve as repositories for a variety of technical and professional information in regard to terrorism have enabled the REM's small groups and individuals to operate relatively effectively for many years.[37]

Another permissive factor that guides the scope of activities of the REM are the social habits and historical traditions of the societies in which the REM operates. If the political or social environment advocates or accepts some degree of violence against the property of corporations or the government, then that type of activity might characterize the activities of an individual REM cell or organization. For example, in the Earth First! movement, which originated in the American West, there was some degree of acceptance regarding violence against property. This attribute of Earth First! corresponded to an historical tradition of the use of violence against property by various groups throughout Western history.[38] The historical social tradition within the United States has certainly embraced the use of interpersonal violence. That acceptance has largely waned today, and the government has been largely effective in curtailing such violence, with the government's actions normally accepted by the population at large. Thus, *The Monkey Wrench Gang*, Edward Abbey's seminal novel of the environmental movement, advocated violence against property but not against people.

Another permissive condition is a government's inability or unwillingness to confront the growth or advent of terrorist activity. Initially, the U.S. government was not active against REM terror groups for approximately a decade. During that time, these groups committed sporadic actions usually involving minor property damage. For law enforcement, these acts of political violence were in most cases easily confused with minor vandalism of property. This was fortunate for the REM in the United States because it enabled the movement to grow before the government became aware of the extent of the problem; the government began to conduct a relatively effective campaign only during the 1990s. In effect, the REM in the United States was able to carry out a multiplicity of direct actions without being apprehended by law enforcement throughout most of the 1980s and part of the 1990s.[39]

Enabling Preconditions

Enabling factors are those societal conditions that serve as a motivation to resist the laws of the state and furnish direction to the movement. Enabling preconditions are a more direct cause of terrorism than permissive conditions. They can include grievances among a society's subgroups and elite disaffection.[40] These two preconditions are pertinent to the REM. In regard to subgroup grievances, the REM serves as a surrogate for the earth, which is regarded as the victim by individuals involved in the REM. The representatives of various terrorist groups, such as the ELF, regard themselves as defenders of the earth who are attempting to gain rights and autonomy from human dominion for the environment. They believe that the environment is being unjustly deprived of its right to life and that there is no moral basis for this deprivation.

The members of the REM could also be described as an elite minority group that has assumed the power to act for the environment in order to give it a voice. This group has become disaffected from society's general populace and regards them as voracious, ignorant, and motivated by self-interest and profit. Members of the REM believe the general populace would support its goals if they were capable of understanding the issues.[41]

Besides enabling and permissive preconditions, terrorist actions are often caused by certain events that act as precipitants to outbreaks of violent action. Unlike preconditions, precipitating events are unpredictable. This is why social and political movements can often fester for long periods of time before one particular event causes an outbreak of group or individual violence against an identified enemy.[42] For example, in 1969, one year before the 1970 Earth Day, Union Oil Company suffered an equipment failure that resulted in oil leaks that dumped five million gallons of crude oil into 800 square miles of ocean off the coast of Santa Barbara. Over 10,000 birds, seals, dolphins, and other species were killed or seriously sickened, and 35 miles of shoreline were contaminated. This occurred at a time when the environmental consciousness of the United States had been raised significantly by Rachel Carson's best-selling book, *Silent Spring*. In addition, citizens in the Santa Barbara area were activists for a variety of counterculture, antigovernment, and anticapitalist groups. One of the communities, Isla Vista, had a citizenry that was very active in war-resistance activities. In 1970, after the complete ramifications of the oil spill became known, a group broke into the local branch of Bank of America and burned it to the ground. At the time, Bank of America directors were known to also sit on the board of Union Oil and were thus connected to the terrible oil spill.[43]

In some terrorist movements, a precipitating event can be excessive repression by governmental force of what would normally be First Amendment–protected activity.[44] The FBI has been extremely successful in its investigations of the REM during the last decade. These investigations have resulted in the successful prosecution and imprisonment of numerous members of the REM. It remains to be seen whether this will curtail the movement or act as a precipitating factor for an increase in REM terrorist activity. So far, it seems that FBI actions have caused a curtailment of activity in the United States and that such actions might, in fact, serve as traditional deterrents to criminal activity as opposed to precipitants to increased activity.

REASONS FOR USING VIOLENCE

The one constant among all terrorist campaigns is the question of whether a particular use of violence will be valuable or politically useful to the cause by engendering popular support. For the eco-warrior who, in the past, has only engaged in acts of civil disobedience and possibly minor acts of vandalism or ecotage, the decision to actually engage in serious acts of violence to property or people may be made for a variety of reasons.

Publicity

Publicity for the cause is one reason for the use of violence. Violence to obtain publicity is a standard short-term objective of terrorist groups. It garners the attention of the media and the public. In some cases, publicity is so important that it can sway the logical thought process of members of a radical organization, causing them to commit an act of violence that can discredit the movement in the eyes of a public that won't accept it.[45] In the United States, once eco-warriors decide to engage in serious physical violence to people or property, they become regarded as ecoterrorists and subject to increased investigative efforts, often led by the FBI's Joint Terrorism Task Forces. In addition, they have exposed themselves to potential penalties that include incarceration on felony charges.

Demonstrate Potency

Another reason for utilizing terror as a tactic is to gain support from a potential constituency and instill fear in an audience defined as the enemy.[46] The prohibition of violence against people, which is currently the position of ecoterrorists, means that they may have difficulty gaining support from desired members of the public. The use of force to instill obedience through fear is an option unavailable to those with a policy of no harm to human beings.

Provocation

Another reason terrorist organizations decide to utilize violence is to provoke an excessive counterreaction from the forces of the government directed against the general population, thus increasing resentment of the government and increasing support for the terrorist group.[47] Provocation is one of the traditional short-term objectives of terrorist acts, but this tactic would not be successful for the ecoterrorist. The small number and size of the cells ensures that the scope and intensity of the government's response would not be so large or intrusive toward members of the general public that it would cause an increase in sympathy for the group.

Failure, Contagion, and Frustration

Reasons for utilizing violence to instill terror can be varied, but the decision is made based upon the specific situation that radical groups face, and, in some cases, it occurs because there is a complete failure of all other alternatives to violence. Another factor that sometimes causes individuals or cells to commit an act of terror is the contagion effect: the knowledge of successful acts of terror being committed by other similar individuals or groups who have gained publicity through their successful actions. Violent actions may also be utilized by REM cells because of impatience or frustration. Small autonomous cells are driven by emotions more than larger organizations that have a review process for decisions to commit an act of violence.[48]

Although the setting for terrorism is conducive and there are reasons for the use of terror, the final determinant as to whether terrorism will be utilized as a tactic involves individual motivations that impel participation in the commission of the terrorist act.

Individual Motivation

What type of person kills innocent people for a political or social cause? Who joins radical organizations? These two questions have engendered many contrasting opinions over a period of 150 years. In regard to subconscious predispositions, no psychodynamic personality characteristics specific to members of terrorist groups have been identified.[49] Terrorist groups are composed of individuals with a variety of personality types and differing expressed attitudes toward society and the government. It is extremely hard to accurately identify attitudes when people are interviewed or furnish their own reports concerning their motivations for committing acts of violence. People often confuse rationalizations with their true motivations for illegal behavior.[50] The motivations of individuals who join a traditional structured terrorist organization may differ from those who join a small autonomous cell or who commit individual acts of terror without belonging to a group. Traditional terrorist groups select their members and may not choose individuals whose motivations they determine are risky for the group, such as thrill-seeking behavior. In regard to the REM, the organizational structure makes it difficult, if not impossible, to select members through a formal group evaluation of their suitability. Members who are involved in the REM are usually self-selected. Inevitably, a movement composed of numerous autonomous cells will attract thrill seekers as a major component of their membership.

To understand the key characteristics of a REM member's mindset, you need to examine the required actions of a terrorist cell member. These actions often involve danger and premeditated violence. The REM, however, because its constituent parts consist of small cells and individuals, will also have a unique group dynamic that could increase the likelihood that the cell will commit increasingly violent acts.[51] On the other hand, individuals and members of small groups without any hierarchical leadership will still, unless psychotic or suffering from severe personality disorder, require the formulation of a pre-offense justification for violent acts. The process of real or virtual group indoctrination as to goals and objectives and the formulation of a justification for the use of violence are components of an instrumental approach to terrorist actions. In theory, this approach is rational and easily analyzed.

From a less instrumental, but more expressive, demographic perspective, REM activists may be predisposed to the commission of terrorist acts not because of indoctrination or a process of moral disengagement but because of age. The highest rates of property and personal crime occur during late adolescence and early adulthood. Subsequently, as individuals age, the steepest decline occurs in the category of property crimes. The available research studies on REM membership show that the majority of activists are teenagers and young adults.[52]

Age is an independent determinant of the propensity to commit crimes. The development of the areas of the human brain that control emotions and understanding extends into late adolescence, with the pertinent areas being malleable throughout life.[53] The relationship between age and judgment is the basis for one highly probable explanation for the propensity of REM activists to commit acts of property damage: they are acting, in some cases, less from a politically instrumental reason to commit their acts and more from a satisfying emotional reason for engaging in acts of violence that have as their proximate target property, rather than human beings. If these individuals are restrained by moral considerations, then their actions against property and not human beings also aid in their justification process for the use of violence. Referring back to Hacker's typology in chapter 4, the criminal terrorist certainly exists among environmental activists at the vandal level. Destroying property, torching cars and buildings, and breaking and entering are activities that can stimulate and intrigue young adults. The psychic appeal of crime, when harnessed to a movement that offers a preexisting philosophical justification for violent acts against property, can act as an inducement to join or initiate a REM cell or engage in individual acts of terrorist violence.

Professor Jack Katz explores the psychic appeal of crime in his perceptive work *The Seductions of Crime*. In examining the individual's motivations for committing criminal acts, Katz breaks the motivational process down into background, determinative factors, and the immediate environmental precipitants of the act itself. To Katz, a powerful precipitant is the emotional attractiveness aspect of a criminal act. For example, property crimes such as vandalism, burglary, and theft are characterized by Katz as "sneaky thrills" and are linked to young people. As Katz explains: "A common thread running through vandalism, joy-riding and shoplifting is that all are sneaky crimes that frequently thrill their practitioners." Katz describes the sneaky thrill experience as "not simply utilitarian and practical; it is imminently magical."[54]

Eco-warriors engaged in acts of animal liberation or environmental protection could certainly find an experience that was magical. For example, Jeff "Free" Luers, a former REM member, whose radicalization pathway is explored further in this chapter, has described having a mystical experience during a tree-sitting campaign while enduring severe weather conditions, "It came to light that the forest understood why I was there, that I was there to protect it. I understood that within this forest I would be safe. I felt this calm and peace wash over me like a kind of magik [*sic*]."[55]

Emotional motivation for criminal acts is not limited to the adolescent age group; even with regard to serious property offenders, instrumental objectives may not be dominant motivational factors.[56] Age, however, may be the master variable in analyzing the reasons for REM activists' commission of property crimes, including arson, bombing, and burglary. It is a given that any analysis of the eco-warrior phenomenon shows that many of the activists are young in age, which, along with the opportunity for thrills, are factors that would cause them to initially join the REM. These factors may not, however, explain the motivation of older individuals who remain active in the REM at a more mature age. The following possible pathway to radicalization can be discerned through studying the autobiographical accounts of career REM activists that are available in print and through Internet sources:

1. Interest in environmental problems
2. Obsessive concern for the welfare of the environment
3. Association with like-minded peers
4. Development of biocentric perspective
5. Identification of an enemy
6. Action imperative accepted

   A. Non violent—civil disobedience and minor acts of monkeywrenching

   B. Violence toward property—serious acts of monkeywrenching; arson and bombings—with warnings to people and mitigation measures taken to prevent harm to all living beings

   C. Violence toward persons—arson and bombings without mitigation attempts; personal assaults and murder

For REM cells and lone wolves, the choice to engage in violence against persons may be highly dependent upon individual personality traits.

In studying individual examples of the radicalization process, Rod Coronado stands out as a mythic figure in the REM. Coronado's life followed the REM pathway to radicalization. While watching television as a boy, Coronado saw baby harp seals in Canada being harvested by being clubbed to death. This created a powerful impression on him and caused him to want to do something to prevent harm to animals. He developed a biocentric viewpoint that equated the lives of humans and animals. When he graduated from high school, he actively solicited Paul Watson's SSCS for membership. In 1986, while a member of the SSCS, he found out that Iceland killed 200 whales every year under the guise of scientific research while there was a moratorium on whaling. Thus, he identified his enemy and accepted an action imperative. This precipitated a trip to Reykjavik, Iceland, where allegedly, he and one associate sank two whaling ships. Through the commission of a violent criminal act, Coronado had crossed a line from radical activist to identification by the government of Iceland as an alleged criminal and terrorist. Coronado escaped from Iceland, and the prime minister of Iceland called him an international terrorist and requested that he be extradited from wherever he was apprehended. He turned up in England, where he was allegedly involved in the sabotage of fox hunts and eventually returned to the United States. Fortunately for Coronado, Iceland never actually charged him for any criminal acts. In 1988, he was recognized at the Earth First! rendezvous by Dave Foreman, the cofounder of Earth First!, as the next generation of eco-warrior. At the time, Coronado had just turned 22.[57]

Subsequently, Coronado gathered evidence of the mistreatment of animals imprisoned on Western fur-ranch installations by sneaking into the buildings at night and videotaping the horrible conditions of the animals. In 1991, Coronado planned Operation Bite Back for the ELF. He and his accomplices broke into animal research facilities and mink farms and released the animals, taking anonymous credit on behalf of ELF. In 1994, Coronado was arrested by the FBI, convicted, and sentenced to 54 months in prison. Coronado never identified his accomplices and adapted well to prison life, even maintaining his vegetarian habits. Coronado's motivation certainly changed during his years as an activist, and his actions had an instrumental motivation based on ideological commitment to the REM. Coronado has always supported the use of sabotage and arson as necessary direct actions if directed only at property but does not advocate the use of explosives.[58]

To understand both the thrill aspect of committing violent acts and the REM pathway to radicalization, a monograph by Jeff "Free" Luers, titled "How I Became an Ecowarrior," offers valuable insight. Luers began his eco-warrior career in 1998 at 19 years of age by becoming a tree sitter to protect and prevent the harvesting of the old-growth forest area in Oregon. Recounting climbing a 200-foot-tall Douglas fir for the first time, he describes his feelings as "scared to death." In describing a nighttime fireside conversation he had with his two companions, he states that they "shared tales of adventure, hopping trains, shoplifting, and running from the cops and in some cases, fighting them."[59]

After depicting sitting at the top of the tree in a heavy rainstorm, he characterizes his experience as a transcending moment: "It is one of those beautiful moments in life that you remember with absolute clarity. At that moment I had no doubt we would save this forest."[60] Describing a long period of tree sitting in volatile weather conditions, Luers interprets his experiences as feeling "the magik [sic] of the forest and of Mother Earth in my blood. I finally truly understood what it was to be a human being and be alive."[61]

Luers's experience in the forest began with a thrill-seeking motivation and ended with his transformation to a fully radicalized individual. He recounts taking a vow to fight for the freedom of all life because he believed "We are all interconnected: we are all made of the same living matter, and we call this planet home. I vow to defend my home; I vow to stand in defense of Mother Earth."[62] Luers had clearly developed a biocentric perspective through his experience with the natural environment. He was no longer motivated by the thrill of his actions. Luers's adoption of the action imperative is shown when he ends his monograph with an impassioned argument for the use of violence in the defense of nature when faced with such a yes-or-no decision.

You have to decide what is important to you—clean water, freedom? You have to decide if you are willing to be a part of something larger than yourself. And you have to decide if you are willing to fight for it. We have already lost too much, we can not lose anymore.

If your answer is "yes," then it is time for you to pick up your spear, draw a line in the ground, and say "you have come this far and you shall come no further. . . . I will not let you rape, murder, and oppress any longer. I am a warrior and I will fight you."[63]

Jeff Luers was young when he wrote this monograph. He has since been convicted of the crime of arson (involving the firebombing of SUVs), has served a prison sentence, and has been released. He intends to continue being an environmental activist but without violating any laws.[64] His monograph portrays the REM radicalization pathway taken by young activists. Luers, however, only harmed property. Despite the fervor of his beliefs, his personality did not have the requisite traits for the commission of acts of violence against persons.

In the first two parts of a three-part series titled "Letters from the Underground," written anonymously and printed in *No Compromise* (an ELF zine), an ELF activist discusses her decision to become a member of ELF and commit criminal acts. There are several key points of her narrative that express the thrill component of her decision to commit an act of ecoterrorism—the interest step in the REM radicalization pathway. For example, in discussing her decision to become an ELF member, the "sneaky thrills" motivational dynamic is apparent: "After reading stories about lab break-ins and fur stores being torched, I too, desperately wanted to join this group."[65] The risk involved in committing break-ins and setting fires emotionally stimulated the author. Her focus is on the thrill of the action, not the underlying cause, as the incentive to join the group. Further in her narrative, she makes a cogent observation about direct actions by ecoterrorists: "There are always plenty of people who want to help in the actual execution of the plan—people are always willing to share in the 'excitement,' but not in the actual work."[66]

Another statement indicates that the author has become immersed in the REM, and the action imperative stage is emphasized: "The more of these types of actions done, the more competent, confident, and experienced you and your cell will become and you can soon 'move up' to bigger and better actions."[67] Direct actions undertaken by cell members serve to increase the commitment to the objectives and goals of the REM and enhance the cohesiveness of the cell.[68]

In examining individual motivation from a rational choice perspective, the personal rewards an individual REM member gains from participating in the commission of violent acts has to be understood. Although his or her motivations are often mixed, there must be some benefit for the individual to decide to commit a criminal act that could lead to severe penalties. Criminals are usually motivated by personal profit, and their actions are usually directed at institutions or individuals that possess valuable items to steal or rob. The targets of ecoterrorist actions will normally not be capable of enriching the individual or cell. The benefits for the REM member can include the good feeling that comes from having performed an altruistic act. Saving the environment or rescuing animals can be an act of altruism that is also a justification for an illegal act. Unlike acts of interpersonal violence committed by other terrorist organizations, the reasons for the commission of violent acts of property destruction by members of the REM serve as justifications that are readily accepted by many members of society. In addition, the benefits may also include an adrenaline-fueled emotional high. The REM's use of violent acts is also a rational strategy for small autonomous groups who desire publicity for their ideological cause.

Rik Scarce, the author of *Eco-Warriors: Understanding the Radical Environmental Movement*, believes, however, that "most eco-warriors have no interest in a well conceived philosophy. . . . It is intuition which spurs them to act, not some clear, rational, deductive thought process. Radical environmentalism emerges out of an ecological consciousness that comes from the heart—not the head—that has experienced the natural world."[69] In fact, Scarce's position is an acknowledgement of "magic"—that the desire to experience magic in their lives can lead individuals to take the ultimate step of committing an act of violence for a cause.

ORGANIZATIONAL STRUCTURE AND METHOD OF OPERATION

The REM is a worldwide movement that is sometimes characterized by the commission of violent actions against property. It is difficult to make generalizations about the REM as a whole because there are varying organizational structures, some of them covert, and methods of operation that distinguish different sectors of the REM.[70]

There are five major REM organizations and all are to some degree international in scope: (1) Greenpeace, (2) Sea Shepherd Conservation Society, (3) Animal Liberation Front, (4) Earth First!, and (5) Earth Liberation Front. In addition, there are a multitude of autonomous self-generating small cells and lone wolves who operate in numerous countries under the banner of the REM. These small cells and lone wolves often profess allegiance to the Animal Liberation Front, the Earth Liberation Front, or to both of them. To understand the organizational structures and methods of operation of the REM, this chapter examines these five major organizations, three of which are aboveground, legal organizations and two that are underground, loosely connected organizations whose exact size and scope of operation are unknown.

Greenpeace Foundation

Greenpeace began in 1969 as a small group of peace activists and Sierra Club members who found a common cause trying to stop nuclear testing conducted by France and the United States. First called the "Don't Make a Wave" committee, they employed direct confrontation as theater and manipulated the media to publicize their actions. Their first action took place in the Aleutian Island chain, specifically Amchitka Island. After their initial antinuclear operations, they began defending whales from illegal harvesting by Russia, Norway, Iceland, and Japan. The organization grew, but internal divisions developed over their tactics.

In 1977, Greenpeace abandoned actions that would destroy property and restricted their members to acts of civil disobedience only, but the acts were well publicized. Today, Greenpeace is the largest environmental organization in the world, with its headquarters in Amsterdam and offices in 23 nations, including the United States. Greenpeace is the only organization to have an office in the Antarctic. Greenpeace has a standard hierarchical structure and does not employ any type of covert group to carry out operations at their behest under a different name. They are an ecological organization that solicits funds, lobbies government organizations, and functions as a multinational corporation.[71]

Sea Shepherd Conservation Society

The Sea Shepherd Conservation Society was founded by Paul Watson in 1977 with financial backing by Cleveland Amory, the director of the Fund for Animals. Originally called Earthforce, Watson's organization has for over 30 years physically intervened to stop the massacre of dolphins, whales, and seals and has, when necessary, damaged or hindered ships engaged in illegal whaling. The SSCS focuses on both marine mammals and the marine ecosystem but uses individual endangered species as the focus of their media campaigns. Their membership has always included individuals from the animal rights movement.[72]

The modus operandi of the SSCS has been to utilize direct actions that have ostensible legal justification along with a powerful moral justification. This operational format has been successful. The major battle facing the organization is in the Southern Ocean against Japanese whalers, who currently operate under a research exemption to the international moratorium on commercial whaling. Japan has often threatened to bring suit against Sea Shepherd for alleged acts of ecoterrorism and piracy and has called Sea Shepherd ecoterrorists, labeling their acts piracy in violation of the UN Convention on the Law of the Seas.[73]

Sea Shepherd's mission statement advocates direct-action tactics, if needed, to stop criminal acts occurring on the high seas. Sea Shepherd also has a written mandate that states they are to engage in policing on the high seas in accordance with the UN World Charter for Nature. Sea Shepherd relies upon the UN World Charter for Nature, specifically section 21 under the heading of implementations, as their authority to take action to enforce international conservation law. This charter is the basis for Sea Shepherd's intervention and acts of physical interference directed against Japanese ships that are harvesting whales in international waters in what Sea Shepherd and Australia consider a protected sanctuary.[74]

The Animal Liberation Front

The Animal Liberation Front was founded in Great Britain in 1976, and its activities spread to the United States by 1979. The ALF organizational system, unlike that of Sea Shepherd, is based on an autonomous cell concept. The cell model used by ALF is the type of structure popularly identified with noted white supremacist and former member of the Ku Klux Klan Louis Beam, who wrote about the concept in a 1983 article titled "Leaderless Resistance." Essentially, the cell structure utilized under the leaderless resistance model dispenses with any type of central organizational body and traditional leadership hierarchy. This type of cell structure has been used for approximately 25 years by various U.S. right-wing terrorist organizations. In Beam's writings, he explains the difference between a cell structure that also has a central control and one in which that central control is lacking, which Beam terms a "phantom cell." According to Beam, the use of a cell-based organization with a central command structure is only possible if the organization has sufficient resources, obtained from outside support, to operate effectively under a command structure. When extensive outside support and funding are not available, Beam's recommendation is to dispense with a central command function. Beam believes this is possible because the cell structure would have unity of purpose, although individual cells would lack the traditional unity-of-organization requirement.[75]

The ALF, although operating under a leaderless resistance or autonomous cell concept, which it implemented prior to the date Beam's article first appeared, does have a Web site presence that serves as a source of ideology, mission, operational guidelines, and tactical instruction. The ALF's mission is to protect the rights of all sentient creatures and to end their status as the property of humans. The ALF guidelines include an introductory section that states: "Any group of people who are vegetarians or vegans and who carry out actions according to ALF guidelines have the right to regard themselves as part of the ALF."[76]

In effect, ALF operations are carried out by autonomous individuals or small cells of terrorists who can claim to be part of ALF and gain publicity for direct actions that comply with ALF's guidelines. ALF utilizes a franchise model: a group can claim to be a member of ALF if the group adheres to the ALF's contractual provisions (ALF guidelines).[77] The ALF guidelines are as follows:

1. TO liberate animals from places of abuse, i.e. laboratories, factory farms, fur farms, etc. and place them in good homes where they may live out their natural lives, free from suffering.
2. TO inflict economic damage to those who profit from the misery and exploitation of animals.
3. TO reveal the horror and atrocities committed against animals behind locked doors, by performing non-violent direct actions and liberations.
4. TO take all necessary precautions against harming any animal, human and non-human.
5. TO analyze the ramifications of any proposed action and never apply generalizations (e.g., all "blank are evil") when specific information is available.[78]

In their use of autonomous cells "the ALF embodies the principle of individuality within collectivity. Individual cells are free to be as creative as they please within the guidelines set by the minimal ALF principles."[79]

When ALF began its operations in the United States, there was not a similar radical organization for the wilderness environment. The environmental movement was a conservationist movement, and the large, bureaucratic organizations involved restricted their strategic approach by allowing only nonviolent tactics. This changed in 1980 with the birth of the first radical environmental organization—Earth First!

Earth First!

In 1980, several conservationists, members of various major environmental organizations who had become dissatisfied with the current status of the environmental movement, formed a new environmental group they called Earth First! In forming Earth First!, the founders were motivated by several issues: (1) the perceived ineffectiveness of the traditional conservation organizations, (2) the Sagebrush Rebellion (attempts by states to claim federal public lands for transfer to private concerns), (3) excessive population growth, and (4) Ronald Reagan's opposition to environmental improvement. By naming the new environmental group Earth First!, they were signifying that it was intended to be a radical organization that would not compromise in protecting the environment.[80]

Earth First!, as a radical organization, adopted a preservationist and biocentric perspective based upon the principles of deep ecology. They intended to adhere to all laws but would encourage others to carry out actions to protect the environment similar to the radical group of eco-warriors in Edward Abbey's *The Monkey Wrench Gang*. Earth First! wanted their organization to be defined by action. The founders wanted a diverse membership and alliances with other social movements. Earth First!, from its inception, was not envisioned as an organization but as a movement. As a movement, it did not have officers, bylaws, or constitutions. It was not incorporated and did not have a tax status. It was essentially anarchistic in structure.[81]

On March 21, 1981, Earth First! held its first gathering, or rendezvous, at Glen Canyon Dam in Colorado. This event garnered a great amount of publicity and the attention of law enforcement primarily because of the previously discussed simulated sabotage of the dam. Since that first gathering, Earth First! has inspired numerous incidents of monkeywrenching—acts of sabotage directed at machinery—that, in adherence to Earth First!'s philosophy, were intended to help save the environment from destruction by man's machines. The movement has also developed an anti-technology slant, and some members advocate a return to a hunter-gather society with a drastically reduced human population. At its core, however, Earth First! is still a movement that addresses the issues of public land usage and wilderness preservation.[82]

Today, Earth First! has become an international movement composed of numerous small, bioregional-based groups. Earth First! advocates the formation of such groups and furnishes instructions on these "affinity groups" on its Web site and through the *Earth First! Journal*, which has its own Web site. Although Earth First! still advocates civil disobedience and monkeywrenching, their Web site emphasizes actions that are legal: "Learn the law. While getting arrested will often bring increased media attention, weigh all the options. Freedom is an important asset. Avoiding jail is sometimes a better strategy."[83]

Differing viewpoints as to the types of direct actions Earth First!ers should commit became a problem within the movement in the late 1980s. Some members had always disagreed with the monkeywrenching concept while others desired to go beyond it. In addition, younger and newer members, although claiming membership in Earth First! and adhering to a biocentric perspective, often had other ideologies. They believed in anarchism and anticapitalism; they were also antigovernment, specifically the United States. The membership divided over ideology and tactics, and some members left the movement.[84]

In 1992, a small group of disaffected members located in England founded another movement. This movement would defend the environment without the restraints placed upon environmental activism by the Earth First! movement. The new movement was the Earth Liberation Front, and it soon expanded to include cells located in the United States.

The Earth Liberation Front

The Earth Liberation Front is an offshoot of the UK's Earth First! movement and possibly arose out of the first UK Earth First! gathering that took place in Brighton, England. The new organization is also believed to have been influenced by the ALF, which was very active in England at the time the ELF movement developed. The new organization developed an ideological approach that included social justice concerns popular in Europe along with its deep ecology core principles. The ELF movement spread to Germany and the Netherlands and to the United States in the mid-1990s. In 1997, ELF activists took credit for their first action in the United States with an arson attack on a Bureau of Land Management horse corral in Oregon and the release of captured wild horses designated for slaughter.[85]

ELF's justification for the arson attack was stated in a communiqué released to the public through a spokesperson: "This hypocrisy and genocide against the horse nation will not go unchallenged! The practice of rounding up and auctioning wild horses must be stopped. The practice of grazing cattle on public lands must be stopped." ELF's first action and the justification for that action show ELF's link to both Earth First! (misuse of public wildlands) and ALF (saving wild animals from slaughter).[86]

ELF utilizes the small, autonomous cell structure of the leaderless resistance model. It is essentially an international movement composed of individuals and cells operating in many countries. In the United States, ELF operates over a wide area but predominantly within the western states. To claim an action and obtain the publicity the ELF's limited aboveground Web site structure can generate, a cell must adhere to the ELF's guidelines. Unlike Earth First!, whose strategic goals are essentially limited to environmental protection, ELF's ideologically based strategic goals are much more revolutionary. In fact, some ELF cells and self-designated spokespersons have advocated a revolutionary insurgency to change existing political structures, particularly the capitalist social system.[87]

Parsons, in a review of ELF's communiqués between 1997 and 2003, agrees that ELF's original focus on deep ecology as the ideological foundation of the movement has changed. ELF's ideology has incorporated other political and philosophical streams of social movement thought, such as green anarchism, anticapitalism, antiglobalization, and social ecology. ELF's written communiqués still incorporate deep ecology, and that alone, with its demand for a decreased human population and a voluntary decrease in the size of the human environmental footprint, could be considered revolutionary.[88]

The ELF operates as an international franchise system with stated requirements: "If you believe in the ELF ideology and you follow a certain set of widely published guidelines, you can conduct actions and become part of the ELF. The ELF guidelines are as follows, (1) to cause as much economic damage to a given entity that is profiting off the destruction of the natural environment and life for selfish greed and profit, (2) to educate the public on the atrocities committed against the environment and life, and (3) to take all necessary precautions against harming life."[89]

The ELF and ALF movements have engendered numerous autonomous cells in many regions of the world. Some are franchisees and claim their successful actions under the banner of the ELF, ALF, or both. Others operate as independent entities, adhering to a variety of guidelines or none at all.[90]

Other Radical Environmental Cells

During the last decade, the underground component of the radical environmental movement has become more diffuse, with individual cells operating under the names of ELF and ALF and other cells operating under a variety of names, all with varied ideological motivations and located in a variety of countries. These radical environmental cells are often rooted in modern anarchist philosophy. Anarchism, with its simplistic concept—eliminate government and everything will be fine—is attractive to the new breed of radical environmentalist who is primarily interested in action, with only a secondary interest in the philosophy that underlies the action. These individuals and cells are merging or cooperating with other cells that link environmental concerns to anticapitalism and antiglobalization. These groups see climate change, as caused by man's greenhouse gas emissions, as the harbinger of an ecological disaster. They often link social and environmental harms, such as climate change, to the capitalist system's destructive power.[91]

In a 2005 Rand report, Chalk and colleagues predicted the radical environmental movement would start to focus on the evils of corporations and on a government that lets those corporations harm the environment.[92] Liddick, in his 2005 book on ecoterrorism, stated that the radical environmental movement has developed an ideological framework that includes a belief in deep ecology; an anarchistic, apocalyptic, and millenarian perspective; and a belief that the human population must be decreased. This belief structure could form an ideological basis for the justification of attacks on people to save the planet.[93]

Organizational Weaknesses of the REM

Revolutionary Ideology

The international scope of the REM has expanded, which has caused the ideological foundations of the REM to change as the movement becomes wider. The original opinion leaders, who traditionally shaped the guidelines of the REM, have become much less influential, and thought leaders from Europe, Mexico, and Australia have increasingly influenced the strategy of the REM. The ideology and strategy of all REM cells have begun to show similar ideological justifications for their direct actions.[94]

This is readily seen by analyzing the communiqués sent out by cells that acknowledge strategic goals that originate from other cultural and political regions. An excellent example of this development is a communiqué from an ELF cell located in Santiago, Chile, and posted on the North

American ELF press office (NAELFPO) Web site, titled "Earth Liberation Front Torches Slaughterhouse." The communiqué states, "We decided to carry out this action, during the international week of agitation for prisoners, given that we identify authority and the exploitation of the land and its beings as the great common enemy of all the battles of anti-authoritarian insurrection."[95] The underlying ideology of the Chilean communiqué clearly expresses an anticapitalist, antigovernment, revolutionary ideology. By incorporating antigovernment rhetoric into the REM ideology and perceiving the REM as engaged in an armed struggle with government forces, the REM becomes a revolutionary threat to individual nations. In democratic nations, this revolutionary, antigovernment motivation will not be supported by the overwhelming majority of the population. In the United States, for example, a limited ideological focus, similar to that of the SSCS and Earth First! during its formative years, appeals to a significant portion of the population. A violent, antigovernment ideology will not achieve even a semblance of support from the U.S. populace and will engender an enhanced law enforcement response to eliminate the movement.

Tactical and Strategic Control of Cells

Based on arrests of REM members for acts of violence against property, there is an operational profile that, although limited, is accurate. REM members, who belong to covert cells or operate individually, are on average in their early twenties, usually in college or graduate school, although they may not be currently enrolled. Internationally, their socioeconomic class varies, although a middle-class background is the median. The operational units are individuals or cells composed of two to six persons. They usually operate at night, and they will travel long distances to carry out operations. They rarely combine into larger units. As a movement composed only of independent cells, there is a limited ability for the REM to ever achieve their stated strategic goal (i.e., to save the environment or liberate animals from human domination).[96]

The REM's covert groups have adopted a variation on the operational model labeled leaderless resistance. This model is "defined by the absence of control or influence at the tactical level, at most weak influence at the operational level, but strategic shaping by opinion leaders within the movement."[97] The covert component of the REM is what Brian Jackson refers to as a "loosely coupled movement," which means it has a common ideology and some general goals but limited operational or tactical control.[98] The REM's covert component is not a pure leaderless resistance movement. As the movement has endured, it has utilized the Internet and new technologies to disseminate strategic goal-directed information and tactical instructions to cell members. The necessity of utilizing Web-based, open-source information is, however, a weakness of the REM. The REM's status as a "loosely coupled" organization makes it necessary for the move-ment, through its Web-based entities, to "broadly disseminate their stra-tegic platform and whatever operational or tactical guidance they expect their members to take into consideration." This type of readily available, open-source information allows an analyst or investigator to gain an un-derstanding of some of the movement's activities.[99]

The main drawback of the REM's operational structure is the lack of tac-tical control the REM can exert over covert individuals and cells. Because these entities essentially operate at will, there is no unity of action—apart from that displayed by individual cells—in the activities of the move-ment.[100] In addition, the current tactical restrictions (e.g., no harm to human or animal life), which are promulgated by the movement's Web sites and other open-source material, may be disregarded by individual cells or indi-viduals. This could and has hurt the movement's goal of influencing public opinion toward the movement. The issue of what tactics should be utilized in direct actions is, at heart, the most divisive issue for the REM.

Vulnerability of Large Cells

In the first decade of the 21st century, the division between the separate domains of the environmental and the animal liberation movements has essentially disappeared. Individual cells, which are the covert operational component of the REM, determine the targets of their actions based on indi-vidual interests and capabilities. A cell may carry out both animal libera-tion and environmental protection actions and claim they are acting for both ELF and ALF under their respective guidelines, or a cell may operate under only one domain.

When cells expand their targets to include both domains, they become less effective because of their limited manpower and enhanced logistical requirements. If they increase their manpower, however, they become more vulnerable to law enforcement penetration and less able to control the ac-tivities of the increased number of cell members.

For example, "the Family," a cell operating under the banner of both ELF and ALF, committed direct actions in Oregon, Wyoming, Washington, and California from 1995 to 2001. This cell, consisting of 12 or more members, committed 25 direct actions and caused property damage in excess of $40 million. The Family operated for a significant period of time and with a great degree of success. The government, predominantly in the shape of the FBI, made their case on the Family by developing a cooperating wit-ness (who agreed to wear a recording device) from among the members. The evidence developed through the cooperative witness subsequently caused the other members to furnish information about their fellow mem-bers as part of the plea-bargaining process.[101]

The Family case displays the weakness of an enlarged ecoterrorist cell system. The ability to commit dramatic and repeated direct actions requires an expansion of the size of the normal two- to six-member operational cell. But this also makes the cell more vulnerable to infiltration by undercover FBI agents and law enforcement's development of weak or compromised cell members as informants and cooperating witnesses. The predominant types of individuals who initially join or create ecoterrorist cells are usually not familiar with the criminal justice system and probably possess a noncriminal orientation to it. Once they are arrested, labeled as criminals, and find themselves facing severe penalties, some will not be able to resist government inducements to cooperate and inevitably will decide to testify against fellow cell members. The Family cell members were easily co-opted by the FBI and accepted governmental plea bargains that required cooperation against other cell members.[102]

Increased REM cell size also leads to difficulty controlling the tactics used by individual members. Even without increased size, the loosely coupled nature of REM cells necessitates the development of specific REM tactics and adaptations to popular terrorist tactics used by larger, traditionally structured terrorist organizations.

REM TACTICS

The tactics used by the REM are generally limited by a restriction on harming animal or human life, especially if the REM cell intends to claim a direct action under the banner of ELF or ALF. Because of the increased use of an antiglobalization, anticapitalism justification for REM actions, along with the increased influence of the green anarchists, the scope of potential REM members is greatly enhanced. This leads to an increased probability that some individuals or cells will adopt violence against humans as a permissible action. This has already occurred and will continue to occur in the future.

In August and September 2003, the revolutionary cells of the Animal Liberation Brigade utilized pipe bombs to attack two companies in northern California because of their business links to Huntingdon Life Science (HLS), the target of the UK's Stop Huntingdon Animal Cruelty (SHAC) organization. The first bombing attack was on Chiron Life Science Center in Emeryville, California, and involved two conventional pipe bombs that caused property damage but no injuries to people. The bombs, however, were set by timers with different detonation times. If intentional, it would have represented a widely known technique used to kill or harm first responders. The second attack, in September, was against Shaklee Incorporated, a subsidiary of HLS's client Yamanouchi located in Pleasantville, California. This attack utilized an ammonium nitrate pipe bomb wrapped with nails. Again, no one was injured, but the pipe bomb was clearly designed to harm human life. After the attack, responsibility was claimed through a communiqué by the revolutionary cells of the Animal

Liberation Brigade and issued through the ALF Web site. The revolutionary cells used violent language in their communiqué: "No more will all
of the killing be done by the oppressors, now the oppressed will strike
back."[103]

The revolutionary cells claimed that they were a "front group for mili-
tants across the liberationary movement spectrum." Their communiqué
also listed their guidelines, which allow the use of violent tactics directed
at human targets:

1. To take strategic direct action (be it non-violent or not) against the oppressive
   institutions that permeate the world.
2. Make every effort to minimize non-target casualties, be they human or nonhuman.
3. Respect a diversity of tactics, whether they be non-violent or not.
4. Any underground activist fighting for the liberation of the humyn [sic],
   earth, or animal nations may consider themselves a Revolutionary Cells
   volunteer.[104]

The revolutionary cells' guidelines do not prohibit harming humans;
instead, they require an effort to "minimize" harm to humans. Although
no one was injured or killed by the revolutionary cells' pipe bombs and
they have not repeated their actions, the FBI charged Daniel Andreas San
Diego, discussed earlier in chapter 1, in connection with both crimes. He is
currently a fugitive and the only environmental activist on the FBI's Most
Wanted Terrorists list.[105]

The SHAC campaign against HLS, their customers, and their associate
businesses displays an evolution in REM tactics. SHAC-related tactics include the basic ALF tactic of releasing animals from facilities that utilize
them for testing clothing or food. SHAC, however, also developed a Web
site–based campaign that portrays itself as an informational media outlet
but, in reality, identified individuals and companies as targets for direct
actions initiated by REM cells or individuals. Individuals and cells could
obtain information, such as the names and addresses of businesses that
were customers of HLS, from the SHAC Web site. The SHAC-facilitated
direct actions taken by ELF, ALF, and affiliated cells and individuals included the following tactics:

1. Threatening letters were sent to company offices and employees.
2. Red paint was poured on residences, and accusations of terrible crimes were
   painted on the homes of targeted individuals.
3. Activists made "home visits" to identify targets and utilized threatening chant-
   ing and signs to intimidate them.
4. Smoke bombs were released in the offices of one of the clients of HLS.
5. Computer and fax jamming techniques were directed at clients and related
   companies.[106]

In the UK, other ALF and ELF-offshoots utilized even more violent tactics during the SHAC campaign, including the following:

1. Threats of murder

2. One case of abduction and branding (ALF letters on the victim's back) of a reporter who had infiltrated ALF

3. Physical assault using baseball bats on HLS's managing director

4. Booby trapped (razor blades) letters sent to employees and researchers involved in vivisection experiments in the UK and the United States[107]

Although bomb and arson attacks have been used by covert REM cells and individuals on an international basis, the primary tactics of the above-ground REM are composed of acts of nonviolent civil disobedience—for example, blocking logging roads and tree sitting. Monkeywrenching, which is generally defined as the destruction or sabotage of equipment or facilities used to destroy or degrade nonhuman life in the natural environment, is a controversial tactic within the REM. Monkeywrenching includes a wide range of actions, involves differing degrees of economic damage, and makes up the majority of direct actions engaged in by covert REM cells.[108]

The book *Ecodefense: A Field Guide to Monkeywrenching* advocates the tactic and recommends that it be accomplished with simplicity, nonviolence, and ethical actions. The ethical prescription is based on the morality of saving the natural environment.[109] Examples of the effective use of monkeywrenching include the following:

1. Tree spiking, used to deter timber sales, is a potentially dangerous tactic that has become controversial among REM activists. In the United States in 1988, Congress passed anti-spiking legislation that allows for severe penalties if anyone is injured even slightly, if property damage occurs that exceeds $10,000, or if an individual is convicted of a second offense even if the offense did not result in physical injury or serious property damage. The minimum penalty of such an act can be up to 10 years imprisonment.[110]

2. Pulling up survey stakes (a felony crime in some states) is used to delay or prevent the building of roads or development projects that affect the natural environment. *Ecodefense* recounts the possible countermeasures the U.S. Forest Service or private development companies can use to apprehend survey stake pullers and advises monkeywrenchers to use a lookout, plan an escape route, be careful of invisible dyes on stakes, and wear disposable gloves.[111]

3. Sabotage of power lines, which in *Ecodefense* is extensively discussed but not recommended, is seldom used because of the severe reaction it engenders from federal law enforcement. However, sabotage of seismic exploration equipment and cables in potential energy exploration sites located in wilderness regions is recommended.[112]

4. Plugging waste discharge pipes is used to stop industries from polluting lakes and rivers.[113]

5. Cutting selected fences in livestock ranching areas to harm the cattle and sheep ranching industries.[114]

6. Sabotaging vehicles and heavy equipment is the classic form of monkey-wrenching.[115]

Arson is the tactic that divides REM members. To most REM members, direct actions that involve physical destruction of property do not violate the "no harm to animal or human life" guideline that the overwhelming majority of REM cells agree to if operating under ELF or ALF guidelines. Arson, however, can also be considered either a direct attempt to harm human life or an unacceptable risk that human or animal life could be harmed even if precautions to prevent such harm are taken. For example, a firefighter could be killed or injured in the line of duty fighting a REM cell's arson attack, or a human or animal present but not discovered by the cell members prior to igniting the fire could be killed or injured. Arson is the tactical choice that affords REM cells the greatest ability to cause extreme property damage but also has the greatest risk to human life. An arson attack on most large facilities will require a three- to six-person cell to safely execute, pre-raid surveillance, and knowledge of arson techniques.

Unfortunately, information on all aspects of accomplishing an arson attack is widely available. *Ecodefense* has fairly extensive information on arson scattered in various sections of the book. In addition, the Internet contains instruction on arson, including the "Arson Around with Auntie ALF" booklet that is found on several Web sites, including ALF's. Arson entails severe penalties if a person is convicted. It was the major tactic used by the Family cell taken down by the FBI in its Operation Backfire. The use of arson enabled the Family to gain extensive publicity for ELF in their 1998 attack on the Vail Ski Resort, which caused $12 million in damage, at the time the most costly action committed by ecoterrorists.

The underground elements of the REM in the United States have allegedly corrected their security procedures to prevent future FBI successes against them.[116] Since the FBI's announcement of its successful Operation Backfire campaign, these groups have continued to operate, both internationally and in the United States. An ELF arson action in 2008 resulted in the destruction of domestic homes in a Seattle suburb, although the homes were vacant and no one was hurt.[117] In September 2009, an ELF cell toppled two radio towers in Washington State.[118] Internationally, the ELF has been active in arson attacks in Mexico: in 2009, a Mexican cell committed a bombing with a subsequently issued communiqué justifying the act because of global warming caused by capitalism.[119]

From 1977 to July 2008, according to the FBI, the U.S. REM has committed over 2,000 criminal acts and has caused economic losses of more than $110 million.[120] In analyzing the tactics used by the REM for over 40 years, the lack of human victims is striking. Unfortunately its ideology, based on philosophies of biocentrism and animal rights, offers a justification for direct attacks on human beings who are perceived as destroying the natural environment and imprisoning animals. An increased use of arson and explosive devices will inevitably lead to the loss of human life, either planned or inadvertent. If isolated individuals and cells see the current strategy and tactics as unsuccessful, then an escalation in the tactics used could be seen as the only means to stop what is viewed as the eventual death of the Earth.

The words of one unknown activist commenting on 40 years of environmental events and direct actions may be a prediction of future escalation:

If we are to make the slightest progress in not nearly slowing down the ecological rapists and murderers, but actually pushing back the assault on nature, the force of our collective response must be greater than the assault. . . .

I, for one, have only a single option; and it has been imbued in my psyche from the moment my ears first heard the song of native birds and the soothing yet determined waters flowing from a Sierra snowmelt. I will bleed for the land that sustains me. I will fight for my home.[121]

CHAPTER 6

Nihilistic Terrorists: Fanatical Cells, Lone Wolves, and Hybrid Groups

> In the very depths of his being, not only in words but also in deeds he has broken every tie with the civil order and the entire cultured world, with all its laws, properties, social conventions, and its ethical rules. He is an implacable enemy of this world, and if he continues to live in it, that is only to destroy it more effectively.
>
> —Sergey Nechaev, *Catechism of the Revolutionist*

On November 2, 2004, in Amsterdam, filmmaker and social critic Theo van Gogh was murdered in the street by Mohammed Bouyeri, a nihilistic terrorist driven by a fantasy-fueled rage who has been characterized as a jihadi.[1] Bouyeri, whose alias is Abu Zubair, was born and raised in the Netherlands and had limited experience with the Islamic religion, but he hated and felt alienated from Dutch society. He is an excellent example of a homegrown terrorist aided in his radicalization process by friends and associates with similar feelings of alienation. Van Gogh had once called Muslims "goat fuckers" and had stated in some of his public pronouncements that the prophet Mohammed was a perverse tyrant. He and Ayaan Hirsi Ali—a female friend and former Muslim who was a Somali-born member of the Dutch Parliament—had made a film, titled *Submission*, directed by van Gogh and written by Hirsi Ali. The film mocked the Koran by showing parts of the text on the body of a seminude girl. Van Gogh was also a columnist and had a Web site on which he had identified himself as a writer of social commentary. He was critical of many elements of European society and was known to be particularly caustic in his approach to commentary.

Bouyeri was a member of a small, jihadi terrorist cell later identified by law enforcement authorities as the Hofstad group. He had been born and raised in the Netherlands and lived in an area that had a high concentration of immigrants from Morocco. He had dropped out of college after attempting to obtain a degree for five years. He had a criminal record, including a conviction for an assault in which he threatened another individual with a knife. He was convicted for that incident and served 12 weeks in jail, where he began to study the Koran.

After his release from jail in 2001, Bouyeri was able to go on Social Security and did not work. He became increasingly involved in a radical form of Islam, holding meetings in his home with other radical, re-Islamized young Muslims who were also citizens of the Netherlands. He became connected to a Syrian preacher, Riduan al Issar (also known as Abu Khaled), whom he met at a phone center. Between 1997 and 2004, Bouyeri had five encounters with the Dutch police. In the last incident, he was arrested after he kicked and struck the police officers. The group of young Muslims he associated with was being watched by the Dutch domestic intelligence agency called the AIVD (Algemene Inlichtingen- en Veiligheidsdienst), but the authorities believed him to be only a peripheral member.

On the day of the attack, Bouyeri awoke at 5 A.M. to pray and have breakfast. He departed the house on his bicycle and met van Gogh, also on a bicycle, in the street; Bouyeri then shot at van Gogh, knocking him from his bike. Bouyeri dismounted from his bike and continued to shoot at van Gogh, who was lying in the street unable to move. After firing all the rounds in his gun, he reloaded his pistol and then drew a knife, which he used to stab the dead or dying van Gogh numerous times. Finally, he cut van Gogh's throat severely in what may have been an attempt to ritually behead him. Bouyeri then took a second, smaller knife; wrote a note; and stuck it on van Gogh's chest with the knife. The note contained Bouyeri's complaints concerning Dutch politics. Bouyeri fled after the attack but was soon caught by the police and, after a gun battle, was shot in the leg and taken into custody. While Bouyeri was killing van Gogh, there were 53 eyewitnesses to his crime. He actually fired 20 shots, 8 of which struck van Gogh.

During the subsequent investigation, the police learned Bouyeri was practicing Takfiri Islam, a radical form of Islam. In his parents' house, the police discovered a large number of photographs of murders, torture scenes, and decapitations. They learned that he was a member of a previously identified jihadi group—a small, self-radicalizing cell the police had named the Hofstad group. Bouyeri had acted alone, however, in his attack on van Gogh and had intended to become a martyr by engaging in a battle with the police, assuming that they would kill him rather than wound him.[2] The jihadi group of which Bouyeri was a part is an example of a domestic, self-radicalizing network of nihilistic terrorists who profess a religious motivation for their actions.

NIHILISTIC-TERRORISM

Nihilistic terrorists are on the margins of every radical movement that has chosen terrorism as a strategy to achieve its goal. This type of terrorist, both group and individual, professes to be motivated by a variety of causes: religion, ethnic separatism, regime change, or other political or social issues. Their terrorist acts, however, are committed for personal motivations: to gain an identity, to expend their anger, or to assuage their grievances against a society they believe has not recognized their value. Their violent acts—including, in some cases, resultant martyrdom—would, they believe, give meaning to their lives. In other words, their acts of violence—like Mohammed Bouyeri's brutal murder of the defenseless Theo van Gogh—make them feel important and send a signal to the world that rejected them.[3]

The term *nihilism* derives from the Latin *nihil*, which means "nothing." The term was used by the 19th-century Russian novelist Ivan Turgenev, in his work *Fathers and Sons*, to portray a younger generation "who valued or recognized nothing as restraining their morals and behavior."[4] Although in Turgenev's view the nihilistic generation was a benign group, the term *nihilist* was given evil connotations in Dostoevsky's novel *The Possessed*, which drew upon Dostoevsky's own experiences as a young, foolish revolutionary in Russia. From Dostoevsky's standpoint, nihilism was "the rejection of all religious and moral principles, often in the belief that life is meaningless."[5] The 19th-century philosopher Friedrich Nietzsche has often been incorrectly characterized as a nihilist "because he questions the value of such ideals as truth and morality, but he does so because they eclipse other, more important values."[6]

The ideological foundation of nihilistic terrorism is found in Sergey Nechaev's work *Catechism of the Revolutionist*, which describes Nechaev's model of a revolutionary. Although Nechaev's work serves as a model for nihilistic terrorism, Nechaev's own career as a revolutionary was very short. In 1868, Nechaev established a small, eight-man cell of alleged revolutionaries. Within two months, however, Nechaev murdered one of the cell members who he believed was a police spy. In committing the murder, Nechaev was assisted by four other cell members but personally strangled the victim, Ivan Ivanov, and shot him in the head. The murderers tried to hide Ivanov's body by sinking it in a pond, but the body bobbed up shortly thereafter, leading to a police investigation and the subsequent arrest of the five men. Nechaev fled to Switzerland but was extradited back to Russia, where he was convicted of the murder and sentenced to 20 years of solitary confinement; he died in prison in 1882, probably of starvation.[7]

The prototype of a nihilistic terror cell was also born in Russia during the reign of Czar Alexander II. A small group of revolutionaries, who termed themselves "The Organization," created a subset of the group called "hell."

The hell cell was led by Nikolai Ishutin and was, in reality, a group of juvenile fantasists who dreamed of assassination and crime. The group, which only lasted from 1864 to 1866, came to an end when one of their deluded members, Ishutin's cousin, Dmitry Karakozov, attempted to assassinate Czar Alexander II in a St. Petersburg park. Karakozov fired at the czar with his pistol but missed his target when a passerby deflected his arm. He then failed to take the poison that was secreted on his person and was taken alive. Karakozov and Ishutin were subsequently hanged by the government.[8]

This chapter examines terrorism's nihilistic fringe—those lone assassins and bombers; autonomous fanatical cells; and anarchistic, criminal-terrorist hybrid organizations that are predominantly driven by feelings of alienation and rage, a fascination with violence, and in some groups, a desire for financial gain. The chapter starts with an analysis of the motivations and organizational systems of three categories of terrorists who often exhibit nihilistic behavior: (1) small, auto-radicalizing cells, (2) lone wolves, and (3) criminal-terrorist hybrids, including an emerging threat—pirates.

ORGANIZATIONS

Nihilistic terrorists usually operate as small, autonomous cells within several radical movements. These cells do not usually have a formal organizational structure with a designated leader. Their membership is amorphous but revolves around a core group of members that have a consistent relationship often based upon prior social or political connections. The lack of central control or a defined leader makes the cell susceptible to unilateral action by individual members or smaller subsets of the group.[9]

The lack of a formal organizational structure in nihilistic terrorist groups complicates both the investigative and prosecutorial processes. The groups can resemble typical groups of friends and acquaintances who meet together in common locations that function as places for recreation. Investigative guidelines in the United States and foreign countries may limit the type of investigative techniques that can be utilized against individual organizations unless the government possesses a defined quantum of proof, such as probable cause, for believing the group or individuals are involved in terrorism.[10]

In addition, the applicability of legal statutes may be based on proving that "an organization" as defined in a pertinent legal code has engaged in criminal or terrorist acts. Unlike formally structured organizations such as the Sicilian Mafia or al Qaeda's central organization, nihilistic terrorist cells do not easily fit the legal definition of an organization. The prosecution of the Hofstad group by the Dutch government was challenged by defense attorneys on the basis that the "group" did not exist. The prosecution had to prove that the unstructured association of individuals fit the definition of an "organization" as required by the Dutch penal code. The Dutch court in Rotterdam resolved the legal issue by finding that the charged individuals were organized around a common intent, thus meeting the definition of a terrorist organization.[11]

Nihilistic terrorists exist within a broad spectrum of the world's political, religious, and social movements. Although their true nihilistic motivation is to express their hatred and gain a sense of importance, their expressed motivation varies according to the cause they have adopted. These causes are diverse but usually involve a belief in irrational conspiracies and are often related to religion, race, antiglobalization, and the environment. When the cause has a nexus with the natural environment, it can include either the destruction or protection of the environment.[12]

Religious Groups

Although nihilistic terrorists exist on the fringes of several religions, jihadi terrorist groups are highly relevant on an international basis, while Christian fundamentalist groups that preach racial supremacy or anti-abortion violence have traditionally posed problems for U.S. authorities. This has changed, however, and currently Salafi jihadi groups are the most significant problem in both the United States and European countries. The Islamic faith has an historical militant tradition. Its concept of jihad is the cornerstone for jihadis who interpret the concept as justification for violent acts directed against those who threaten Islam.

Ideology

In the modern era, radical followers of the Sunni Islam tradition uniformly adhere to the teachings of Sayyid Qutb (1906–66), whose most significant work, *Milestones*, was published in 1965. In *Milestones*, Qutb calls upon Muslims to fight a holy war against those who threaten Islam. He justifies the use of violence and teaches that other religions are evil. Qutb, who lived in the United States for two years as an exchange professor, believed the West to be an enemy of Islam. In *Milestones*, he claims that all existing Islamic states were not adhering to the true principles of Islam and that their leadership were pagans. Qutb, a member of the Muslim Brotherhood, was imprisoned for many years by Egyptian authorities, was released in 1964, and was subsequently imprisoned and hanged because he had been part of a conspiracy to assassinate Egyptian ruler Gamal Abdel Nasser. Today, Qutb is considered a martyr, and his teachings are used by Salafi jihadis to justify acts of terrorism.[13]

Although Qutb's influence remains strong, other jihadi leaders use the Internet to provide guidance to the decentralized network of jihadi terrorists. Abu Musab Al Suri, the nom de guerre of Mustafa Setmarian Nasar, is a senior al Qaeda ideologue, currently in custody, who is influential in the Salafi jihadi movement. He concentrated on the jihad concept and how jihadis could maximize their success. Al Suri advocated the use of media campaigns and communications technology to justify the Salafi jihadi movement's "use of violence to the public particularly to the young, Muslim men around the world in search of ways to participate."[14]

In Europe and the United States, the greatest threat in the last decade has been homegrown groups who profess to be motivated by a distinct fundamentalist movement within the Islamic faith referred to as Salafism. The term *Salaf* in Arabic means "the ancient ones." Salafism is based on revivalist ideology, which advocates a return to the original Muslim community as it existed in the seventh century after the revelations made to the prophet Mohammed. This golden age, in which Islam made great advances through military means throughout North Africa and into Europe, was a community governed by Sharia law, which is based on the Koran. Those who follow the Salafist ideology as interpreted and expressed by Qutb and Al Suri are essentially a terrorist sect within the Salafist movement.[15]

Marc Sageman, in his book *Leaderless Jihad*, characterizes the young people who are on the fringes of the nonviolent Salafist movement but will eventually resort to terrorism as romantics with an inflated and unrealistic vision of themselves and their society. Sageman equates these Salafi jihadis with Russia's 19th-century anarchists as to their self-image and personal sense of sacrifice: "My data shows that they are generally idealistic young people seeking dreams of glory fighting for justice and fairness."[16]

Although many of al Qaeda's followers may be looking for a just, utopian society under an Islamic caliphate, homegrown nihilistic jihadists are not interested in the complexities of a caliphate based on Sharia law. For these alienated individuals, bin Laden's communiqués and the writings of al Qaeda's fundamentalist ideologues offer "simplistic conspiracies to explain their world."[17]

Domestic Salafi jihadi cells are self-organized and radicalized in the home countries of their members. The NYPD study of homegrown terrorism conceptualized a four-stage process in the organization of a domestic Salafi jihadi group: (1) pre-radicalization, (2) self-identification, (3) indoctrination, and (4) jihadization.[18]

The NYPD's four-stage process comes with caveats:

- Each of these phases is unique and has specific signatures.
- All individuals who begin this process do not necessarily pass through all the stages.
- Many stop or abandon this process at different points.
- Although this model is sequential, individuals do not always follow a perfectly linear progression.
- Individuals who do pass through this entire process are quite likely to be involved in the planning or implementation of a terrorist act.[19]

The NYPD identifies three factors that are usually essential to the unfolding process of radicalization: First, an individual who has begun to explore Salafi Islam must experience a personal crisis that causes him to begin the development of a new mindset. Second, the indoctrination phase usually needs to be guided by a "spiritual sanctioner." Third, the process needs to be undertaken with other friends and associates who are also on the pathway for the process to take full effect.[20]

RAND researcher Kim Cragin, in testimony before the U.S. Congress on December 15, 2009, stated that in general the radicalization process had three phases: availability, recruitment, and commitment to action, but "research conducted at RAND and elsewhere suggests that no single pathway toward terrorism exists."[21] Marc Sageman's research concerning Salafi jihadism determined that joining a terrorist network was "a collective process based on friendship or kinship" and that this process involved intimate networks of individuals that were structured as in-person groups and "virtual online groups."[22]

The FBI points to the Internet and social networking as linked in serving as a conduit for the radicalization of extremists.[23] Social network analysis (SNA) is an essential tool for understanding nihilistic terrorism, including hybrid crime and terror groups. When movements adopt a leaderless resistance structure that relies on networking principles fostered by modern technology, SNA offers the best hope of understanding their operational characteristics. Unlike overt groups and movements, however, covert groups prove difficult for SNA experts to accurately map. The use of SNA is a countermeasure to the operations of nihilistic terrorists and is discussed more thoroughly in chapter 8.[24]

CASE EXAMPLE—EUROPE: THE HOFSTAD GROUP

The jihadi cell informally referred to by Dutch authorities as the Hofstad group began and ended with an Amsterdam teenager named Samir Azzouz, who initially came to the attention of Dutch authorities when he attempted to travel to Chechnya to fight as a mujahideen against the Russians.[25] He never made it into Russia and was arrested and sent back to the Netherlands by Ukrainian authorities, where he was first interviewed by the Dutch police. He was released after the interview as the Dutch authorities did not have enough information to charge him with a crime. Azzouz settled in Rotterdam, where he began to visit various social networking sites, the most prominent being a phone center in the Rotterdam suburb of Schiedam.

The phone center was frequented by a group of young Muslims, who used it to watch videos of terrorist attacks, pray, and discuss their aspirations concerning Islam and jihad. While there, Azzouz gathered a group of friends. Jason Walters was also born in Amsterdam to a native Dutch mother, who was divorced from his father, a former American serviceman. Walters was a Baptist, but, in 2000, he and his brother Jermaine converted to the Islamic faith. Walters became active on the Internet and soon came into contact with other cyber jihadis. By this time, his views had become more radical, and the mosque he was attending asked him to no longer attend services because he had become too radical. The number of acquaintances Azzouz and Walters attracted at the phone shop grew, and they began other meetings at the more radical Tawheed Mosque and private apartments of the various friends in their network.

One of those friends was Mohammed Bouyeri, the eventual killer of Theo van Gogh. Bouyeri became a magnet for additional new members after he left his parents' home in Amsterdam for his own apartment in a poorer section of Amsterdam West. His roommate, Nouredine ael Fatmi, an illegal immigrant from Morocco, had worked in the Schiedam phone center.

The phone center was significant in the activities of the group because of the presence of a Syrian named Riduan al Issar, who actually lived in a room above the phone center. Al Issar claimed to be a mujahideen and gave lectures to the other young men who frequented the phone center. Bouyeri and ael Fatmi hosted al Issar in their Amsterdam apartment, and these meetings were attended at various times by a group of 40 to 50 young Dutch Muslims who lived in various cities. Al Issar was an attraction for these young Muslims, and Bouyeri and ael Fatmi's apartment became a hub for the Hofstad group. By 2003, the Hofstad group had a core membership of approximately 15 to 20 members.

In 2004, Samir Azzouz was arrested by Rotterdam police. A search of his apartment turned up bomb-making materials, weapons, and a bulletproof vest. The police also found maps and floor plans of an airport and a nuclear power plant along with government buildings in The Hague. Then, in November, Bouyeri killed Theo van Gogh. After Bouyeri's arrest and confinement, the Dutch authorities arrested other members of the Hofstad group. The police were attacked when they attempted to arrest Jason Walters and his roommate in their apartment, and three officers were wounded by hand grenades.

Subsequently, the police gained information that Samir Azzouz, who had been released from jail after serving three months for possession of a firearm, had begun planning attacks with a small remnant of the Hofstad group. On October 14, 2005, Azzouz and six others were arrested and charged with various crimes using a new antiterrorism statute. In March 2006, the court in Rotterdam determined that the Hofstad group was a terrorist organization, and the group's members were convicted of various crimes.

The Hofstad group demonstrates the characteristics of a nihilistic terrorist group: (1) they lack a defined organizational structure; (2) they do not have a formal recruitment process; (3) the radicalization of the members is autonomous and does not rely upon a recruiter; (4) there is no formal affiliation to international terrorist organizations; (5) they often have an egalitarian, informal authority structure without a formally designated leader and the individual cell members are capable of acting independently; and (6) there is a lack of realistic goals, with the membership "seemingly driven more by a nihilistic attraction to violence than by a concrete political goal."[26]

The psychological state of nihilistic individuals and groups is best described as fantasy driven. For example, the Hofstad group wanted to overthrow the Netherlands' government and impose an Islamic state governed by Sharia law. An overall strategy for accomplishing this goal was never part of the group's planning process. The group was action oriented and driven by the desire for revenge upon Dutch society more than by an intellectual desire to achieve a better, more utopian society. They also engaged in the demonization of people of other faiths, including those Muslims who did not agree with their radical interpretation of Salafist Islam. "The group's members were quintessentially nihilistic, certain about what they hated but unclear about what they wanted."[27]

The Dutch AIVD characterized the Hofstad group as a jihadi network that was distinct from other terrorist groups and organizations. As a network, rather than an organization, it was not structured like a pyramid and its membership fluctuated. These networks contain a subset of dedicated members, but the majority of the membership is loosely attached and changeable. The members of the Hofstad group were linked only by a common mindset. They acted independently, and their direct actions were committed by single individuals or small subgroups.[28]

The nihilistic jihadi groups that operate in Europe and the United States are characterized by their loosely coupled organizational structure, lack of defined leadership, possession of a consistent set of stated anti-Western goals, and an unrealistic, violent strategy that bears little relationship to their stated goals.

Environmental Antiglobalization Groups

As with jihadi groups, environmental antiglobalization terrorist groups are also a fringe element of a broader movement, in this case both the environmental and antiglobalization social movements. These social movements are predominantly nonviolent or engage in civil disobedience, including vandalism of property. The terrorist groups, on the other hand, exhibit more violent tendencies, including the routine destruction of high-valued private and public property and occasional acts of personal violence.

In regard to acts of personal violence, environmental antiglobalization groups have not exhibited the consistent violence against people that religious groups routinely demonstrate. They are, however, responsible for many more acts of terrorism directed against property, and, to a lesser

degree, against people, but without the murderous armed assaults and suicide bombing attacks that have been carried out by some religious terrorist groups. The complex ideology of the environmental antiglobalization
groups explicitly identifies targets for cell members and demonizes the
various individuals and organizations that harm the environment, including its human social structure.

Ideology

Environmental antiglobalization groups have an ideology that combines
the existing ideologies of separate movements. The environmental movement has at its core the principles of deep ecology. The dangerous component of this biocentric ideology is its principle that the "flourishing of
human life and cultures is compatible with a substantial decrease of the
human population" and that "the flourishing of non-human life requires
such a decrease."[29] If you combine this principle with the nihilistic belief
that human life is without objective meaning, purpose, or intrinsic value,
the elimination of human life could become the solution to a problem.[30]

The followers of deep ecology have a religious perspective toward the
environment and perceive an eventual apocalyptic ending for the world
unless action is taken to reverse the current anthropocentric and technological models for our existence.[31] Correspondingly, adherents to deep ecology
principles believe they "have an obligation to try to implement the necessary changes."[32] Once human life has been devalued and demonized, terrorist actions that injure and kill humans can be easily justified by inherently
violent individuals and groups.

This deep ecology ideological thread has increasingly become inter-
twined with an antiglobalization thread, which serves as a link to several
radical ideologies, such as antiglobalism, anticapitalism, and antigovernment. These are the main ideologies incorporated into the antiglobalism social movement, which advocates against free trade and the Westernization
of the world. It also includes individuals who are against U.S. involvement
in the United Nations and who believe the United States has become sub-
servient to a new world order.[33]

Some REM groups merge antiglobalization with deep ecology by cast-
ing capitalism as the means that powerful corporations and government
supporters use to dominate and destroy nature for economic profit. In deciding to attack the economic system of capitalism, these REM cells move
from special interest terrorist organizations with restricted goals to revolutionary organizations whose goal is to replace the Western economic model
of capitalism. With this revolutionary goal, radical environmental cells become a hypothetical threat to the governments of most nation states.[34]

Of course, the small, decentralized cells that comprise the REM are incapable of successfully attacking a modern nation state. This reality, however, does not cause these groups to rethink their strategic goals, despite

the fact that the antiglobalism social movement does not support terrorism. For example, a recent (2010) article by Leslie James Pickering, formerly an ELF spokesperson and head of their press office, contained the following observations:

Many ELF actions, including a number of very significant actions, remain unsolved and at least some strategic evolutions have apparently taken place to better prevent a repeat of Operation Backfire. The organization continues to engage in guerrilla sabotage in the defense of the Earth, including the toppling of two controversial AM radio towers in Washington with a commandeered excavator on September 4, 2009 and a series of recent high-profile strikes and arsons in Mexico.

EMETIC took the seemingly scattered and isolated incidents of "monkey-wrenching," popular in the 1980s, to a significantly more organized and powerful level. The *Earth Liberation Front* has built an extensive legacy of very costly guerrilla strikes and has frequently incorporated liberation philosophies outside the realm of environmentalism. Looking back to the early 1970s, the *Revolutionary Force 9* bombings are a solid example of how Earth liberation politics can be effectively integrated into a revolutionary struggle.[35]

Pickering, although no longer representing ELF, has been an observer of the REM for many years. His comments concerning Evan Mecham Eco-Terrorist International Conspiracy (EMETIC) and Revolutionary Force 9 are furnished as examples of how a limited, single-issue strategy can be converted to a much broader and more radical strategy of revolution. EMETIC involved a dangerous three-year campaign of sabotage of the nuclear power industry in the southwestern United States. The results of EMETIC were significant in terms of property damage, but no humans were killed or injured. Revolutionary Force 9 refers to a domestic terrorist group responsible for the bombings of the headquarters of several major corporations based in New York City during 1969–70. Although the bombings caused serious property damage, no one was physically harmed, and prior warnings to evacuate were given to the police before the bombs exploded.[36]

The essential nature of small, self-radicalized groups is irrational, nihilistic behavior. Today, however, the availability of powerful weapons and the ability to use the media as a force multiplier for environmentally linked attacks make these small, nihilistic cells a probable threat even to powerful nations. The fear engendered by terrorist attacks has been recognized by terrorists as a psychological weapon as powerful as conventional explosives in its economic damage.[37]

Nihilistic environmental cells operate in accordance with the principles of leaderless resistance and franchising as described in chapter 5. They are true self-generating organisms that are part of the social networks prevalent in both the environmental and antiglobalization movements. The leadership component of these nihilistic groups is not always well delineated, which may be a major reason for the lack of success of many of these groups. The NYPD study of jihadi groups concluded that leadership was the major factor in the effectiveness of terrorist groups and that leadership needs to be both operational and charismatic. One leader may incorporate both traits, or the respective qualities of leadership can be shared by two cell members.[38]

The nature of the leaderless resistance concept practiced by environmental antiglobalization cells seems less authoritarian than the jihadi groups and may be one reason for their lack of violent acts directed against people, in contrast to the Salafi jihadi cells, which prefer human targets. For the leadership resistance concept to work, the members of a cell must be in sync with one another in respect to their mindset. If they are not, and because of the "no leader concept of organization," these cells are inherently prone to dissolving into networks of lone wolves.[39]

This lack of authoritarian leadership and an ideological doctrine that explicitly rejects the use of interpersonal violence may be the reasons non-nihilistic, REM cells have engaged in few acts of violence against people. The potential, however, for nihilistic, ecoterrorist cells to commit extreme acts of violence has been demonstrated on at least one occasion.

CASE EXAMPLE: RISE

The ecoterrorist cell identified by the name RISE, or the Rising Sun, was formed in 1971 by two somewhat disturbed Chicago college students.[40] The cell was the quintessential small nihilistic cell with a core membership of only two active conspirators—Allen Schwander, who was 19 at the time of his arrest in 1972 and Steven J. Pera, 18 at the time of his arrest in 1972—and a small group of friends and associates. The strategic objective of the group, or, more likely, that of Schwander and Pera, was to eliminate a large part of the human population in order to preserve the environment.

The method they selected to accomplish this goal was a biological weapon attack. Schwander planned to use an aerosol spray to disperse a biological agent over major cities. Pera used social engineering to gain access to laboratory facilities and acquire microbial pathogens.

Schwander and Pera envisioned three techniques for disseminating their biological agents: the use of aerosol sprayer technology for airborne dissemination; direct contamination of water supplies; and food contamination, also through the use of an aerosol sprayer. The group developed a very basic sprayer that was to be utilized by dumping bacteria in a glass container and spraying it around an enclosed area.

Fortunately, the group began to self-destruct in December 1971, when Pera lost his access to the hospital and the biological cultures he was working on were taken away. Then, one of their recently recruited members went to a hospital emergency room in January 1972 and advised the attending personnel about the group and its plans. This caused the Chicago

Police Department and eventually the FBI to become involved. Police arrested Schwander and Pera on January 17, 1972, which brought an end to their career as ecoterrorists.

The only members of RISE who took an active role were Schwander and Pera, although there were probably an additional six to eight people associated with the group. In sum, the strategic goal of the RISE group, specifically Schwander and Pera, seemed ominous, but their incapability of carrying out the envisioned biological attack made their goal a delusion. If, however, Pera had possessed a better scientific background and had been able to obtain a sufficient amount of an appropriate biological agent, the group might have been able to carry out an attack that could have resulted in the deaths of human beings. Even an unsuccessful attack, had the cell members not been apprehended and the scope of their activities and abilities ascertained, could have caused a panic in the city of Chicago that may have resulted in a variety of unpleasant consequences.

THE LONE WOLF

On November 19, 2009, in testimony before the U.S. Senate's Committee on Homeland Security, Brian Jenkins of the RAND Corporation addressed the committee concerning the mass murders by Major Nidal Malik Hasan that had occurred at Fort Hood:

The path that takes Hasan to the Fort Hood slayings include many of the signposts identified in the radicalization process: the search for meaning and spiritual guidance, his engagement via the Internet with jihadist ideology, his adoption of the jihadist view that the West and Islam are irreconcilably opposed, the broadening of his sense of grievance from the personal to what he saw as a besieged Muslim community, his reported on-line encounter with an enabler—a jihadist imam whose writings would morally validate and reinforce Hasan's own feelings of anger and aggression, his expression of extremist views, and at some point, his decision to kill. If some of the markers of radicalization and recruitment are missing, it is because, except for Hasan's reported correspondence with the imam, Anwar al-Awlaki, his journey may have been entirely an interior one.[41]

Since the 9/11 attacks, the only other successful terrorist attacks that have resulted in the deaths of individuals on U.S. soil were committed by individuals acting alone, otherwise known as lone wolves.[42] The FBI states that the lone offender is represented in all types of domestic terrorism. The Bureau defines the lone offender as the "single individual driven to hateful attacks based on a particular set of beliefs without a larger group's knowledge or support."[43] Lone wolves cross ideological and religious boundaries. Their unifying theme is leaderless resistance, which advocates individual acts of terror without any form of centralized coordination rather than actions coordinated by others.

Lone wolves sometimes deliberately choose their solitary actions, but in other cases the lone wolf's underlying pathological personality makes membership in even small autonomous cells impossible. In other instances, individual members of small cells break away from those cells and act alone, outside the scope of control or knowledge of the other cell members. This may occur because of an impulsive need to commit a violent act that other cell members may have questioned and that the lone wolf feels is imperative.[44]

The most significant lone wolf in U.S. history was Timothy McVeigh, who bombed the Murrah Federal Building in Oklahoma City on April 19, 1995. McVeigh's truck bomb took the lives of 168 people, including 19 children. McVeigh hated the government and believed it was conspiring to take away the second amendment rights of U.S. citizens. He was self-radicalized and probably inspired by William Pierce's book *The Turner Diaries*, which deals with the themes of racism, white supremacy, anti-Semitism, antigovernment, and new world order conspiracy theories.[45]

Pierce, who is now deceased, also furnished a fictional portrayal of a lone wolf in a subsequent book, *Hunter.* Pierce dedicated *Hunter* to Joseph Paul Franklin, a serial murderer who used sniper attacks to kill at least 20 victims. In *Hunter,* the lone wolf is portrayed as a white supremacist who decides to take direct action without external leadership to combat what he perceives as the government's threat to the white race. Pierce's protagonist, Oscar Yeager, is described as alienated and frustrated with actions the government has taken concerning racial relations. Yeager (which means "hunter" in German) independently decides that the solution to the problem of racial integration is to shoot mixed-race couples as a primary tactic. He reasons that this tactic will be successful because it will be a symbol to other white Americans, because the violent act will be therapeutic for himself, and finally because sniper-type attacks could be easily imitated by others. Yeager advocates assassination of individuals in key positions as a tactic that will keep society in turmoil and influence other societal problems.[46]

McVeigh himself, after his arrest, became intrigued with the tactic of assassination through a book by John Ross titled *Unintended Consequences.* Ross's book is the story of a team of assassins who murder agents of the federal government because of their attack on members of the gun culture. McVeigh told the reporters who interviewed him in prison that if he had read the book (which was published in 1996) before his bombing of the Murrah Building, he could have adopted another strategy.[47]

CASE EXAMPLE—LONE WOLF:
JOSEPH PAUL FRANKLIN

The prototype for the lone wolf, who is driven by personal pathology but has a poorly conceived or impossible political or social goal, is Joseph Paul Franklin (born 1950), currently on death row at Potosi Correctional

Center in Missouri.[48] Franklin was born in Alabama and named James Clayton Vaughn. He had a disadvantaged childhood, lost his sight in one eye through a childhood accident, and developed into a delinquent who failed to finish high school. Franklin, while an adolescent, developed white supremacy ideas, believed in Nazism, and changed his name to Joseph Paul Franklin in honor of Joseph Goebbels, the Nazi war criminal, and Benjamin Franklin. Joseph Paul Franklin has been a member of the Ku Klux Klan, the American Nazi Party, and the National States' Rights Party. Although he was a fanatical member who wore a swastika on his clothing, he was a loner in all these groups and left them because he felt they were not sufficiently action oriented.

Franklin began murdering African American men and mixed-race couples involving black men and white women. Concurrently, Franklin became a skilled bank robber and conducted robberies while engaging in racially motivated terrorism. The most famous of Franklin's numerous victims were Vernon Jordan, the civil rights leader who survived Franklin's attack, although he was seriously wounded, and Larry Flynt, the former publisher of *Hustler* magazine, who was paralyzed by Franklin's bullet.

According to John Douglas, former FBI profiler, Franklin believed that by murdering black people he would cause other white people to imitate his acts.[49] Franklin was eventually arrested and convicted of multiple murders and is widely considered a serial killer. His murders did, however, have a political element, and the National Center for the Analysis of Violent Crime's *Crime Classification Manual* lists Franklin under the category of "political extremist homicide."[50]

Although Franklin specialized in sniping attacks using rifles and handguns, other successful lone wolves have utilized diverse weapons ranging from actual biological weapons (Dr. Bruce Ivins) to the use of package bombs (Theodore Kaczynski) and pipe bombs (Eric Rudolph). The lone wolf is distinguished from the cell member who carries out an individual assignment. The lone wolf acts on his own volition without any form of external command or control. Recent suicide bombings by lone individuals commanded by jihadi organizations may be attributed to a recognition by those organizations that one-man suicide missions are simpler and have a higher likelihood of success and catastrophic loss of human life than attacks by armed groups.

CRIMINAL-TERRORIST HYBRID GROUPS

The need for cash causes the incorporation of criminal objectives within the strategic approach of terrorist groups. These criminal objectives are fostered by the inevitable presence of members within the group who possess criminal rather than crusader orientations.

Terrorist organizations have three types of criminal involvement with legitimate society. First, they act as predators by committing violent crimes to obtain money for their operations. The crimes of robbery (usually of banks and armored cars) and kidnapping for ransom are traditional predatory crimes, historically referred to by leftist groups as expropriations. If the money gained through crime is used to help achieve political goals, the group's orientation remains that of the crusader. If not, and the group members are using the money for their own benefit, then the group is developing a criminal orientation. Terrorist groups that start out with the traditional strategic goal of political change can, with the sudden possession of wealth, develop a criminal rather than a terrorist orientation.[51] A well-known example of this occurrence was Germany's 1970s terrorist group, the Red Army Faction. In order to raise operational funds and gain publicity for the group in the hope of increasing their recruitment, the RAF conducted a series of successful bank robberies. Although the money helped fund the organization, the new recruits were more interested in money rather than revolution.[52]

Northern Ireland's loyalist paramilitary organization, the Ulster Defense Organization, made so much money from their criminal activities that they did not return the majority of the money to their organization. Instead, individual members kept it for themselves, thus destroying the effectiveness of the group as a reactionary terrorist organization.[53]

Predatory acts used to enrich the group's members are the only logical type of crime that small cells of nihilistic terrorists can successfully engage in. These nihilistic cells easily degenerate to a disorganized mixture of political rhetoric and criminal activities. Some members of these small hybrid cells may also exhibit severe personality disorders.[54]

CASE EXAMPLE—HYBRID GROUP: ARYAN REPUBLICAN ARMY

The Aryan Republican Army (ARA) is a textbook example of a nihilistic, criminal-terrorist hybrid group.[55] The ARA used guns and bombs to rob banks in the Midwest in imitation of the bank robbery gang portrayed in the popular movie *Point Break*. Like the gang in *Point Break*, the ARA also wore masks that impersonated various U.S. presidents. The leaders of the ARA were Peter Langan, a violent transsexual ex-convict who believed in Christian identity theology, and Richard Guthrie, a violent, intelligent, dishonorably discharged former sailor with some military explosives training. These individuals met in Cincinnati in 1991 because of their similar interests in white supremacist movements. They visited the Aryan Nations, a white supremacist, antigovernment organization located at Hayden Lake, Idaho. At the Aryan Nations, Langan and Guthrie decided to start their own terrorist group because they believed the groups that were part of the Aryan Nations community were not active enough; Langan and Guthrie were interested in action, not talk. Eventually, Langan and Guthrie recruited three other individuals as members of the ARA and began their operation as a criminal terrorist hybrid group.

The ARA decided to obtain money for their cause by committing bank robberies. During their robberies, they showed a unique amount of organizational skill. Although they had revolutionary goals that were related to their antigovernment, white supremacist ideology, they were actually more enamored with obtaining money than in being terrorists. Their robberies accumulated over $300,000 for the group, which they actually believed should be used, in part—probably a very small part—to accomplish their strategic goal of overthrowing the U.S. government.

However, on June 15, 1996, their organization started to unravel. The FBI arrested Guthrie in a suburb outside Cincinnati. Guthrie immediately informed on Langan, furnishing the FBI with his location in Columbus, Ohio. The FBI arrested Langan but only after a shootout with the FBI SWAT team that left Langan covered with glass and shaken up but essentially unharmed. Guthrie pled guilty to 19 bank robberies in seven states. He subsequently hanged himself with a bed sheet in his prison cell in Covington, Kentucky. Langan was found guilty of numerous crimes and sentenced to life in prison.

The ARA was a group with a strategy but no feasible way of achieving its strategic goal. The lack of an obtainable end goal did not deter the group from engaging in crimes to fund their alleged revolution. The acts they committed were personally satisfying to Langan and Guthrie, and they obviously received an additional psychic benefit from their belief that they were terrorists.

Hybrid Group Strategies

Unlike small nihilistic cells, larger terrorist groups can move from their initial predatory acts to a parasitic strategy in which they take a share of the wealth possessed by members of the public. This entails "revolutionary taxes" on members of the public who are wealthy, own a prosperous business, or are criminal groups who require the services of the terrorist organization.[56] The best example of a parasitic strategy is that developed by the Revolutionary Armed Forces of Columbia (Fuerzas Armadas Revolucionarias de Colombia), which was founded in 1960 as the armed wing of the insurgency of Colombia's communist party. The FARC was a relatively unsuccessful guerilla and terrorist force throughout the 1970s. During that period, the size of the FARC was approximately 100 to 200 members. In the early 1980s, the FARC leadership made a deal with the drug organizations operating in the jungles of Colombia. They offered protection for the growers, smugglers, and those operating the refining plants. The FARC required a 10 percent protection payment from the local growers, which equated to millions of dollars for the FARC's coffers. The increased funding enabled the FARC to expand their size and influence in Colombia. By 1984, the FARC was estimated to have 2,000 members and soon became the most powerful terrorist organization in Colombia.[57]

Large, well-established criminal terrorist hybrid groups can move from parasitic relationships with their societal victim to symbiotic relationships. The symbiotic relationship can result in environmental resources becoming targets of the hybrid group because of their value. For example, the Karen National Liberation Army (KNLA), an insurgent group in Burma until the mid 1990s, taxed the illegal cutting and export of teakwood to Thailand and China by legal businesses engaged in illicit transactions. The KNLA was also involved in establishing sawmills to increase cutting the endangered teakwood forest within Burma. In effect, the KNLA became a business partner in an illegal business involving the degradation of a nation's valuable natural resource.[58]

Generally speaking, the major source of illicit income for criminal terrorist hybrids is the narcotics trade. Terrorist groups can participate in this trade as predators by robbing dealers, as parasites by being paid to offer security for processing facilities, or as a symbiotic component of the illegal trade by becoming exporters of the product. Cocaine, opium, and marijuana are valuable natural resources that cause groups to engage in conflict in some areas of the world. As other natural resources become exceptionally valuable as a source of illegal profit, criminal terrorist hybrid organizations will develop symbiotic relationships with the region in which the resource is located and will aid in the eventual degradation or depletion of the resource for profit.

It is also possible for criminal organizations to begin espousing revolutionary goals for the purpose of gaining public support and protection for their criminal activities. In addition, for nihilistic terrorist groups where the expressed motivation is not the real internal motivation of the members of the group, it is easier to switch to a criminal orientation while still espousing a political goal. There is one group today that is difficult to evaluate as to their future status—pirates.

PIRATES: AN EMERGING RISK

On October 7, 1985, six members of the Palestinian Liberation Front (PLF), a Middle Eastern terrorist organization, took control of an Italian cruise ship, the *Achille Lauro*, during the 6th day of a 12-day cruise. The vessel was on its way from Alexandria, Egypt, to Port Said, Egypt. The terrorist pirates were armed with automatic weapons and took over the ship without incident. They then used the ship's radio to state their demands to the authorities in Port Said. They demanded the release of 50,000 Palestinians who were being held in Israeli prisons. They threatened to execute their hostages, starting with the Americans, and said they would blow up the ship if any rescue was attempted. The taking of the *Achille Lauro* was the first recorded piracy of a ship by a terrorist group.[59]

Historical Overview

The possibility of a terrorist group engaging in an act of piracy is not an open question. They already have and will certainly do so again. As terrorists look to the environment as an increasingly valuable target, they will realize that "acts of piracy have the potential to cause major environmental damage, especially if they take place in crowded sea-lanes against heavily laden petroleum tankers."[60] Historically, pirates have always been a thorn in the side of empires and nations. Three critical periods of pirate activity offer instructive insights into what the United States and other nations are facing in several areas of the world.

The first critical period lasted for three centuries. From the 17th through the early part of the 19th century, the Mediterranean was dominated by rival pirate fleets—the Barbary (Muslim) and Maltese (Christian) corsairs. The Barbary corsairs operated from the Ottoman Empire's Barbary states' Muslim ports on the North African coast. The Maltese corsairs operated from the island of Malta and were under the control of the Knights of the Order of St. John. The two groups of corsairs were organized businesses engaged in the plunder of ships, but their respective religious hatred was a factor in deciding what ships they would plunder and who they would take captive as slaves or for ransom. Maltese corsairs plundered Muslim ships, and Barbary corsairs plundered Christian ships. Barbary corsairs also plundered U.S. ships after the United States had gained independence from England. The Maltese corsairs were eliminated in 1798 by the actions of the French government. The Barbary corsairs were stopped in 1830 through a combined effort of the United States, England, and France.[61]

The second critical period occurred in China during the early 1800s. Piracy reached its highest historical development during this period. Because China was a weak state, government forces were incapable of aggressively moving to stop the endemic practice of piracy by numerous small pirate organizations operating in China's offshore waters. The weakness of the Chinese government and the organizational skills of two pirates, a husband and wife team named Cheng I (the husband) and Shih Yang (known as Cheng I Sao, the wife of Cheng I), allowed the unification of numerous small pirate organizations into one powerful confederation. The confederation had over 400 ships and thousands of pirates. It developed a protection racket in which merchants engaged in trade were required to pay for pirate escorts. This practice began with the advent of the trade in salt and expanded to all types of trade merchants were engaged in with China.[62]

Cheng I died in battle in 1807, but, upon his death, his widow, Cheng I Sao, took command of the confederation. She led 50,000 pirates, the largest pirate force ever assembled anywhere in the world. Cheng I Sao continued Cheng I's practices, including the kidnapping for ransom of people and vessels and the trade-protection racket. When Chinese government forces decided they had to regain authority over their waters, they requested help from the United States in attempting to destroy the confederation.

Unfortunately, the pirates successfully stopped the government forces. In 1809, the confederation dissolved because of disputes between the leaders of the various pirate groups and the retirement of other key leaders.[63]

The confederation was never destroyed by the government of China, but neither was it ever strong enough to overthrow the government. The confederation was "the world's most significant instance of piracy qua piracy: without some other overarching political, economic, or social reason for its existence." The pirates of the confederation "had no other reason for existence than the sheer force of strong leaders who, for nearly a decade, outperformed the [Chinese] state's own officials in extracting resources from the local economy and enforcing their 'right' to do so with military power."[64]

The third critical period of piracy extends from 1980 to the present day. Today's piracy in East African waters and the Gulf of Aden is a resumption of pirate activity that began "in the Arabian Gulf as early as 1600 BCE."[65] The previous high point for attacks in this region occurred in the 1690s, when pirate forces from several countries established bases on various islands in the Arabian Sea and Indian Ocean. Madagascar Island was the main base for pirate activity during this period. American pirates such as Captain Kidd and Black Bart operated in this region and traded with colonial traders in the United States and Virgin Islands who also, in some cases, financed the pirates' expeditions. U.S. pirates plundered the Moorish ships owned by the Islamic ruler of Hindu India known as the Great Mogul.[66]

Modern Piracy

The age of modern piracy began in 1980 with attacks on fleeing Vietnamese boat people by local fishermen from nearby nations. In 1981, Nigeria was believed to have the most dangerous coastline, according to the International Maritime Organization (IMO). Piracy in the 1990s occurred frequently in Southeast Asian waters, particularly the Strait of Malacca.[67]

Today, the most active pirate area is off the coastline of Somalia and in the Gulf of Aden. The Gulf of Aden is of great strategic importance: 22,000 vessels go through the Gulf annually, encompassing 8 percent of the world's trade and 12 percent of the total volume of oil. Between January and December of 2008, 90-plus vessels were attacked in the Gulf of Aden (a 100% increase from 2007).[68] In 2008, there were also 135 attacks off the coast of Somalia, and pirates seized 44 ships and 600 seafarers were kidnapped and held for ransom in this area. The pirates obtained $30 million in ransom during this period.[69]

In 2009, there was an increase in naval vessels deployed in the Horn of Africa region, and the UN Security Council has passed security resolutions allowing increased international jurisdiction over piracy. The pirates, however, increased their actions in 2009 for a total of 214 Somalia pirate attacks on vessels and the seizure of 47.[70]

A high incidence of pirate attacks points to a linkage to criminal organizations that have the contacts and networks to dispose of property seized by pirate groups. In Somalia, piracy may have begun as a response to illegal fishing by foreign nations in Somalia's national waters. Allegedly, fishermen were angry over these incursions and began extorting license fees from foreign fishing trawlers. This activity expanded to the seizure of vessels and their cargos when criminal gangs, such as the Somali marines, saw a golden opportunity for profit. Most pirates today are young, and their numbers may be as high as 1,000.[71]

The greatest potential for an environmentally linked pirate attack is in international waters off the East African coast. The probable scenario will involve the seizure of an oil tanker headed to the United States. The tanker will be held for ransom by terrorists claiming allegiance to al Qaeda, allegedly as a response to America's exorbitant use of the oil that contributes to the global warming that is negatively affecting the countries of Africa. The resultant ransom money could be split among group members, the operational needs of the pirate groups, and Islamic charities. In November 2008, Somali pirates hijacked a Saudi Arabian Aramco-owned ship, the *Sirius Star*. The *Sirius Star* carried over $100 million worth of oil and was taken 400 miles from shore and motored back to Somalia.[72]

Another possible scenario is for a pirated oil tanker to be destroyed in one of the key straits or ports of the world. The destruction of a tanker with its load of crude oil would cause environmental devastation to the affected region. Another option would be a suicide attack on an oil-carrying super-tanker, which could possibly be accomplished by driving a fast boat filled with explosives into the side of the tanker.

The often-stated axiom that criminals and terrorists cannot coexist because of their different motivations should be changed to a statement that terrorist groups can engage in criminal activities either as hybrid crime-and-terror organizations or in limited partnerships with a criminal organization. In regard to piracy, terrorists can operate in both fashions, either of which can result in environmentally linked attacks. Generally, pirate attacks will be for monetary and nonideological purposes, but the potential for such attacks by terrorists for propaganda or funding purposes has to be considered highly probable because such attacks are both achievable and logical.

NIHILISTIC STRATEGY

Within the spectrum of terrorism, nihilistic cells and individuals occupy the outer band of the spectrum. At the band's inner margin, small cells are loosely coupled to an active, international social movement by the Internet and other social nodes that furnish doctrinal guidance, tactical training, and motivation. At the middle, they are small, autonomous cells, lacking a link to a broader social movement, that make decisions in an atmosphere dominated by group dynamics that take place under the pressure of their cell's isolated existence. At the outer margin exists the lone wolf, normally with a severe personality disorder or driven by irrational beliefs based on hatred of a demonized group or individuals. The strategic direction of these respective cells and individuals will vary greatly. The small groups that have either developed from social networks or lack any connection to a social movement will have a changing, situationally based leadership lacking a strategic vision. The strategic direction of these cells is developed through a participatory rather than authoritarian process and is influenced by emotional desires of individual members. The strategic direction for lone wolves will be influenced by Internet communications and motivational books, such as William Pierce's *Hunter* and *The Turner Diaries* or the Phineas Priesthood works by Richard Hoskins, such as *Vigilantes of Christendom*, that furnish justification for the pathological beliefs and goals of the lone wolf.

The strategic approach of nihilistic cells and individuals will always be based on internal, expressive motivations rather than a rational, instrumental approach. The logic will be dominated by the strategies of attrition and intimidation, but these strategies may not be based on a realistic assessment of the capability of the terrorist group. For these types of strategies, the small size of the group requires the use of a weapon of mass destruction or an attack that will result in similar psychological effects. The strategic approach, however, will be dominated by a bias toward action more than accomplishment. The strategic goals of these cells and individuals will vary, but the predominant goal will be social control. This particular goal will be chosen because the core motivational factor of these groups and individuals is hatred of an external enemy whose behavior the group desires to restrain or eliminate. For some right-wing groups, the strategic goal will be status quo maintenance, or the desire to protect the existing political order from a perceived revolutionary threat that is usually expressed by a nascent political movement.[73]

To be successful, nihilistic groups and individuals should formulate a strategy and select tactics that will achieve strategic goals that fit their operational capability. Fortunately, these nihilistic cells, groups, and individuals rarely follow such a rational process. When they do, however, their success often has grave consequences.

TACTICS

It is midnight, July 4, 2012. The Gulf Coast is preparing for the arrival of a Category 4 hurricane forecasted to reach landfall within 24 hours. A speedboat, loaded with C4 military explosive and containers of gasoline, is racing through the night from the direction of New Orleans. In a southern state, a backpacker in the state's forest system has set the last of six firebombs with electronic ignitions and is walking toward the trailhead where she left her car. At a large, well-known resort hotel in a major southern city, a recently hired maintenance employee has emerged from a hiding place near the heating and air conditioning system carrying a sealed container filled with anthrax spores.

At 12:15 A.M., the speedboat strikes the largest deep-water drilling platform in the Gulf of Mexico and explodes, causing other explosions on the drilling rig that result in outbreaks of fire throughout the platform. At 12:30 A.M., six firebombs explode at various locations scattered throughout 1000 acres of wilderness forest that intersects with extensive residential subdivisions 5 miles from where the closest firebomb exploded.

At 6 A.M., a communiqué is e-mailed to the major news media headquarters in New York, Miami, and Washington, D.C., claiming credit for the destruction of the drilling platform and the wildfire arson in the state forest. The communiqué also states that the next attack will be to infect the guests at a resort hotel located in a large southern city with anthrax. The communiqué is signed "Al Qaeda in America."

The hypothetical, nihilistic terrorist cell grandiloquently calling itself "Al Qaeda in America" may not actually be successful in carrying out a combined attack of this nature. It could, however, try, and the attempt itself would change the way we look at our energy infrastructure, vulnerable environmental areas such as residential areas that intersect wildlands, and the air we breathe within our buildings.

Striking at the natural environment's nexus with human life is an effective tactic. Three tactics offer nihilistic terrorists the ability to maximize their potential capability to instill fear in their intended targets with limited risk of detection and apprehension by law enforcement:

1. Arson attacks on the wildlands-built environment junction
2. Sabotage or bombings of oil and natural gas facilities and transports located within environmentally sensitive areas
3. The use of biological toxins and agents to attack our air, food, and water

Arson Attack on Wildlands

Arson attacks on wildlands and on the intersection of wildlands and the built environment (e.g., housing subdivisions and resort hotels) occur frequently in many areas of the world. These attacks are often due to malicious mischief or the psychological desire for excitement linked to fire setting, but many are intentionally caused for a variety of criminal reasons. From the standpoint of terrorism, arson has been used as an asymmetrical tactic by terrorist groups and lone wolves.[74]

From an international perspective, terrorist attacks on forests have already occurred and offer a low-risk, high-value method of attack that requires a minimal amount of equipment, usually only an ignition device and highly combustible fuel. Changing climate has exacerbated the flammability of wildlands in many regions of the world, including the United States. Jihadi groups are well aware of how to use arson as a tactic. Israel's forests were subject to numerous arson attacks implemented by Palestinians during the first Intifada (1987–93). The Israelis termed these attacks "pyro-terrorism."[75]

Spain in 2006, Estonia in 2006, Greece in 2007, and Australia in 2008 had extensive forest fires, and their governments initially characterized those fires as possible acts of terrorism. The motives of the individuals who set the fires in Spain and Greece are uncertain. Estonia's forest fires were possibly started by a nihilistic terrorist group with a seemingly specious motive—anger at the government's refusal to remove a Soviet monument from the capital city of Tallinn. Calling themselves the Forest Incinerators, the alleged terrorist group seems to have overreacted by conducting an irrational attack that was not successful in achieving its goal of monument removal. Although pyro-terrorism has been suspected as one cause of Australia's extensive forest fires, the government has not been able to prove that terrorist actions actually occurred.[76]

In the United States in 2003, USA Today reported that an al Qaeda detainee had revealed an al Qaeda–directed plot involving three or four people who would use timed ignition devices to start wildfires in Colorado, Montana, Utah, and Wyoming. The FBI sent a memo to certain law enforcement agencies stating that the detainee's credibility could not be confirmed. The wildfires never occurred, and it is obvious from the facts recounted by USA Today that the FBI did not regard the threat as credible.[77]

Overall, pyro-terrorism remains a high risk for use by nihilistic terrorists, especially lone wolves, who would find this type of tactic within their limited operational capabilities.

Biological Weapons

America's worst act of biological terrorism occurred one week after the 9/11 al Qaeda attacks on targets in the United States. The weapon was dried, powdered spores of Bacillus anthracis, the bacterium that causes anthrax. The vehicle was letters sent through the U.S. mail system. Targets were the media and selected U.S. senators. The results of the attack were deadly and costly: five people died from inhalation anthrax; several buildings and postal service facilities were contaminated (two of the deceased victims were postal service employees); the facilities of the U.S. Senate were shut down; the safety of the U.S. mail system was questioned by citizens; and hundreds of false alarms over benign powders maliciously sent to people through the mail threatened the public's belief in the safety of the U.S. Postal Service.[78]

After a multiyear investigation, the FBI used traditional investigative methods and a novel approach to the new field of microbial forensics in concluding that the perpetrator of the anthrax attacks was Dr. Bruce Ivins, a microbiologist employed at the U.S. Army's Medical Research Institute of Infectious Diseases (USAMRIID).[79] Only two credible questions remain concerning the FBI's determination of Ivins's guilt. First, Ivins was limited to working on liquid formulations of anthrax spores, not the powdered spores that were sent through the mail system. Second, Ivins committed suicide in late July 2008 as the U.S. government was moving toward an indictment of him, and, thus, the evidence against him has never been tested in a criminal trial.[80]

One of the major benefits of using a biological weapon is the anonymity of the attack. The weapon can be delivered covertly, and the deadly results will surface hours (if a toxin) or days (if an agent) after the attack. Even then, medical and law enforcement authorities may believe that any resultant deaths and illnesses occurred as a result of a natural disease or poisoning that was acquired through accidental contact with the organism or toxin.[81] Thus, the number of people killed by the anthrax attacks could have been significantly larger if the attacker had disseminated the anthrax spores by a more covert method. For example, a mechanical aerosol sprayer could have been used in a movie theater without any of the people being aware they had inhaled anthrax spores.

If Ivins had not sent any type of communication with the spores, he might not have been caught. The initially unknown perpetrator of the anthrax letter attacks sent notes with the spores, and terms in the notes related to Islam. Initially, this caused elements of the U.S. government to believe the attacks may have been implemented by Iraq. The FBI, however, performed a linguistic and behavioral analysis of the three letters and transmittal envelopes and a behavioral assessment based on a hypothetical perpetrator's use of anthrax as a weapon. The key elements (paraphrased) of the assessment were as follows:

1. Adult male
2. May work in a laboratory and possibly has at least a strong interest in science
3. Has access to a source of anthrax and the ability to utilize it as a weapon
4. Has access to the necessary laboratory equipment
5. Holds grudges[82]

Ivins fit the profile, and the profile helped the FBI focus their investigation on him as a lone wolf with the requisite scientific background and access to anthrax spores.

Nihilistic individuals and small cells are likely to regard biological weapons as an effective and appropriate method of attack. An attack with a potent biological weapon has the capability of causing large losses of life. If the agent or toxin used is not a true biological weapon, it can still be a weapon of fear and chaos. According to Jessica Stern in her work *The Ultimate*

Terrorists, the types of terrorists who would select bioweapons would do so because those weapons inspire dread, and they would regard the formation of chaos as a successful attack. Stern believes "the groups most likely to use these weapons are groups with amorphous constituencies, including religious fanatics, groups that are seeking revenge, and groups that are attracted to violence for its own sake."[83]

According to Jonathan Tucker of the Center for Nonproliferation Studies, the hurdles for terrorists to overcome in choosing a biological weapon attack using an infectious agent or toxin are many:[84]

1. The biologic agent that is selected needs to be sufficiently virulent.[85]

2. The terrorist or terrorist cell members must have sufficient knowledge, training, and equipment relevant to microbiology.[86]

3. Dissemination for large-scale attacks would need an aerosol delivery system, which would create difficulties and also be subject to the atmosphere and wind conditions.[87]

Tucker believes the problems inherent with aerosol delivery are beyond the ability of most terrorists. He describes the problem thusly: "To infect through the lungs, infectious particles must be microscopic in size— between one and five microns (millionths of a meter) in diameter. Terrorists would therefore have to develop or acquire a sophisticated delivery system capable of generating an aerosol cloud with the necessary particle size range and a high enough agent concentration to cover a broad area."[88]

Opposed to Tucker's viewpoint, Michael Osterholm and John Schwartz, in their book *Living Terrorism,* state, "Experts in the burgeoning field of aerosol technology disagree, say that the achievements of their discipline would make aerosol distribution simple and that these technologies have been well described in the scientific literature." Stern, in her review of the aerosol dissemination issue, believes that the truth is "probably somewhere between these two viewpoints."[89]

The only logical attack venue for small cells and lone wolves would be an enclosed space, such as a hotel, mall, train, subway, or plane. "Such an attack, if it involves respirable aerosol, might infect thousands of people, but even here the technical hurdle would be by no means trivial."[90] Despite the difficulties inherent in an attempt to use bioweapons, a variety of terrorist groups have demonstrated an interest in their usage. Al Qaeda is undoubtedly the greatest threat. Bin Laden has consistently, over many years, displayed an awareness of the benefits of bioweapons and is believed to have implemented plans to obtain or develop such weapons.[91] The reality is that bioweapons have failed as a tactic for causing mass casualties when used or attempted to be used by terrorist groups. They do, however, possess an inherent capability to engender fear and possibly panic on the part of the public. Forecasted projections of deadly epidemics and mass casualties are only theoretically possible.[92] The use of such tactics, however, does meet the strategic goals of provocation and intimidation. Even an unsuccessful attack, if combined with the force multiplier effect of consistent media interest in publicizing the attack, would cause the targets of the attack to reasonably become panicked.

The drawbacks to the use of such weapons are such that individual terrorists who do not desire a slow, painful death may not wish to use these weapons. The handlers of bioweapons face a high risk of being infected. A resultant death would not be rapid in most cases of infection with biological agents. If poisoned with certain toxins, death would be fast, but painful. Terrorists are imitative, however, and the successful anthrax letter attacks could cause terrorists to try to improve on Ivins's work.[93]

Certainly, Ivins could have increased the severity and frequency of his attacks if he had wanted to. Ivins's motivation seemed to be inherently personal, and he seems to have wanted more governmental focus to be given to biological weapons and to his own position. By utilizing the tactic of biowarfare, he refocused the nation's interest on anthrax as a weapon of terrorism, and, thus, his own position became more important to the government that employed him.[94]

A bioterrorism attack could also be used to target agriculture. "A major act of agricultural terrorism, one that causes over one billion dollars in damages, could be produced by a series of limited infections triggered by pathogens delivered by simple methods."[95] There are several advantages to an attack on agriculture over committing an attack on humans:

1. It is easier to produce animal and plant pathogens from natural sources than it is to produce human pathogens.
2. It is easier to obtain plant and livestock pathogens from micro-libraries.
3. The most dangerous animal and plant pathogens are easier to obtain from the environment than to acquire from a laboratory.
4. Weaponization of the pathogen is not required.
5. It is easier to disguise an attack on agriculture than it is to disguise an attack on humans.[96]

Terrorists could target both crops and animals, but different techniques for the respective targets would have to be used to disseminate the disease. Such an attack on agriculture could cause devastating economic and psychological damage. Nihilistic ecoterrorists could conceivably use this type of attack because of their belief that modern agricultural methods are deadly to the environment. Animal farms would probably be the chosen target, as "this concentration of animals combined with communicability of livestock diseases suggests that a handful of attacks could cause widespread devastation to an important sector of the U.S. economy."[97]

The list of critical bioweapon threats compiled by the Centers for Disease Control and Prevention include those that might be foodborne: (1) *Clostridium botulinum* neurotoxin (the most lethal substance known),

(2) *Salmonella typhi*, (3) *Shigella dysenteriae*, (4) *E coli O157:H7*, and (5) *Vibrio cholerae* 01. Because the food supply "is characterized by centralized production and processing and widespread distribution," a bioweapon attack on the critical centers or nodes could have cascading effects that could panic the population.[98]

Bioweapon attacks on water supplies have been planned or conceived by several U.S. terrorist groups in the past. Although the success of such an attack is possible, it would be extremely difficult to accomplish.[99] The security measures in regard to water supplies make such an attack unlikely in regard to municipal treatment centers and large, urban reservoirs. The water distribution networks might be logical targets for small-scale attacks, and remote, small reservoirs that service a restricted population could be possible targets for a nihilistic terrorist cell or individual.[100] The Rajneeshee cult that employed biological agents against people in the small Oregon town called The Dalles during August and September of 1984 included the attempted contamination of the town's reservoir among their direct actions.[101]

Attacks on Junctions of Built and Natural Environment

To maximize the effects of an environmentally linked attack, nihilistic terrorists will attack facilities that are economically important and adjoin critical areas of the natural environment. The methods of attack will be sabotage, bombings, and arson. The most frequent attacks on vulnerable built-environmental areas will be directed at energy facilities and infrastructure, such as oil and gas pipelines. These pipelines and other oil and gas facilities are located on both land and water, specifically in our rivers, oceans, and seas.

Attacks on drilling platforms and oil tankers will be increasingly attractive in the foreseeable future. The explosion of the deep-sea oil-well drilling rig *Horizon* and the resulting damage to the Gulf's already damaged ecosystem has, once more, focused the concern of governments and citizens on the environment. The damage that can be caused by the destruction of drilling rigs and the failure of the fail-safe technologies used to prevent devastating fires and well blowouts exposed a vulnerability that could be exploited. The risk that nihilistic terrorists could utilize a small craft loaded with explosives and attempt to destroy an ocean well-drilling rig or large, oil-carrying tanker is apparent, and the probable environmental damage could be much worse than the financial loss due to the destruction of the rig or tanker. An example of such an incident occurred on October 6, 2002, when a French oil tanker, the MV *Limburg*, was attacked in Yemeni waters by an explosives-packed boat operated by suicidal members of the Aden-Abyan Islamic Army. The attack was unsuccessful, as the targeted ship did not sink, and the spilled oil, approximately 90,000 tons, was successfully contained. The attack also only caused one casualty. The attack, however, did negatively affect the stock market because of concerns by oil industry investors, and it serves as a model for other nihilistic terrorist groups.[102]

The most frequent targets of terrorist attacks are the pipeline systems for crude oil, refined petroleum, and natural gas that exist in most of the world's countries. Among the most frequently targeted pipelines are those located in Colombia, Russia, Turkey, Sudan, India, and Nigeria. Colombia has the most extensive history of pipeline attacks. Occidental Petroleum's 480-mile Cano Limon-Covenas oil pipeline has been bombed over 900 times, costing the Colombian government $2.5 billion in lost revenues.[103]

The United States has 470,000 miles of oil and gas pipelines, with the greatest concentration in the southern (energy production) and northeastern (energy consumption) regions. These pipelines cross the United States and link to pipelines in Canada and Mexico. Most U.S. pipelines lie underground, but there are required markings above them in order for repairmen and other first responders to locate them.[104] On an international basis, more than half of all pipelines are aboveground. Generally, pipelines are located in areas that follow existing roads or traverse wilderness areas. Pipelines are difficult to protect and are commonly attacked with improvised explosive devices (IEDs) placed directly on the line. Increased security measures, such as a patrolling unmanned aerial vehicle (UAV), make IED attacks more problematic, and the use of standoff weapons, such as rocket-propelled grenades and mortars, has become more common.[105]

Attacks, even those carried out by single individuals using easily obtained weapons, can be highly damaging. Although common in other countries, attacks on U.S. pipelines are rare. In 1999, however, a former member of the U.S. Army's Special Forces was arrested in possession of high explosives and 14 timing devices. He planned to blow up a section of the Trans-Alaska Pipeline in order to make a profit in oil futures.[106] In 2001, vandals attacked the Trans-Alaska Pipeline with a high-powered rifle, causing a two-day shutdown of the pipeline and ecological and economic damage.[107]

The difficulty in stopping energy infrastructure attacks was recently demonstrated by the inability of Canadian authorities to capture the group or individual who has bombed six natural gas installations in Alberta, Canada, since October 2008. Canadian authorities believe the bombings have been committed by ecoterrorists. The victim of the attacks is Encana, North America's largest natural gas company.[108]

Attacks on targets that lie within the intersection of the built and natural environment are attractive to nihilistic terrorists with varying mindsets. Terrorists motivated by environmental protection concerns regard these facilities as a desecration of the natural environment. Nihilistic terrorists who lack such concerns see these attacks as a way to strike at the government and corporations, both economically and ecologically. Jihadi cells may also be aware that al Qaeda and its affiliates have called on their cohorts, via the media, to strike at the oil and gas industry in order to disrupt oil supply to the United States.[109]

There are many attractive targets that have an environmental nexus, and they are often located in areas of the world in which ecoterrorists and nihilistic terrorists operate. It is the responsibility of government and private enterprise security planners to protect their nations or organizations from these attacks through accurate risk assessment and effective security planning to both detect and prevent such attacks.

CHAPTER 7

The Risk of Terrorism

In strategy, it is important to see distant things as if they were close and to take a distance view of close things. It is important in strategy to know the enemy's sword and not to be distracted by insignificant movements of his sword. We must study this.

—Miyamoto Musashi, *A Book of Five Rings*

On April 20, 2010, in the Gulf of Mexico, a deep-sea oil well located 5,067 feet under water blew out, sending flammable gas and oil up the well shaft onto the attached drilling vessel, the *Deepwater Horizon*. The resultant explosion and structural fire created chaos and destruction. Personnel on the bridge delayed activating the vessel's emergency disconnect, which was designed to disconnect the vessel from the well and stop the eruption of gas and oil. When the disconnect system was finally activated, its blowout prevention device failed to stop the cascade of fiery gas and oil. The vessel's crew could not stop the well's eruption or fight the raging fire, and the captain ordered them to abandon ship. The surviving crew members loaded onto the two life boats or jumped from 75 feet into the black, oil-slick waters. Fortunately, a 260-foot ship, the *Damon Bankston*, was at the scene and possessed a fast recovery craft that was used to rescue the survivors in the water. The Coast Guard arrived at 11:15 P.M., but, by that time, 115 survivors were already aboard the *Bankston*, 11 crew members were dead, and 17 were injured. The *Deepwater Horizon* continued to burn for over 36 hours before eventually sinking into the ocean's depths.[1]

This tragic loss of human life and property was the beginning of one of the worst environmental disasters in U.S. history. Unfortunately, the well's owner, British Petroleum (BP), and the U.S. government did not know the magnitude of the crisis they were facing in the Gulf. They had not foreseen such a disaster, and BP's existing emergency plan was soon proven to be shockingly inadequate.

With the *Horizon* on the ocean's floor and the toxic oil gushing, the U.S. government and BP began to respond to the environmental crisis—the unceasing spread of oil that would create an ecological disaster for the entire Gulf region. As they fought the oil spill, BP and the U.S. Coast Guard, whose Department of Homeland Security had final oversight and control of the disaster response, realized that the existing emergency response plan had numerous deficiencies. Even worse, the plan's equipment requirements were based on flawed government assessments regarding the probability of oil reaching landmass as the result of a spill.[2]

Almost immediately after the *Horizon* tragedy gained national attention, questions arose as to the possible causes of the disaster. Right-wing commentators and the blogosphere raised the possibility that the *Horizon* had been destroyed by ecoterrorists. Although this has been debunked by information gained from survivors and later scientific analysis of the explosion, the belief that terrorists would attack an oil-well drilling ship is not improbable.[3] BP's emergency response plan, however, did not consider the probability of a terrorist attack, and there is no information that such an attack had ever been assessed to determine its likelihood. Although the idea of an ecoterrorist attack on the *Horizon* oil-well drilling ship may perpetuate in the minds of conspiracy theorists, the technical requisites for a successful attack would, more than likely, have been beyond the capabilities of any known ecoterrorist group.

Although the BP response plan has been criticized for its inadequacy, BP's management defended their emergency preparedness in a May 10, 2010, *Wall Street Journal* article. They based their failure to stop the blowout on a lack of prior incidents under similar circumstances: "You have here an unprecedented event. Never before have you seen a blowout at such depth and never before has a blowout preventer failed in this way."[4]

Although worse than the *Deepwater Horizon* catastrophe, the 9/11 al Qaeda attack against the U.S. homeland revealed a similar lack of risk assessment and security planning. After that attack, government intelligence agencies were asked by the 9/11 Commission if they understood the risk of such terrorism, if they had planned responses and defenses, and if they knew their planned responses and defenses might not succeed. The agencies defended themselves but the 9/11 Commission concluded that the U.S. government's leaders did not understand the magnitude of the threat they were facing.[5] The 9/11 Commission, in the last recommendation of their final report, stated that the government should "regularly assess the types of threats the country faces to determine (a) the adequacy of the government's plans—and the progress against those plans—to protect America's critical infrastructure and (b) the readiness of the government to respond to the threats that the United States might face."[6]

Corporations—an integral part of our physical and economic infrastructure—and the U.S. government have the responsibility to plan the protection of governmental and corporate operations within the United States and foreign countries. Because the threat of terrorism is not improbable, the mission for government and corporate security planners is to determine the likelihood of a terrorist attack, the targets of the attack, the vulnerabilities that can make such attacks successful, and the possible severity of such attacks. These determinations are difficult to make but are necessary and required for a multitude of possible terrorist attackers.

This chapter examines the difficult process of terrorist risk assessment. The approach to this subject begins with an overview of the general concept of risk and, more specifically, risk in relation to terrorism. Then, the basics of risk analysis methodology are presented as they are applied by both governmental and private enterprise analysts. Further, selected key elements of the risk assessment process are examined in relation to environmentally linked terrorist attacks. Finally, some of the more critical problems with analysis and prediction of rare events, such as terrorist attacks in most areas of the world, are presented.

RISK

Al Qaeda's founders have been consistent in decrying the presence of U.S. interests in the Islamic countries of the Middle East. They have pledged to destroy that presence and establish a caliphate in the region.[7] When a U.S. multinational corporation establishes operations in the Middle East, they face the possibility of a terrorist attack, which could entail the murder of their employees and the destruction of their facilities. Today, that possibility is referred to as the risk of an attack, and some individuals believe that with sufficient, accurate information, it is possible to assess with an actionable degree of probability the risk that terrorists, such as al Qaeda, will launch an attack against a defined target. Such a risk assessment is a relatively modern concept based on the belief that we can predict the future with some degree of success and thus influence its outcome by our activities.

Risk, from an organizational standpoint, is defined as the "potential for loss or harm to systems due to the likelihood of an unwanted event and its adverse consequences."[8] The term derives from the early Italian *risicare*, which means "to dare" and signifies a choice rather than a fate.[9] Today, risk is intimately connected to the ideas of probability and prediction. In the past, at least in the Western world during the centuries before the Renaissance, human beings believed that their lives in relation to the future were determined by impersonal fates whose decisions they hoped could be influenced by offerings or sacrifices to various deities or natural forces. An example of this practice was the ancient Greeks' solicitation of the providence of the winds, which they believed could influence their lives.[10] The failure of the Greeks to develop a rational system of thinking about the future was based on their belief that life on earth was under the control of irresponsible, unpredictable forces.[11] Today, because of developments in mathematics over the centuries, risk has become linked with the modern term *probability*, which has two accepted meanings: (1) the degree of doubt concerning an opinion because of a lack of human knowledge, termed *epistemic uncertainty*; and (2) events whose occurrence or outcome is uncertain because of their random characteristics (e.g., the game of craps)—termed *aleatoric uncertainty*. The development of mathematical concepts and their application to situations of aleatoric uncertainty led to the discovery of the laws of probability, which allowed human beings to quantitatively measure the likelihood of a future event or its adverse consequences.[12]

The concept of risk is also divided between situations involving the chance of suffering either a loss or gain when a specific event occurs—such as the throw of the dice in a game of craps, termed *speculative risk* (e.g., gambling)—or situations where, if an event occurs, it could be a loss, but if the event does not occur, there will be neither a loss nor a gain—termed *pure risk*. Events involving pure risk are typically insured events and are the focus of the field of risk management.[13]

Risk Management

The assessment and management of pure risk in the area of security planning for terrorism is engaged in by both governments and private enterprises. Randall Nichols and colleagues, in *Defending Your Digital Assets against Hackers, Crackers, Spies, and Thieves*, defines risk management as "applying reason in choosing how much risk we can accept and, hence, how much security we can afford."[14] Peter Bernstein, an historian of the concept of risk, states that "the essence of risk management lies in maximizing areas where we have some control over the outcome while minimizing the areas where we have absolutely no control over the outcome and the linkage between effect and causes is hidden from us."[15]

The process of accomplishing the objectives identified by Nichols and Bernstein is based upon the assumption that there is a rational method for determining the existence of certain risks and the belief that there are other risks beyond the purview of the risk management process. The assumption of rationality occurs when there are known historical instances of loss-causing events. As James Broder states in his comprehensive book on risk analysis, "when experience (history) has provided an adequate data base, loss expectancy can be projected with a satisfactory degree of probability."[16] The two universal, preliminary steps in the risk management process are to understand the mission of the organization and to accurately identify the assets of the organization that need to be protected. Once these have been accomplished, the risk to the success of the mission and security of the assets can be analyzed and assessed.

Risk Analysis

In chapter 6, a hypothetical scenario was presented that dealt with the threat of a multifaceted terrorist attack involving three distinct threats: a suicide attack on an oil-well drilling vessel utilizing a speed boat and explosives, a pyro-terrorism attack on a wildlands-built environment junction, and a biological weapons attack on the occupants of a resort hotel. These three scenarios are all possible attacks, but how probable are they? Which attack is worse in terms of actual loss and psychological harm? What would it cost to defend against each attack? Which attack is easiest to defend against? How do you know your estimates of threat, vulnerability, and consequences are valid? These are tough questions to answer, and any security professional who has conducted a risk analysis for a government or private enterprise knows the difficulty in finding certainty in the assessment process. Within private industry and the government, there are approximately 200 risk assessment methodologies currently in use.[17] These methodologies usually employ either a qualitative (intuitive) or quantitative (mathematical) approach but can blend both approaches. The various methodological approaches utilize techniques that are often similar in regard to the basic algorithms employed. For example, ASIS International has published their "General Security Risk Assessment Guideline," which covers both quantitative and qualitative assessments. This guideline, which is highly influential with private security consultants and security officials of major corporations, portrays the following algorithm, which is used in quantitative assessments to assess loss event probability or frequency:

$$p = \frac{f}{n}$$

where:

p = the probability that a given event will occur

f = the number of actual occurrences of that event

n = the total number of experiments seeking that event[18]

Nichols, in *Defending Your Digital Assets*, recommends the following algorithm but advises that it is not a mathematical equation that can be used to quantitatively determine the percentage of risk; however, it can be used to assess the qualitative level of risk for varying scenarios.[19]

$$Level\ of\ Risk = \frac{(threat \times vulnerability)}{(countermeasures)} \times Impact$$

When conducting risk assessments without factoring in countermeasures, the equation used in most systems is expressed as follows: risk = threat × vulnerability × criticality. Colonel Joel Leson, in *Assessing and Managing the Terrorism Threat*, explains this basic formula: In this equation, risk is defined as the extent to which an asset is exposed to a hazard or danger. Threat times vulnerability represents the probability of an unwanted event occurring, and criticality equals the consequence of loss or damage to the critical infrastructure or key asset.[20]

Dealing with risk in some large organizations can be viewed as a four-part system: enterprise risk management, standard risk management, risk analysis, and risk assessment. Enterprise risk management requires a top-level process driven by senior organizational executives. Its focus is on the strategic goals and value centers of the enterprise, and it addresses all aspects of its risk exposure, including pure risks—such as crime, natural disasters, and terrorism—and traditional business and political risks. Standard risk management is an older system of risk management that focuses on lower-level operational units (e.g., departments and units) and the control of casualty risks linked to insurance.[21] The terms *risk analysis* and *risk assessment* are often used interchangeably, but they have distinct meanings.

Broder refers to risk analysis as "a management tool, the standards for which are determined by whatever management decides it wants to accept in terms of actual loss." Risk assessment is a subset of risk analysis and is the method used to identify problems and determine probabilities.[22] According to the Society for Risk Analysis, risk analysis is comprised of both risk assessment and risk management.[23] The focus of this chapter now shifts to the risk assessment process in relation to terrorism.

ASSESSING THE RISK OF TERRORISM

Regardless of the methodology employed, a comprehensive terrorism risk assessment always involves three factors: threats, vulnerabilities, and consequences. Within the United States government, the Department of Homeland Security (DHS) is the main player in the area of terrorist risk assessment. Other departments and agencies also conduct terrorist risk assessments using a wide variety of methodologies. Even within DHS, various organizations with distinct mission needs employ a diverse set of methods that "range from formal analytic methods and models or simulations to more generic applications of basic concepts of risk assessments."[24]

The DHS's approach to terrorist risk assessment is based on the aforementioned three variables—threat, vulnerabilities, and consequences. The starting point in the terrorist risk assessment process is the evaluation of the threat. In evaluating the threat of a terrorist action, the analyst must identify probable terrorist attackers and determine the intent and capability of these groups and individuals. Then, an analysis must be made of the vulnerabilities of the targets these groups could possibly attack. Vulnerability refers to the probability a terrorist attack will strike and damage the target. The "likely" effects of a terrorist attack against the target are the "consequences."[25]

From a private enterprise perspective, the methods of risk assessment will also assess the threat, vulnerabilities of the target, and the potential consequences of a successful attack. However, private industry methodologies require an examination of the use and cost of countermeasures and a cost-benefit analysis that includes both the cost of the countermeasures and the probable benefits to the enterprise if the countermeasures prevent a successful attack. Although cost is a factor in governmental risk assessments, the national security mission makes cost a peripheral matter once a countermeasure is determined to be necessary to counteract a specific attack. Private enterprises, however, have the goal of achieving an "economic balance—between impact of risks on the enterprise and cost of implementing prevention and protective measures."[26] Thus, countermeasures have to be cost effective from a private enterprise standpoint.

From both governmental and private enterprise perspectives, the most important and difficult component of the assessment process is determining the potential threats that have the requisite intent and capability to attack the target. This chapter is limited to threat and vulnerability assessment. Assessing consequences is beyond the scope of this work.

The Threat

The assessment of conventional risks (e.g., natural disasters and accidents) by private and governmental enterprises relies on a standardized portrait of the specific risks and usually leads to the implementation of a generic set of objective countermeasures. Terrorism does not permit one generic portrait of the threat (group or individual) or a corresponding set of standardized countermeasures to protect against the threat. Terrorists, and criminals to a lesser degree, need to be able to adapt to the security environment in order to survive. They must have the ability to learn on both strategic and tactical levels in order to adapt. "The greater a group's learning capabilities, the more threat it poses to its adversaries. . . . In the face of this threat, the law enforcement and intelligence communities must try to stay one step ahead of the enemy."[27] Assessing a terrorist threat will have a subjective component that makes it essential for the individual or group that conducts the assessment to be an expert on the subject matter.[28]

The intelligence analyst or security planner conducting the assessment will be required to determine the likelihood of a successful attack by specific terrorist groups or individuals. In essence, their job is prediction. Prediction can be strategic, in which the analyst forecasts threats and trends without precise information as to date, time, place, and method of attack, or it can be a point prediction, which is expected to predict attacks in the immediate future with preciseness. In reality, point predictions are much more difficult to formulate with a high degree of certainty than long-term strategic predictions.[29] The basic components of a threat assessment are intent and capability, but the mindset of the group and external situational factors, relative to the social, political, and natural environment, should also be factors in the assessment. The sheer complexity of threat assessment can result in uncertain predictions because of the frequent inability to obtain accurate, relevant data.[30]

Despite the difficulty in prediction, there are methodological principles that planners and analysts should consider in conducting terrorist threat assessments:

- In making a strategic prediction as to the likelihood of terrorist attacks, take an historical retrospective in determining future trends. This historical review should encompass not just the recent past, but, even more importantly, a perusal of the recorded history of political warfare and violence as far back as Thucydides's *History of the Peloponnesian War*. For example, the proposition made in chapter 6 that there is an emerging threat of terrorist pirate hybrid groups could be criticized if one takes a short-term view of history and only looks at pirate attacks during our 20th-century experience with piracy. During this time period, piracy has usually been limited to small-scale banditry. An analysis restricted to only a review of the 20th century would probably not be concerned about a present-day threat of terrorist pirate hybrid groups engaging in catastrophic attacks against vulnerable targets in the maritime environment. If, however, one looks to the 17th and 18th centuries, a different perspective emerges of the real potential of piracy as a terrorist threat. The Christian and Muslim corsairs operating in the Mediterranean during the 17th and 18th centuries were operating not only as hostage takers and cargo robbers but also as opposing religiously inspired forces with political objectives. Their respective religious ideologies undoubtedly furnished justifications for their violent depredations, although the potential profit may have been an even greater motivation for their actions.[31] History does sometimes repeat itself, and the history of piracy is instructive for a current analysis of its potential as a terrorist threat.[32]

- Point prediction from a tactical perspective is the predominant level of analysis used by security planners. Brian Jackson and David Frelinger, RAND Corporation researchers, advocate a methodology for tactical point analyses composed of three steps: (1) determine the "terrorist group's capability and resources," (2) determine the group's ability to adapt to the "requirements of the operations the group previously attempted and the current operation it is planning," and (3) evaluate the "relevance and reliability of security countermeasures."[33] Although the three components of this methodology are used routinely in risk assessments, the way the three elements are evaluated in Jackson and Frelinger's work is novel. They do not consider the determination of absolute values for the individual elements as being excessively important. Rather, they advocate an evaluation of the relationships between the three elements as the critical factor in predicting the likelihood of success or failure of a terrorist attack. Even within their own analytical framework, Jackson and Frelinger do not furnish definitive predictions. They are concerned with degrees of probability of risk rather than deterministic factors of operational success or failure.

Jackson and Frelinger correctly recognize that a terrorist threat assessment will offer security planners information that will improve their likelihood of success but will never eliminate uncertainty because of variables that are unknown or uncontrollable. With this caveat, we can examine the application of two of the three factors—capabilities and resources, and ability to adapt to operational requirements (i.e., learning ability)—in a limited threat analysis (countermeasures are examined in chapter 8) of ecoterrorists and nihilistic terrorists.

Terrorist Group Capabilities and Resources

Ecoterrorists who operate in accordance with the guideline of not harming human or animal life have a limited set of tools to carry out their operations. Their attacks on facilities consistently involve vandalism, sabotage, and arson. Their most destructive tool is arson. These groups do not attack security officers or law enforcement and chose targets that do not have effective physical security. Their attacks are almost always at night, when the targeted facilities are unoccupied by people. The groups, usually small cells of two to six or single individuals, utilize simple techniques. These techniques, however, are easy to master, and, at the right location and appropriate facility, ecoterrorist groups such as the Family have been able to unleash highly destructive attacks resulting in large economic losses. Their leaderless resistance cell structure limits their operational capacity, however, as their cell size determines not only the type of attack but also the approximate scale of the attack.

Nihilistic terrorist cells and individuals are also limited by size and capability in regard to their operational units. However, the mindset of nihilistic terrorists incorporates the desire to kill a demonized enemy. Thus, they are capable of committing deadly, highly consequential attacks that require only a small group or a single individual, such as sniper attacks, bombings, and suicide attacks involving armed assaults or bombings. Their success with these styles of attack will depend, however, on their skill and training in a variety of areas. In looking at terrorist group capabilities, Jackson and Frelinger believe the degree of operational skill in regard to the areas of security and planning will influence a group's overall chance of success.[34]

The alleged terrorist group self-identified as the Hutaree, discussed in chapter 4, is an example of a nihilistic militia cell whose operational skills for security and planning were not equivalent to the law enforcement force opposing it. The Hutaree engaged in training for their planned attack on law enforcement but possessed a weak operational security apparatus and, in addition, did not have the technical expertise to match their operational plan. Their plan allegedly involved an IED they intended to use to kill law enforcement officers, who the cell believed would be attending the funeral of a police officer the cell had previously assassinated. The militia cell did not possess the ability to construct the required IED and had to contact another person, outside the cell, for assistance in manufacturing the explosive device. This breached their operational security and led to the cell's penetration by an undercover FBI agent. In addition, the plan itself was obviously beyond the group's capabilities. They had no prior experience in carrying out such a complex plan of operation that included the use of additional IEDs in an ongoing battle with governmental forces.[35] This alleged nihilistic terrorist group motivated by paranoia, social alienation, conspiracy theories, and fanatical hatred exhibited deficiencies in operational planning and security. Other nihilistic groups, however, have shown an ability to enforce operational security and employ logical planning in relation to the limited scope of their tactical operations. The small size of their cells and their decentralized, loosely coupled structure reduces the scope of potential operations and the corresponding requirements for security and planning.

For nihilistic terrorists, even a simple suicide attack using black powder IEDs can be within the technical parameters of their operational capability but still be beyond their security or planning capabilities. An excellent example of this defect was exhibited by two Palestinian terrorists, Gazi Abu Mezer and Lafi Khalil, who planned an attack on a New York City subway in July 1997. The two Palestinian natives of the West Bank had planned to attack a subway station using five black powder IEDs. The two terrorists were characterized by acquaintances as not being particularly religious and interested more in women and money. During the investigation, Mezer told investigators that the reason for picking the Penn Avenue subway station was because he wanted to murder Jewish people. The FBI analysis of the terrorists' bomb-making expertise concluded that they were technically proficient, and the FBI subsequently reconstructed a similar weapon for testing that functioned properly as designed. The overall planning process of the terrorists was adequate to accomplish the task. They had selected a target that was within their capability of attacking. They could have successfully accomplished their attack, but a deficiency in operation security ended their mission. On the evening before the attack, Mezer showed the IEDs to a friend, another Arab immigrant who resided with the terrorists in the same apartment, and told him of his plan to blow up the train. That man, the next day, notified the police and furnished a key to the apartment, diagrammed the layout of the apartment, and led the police to its location. The police entered the apartment and during a struggle with Mezer and Khalil, shot both of them, although not critically, because the two individuals were attempting to detonate the IEDs during the police raid.[36]

Operational security, in this case the lack of it, caused this nihilistic terrorist cell to fail in their mission. This is an example of the importance that operational security has for successful terrorist actions. For terrorists groups, both ecoterrorist and nihilistic, to be capable of functioning over an extended period of time as a viable threat, they must be able to continually adapt to the techniques and countermeasures employed by law enforcement. The continued operation of some terrorist groups is an indicator that they possess organizational learning ability.

Learning Ability

Brian Jackson and fellow RAND researchers believe that the ability to learn and adapt to their operational environment determines the resilience of terrorist groups. They propose that groups with a history of committing attacks should be analyzed to see if they possess a high degree of adaptability. If the adaptability factor of a group is strong, it means the prior history of the group has limited applicability as to the group's current capability. This factor should also be considered by the analyst in determining the likelihood of a successful attack, as Jackson and his team believe that the greater a terrorist group's ability to learn, the more adaptable the group is, and the greater the threat the group poses to law enforcement and intelligence agencies. They posit that group learning occurs at both strategic and tactical levels.[37] In Horace Trujillo's examination of attacks committed by terrorist cells of the REM, he arrives at the following conclusions:

- The REM's terrorist groups have demonstrated a relatively low level of organizational learning.[38]
- The REM's virtual and social integration of their autonomous terrorist cells aids their ability to learn.[39]
- The REM terrorist groups' strategic learning capability is demonstrated by the shifting of their targets from the forest to both the streets and the wildlands-suburban nexus.[40]
- The REM terrorist groups' strategy in regard to targeting has shifted their focus from the proximate victims of a terrorist attack to the wider audience of the attack—the public and those individuals and organizations that would be the target for demands made by the group (i.e., public officials).[41]
- The REM terrorist groups use a low technology approach tactically because it is the best approach in regard to their capabilities and ideological restrictions.[42]
- The REM terrorist cells' direct actions may be subject to the J-curve theory, normally applied to revolutions, that posits that incidents of terrorist actions should be expected to increase when a period of political and social progress, from the perspective of an activist, is reversed through a change in governmental policies.[43]
- Although the language used in communiqués transmitted by self-identified REM spokespersons and anonymous terrorist cell members has taken an

increasingly violent and apocalyptic tone, it is probable that lethal violence would appeal only to that small extremist fringe of the movement with the greatest risk for violence against persons—namely, the lone wolf.[44]

The last two of the aforementioned conclusions relate not to the learning ability of terrorists but to their motivation for the commission of acts of violence.

Motivation

The motivation of identified terrorist groups operating in a specific jurisdiction or region is a factor in analyzing the likelihood of an attack. Motivation is usually linked to the stated reason for terrorists' violent actions. Ecoterrorist and nihilistic terrorist groups will usually espouse distinctly different motivations. The "environmental destruction by human beings" causal factor, however, is always a motivational factor with REM terrorist cells and for some nihilistic lone wolves, such as Theodore Kaczynski, and groups, such as the revolutionary cells.

Standard analytical methodology requires a determination of motivation, often by analyzing written and oral statements of a terrorist organization's political or social goals—that is, their platform for change. This method has two problems analysts and planners must be cognizant of in preparing threat assessments. First, if identified terrorist threats within the analysts' sphere of responsibility (private enterprise analysts or planners) or jurisdiction (law enforcement or intelligence analysts) are part of a larger movement with a published political goal, the strategic goals of the larger movement may not be the motivational goals of the local terrorist group. This is true for both domestic and international terrorist groups. Second, significant research casts doubt on the validity of the proposition that terrorists are always rational actors who are motivated by the strategic goals they espouse. Because of these two problems, determining the motivation of terrorist groups is a more nuanced process than some analysts might currently realize.[45]

The cause-based motivations of nihilistic terrorists vary greatly, depending upon the group's political or social focus, but can reflect the goals of a broader social movement. For example, the Islamic fundamentalist movement, which influences jihadi groups, uniformly states as one of its goals the creation of an Islamic Palestinian state and the elimination of "Jews residing in the Holy Land."[46] The far-right movement in the United States, which generally incorporates nihilistic groups, generally espouses anti-government beliefs.[47] However, this linkage between movement goals and individual terrorist group motivation can be weak or nonexistent.

For example, in examining the Salafi jihadi movement led by al Qaeda, the movement's strategy involves (1) eliminating the U.S. presence in the Islamic areas of the Middle East in order to establish a Pan-Islamic caliphate in Egypt and (2) conducting a jihad against the West.[48] This strategy may not coincide with the actual goals desired by various local jihadi groups.

According to counterinsurgency expert David Kilcullen, al Qaeda does not control the operation of the numerous cells that claim a direct connection or at least allegiance to it. Kilcullen believes that al Qaeda is more of a sponsor of terrorist action but that local groups gather intelligence and select targets that are driven by local causes. These causes may have no relationship to al Qaeda's strategy for a global jihad. Kilcullen believes that the al Qaeda global jihad "appears to function more like a tribal group, organized crime syndicate or extended family, than like a military organization."[49]

Kilcullen posits that al Qaeda has inserted itself into local and regional conflicts as a patron that wants its goals melded with local issues. For Kilcullen, the key to weakening al Qaeda is to weaken it as a global force through the destruction of its links with regional terrorist groups—"a strategy of disaggregation."[50] Kilcullen's concern is with the overall threat of al Qaeda's global insurgency. He believes that al Qaeda has identified and established links with regional terrorist groups that can aid in the global insurgency. In regard to local groups, he believes that al Qaeda "seems not to have direct dealings with local insurgent groups, but to deal primarily with its regional affiliates in each theatre."[51]

Kilcullen's approach to countering al Qaeda's reach is to cut it off from regional actors as a way to eliminate its power and allow local governments to deal with the clearly identifiable local issues that really motivate local insurgent movements. Kilcullen, in his approach to counterterrorism, believes that you eliminate an insurgency by eliminating its ability to spread its revolutionary ideology. From an operational standpoint, Kilcullen believes it is essential that the military and diplomatic forces engaged in the global insurgency include individuals with a deep understanding of cultures and languages and with the interpersonal skills to facilitate personal relationships with key individuals from other Islamic countries and regions. The primary skill of these political and military operators should be foreign language ability. This ability is essential to develop the necessary interpersonal relationships and to understand the often-nuanced motivations that drive politics in these areas.[52]

Kilcullen's look at al Qaeda assumes that its strategic goals are motivators for its actions. He knows, however, that local groups will be driven by other causes and may have unique objectives. One of the premises of this book is that some terrorist groups with an environmental nexus may be influenced by nonideological reasons and that such groups and individuals may have highly idiosyncratic reasons for committing acts of terrorism. Thus, when an analyst examines the motivation component of a threat assessment, it is necessary for the analyst to ask what the terrorist group really wants.

In regard to al Qaeda, the answer to the question of what they want may be uncertain. In 1988, after the USSR began withdrawing troops from

Afghanistan, the dominant leaders of the Afghan jihad—Osama bin Laden and Abdullah Azzan (a Palestinian cleric who partnered with bin Laden in obtaining Arab recruits for the Afghanistan jihad)—and other jihad leaders were faced with a choice about what to do next, as they had achieved their original objective. They decided that their organization—the Bureau of Services, created specifically for Afghanistan—"should not be allowed to dissolve," and they then transformed the Bureau into a "general headquarters for future jihad" that they named al Qaeda, or *base* in Arabic.[53]

The decision by al Qaeda's founders to continue a jihad without formulating a strategic platform based upon a causal condition illustrates the difficulty in determining the motivational component for terrorism. Max Abrahms, in his prescient article on counterterrorism strategy, "What Terrorists Really Want," criticizes what he calls the "classical strategic model." He believes that the classical model bases its analysis of the motivational component of terrorism on three assumptions: (1) terrorist political platforms state consistent goals, (2) terrorists are rational actors and utilize a utilitarian calculus in deciding upon their courses of action, and (3) terrorists utilize the "logic of consequences" in selecting their strategic options.[54]

Abrahms's position is that these assumptions are flawed. He buttresses his position by empirical evidence, a rarity in the field of terrorism studies. He states that the assumptions of the classical model are simply false and explains why. In regard to the consistency of their goals, Abrahms states that terrorists are actually inconsistent. Their goals are protean, which makes it impossible for any government to rationally bargain with them over their platform. Abrahms furnishes examples of how readily terrorist groups reject government proposals that meet their previously stated goals.[55]

As to the second assumption, that terrorists utilize a utilitarian calculus in their choice of actions, Abrahms states that terrorists do not always do so. He believes they do not seize opportunities to achieve their goals through nonviolent means. The majority of their attacks are anonymous, which negates their ability to use attacks calculated to affect public opinion or to obtain beneficial policy concessions from the government. If the public is unaware that the group has committed a specific act, they lose the public's ability to change the government's approach. Lastly, Abrahms shows that terrorists put the survival of the group over the achievement of their stated goals.[56]

Abrahms believes the classical, goal-centered strategic model should be replaced when analyzing terrorist motivations. He uses organizational theory to support his position. Because terrorist groups are organizations, Abrahms reviews the natural systems model, formulated by Chester Barnard in the 1930s, as a correct strategic model for terrorism. Barnard was the founder of the human relations approach to organizational theory and emphasized that personal benefits are an inducement to joining organizations. Barnard believed that people gain a desired sense of community from working with other people on a task. According to Abrahms, the natural systems model applies to terrorist groups because there is strong empirical evidence that "individuals participate in terrorist organizations not to achieve their political platforms, but to develop strong effective ties with fellow terrorists."[57]

Abrahms cites several empirical studies that attempted to determine why individuals join terrorist organizations. The consensus opinion, according to Abrahms, is that individuals join terrorist organizations because they are already lonely, rejected, and alienated from their society and possess social or family linkages with other similarly alienated individuals. The necessary social connection to terrorists develops through these linkages if one or more of these friends or associates are already involved in some peripheral manner or are actual members of a terrorist organization. This social connection to terrorists can cause certain individuals from the larger pool of alienated, lonely people who are present in any society to join a terrorist group. The social linkage with terrorism precedes any ideological commitment to the group.[58] Supporting Abrahms's theory, Jerrold Post, in his book *The Mind of the Terrorist*, comments briefly on the main strategic goal of ecoterrorists: "To preserve the environment suggests that the cause is not the cause. Rather it is the justification, the rationale for frustrated, alienated individuals who have had their frustration channeled against a particular group."[59]

For the analyst, Abrahms's position, if correct, means the common counterterrorism strategies, designed to reduce terrorism by reducing its value as a productive strategy, may not be effective in at least some situations. Abrahms offers a solution based on the importance of social bonds as a factor in the analysis of terrorist groups. He recommends the utilization of social network analysis to map the social connections originating from known or suspected terrorists. Once this information is organized, the objective of a counterterrorism strategy would be to disrupt the linkages between members of a group by attacking the social bond. The easiest way to affect the cohesion of social ties is by destroying the trust social relationships are based upon. One technique is to target vulnerable members of terrorist groups who have been charged with crimes or who are already in prison facing long sentences and offer them a deal with the government. The deal would entail their testimony against the group or their agreement to become informants for the purpose of gathering information about planned attacks and evidence that would eventually be used against other group members. This strategy has two purposes: (1) to obtain evidence for eventual prosecution and information about attacks for the purpose of interdiction and (2) to cause the group to distrust one another, thus making the group ineffective as its social bonds decay.[60]

The FBI, in their investigation of the ecoterrorist group known as the Family, utilized this strategy in disrupting, arresting, and obtaining convictions of the Family's members, after the group had ceased operations, for the most serious acts of property destruction committed by any ecoterrorist group. The FBI compromised one former group member, whom they had record conversations with other former members of the Family. The information gained resulted in the successful indictment of several of the Family's members. After their arrests, subsequent plea bargains in return for testimony against other Family members resulted in further destruction of any bonds the group once had. Not all members participated in plea bargaining if it required furnishing information or testifying against former members, but those who did finished off the group.[61]

Social network analysis is a technique security planners should consider utilizing as part of their overall methodology. It can aid in determining the actual extent of a network of individuals that composes an identified terrorist group. This technique can be controversial, but, if applied correctly, it may shed considerable light on the extent of the threat posed by terrorism in a particular jurisdiction or area. This technique will be discussed more thoroughly in the following chapter on security planning.

Once a terrorist group or individual has been identified and assessed in regard to capabilities, resources, adaptability, and motivation, the next step is to begin gathering intelligence, including conducting surveillance of both terrorists and their probable targets, for the purpose of identifying indicators that the group intends to commit a future attack.

Pre-Attack Indicators

Pre-attack indicators are often the illegal actions committed by terrorists for the purpose of obtaining operational funds and living expenses for individual members of the terrorist group. The classic form of pre-attack preparation is institutional robbery. All types of terrorist groups perceive robbery as a potential method to obtain needed funds. In addition, the planning and commission of robberies serves as a bonding and training exercise for terrorist group members. The stress, danger, and violence of a robbery are excellent preparation for direct actions involving armed assaults. The joint planning and operational requirements instill teamwork and, if the robbery is successful, will build the requisite group solidarity necessary for a functional terrorist unit. The use of robbery as a primary criminal activity applies particularly to nihilistic terrorists. Because of their lone wolf or small-cell organizational profile, involvement in typical organized crime activities, which can be more lucrative with less risk of arrest, is unlikely. This is due to organizational deficiencies, such as the lack of a network of collaborators, or personality requirements, such as the desire for the emotional "rush" that accompanies a violent robbery.[62] Another reason nihilistic cells might prefer robbery over safer and more lucrative organized crime or financial fraud is the strategy of presenting the illusion of the strength and activity of the terrorist group to the public and governmental authorities.[63]

For the private enterprise risk manager who is involved in the threat assessment process, the issue is relevance. How can information about pre-incident activity on the part of suspected terrorists be of value to a security planner whose area of interest is usually a city, small regional area of the United States, or overseas location? Research conducted by Brent Smith and colleagues for the National Institute of Justice (NIJ) and reported in two published studies looked at the length of time it took international and ecoterrorists to plan their attacks, where they planned their attacks, and where their residences were in relation to the targets of their attacks. Based on their first NIJ study, which involved four types of U.S. terrorists, Smith's team reached the following conclusions:

- A significant percentage (44%) of all terrorists resided near their targets.[64]
- The international terrorists selected targets close to their residences, but right-wing terrorists selected urban targets and resided further away in rural areas.[65]
- Prior to an attack, terrorists utilized pre-operational surveillance and intelligence to gather information about the planned target. These activities "took place relatively near their homes, which, in turn, were close to the targets."[66]
- The single-issue terrorists generally committed preparatory acts relatively close to their targets. This predilection could be the result of "local targeting by 'lone wolves' sympathetic to the cause."[67]

In their second (2006) study, Smith and his fellow researchers analyzed the distance between 250 ecoterrorist and international terrorist homes and their targets. Their analysis found as follows:

- Approximately "half of the environmental terrorists and nearly three-fifths of the international terrorists lived within 30 miles of their targets."[68]
- "Sixty-five percent of the environmental (ecoterrorists) terrorists and 59 percent of the international terrorists prepared for their attacks within 30 miles of their target sites."[69]
- Although both types of terrorists committed the majority of "their preparatory offenses near their homes, they committed robberies, burglaries and thefts much further away—an average of 429 miles from home."[70]
- The data indicates that environmental and international terrorists generally live and operate close to residences and targets. "Major crimes to procure funding for the group—like thefts, robberies and burglaries—however, are intentionally committed many miles away to avoid drawing attention to the group's location and target choice."[71]

Smith and his team also examined the time it took from the beginning of pre-attack preparatory behavior to the actual attack. The researchers concluded, "Preparations generally began less than six months before the attack and ended with a flurry of actions a day or so before. This pattern varied by group type. Single issue and right wing terrorists engage in substantially less preparatory crime over a shorter period—once again most likely reflecting the use of 'leaderless resistance' and 'lone wolf' strategies. The planning cycle of international terrorists tended to be longer."[72]

The most important conclusion for security planners that can be drawn from these two studies is to think locally about pre-attack indicators. There is a likelihood that terrorists targeting a critical asset within your area of responsibility could live within 30 miles of the target. In addition, preparations for a planned attack will take place somewhere within a short driving distance from the target.

According to Smith, "knowledge of the threat—for example, understanding how long environmental or international terrorists prepare for their attacks—will affect the manner in which local officials respond. Identifying preparatory actions by environmental terrorists may signal that an attack is imminent, whereas similar behavior by an international group might suggest that an attack is still several months away."[73]

A specific type of pre-incident behavior that should be looked for by analysts and planners is the communication of threats concerning a target, which can be a person, property, or institution. The variety of online periodicals and zines prevalent within the REM are often used to indicate that terrorist cells and individuals are planning attacks and to announce successful attacks. Nihilistic groups and individuals vary as to their propensity to issue pre-attack threats in written or oral form. As a general rule, the quantity of threatening communications from terrorists, part of the "chatter" analysts have to review, does not correspond to the much smaller number of attacks. This general rule is also applied by analysts who evaluate the threats made by assassins and potential assassins of prominent officials or public figures. Despite the general rule, threatening communications, in all forms, cannot be disregarded by security planners. Threats made by lone wolves and small nihilistic cells are particularly problematic. Assassination—the targeting, stalking, and murder of political leaders, government officials, and public figures—has historically been a favored tactic of terrorists, and security planners should understand the who, why, and how of this act.

The authoritative U.S. Secret Service's study on the subject of assassination looked at 83 individuals who were grouped as assassins, attackers, and near-lethal approachers. The Secret Service's Exceptional Case Study Project (ECSP) specifically examines seven questions, two of which are relevant to an analysis of pre-incident indicators as applied to nihilistic individuals and groups whose mindset involves hatred of a demonized enemy. The first involved interest or membership in a militant/radical organization.

The second involved the communication of threats by the subjects of the study.

Of the 83 subjects of the study, 52 were either involved at the time of the incident, had a history of membership, or had a history of interest in militant/radical organizations. Although most of the actual attackers had an interest in belonging to military/radical groups, most were not members at the time of their attacks. This pattern is similar to terrorist attacks by lone wolves, who often have prior histories of involvement in radical organizations before leaving those groups and acting on their own. The actual attackers in this study were "more likely to have histories of interest in these groups and of joining them than were near-lethal approachers."[74]

In regard to the communication of threats by the 83 subjects, the subjects rarely communicated threats directly to the targets or law enforcement authorities (10% of offenders). But, "about two thirds of the subjects did make an implicit or explicit threat about the target before the principal incident," but these threats were communicated to friends, associates, and others known to the subjects or were written in the subjects' diaries or journals (9% of the offenders).[75]

The receipt of threats concerning the target are important indicators, and sources tangential to the target, individual or institutional, should be surveyed for information concerning such threats; if there are threats, attempts should be made to identify the source. In addition, an individual with a prior history of involvement with the REM or another radical organization and who has ceased participation in these movements should not be automatically classified as rejecting the group's ideology. This individual might be dissatisfied with the group because its ideology was not extreme enough or because the group did not offer the desired amount of action. In addition, almost all the individuals in the ECSP had difficulty dealing with problems of daily living. They saw murdering their targets as a solution. The authors of the study state, "It seems obvious and it is true: persons who see themselves as doing well in life rarely attempt assassinations. Almost all American assassins, attackers, and would-be attackers were persons who had—or believed themselves to have had—difficulty coping with problems in their lives."[76]

The ECSP's documented facts surrounding the attacks often reveal preattack indicators. For example, Lynette "Squeaky" Fromme attempted to assassinate President Gerald Ford in 1975 because she was angry about the U.S. government's imprisonment of Charles Manson and also wanted to make a statement about the actions of corporations and the U.S. government that she believed threatened the environment. Prior to the attack on President Ford, Fromme, along with Sandra Good, another Manson family member, created a fictitious organization, called the International People's Court of Retribution, for the purpose of threatening executives whose companies they believed were harming the environment. Manson had given Fromme the nickname Red, as it was her job to save the redwood trees. At her trial for the attempted murder of President Ford, Fromme only spoke about the environment.[77]

Another attacker, who is not identified by name in the study, mistakenly attacked a government official on the U.S. Capitol grounds while the official was being interviewed by a television reporter. The attacker had reasoned irrationally that his victim was another government official with whom he was angry. The reason for his attack was to "warn the world of an impending environmental catastrophe."[78]

The Secret Service also determined that the subjects of the ECSP engaged in some planning prior to their attacks. The most meticulous planners, however, were not those who had political motives but those whose motives were money—paid assassins. There was one nihilistic group analyzed by the study. This well-known group had identified itself as the Order. It included Robert Jay Mathews, Bruce Pierce, David Lane, Jean Craig, and Richard Scutari. The Order was a right-wing, antigovernment, anti-Jewish organization that, in 1984, spent months preparing to assassinate Alan Berg, a Jewish talk-radio host. Berg's on-air comments and Jewish heritage had enraged the group and made them decide to target him. The group engaged in extensive pre-attack surveillance prior to successfully assassinating Berg.[79]

The ECSP also analyzed the prior communication of threats by the subjects of the study. The ECSP's authors reached the following conclusions:

- "No assassin or attacker communicated a direct threat about their target to the target or to a law enforcement agency before their attack or near-lethal approach."[80]
- "Almost two-thirds of the subjects are known to have made some threat about their targets in the days, weeks, and months before their attack or near-lethal approach. . . . Some subjects told family members . . . others mentioned their aims to co-workers or friends; still others kept detailed journals in which they recorded their hopes and plans."[81]

The attackers did not send direct warnings to their intended victims before mounting their attacks because they wanted to succeed. The findings of the ECSP that are relevant to security planners are the following facts: the subjects of the ECSP engaged in target surveillance, they practiced with weapons prior to their attacks, and they attempted to gain information about the security of their targets. This is important and points to the necessity of obtaining intelligence about suspicious individuals or groups that engage in unusual amounts of practice with firearms, particularly in covert or out-of-the-way locations.[82]

From another perspective on the communication of threats by terrorists, Jonathan Tucker, in the book *Toxic Terror*, asserts that even hoaxed threats are important indicators of possible terrorist attacks using chemical or biological weapons. According to Tucker, "even if a threatened attack turns out to be a hoax, it still means the terrorist was thinking seriously enough about chemical or biological weapons to develop credible scenarios for their use."[83]

Case Analysis

Ecoterrorist cells and individuals, unlike nihilistic groups and individuals, have self-imposed limitations on their tactical approaches. By far the most successful ecoterrorist group, in terms of economic loss to the government and private industry, has been the Family, the subject of a long-term FBI investigation for crimes committed by this group from 1995 to 2001. An examination of pertinent trial documents concerning the Family reveals a limited but consistent and effective set of pre-incident steps that subsets of the Family undertook in planning their operations.[84] The following are the steps that could be vulnerable to detection through a comprehensive, all-hazards security planning process:

- A subset of the cell's members (all members did not participate in the individual direct actions) physically met at locations distant from their residences prior to engaging in direct actions. The meetings were also used for hands-on training in lock picking, computer security, encrypted messaging, and the manufacture of improvised incendiary devices (IIDs).
- The cell conducted a pre-attack reconnaissance of both the selected target and for the purpose of locating a staging area near the location of the planned attack.
- The cell purchased equipment near the location of the target, prior to the direct action, that would include some or all of the following items: petroleum products (gasoline was recommended but diesel and kerosene were also acceptable) for use as accelerants; model rocket engine igniters; matches, kitchen timers, and alarm clocks; five-gallon buckets; one-gallon jugs; hydrochloric acid (to destroy evidence); candles and incense sticks; shrink tubing; alkaline batteries, nine volts or more; battery snaps for nine-volt batteries; digital multi-meters; cloth and latex gloves; portable soldering irons; tents; and bullet or snap-on connections.
- The cell prepared their IIDs at the staging area or another location (a tent would be utilized in forested areas) that could be prepared as a clean room to hamper any subsequent DNA analysis of evidence recovered during a search by law enforcement agencies. The cell members also wore surgeon's masks to guard against depositing saliva-based DNA, and they stored the constructed IIDs in zip-lock bags and plastic storage containers.
- The group purchased dark clothing, shoes (larger than the wearer's actual size), ski masks, surgeon's masks, shower caps, and painter suits.
- The cell utilized bolt cutters, if necessary, to cut locks and fencing and carried two-way radios with earpiece attachments and a radio scanner to intercept police response traffic.

- At the conclusion of a direct action, the cell returned to the staging area. In several cases, they buried their clothing and shoes after pouring acid on them. After one raid, a cell member returned to the staging area in order to recover the buried clothing. (Discovering staging areas either before an attack, as part of the security planning process when a terrorist threat has been identified, or after an attack, as part of the response plan, is essential.)
- The Family used subsets of three to seven members for their attacks.
- Family members carried false identification and used code words and code names as part of their tradecraft.

Ecoterrorist cells look for soft targets because their modus operandi is sabotage and arson, not armed assaults or high-explosive bombing attacks. These cells, like the Family, are not a threat to facilities with layered security systems or trained, 24-hour security personnel. As Clint Eastwood so famously said, "A man must know his limitations," and when these cells work within their limitations, their tradecraft is often superior to other terrorist groups.

Once the terrorist threat has been identified and analyzed, the next step in the assessment process is to determine the vulnerability of the potential targets of identified terrorist groups.

Target Vulnerability

A vulnerability assessment in relation to a terrorist threat examines the various attributes of a security system in order to determine the likelihood of withstanding various attacks.[85] Generally, a vulnerability is a characteristic of a particular situation, security system, or facility that "can be exploited by a threat to do us harm"[86] and that can occur in the "design, implementation, or operational practices" of the relevant system.[87]

Various conditions that can increase the vulnerability of a target generally fall into five categories: (1) physical environment, (2) social environment, (3) political environment, (4) historical experience, and (5) terrorist capabilities. The fourth and fifth categories are problematic for the assessment process. In most regions of the world, there is not enough historical data concerning terrorist attacks to forecast the likelihood of attacks when directed at a specific target. This lack of data also influences the accuracy of the assessment of terrorist capabilities. Because of uncertainty in the background conditions, "the standard loss event probability equation is impractical when attempting to determine the probable amount of loss for terrorist actions directed against specific assets."[88]

To increase the degree of certainty in the assessment process, the analyst should consider the following four factors when determining asset vulnerability:

- Location: Geographic location of potential targets or facilities and routes of ingress and egress; location of facility or target relative to public areas, transportation routes, or easily breached areas

- Accessibility: How accessible a facility or other target is to the adversary (i.e., disruptive, terrorist, or subversive elements); how easy it is for someone to enter, operate, collect information, and evade response forces

- Adequacy: Adequacy of storage facilities, protection, and denial of access to valuable or sensitive assets such as hazardous materials, weapons, vehicles, or heavy equipment, and explosives or other materials that some person or organization could use deliberately or in an opportunistic manner to cause harm.

- Availability: Availability of equipment, adequacy of response forces and of general physical security measures.[89]

The vulnerability assessment for terrorist threats has three steps: (1) the security system components (e.g., guards, locks, fences) are individually evaluated to determine the likelihood of defeat by different types of attack; (2) the techniques (how) an attacker could use to compromise critical assets in order to disable the system are identified; and (3) the pathways or routes of approach an adversary could take to be in a position to compromise critical assets are identified.[90]

Step one of the vulnerability assessment methodology is self-explanatory. Step two requires an understanding of both the identified threat's known tactics and other tactical methods that are within the threat's capability to utilize effectively. Step three recognizes that in possible terrorist scenarios, once a primary asset is identified as vulnerable to terrorist attack, there are steps that must be completed and conditions that must be met by the attacker prior to a successful attack on the asset. To accomplish a complete vulnerability assessment after the aforementioned three steps have been accomplished, the standard approach is to construct a risk matrix. This can be done by the individual security planner utilizing standard printed forms or as a computerized assessment process using software designed to estimate the relative risk of each critical asset in relation to (1) the probability of the successful attack and (2) the criticality of the loss of the identified asset. The answers to the questions of probability and criticality are determined based upon the situation at the time of the assessment and do not factor into planned countermeasures. In conducting vulnerability assessments, the process involves one or more of the following assessment tools:

- Checklists and questionnaires are used as part of a qualitative evaluation of subsystems.

- Ratings/scoring matrices are criteria-based and non-probabilistic but provide a quantitative evaluation of components and systems.

- Testing using exercises involving simulated attacks on security systems is used to analyze vulnerability.

- There is an increasing use of software that employs mathematical-based modeling, which simulates attacks on security systems and their vulnerability to those attacks.[91]

The last phase of the assessment process involves the consequences of a successful attack; although important, this phase is beyond the scope of this book.

Methodologies

A major issue for analysts and security planners faced with assessing a terrorist threat is the adaptive nature of human adversaries, whose evolving tactics force security planners to prepare responses based on speculation. The increasing complexity and connectivity of our energy, agricultural, technological, and economic systems make it difficult for analysts and security planners to determine vulnerabilities and consequences. This is due to the uncertainty of judgments as there will almost always be a lack of relevant and accurate data concerning the integration of various systems. It is important for analysts to understand the possible cascading effects of a terrorist attack on a critical node that serves as a linkage between various systems.

To assist in resolving assessment problems caused by the increased complexity of security systems, a multitude of assessment methodologies have been developed. These assessment tools have proliferated throughout private industry and the federal government. They range from highly quantitative stochastic modeling to the intuitive technique of expert-opinion elicitation.

These methodologies are not only extremely diverse, some are difficult to understand without possessing advanced mathematical skills. A review of the majority of these new methodologies is beyond the scope of this book. There are two methodologies, however, that will be used in almost any terrorist risk assessment. Unfortunately, they are often used incorrectly. These methodologies are (1) threat scenario analysis and (2) the use of threat attack trees. Using both of these assessment tools greatly facilitates the threat and vulnerability assessment process.

Threat Scenario Analysis

Threat scenario analysis utilizes both real prior incidents and hypothetical scenarios. It is a team project and usually begins with a brain storming session. A realistic perception of the capability of pertinent terrorist groups and a "what if" mentality should be possessed by all members of the planning team. Some members should be involved actively in the operation of the current security systems that are being analyzed. Once the scenario has been constructed by the planning team, it should be evaluated by a separate team drawn from employees familiar with the target. Scenarios are also used as a starting point for complex practical exercises. In this case, the practical exercise will incorporate a simulation cell that will introduce injections (pre-scripted messages introduced by telephone, e-mail, or other methods) of changing circumstances into the scenario in order to simulate an adaptive adversary and changing environmental conditions. A practical exercise, if properly conducted, will use an evolving scenario to force the individuals and units that are being evaluated to respond.[92]

Attack Tree

When the assessment process identifies a primary vulnerability of the potential target of a terrorist attack, there will always be preliminary steps and conditions that must be achieved prior to a successful attack.[93] The model that displays the steps necessary to achieve a successful attack on a protected target is termed an attack tree. Building an attack tree offers the security planner a method to disrupt possible attacks before terrorists achieve their objective. An attack tree utilizes threat logic to build the tree by looking at the various steps an attacker must negotiate before achieving success. Threat logic refers to the various ways to perceive and display the options encountered by an attacker at various stages during the attack process in relation to target vulnerabilities.

The threat logic steps and the options presented to the attacker are represented through the use of specific words. The following examples illustrate threat logic terms and their definitions:

- And: Two steps simultaneously
- And, but X before Y: All must be taken in a stated sequence
- Or: Any step alone must be taken
- Or, but, if X then not Y: Any step alone but not all together or in a stated sequence[94]

The attack tree will have complex schematics if the threat combines several tactics or if there are numerous steps that must be taken after the threshold vulnerability has been breached. In one method of constructing the tree developed by security expert Ted Almay, the overall tactical goal of an attack is the trunk. The branches begin at the top with the initial method of attack, which exploits the threshold vulnerability of the target. For example, the threshold vulnerability could be the entrance to a facility's fenced-in grounds. The branches are pruned after the tree has been constructed based upon existing countermeasures that eliminate the vulnerabilities displayed on the branches.[95]

An attack tree is a visual threat model, a picture that aids security planners in determining where countermeasures should be applied most effectively to eliminate vulnerabilities. The tree aids security planners in using the leverage principle for cost effectiveness by displaying the locations for applying countermeasures that will neutralize those vulnerabilities that are common to two or more methods of attack.[96]

Software programs that model the attack tree process exist, but a tree can be constructed by a planning team without utilizing a software program.

The mental and physical process of building an accurate tree furnishes insight into the mind of a potential attack planner and may be more valuable than the tree itself. For an example of a terrorist threat attack tree, see appendix A.

Countermeasure applications are part of both the risk assessment and security planning processes. Although some have been introduced in this chapter, they are examined comprehensively in chapter 8. Before ending this examination of the risk of terrorism, a significant problem has to be addressed. This problem exists at the level of the analyst or security planner and involves a process of assessment that assumes a level of certainty in prediction that may be impossible to achieve.

The Problem with Prediction

A terrorist attack is an unusual event in the Western world. Al Qaeda's 9/11 attack on the United States's economic and political centers was a shockingly catastrophic event. In fact, no other act of terrorism by a non-state actor approaches the magnitude of the 9/11 attacks. The Central Intelligence Agency (CIA) and the FBI were excoriated for their failure to accurately predict the attack. The consensus opinion of experts and the widely held opinion of the majority of the public were that the attacks should have been predicted and that a similar attack in the future could be predicted if the FBI and CIA, along with other members of the intelligence establishment, improve their capabilities.[97] This opinion is fallacious. A catastrophic act of terrorism is the type of event that philosopher and economist Nicholas Taleb has referred to as a "black swan." Taleb characterizes a black swan as something (an event) that is rare, has an extreme impact, and possesses the attribute of "retrospective predictability."[98]

Human Cognitive Problems

Intelligent human beings believe they should be capable of predicting rare events. We base our beliefs on our great achievements as a species and our knowledge that experts in various fields have the power to forecast certain events by reviewing the historical past and using the power of rational thought. There are several problems with this position. First, we do rely on experts, usually in the government, military, or academia, to be the oracles of modern-day society. But experts, when tested on their prediction ability, have error rates much greater than the rate of error they predicted they would have.[99] After failing tests of their abilities, experts routinely advance excuses in their defense—or, as Taleb states while reflecting on human nature, even that of experts: "We attribute our successes to our skills and our failures to external events outside our control, namely to randomness."[100]

Another problem with prediction lies in the concept of mathematical probabilities. We rely on this concept to predict events and believe we can determine the probability of an event occurring in the future based on other occurrences of the event in the past. This conceptual basis for our predictive ability is valid, but only when we utilize past events that are a set of independent observations. These observations also must be numerous. If those two conditions are met, we can make predictions of the same event occurring in the future with varying degrees of exactitude. In real life, history may not be so helpful. The event we are trying to predict probably did not occur as an independent event but was one of a sequence of interrelated events and may only have occurred on rare occasions.[101] Taleb believes that our "mistaking a naïve observation of the past as something definitive or representative of the future is the . . . cause of our inability to understand black swans."[102]

Humans also have a tendency to believe human-directed events possess a rational nature. We desire to use the rational part of our intellect to reduce the uncertainty in our lives. Some of us (possibly most of us) believe we can calculate the probability of success or failure in our various endeavors. This is a false belief. We can never have sufficient information concerning human actions or the randomness of human responses to develop a rational calculation of probability. We can do this with many natural events (e.g., the skies are overcast and gray so it will probably rain today), but we routinely fail to do so in situations involving the actions of human beings, including ourselves. Today, adherents of game theory assume that human beings are rational actors, and the belief that "such behavior can be measured and expressed in numbers has unleashed a flood of exciting theories and practical applications."[103] Game theory believes in the power of humans to predict the responses of humans. However, the extent of our powers of rationality is subject to doubt. A theory of decision making developed by Daniel Kahneman and Amos Tversky,[104] called "prospect theory," proposes that man possesses two shortcomings in regard to rationality: (1) our emotions overwhelm our self control and (2) we have problems with cognition—our decision making is subject to a variety of deficiencies and biases. Overall, "the evidence . . . reveals repeated patterns of irrationality, inconsistency, and incompetence in the ways human beings arrive at decisions when faced with uncertainties."[105]

Richards Heuer, a former CIA analyst and the author of *Psychology of Intelligence Analysis,* believes that our cognitive biases cause our analytical abilities to be flawed, that we mistake causes for accidental and random events, that we desire to structure our environment, and that we overestimate the rationality of individuals and give too little credence to the situational aspects of an actor's behavior.[106]

Mathematical Models for Risk Prediction

Today, the emphasis is on mathematically based software models for risk assessment and prediction. Our mathematicians and computer scientists have purportedly made great strides in search of the holy grail of mathematical modeling—a model that can predict the actions of human terrorists. The latest development in mathematical modeling comes from the field of physics, where some scientists believe the behavior of subatomic particles and terrorists have some similarities. By treating terrorists as irrational, individual particles subject to changing influences on their behavior as a collective body that is beyond individual control, scientists believe that terrorist actions should create distinct mathematical patterns that are discoverable. Mathematical modeling is based on a perspective on human nature that rejects the belief that human behavior is so complex and unique that it is unpredictable.[107]

The belief that advances in computer modeling of human behavior have reached the stage where that behavior can be reduced to a mathematical formula may not itself be a rational belief. There are probably many members, however, of various national and homeland security agencies who believe the plethora of mathematical approaches to assessing risks of terrorism are a viable solution to the prediction problem. Few law enforcement and intelligence community professionals understand how mathematical models work or what problems might exist with the theories that underlie their operational results. Our belief that experts will have a solution has led us astray on numerous occasions in the past. It may be a mistake to assume that our new experts' belief in the validity of their models is reasonable. In looking at mathematical modeling, Taleb states that the "gains in our ability to model (and predict) the world may be dwarfed by the increase in its complexity—implying a greater and greater role for the unpredicted."[108]

The novelist and essayist G. K. Chesterton, writing almost three-quarters of a century ago, perceived the problems with predicting rare human events, such as terrorist attacks, through the use of mathematical modeling:

The real trouble with this world of ours is not that it is an unreasonable world, nor even that it is a reasonable one. The commonest kind of trouble is that it is nearly reasonable, but not quite. Life is not an illogicality; yet it is a trap for logicians. It looks just a little more mathematical and regular than it is; its exactitude is obvious, but its inexactitude is hidden; its wildness lies in wait.[109]

CHAPTER 8

Security Planning for Environmentally Linked Terrorism

Now if the estimates made in the temple before hostilities indicate victory it is because calculations show one's strength to be superior to that of his enemy; if they indicate defeat, it is because calculations show that one is inferior. With many calculations, one can win; with few one cannot. How much less chance of victory has one who makes none at all! By this means I examine the situation and the outcome will be clearly apparent.
—Sun Tzu, *The Art of War*

On October 18, 1998, several structural fires erupted on Vail Mountain in Vail, Colorado, a resort town located approximately 100 miles west of Denver. The fires overlooked a national forest area where Vail Resorts, Inc. planned an 885-acre expansion that would entail the destruction of a forested area. The fires, which burned so strongly that the responding fire department was unable to extinguish them, destroyed or damaged two restaurants, a ski lodge, and the ski patrol headquarters for Vail Mountain.

For months prior to the fire, Vail Resorts's decision to expand the ski resort had been controversial, engendering arguments at volatile public meetings where environmentalists, backcountry skiers, and residents of Eagle County wanted to block the planned expansion. Environmental groups accused Vail Resorts of trying to destroy old growth habitat, which would harm wildlife migration and destroy the mountain lynx. The week before the fire, at the U.S. Court of Appeals for the 10th Circuit in Denver, an action for an injunction to stop Vail Resorts's plan to expand, brought by a variety of environmental groups, was denied. Once it was denied, Vail had began their preliminary work of building fences and clearing trees for trails.[1]

On October 21, the Earth Liberation Front sent an e-mail communiqué claiming they had set the fires atop the mountain. The communiqué read as follows:

On behalf of the lynx, five buildings and four ski lifts at Vail were reduced to ashes on the night of Sunday, October 18th. Vail, Inc. is already the largest ski operation in North America and now wants to expand even further. The 12 miles of road and 885 acres of clear cuts will ruin the last, best lynx habitat in the State. Putting profits ahead of Colorado's wildlife will not be tolerated. This action is just a warning. We will be back if this greedy corporation continues to trespass into wild and unroaded areas. For your safety and convenience, we strongly advise skiers to choose other destinations until Vail cancels its inexcusable plans for expansion.

—*Earth Liberation Front*[2]

On October 22, federal agents concluded the fire was caused by arson. The investigators had found empty plastic jugs that had been filled with gasoline and used to ignite the fires at several locations on the mountain. The consequences of the arson were estimated to be $12 million—at the time, the most expensive and infamous act of sabotage by an environmental group in U.S. history.[3]

Vail Resorts had little or no security at the site of the arson attack. The company was not prepared for such an attack and had not been alerted by any pre-attack incidents committed by the attackers. Vail Resorts should, however, have picked up some obvious warnings that such an attack could occur. First, the plan for expansion, which had been approved by the federal government, was vigorously fought against and had been in litigation for two years. The denied injunction had been filed by a coalition of environmental groups to specifically stop the expansion and protect the lynx's natural habitat. Once the appeal was denied, it cleared the way for a very large expansion. The fires were set the night before construction was to begin. The arson perpetrators expressed motivation for the attack was shared by numerous people who were concerned about the impact the expansion would have on the local environment. The Earth Liberation Front, by using arson to destroy the resort's property, was attempting to influence the government by an act of violence. This met the federal government's definition of terrorism, and the FBI began its investigation.

The investigation lasted eight years. The case was resolved on January 19, 2006, when the FBI's Operation Backfire resulted in the issuance of an indictment, obtained by the U.S. Attorney's Office in Eugene, Oregon, that charged 11 people with criminal conspiracy related to a multitude of successful attacks on a variety of targets that included the Vail Ski Resort.[4]

The Vail Mountain arson was an act of domestic terrorism. It was committed because an ecoterrorist group believed a local corporation's activities would harm the natural environment. The act of violence was directed at the site of the allegedly harmful activity. Corporations have also suffered the consequences of international acts of environmentally linked terrorism when their allegedly harmful acts occurred in one country yet engendered subsequent acts of terrorism at their facilities in other countries. The impetus for two such attacks was the single deadliest chemical leak in human history, which occurred on December 3, 1984, at the Union Carbide pesticide plant in Bhopal, India. In the morning hours, a poison gas produced by the plant, called methyl isocyanate (MIC), leaked from the plant and drifted over the town of Bhopal for one hour. Although the exact number of deaths caused by the deadly leak is uncertain, the estimates range between 2,000 and 4,000 people and with an estimated 200,000 injured. The injuries included blindness and lung damage. Twenty years after the incident, 14,000 deaths were linked to it, along with hundreds of thousands of injuries.[5]

The reasons for the disaster were varied but can be summed up as negligence, inadequate safety procedures, a lack of emergency response planning, and poor overall strategic planning. The plant's safety procedures should have included furnishing information to nearby city residents concerning the dangerous chemicals produced by the plant. For example, the inhabitants in the surrounding neighborhoods in Bhopal had never been informed about the danger of a leak from the plant and believed the chemicals made by the plant were harmless. The residents had never even been informed of a simple life-saving technique, a wet cloth held over the mouth and nose, that could have saved many lives.[6]

After the incident in Bhopal, Union Carbide was excoriated by the international media. This occurred for months, and the resulting civil litigation kept the case before the courts and in the media for years. In December 1984, soon after the news concerning the incident had been spread by the media, two gasoline firebombs were placed in the Union Carbide factory at Milstedt, Germany. One of the firebombs exploded, but the other failed to detonate. No injuries occurred, and there was little damage to the factory. An anonymous caller indicated the attack was in retaliation for the Bhopal gas leak. There was also graffiti at the building site, using the terms "slime" and "poison killers."[7]

Then, seven months after the Bhopal incident, a bomb exploded outside a Union Carbide plant that manufactured flashlights in Rosebury, a suburb of Sydney, Australia. After the incident, responsibility for the bombing was claimed by the Peace Conquerors as retribution for the collective murder at Bhopal.[8]

The bomb attacks subsequent to the initial Bhopal incident were an international response to an event that only harmed local residents of Bhopal. The terrorists did not allege that the local environment of the other locations had been harmed by Union Carbide. Terrorists in Germany and Australia seized on a significant foreign event as a cause and took local action in revenge for the catastrophic effects of the incident in India.

Another way a corporation operating internationally can become the victim of an environmentally linked terrorist attack was exemplified by a kidnapping that took place in Ecuador in 1997 as described by Ann Hagedorn Auerbach in her comprehensive book on international kidnapping. On February 15, Mark Thurber, a geologist, was conducting an environmental study with a small team in the rugged countryside 100 miles from the city of Quito. Thurber was a contractor for an American environmental company that was, in turn, working for a petroleum corporation (Compania General de Combustibles); his job was determining which areas of an oil reserve should be open to drilling and which areas should be preserved from this type of activity. Thurber and his team were working at the remote site when they were abducted by members of the Achuar indigenous community, which was upset over what it perceived as exploitation of its land by oil companies. The community was particularly angry at Texaco, who had been operating in its territory for several years. In 1992, the Achuar, along with many other Amazon indigenous communities, had filed a class-action suit against Texaco for alleged environmental damage to their land and people. The kidnappers of Thurber wanted money, scientific data from the study being conducted by the victims, and a commitment from the petroleum company to stop oil production in the Achuar territory. Thurber and one other team member were eventually released on February 23. According to Hagedorn Auerbach, it was not clear exactly what caused their release, although it is highly probable ransom was paid to the kidnappers.[9]

The kidnapping of a corporation employee for an actual or alleged environmental harm caused by the company is a tactic employed by terrorists, criminals, and hybrid groups, all of which have been using kidnappings as a means to gain money for their operations since the 1960s. Kidnapping is a tactic that is usually successful because the victim's location is not known during the negotiation period, and there is enormous pressure on the affected companies, governments, and families to pay the kidnappers.[10] Personnel are the most critical assets of an organization, and their protection is the highest priority for security planners.

SECURITY PLANNING PROCESS

Today's security planners for government agencies and multinational corporations often have a common duty of protecting the critical assets of the nation. Corporations also have a duty to protect the interests of their stockholders, and, when engaging in security activities, corporations are increasingly expected to serve two masters. The question is, can they do so effectively?

Private Enterprise Perspective

In examining the subject of security planning, it is apparent that the terrorist attacks on 9/11 and the ensuing *9/11 Commission Report* caused major changes in the way both the public and private sectors handle their security responsibilities. Under the general heading of private sector preparedness, the 9/11 Commission stated the new paradigm:

The mandate of the Department of Homeland Security does not end with government; the Department is also responsible for working with the private sector to ensure preparedness. This is entirely appropriate, for the private sector controls 85 percent of the critical infrastructure in the nation. Indeed, unless a terrorist's target is a military or other secure government facility, the "first" first responders will almost certainly be civilians. Homeland Security and national preparedness therefore often begins with the private sector.

Preparedness in the private sector and public sector for rescue, restart, and recovery of operations should include (1) a plan for evacuation, (2) adequate communications capabilities, and (3) a plan for continuity of operations. As we examined the emergency response to 9/11, witness after witness told us that despite 9/11, the private sector remains largely unprepared for a terrorist attack. We were also advised that the lack of a widely embraced private-sector preparedness standard was a principle contributing factor to this lack of preparedness.[11]

Security planning starts with the individuals charged with the responsibility. They should have an attacker's mindset, often termed a "what if" perspective. They should be capable of envisioning attacks that exploit the vulnerabilities of the targets they protect. Security consultant and author Bruce Shneier believes this type of mindset is possibly innate and very hard to inculcate in an individual who is not already inclined to look for weaknesses in security.[12]

Security planning fits within the overall process of an organization's strategic planning, which is defined as "the process of establishing objectives and choosing the most suitable means for achieving these objectives prior to taking action."[13] Leonard Goodstein, Timothy Nolan, and William Pfeiffer, in their influential work *Applied Strategic Planning*, state that planning for contingencies begins with the strategic planning process by which the guiding members of an organization envision its future and develop the necessary procedures and operations to achieve that future.[14] In carrying out the strategic planning process, they also believe the planner must answer three questions: (1) Where are you going? (2) What is the environment? (3) How do you get there?[15] In answering the question of destination, or, as Goodstein and colleagues termed it, engaging in "down board thinking," predictions concerning climate change should be factored in because of the implications such change could have for an organization's operations. For example, the high probability of an increased scarcity of natural resources, such as water or natural sources of fuel, might impinge on a decision to build facilities in regions where such a scarcity is predicted as likely to develop in the future. The authors' concept of strategic planning is not synonymous with long-term planning. Strategic planning looks to the future to visualize responses to the organization's actions and how the organization's actions can change that future by actions taken now and in the future.[16]

In answering the second question—what is the environment?—the planning team must examine the relevant strengths, weaknesses, opportunities, and threats currently facing the organization and as envisioned in the future. Among the threats facing any organization that operates in many nations and regions is the certainty of significant environmental change and, in most regions of the world, the rare but consequential threat of terrorism. The nexus of terrorism and the natural environment is an issue the strategic planning process should address, not only during the planning phase but also during the implementation phase.[17]

As part of the implementation of the strategic plan, or getting there, the macroenvironment has to be monitored for social, technological, and political developments, along with macroeconomic trends in the regions or areas of the world where the corporation operates.[18] The monitoring of trends can identify emerging problems that can be critical for the profitability or even survival of an organization. With certain trends, an organization should institute a point when the trend becomes significant enough to become dangerous to the operational ability of the corporation. For example, political trends in Venezuela, currently under the leadership of Hugo Chavez, indicated an increase in the degree of resentment displayed toward Western-owned petroleum companies. Chavez's negative actions and comments concerning oil companies occurred prior to his nationalization of the petroleum industry within the country of Venezuela.[19] In the summer of 2010, Moscow suffered from extreme temperatures and wildfires, and the U.S. State Department decided, based upon their monitoring of the environment, that the worsening weather conditions had reached the unsafe point and recommended that the families of Foreign Service personnel return home.[20] Similarly, the J-curve theory, discussed in chapter 7, could be integrated into the macroenvironmental scan as a way to determine the point when a change in political conditions signals an increased possibility of a terrorist attack. This would allow an organization to take actions that could avert the possible attack and the negative results that would follow.

In the strategic planning process, a terrorist attack is a threat that is handled as a specific contingency by organizations that have an identified likelihood of facing such a threat. Normally, contingency planning should start with a consideration of those events that the risk assessment process, described in earlier chapter 7, has identified as probable. However, unless a terrorist event is assessed as impossible, the potentially serious consequences of such an event will make it a contingency that must be planned for, and trigger points must be established to indicate when developments necessitate intervention by specific actions. These actions can include higher-level monitoring of the situation or actions specific to the event.[21] Goodstein and colleagues believe that in deciding which events should be planned for as contingencies, it is important to include those events that would have severe consequences for the organization and involve "other than the most likely scenarios." An act of terrorism would usually be this type of event.[22]

As part of the ongoing strategic planning process, contingency planning for the unforeseen development of problems with an organization's security system is of the highest importance from both an operational and legal standpoint. To reduce problems when designing or evaluating security systems, Bruce Schneier recommends a five-step process: (1) identify valuable assets, (2) identify and assess the risks to those assets, (3) evaluate if risk is reduced by the current or planned security system, (4) find out if the security solution will cause other risks, and (5) quantify the cost-to-benefit ratio of the security solution.[23] Schneier's methodology can be utilized from the perspective of both a private company's and a government agency's security planning team. In relation to environmentally linked terrorism, the assets to be protected will include people, property, natural resources (e.g., forests), public symbols, infrastructure (e.g., water systems), and the "feeling of safety" possessed by the targeted population. The targets at risk can be generalized as physical, economic, social, and emotional targets.[24]

Security systems need three qualities to ensure that even the existence of vulnerabilities will not make the security scheme easy to penetrate: "Defense in depth ensures that no single vulnerability can compromise security. Compartmentalization ensures that a single vulnerability cannot compromise security entirely. And choke points reduce the number of potential vulnerabilities by allowing the defender to concentrate his defenses."[25] Above all, security systems must be dynamic, capable of responding to novel attacks and an innovative enemy. Computer-based systems, although having many benefits, lack the dynamism only human beings can bring to the system.[26]

For some organizations, the security system component of the planning process will involve the protection of the nation's critical infrastructure and key resources (CIKR) from man-made and natural disasters and intentional attacks. These private sector organizations are currently not required, but are encouraged, to develop contingency plans for threats to CIKR under their control. The federal government encourages the interaction of state, local, and private enterprise security planners with it to ensure their plans are consistent with the national planning system's requirements.[27]

Public-Private Partnership

The current relationship between the U.S. government and private organizations in regard to security planning is based on the joint recognition of the importance of protecting the critical infrastructure of the United States. The importance of the U.S. infrastructure to national security and the identification of the critical elements of that infrastructure were formally set out by a 1997 report from the President's Commission on Critical Infrastructure Protection. The commission recognized that the national infrastructure essential to U.S. security was mainly privately owned and operated. Based on this fact, the commission concluded that critical infrastructure protection was a shared responsibility of the public and private sectors. The commission proposed the fostering of public-private partnerships in which the objective was for private industry to focus on protecting themselves with the government's help. The commission also proposed that a national policy be crafted for the protection of critical infrastructure.[28]

Subsequently, on May 22, 1998, President Clinton issued Presidential Decision Directive 63, Protecting America's Critical Infrastructure. The directive sets out several goals, of which the following two are relevant to the current relationship between the U.S. government and private industry: (1) ensuring the capability to protect critical infrastructure from intentional acts by 2003 and (2) seeking the voluntary participation of private industry to meet common goals for protecting our critical systems through public-private partnerships.[29]

Today, the United States is still in the process of fulfilling both goals, and the current National Strategy for Homeland Security incorporates the concept of a public-private partnership:

The private and non-profit sectors also must be full partners in Homeland Security. As the country's principal providers of goods and services, and the owners or operators of approximately 85 percent of the Nation's critical infrastructure, businesses have both an interest in and a responsibility for ensuring their own security. The private sector plays key roles in areas as diverse as supply chain security, critical infrastructure protection, and research and development in science, technology, and other innovations that will help secure the homeland. The non-profit sector, including volunteer and relief groups and faith-based organizations, provides important support services for the Nation, including meals and shelter, counseling, and compassion and comfort to Americans, particularly in the aftermath of an incident.[30]

The National Strategy identifies 17 sections of critical infrastructure and key resources. Of these 17, the following are attractive targets within the capabilities of some nihilistic terrorist cells: agricultural and food; government and commercial facilities; energy; drinking water and treatment systems; and small dams.[31]

The National Strategy explains the importance of private sector participation in safeguarding these 17 sectors. It stresses the fact that the private sector owns and operates the majority of America's critical infrastructure and concludes that because of "the multiple and essential roles the private sector plays across all areas of Homeland Security, continued collaboration and engagement with the private sector to strengthen preparedness is imperative."[32] The strategic importance of protecting our national infrastructure is demonstrated by the U.S. government's development of a comprehensive plan to protect that infrastructure.

The current 2009 National Infrastructure Protection Plan (NIPP) has as its overarching goal "to build a safer more secure and more resilient America by preventing, deterring, neutralizing, or mitigating the effects of deliberate efforts by terrorists to destroy, incapacitate, or exploit elements of our nation's CIKR and to strengthen national preparedness, timely response, and rapid recovery of CIKR in the event of an attack, natural disaster, or other emergency."[33]

The drafters of the NIPP examined the vulnerability of the U.S. infrastructure and concluded that its great diversity and redundancy would allow it to survive and recover even if a successful terrorist attack were to take place. On the other hand, according to the NIPP, our highly integrated and complex system also presents a very attractive target to terrorists. If a terrorist group has the ability to hit certain targets within the overall infrastructure system, it could have a cascading effect and drastically enhance their ability to inflict great damage with a relatively minor attack.[34] The NIPP states that some of the terrorist groups identified as threats to the United States have proven to be "relentless, patient, opportunistic, and inflexible, learning from experience and modifying tactics and targets to exploit perceived vulnerabilities and avoid observed strengths."[35] The NIPP further notes that terrorists will focus on both domestic and international CIKR as targets, but as security is enhanced around those targets that have been hit before, terrorists are likely to shift their focus to targets that have been left relatively unprotected. Based on this assessment, the NIPP's advice in regard to the use of countermeasures is to look for target shifting as countermeasures increase around formerly attractive targets.[36]

The NIPP also posits that terrorists are taking an approach that measures the consequences of their attacks on a variety of critical infrastructure. Their objective is to focus their efforts on those areas of U.S. infrastructure in which attacks can "result in mass casualties, weaken the economy, and damage public morale and confidence."[37] Terrorists have conducted numerous successful attacks and will do so in the future. Planning must include a robust response to such attacks.

The National Response Framework (NRF), another Department of Homeland Security document that private sector security planners should be thoroughly familiar with, is a guide to conducting an "all hazards" response to terrorism. The term *response*, as used in the NRF, includes "immediate actions to save lives, protect property and the environment, and meet basic human needs."[38] The NRF "commits the Federal Government in partnership with local, tribal, and state governments and the private sector to complete both strategic and operational plans for the incident scenarios specified in the National Preparedness Guidelines."[39] The NRF is based on five response doctrine principles: "(1) engaged partnership; (2) tiered response; (3) scalable, flexible, and adaptable operational capabilities; (4) unity of effort through unified command; and (5) readiness to act." By the first principle—engaged partnership—the NRF stresses the concept of preparedness, which is fostered through the use of practical exercises to test the capability of the combined forces of federal agencies and private organizations to respond to the various threats portrayed in the federal government's incident scenarios.[40]

The NRF has numerous requirements in regard to planning and states, "Emergency planning is a national priority as reflected in the National Preparedness Guidelines."[41] The NRF identifies seven specific criteria that it recommends to measure response planning: (1) acceptability, (2) adequacy, (3) completeness, (4) consistency and standardization of products, (5) feasibility, (6) flexibility, and (7) interoperability and collaboration.[42] The NRF also identifies the likely incidents for which planners, in both the private and government sectors, should formulate contingency plans. The NRF breaks these specific incidents down between scenario sets and planning scenarios. The key scenario sets are the following: (1) explosives attack—bombing using improvised explosive device; (2) nuclear attack; (3) radiological attack—radiological dispersal device; (4) biological attack—with annexes for different pathogens; (5) chemical attack—with annexes for different agents; (6) natural disaster—with annexes for different disasters; (7) cyber attack; and (8) pandemic influenza.[43] The predicted biological attacks involve aerosol anthrax, plague, food contamination, and foreign animal disease. In regard to chemical attacks, the planning scenarios include blister agents, toxic industrial chemicals, nerve agents, and chlorine tank explosions.[44] The NRF, along with the NIPP, recommends that the general thrust of all Homeland Security planning should be an "all hazards" approach and that the public and private sectors should be integrated in all aspects of both the planning process and the evaluation process, via the exercises.[45]

Implementing the various requirements for security planning as set out in the NIPP and NRF is difficult and requires a high level of commitment on the part of both public and private partners. In preparing and planning, it is necessary to utilize a planning team. Goodstein and colleagues, in their book *Applied Strategic Planning,* are emphatic that no less than 5 and no more than 12 persons should constitute a security planning team. They furnish the following basis for recommending that 7 to 9 persons constitute the planning team: "Significant amounts of research indicate that groups of five are typically the most effective in problem solving, and our experience tells us that groups larger than twelve are difficult to 'read' in terms of group process; furthermore, a group larger than twelve limits each person's 'air time' to the degree that it is difficult for every member to make appropriate contributions."[46]

As part of the strategic planning process, the design (evaluation or plan) of the security system should be integrated into the process. If one of the identified threats to the organization is terrorism, the planning team should be cautious about reducing the number of security personnel in the interest of cost control. As experienced security managers know, one of the easiest ways to cut down on the cost of security is to replace people with technology, such as increased closed-circuit television coverage of company property and assets. A terrorist threat could make such a decision a highly consequential one. The best defense against an adaptable threat is an adaptable defense. Only a strong human component can make a security system capable of responding to a human threat that can react in several ways to a fixed, technology-based security system.

Bruce Schneier has several observations on the importance of the human component of a security system. Schneier believes "a good security system leverages the benefits of 'trusted people' while building countermeasures to prevent them from abusing that trust."[47] He believes the most important component of a security system is the human one and that the motivations of security personnel are as important as the motivations of attackers. Schneier, although believing that "trusted people" form the keystone of a security system, cautions that they are also the weak link of the system. People are vulnerable to social engineering techniques used to manipulate people on an interpersonal basis. Knowing the necessity of trusted people to the system, Schneier recommends that aside from routine, comprehensive background checks, security systems should also be compartmentalized and countermeasures should be employed to protect systems from insiders, or trusted people, who decide to exploit their trusted status. He also believes all trusted people should have overlapping responsibilities.[48]

The two most important factors for security planners who have responsibility for critical infrastructure located in foreign areas are knowledge of their operational environment, especially if that environment includes dangerous regions, and the utilization of appropriate countermeasures for identified threats to those infrastructure assets that are considered attractive targets.

DANGEROUS REGIONS, HOT SPOTS, AND ATTRACTIVE TARGETS

The component of the security planning process that identifies the linkage between terrorism and the natural environment is the strategic environmental scan that should include the external environment. This macro-level evaluation should include an examination of the political and social problems of pertinent geographical regions and the possible natural environmental linkages to those problems. There are certain regions of the world where environmental characteristics are sufficiently imbued with dangerous qualities that they should receive serious attention during the security planning process.

Specifically, when a multinational corporation is considering building facilities or investing capital in a new region of the world, the criteria for selecting that region will always include the laws, regulations, and political stability of the region. The social and physical climate, however, should also be evaluated for suitability and stability. The natural environmental conditions in certain regions of the world are fragile, and climate change will exacerbate those ecological weaknesses.[49] This can affect resources, and a scarcity of renewable resources (e.g., forests, crops, and water) can, in some circumstances, "contribute to diffuse, persistent, subnational violence, such as ethnic clashes and insurgencies."[50] Multinational corporations and non-government organizations (NGOs) operate in some of the most volatile regions of the world. International businesses may see opportunities for great profits and believe the risks are worth it. NGOs and relief organizations may operate in these regions for humanitarian reasons or in conjunction with a variety of international projects.

There may be targets in these dangerous regions that if successfully attacked by terrorists, coupled with the intrinsic social and political factors that made the attack possible, would severely affect both the natural environment and human life. Other terrorists—believing that private or public organizations are currently, or are considering, engaging in actions that harm the natural environment—could launch damaging and destructive attacks on those organizations. In the more dangerous regions of the world, these types of attacks are either already occurring or will be more likely to occur in the future, and the ramifications of such attacks are more severe than in other areas of the world.[51]

Terrorism Statistics

This book examines two dangerous regions of the world based on their potential for violent conflict, the importance of their natural resources to the world economy, and their importance to U.S. national security. The regions are Africa, specifically the Democratic Republic of the Congo (DRC) and Nigeria, and the maritime region—our world's seas and oceans. In determining the dangerous regions of the world, the frequency and severity of terrorist activity was one criterion examined. An analysis of terrorism data, compiled and maintained by the National Counterterrorism Center, was conducted during the preparation of this book.

Number of Attacks

In 2009, on an international basis, there were approximately 11,000 terrorist attacks that occurred in 83 countries, resulting in over 58,000 victims and nearly 15,000 fatalities. The amount of deaths and attacks decreased from 2008.[52] In Africa, 850 attacks occurred, approximately 700 of which were in connection with situations in Somalia and the DRC. Compared with 2008, the number of attacks in this region rose by 140 (19%), and the amount of fatalities increased by over 250 (8%).[53]

Attackers

On an overall basis, approximately 50 percent of the attackers were Sunni Islam jihadis. The largest non-Sunni group of attackers was the Lord's Resistance Army (LRA), who were responsible for murdering 400 people by assaults and incendiary attacks in the DRC. In addition, the Forces for Liberation of Rwanda (FLR) murdered 86 individuals in the DRC, including 25 children.[54]

Statistical Totals in 2009

In looking at the countries of the world, the majority of the deaths caused by terrorist attacks occurred in Iraq, Afghanistan, Pakistan, Somalia, and the DRC.[55]

Africa

Although Africa has many dangerous regions, the two most closely connected with environmentally linked terrorism are Nigeria and the DRC. Africa will have great strategic importance for the United States in the future because of the abundance of both renewable and nonrenewable natural resources that are important to our changing technological needs. There are four important resources that Africa has in abundance: oil, minerals, gems, and timber. The minerals are the key resource for the future. Africa has large reserves of valuable minerals such as bauxite, cobalt, gold, platinum, and uranium. Because of this abundance of resources, the main focus of multinational companies has been in the mining area.[56]

Africa's old-growth timber is another key resource for the world. After the Amazon, Africa has the next largest rainforest located in its central region. The 2010 National Security Strategy (NSS) refers to Africa's vital carbon sinks. Finally, Africa is also rich in oil and gas reserves and has agreements with several multinational corporations to develop their petroleum industry. The 2010 NSS recognizes Africa as a future partner in clean energy endeavors. The major African country in regard to oil and gas exploration is Nigeria. The major country in Africa in regard to mineral wealth is the DRC. Nigeria and the DRC are "hot spots" of environmentally linked terrorism.[57]

According to Michael Klare in his book *Resource Wars,* Africa is in danger of becoming the site of increased conflicts over resources. Klare believes all the preconditions for conflict are present in Africa: "Large concentrations of vital minerals, numerous territorial disputes in areas harboring valuable deposits, widespread political instability and factionalism, the presence of private armies and mercenaries, and a history of collaboration between foreign resource firms and local warlords."[58] For example, according to Klare, the DRC has been forced to accept coalitions between powerful interest groups that have developed plans to take over the DRC's reserves of oil, timber, gems, and minerals.[59] The DRC has over 250 tribes and contains over 900,000 square miles of territory. It is Africa's third-largest country, with the eighth-largest river in the world. The DRC also has 70 percent of the world's cobalt, and more than one billion dollars worth of gold is mined in the Congo each year. Although the DRC has large deposits of valuable natural resources, Robert Young Pelton, the author of *The World's Most Dangerous Places*, refers to it as "everyone's favorite hell hole—corrupt, fetid, dangerous, and deadly."[60]

In recent history, the Congo's key figure has been Joseph Mobutu, who seized power via a military coup in 1965. He later changed his name to Mobuto Sese Seko and the country's name to Zaire. Mobuto nationalized the mining industry in 1966 and had close relationships with the United States, although he was totally corrupt. In 1997, Mobuto was overthrown and subsequently died in exile in Morocco at 66 years of age. He was replaced by Laurent Kabila, a long-time revolutionary who spent years in the jungle, and the country was renamed the Democratic Republic of the Congo. Since Kabila took power, the Congo has been the scene of an endemic resource war that has resulted in thousands of deaths. Today, with the revolutionary growth of the information technology area, the DRC has an even greater value as a source of resources. It has large amounts of gold, coltan, cassiterite (tin ore), and tungsten (used in cell phones and light bulbs).[61]

Rwanda and Uganda are two countries that have been involved, along with the DRC, in a rare interstate war—the first continental war in Africa over nonrenewable resources. It began when the governments of Rwanda and Uganda tried to overthrow Kabila, who was aided by other African nations that were offered mining concessions for their support. Warlord-controlled rebel groups also proliferated in the DRC. In 2001, Laurent Kabila was assassinated but was succeeded by his son, Joseph Kabila. A peace accord between the warring nations was signed in 2001, but the warlords still fought until 2006, when the United Nations arranged the first free election since 1960. Joseph Kabila won the election and merged the former warlords still active in the country into his army and administration. Then, in 2007, the Ebola virus struck the Congo further disrupting the social system. Regardless of the DRC's volatility, China has invested nine billion dollars into the Congo for mining concessions, and multinational corporations have returned to the DRC, investing and setting up operations in the industrial mining area. The DRC has privatized the former nationalized companies that were involved in mining. Armed guards are still necessary in this area, and another investment opportunity has been the international security firms.[62] To review a map of the Democratic Republic of the Congo, see Map 1 in appendix B.

The major terrorist threat, and also a classic nihilistic threat, is the Lord's Resistance Army. The LRA initially based their insurgency on a desire to change the government in Uganda to one based upon the biblical Ten

Commandments. The LRA fights throughout the nations of Uganda, Sudan, and the DRC. Since 1992, when it was first formed, the LRA leader has been Joseph Kony, who is renowned for an exceptional brutality that often involves the crimes of rape and torture along with numerous murders. The LRA is also known for its use of child soldiers and for capturing young girls for use as sex slaves. The basic strategy of the LRA is to use fear to obtain the support of the populace for the operations of the group. Kony is currently believed to be hiding in the Ugandan jungles, but the LRA continues to rampage throughout the rural regions of these three African nations. The LRA's goal is survival, and its various commanders have stated that they will target U.S. citizens. Recently, the LRA is believed to be seeking shelter in the DRC's Garamba National Park.[63]

Nigeria is another African state with great potential for development and of strategic importance to the United States. Nigeria has the largest population in Africa and is the country's top oil-producing state. It is historically known for its corruption and has, for several years, been experiencing conflict in the Niger Delta region between multinational oil companies, supported by the government, and a variety of rebel groups, the largest of which is the Movement for the Emancipation of the Niger Delta (MEND).[64] The goals of MEND are to expel the foreign oil companies and Nigerians not indigenous to the Delta region from the Niger Delta and to use the oil to benefit the inhabitants of the region. They have utilized armed assaults, bombings, and hostage taking. This region, however, is the home of numerous other small terrorist groups numbering approximately 100 or more. MEND, however, has incorporated many of them and is by far the region's largest and most significant threat to the operations of multinational corporations.[65]

The political movement in the Niger Delta region is led by an organization called Movement for the Survival of the Ogoni People (MOSOP). The Ogoni people populate the region of the Niger Delta and believe their region has been severely harmed by the multinational oil companies. This aboveground organization has mobilized strongly in protest over the oil corporations' practices and what they consider the destruction of farmlands. In 2009, Royal Dutch Shell, the third-largest petroleum company in the world and the most significant company operating in the Niger Delta, reached a settlement in a lawsuit filed against Shell by the Ogoni people. The settlement involved a $15.5 million payout. After the settlement was announced, however, bombings occurred at three different Shell installations in the Niger Delta. Also in 2009, MEND stated they would not allow the trans-Saharan gas pipeline project to link Nigerian oil fields with Europe.[66] The government of Nigeria reached what they thought was an amnesty agreement with MEND in 2010, but in June of 2010, MEND attacked an oil facility in the Niger region.[67]

In July 2010, Julia Baird, in a *Newsweek* essay titled "Oil Shame in Africa," said, "Each year since the 1960s, there has been a spill the size of the Exxon Valdez's into the Niger Delta. Large purple slicks cover once fertile fields, and rivers are clogged with oil leaked decades ago. It has been called the 'black tide': a stain of thick, gooey oil that has oozed over vast tracts of land and poisoned the air for millions of Africans. In some areas, fish and birds have disappeared: the swamps are silent."[68] Nigeria is a volatile mix of valuable resources, terrorist groups, and opportunities for huge profits. The oil companies have increasingly invested in offshore oil fields, which the Nigerian government believes will cut down on attacks by rebels. The rebels, however, now use speedboats to attack offshore oil-drilling platforms located in the open ocean.[69] In the years to come, Nigeria will maintain its status as a dangerous area, one of the world's hot spots. To review a map of Nigeria, see Map 2 in appendix B.

Maritime Region

Our world has an ocean region that is larger than our land region. Oceans cover roughly 75 percent of the world and have a tremendous influence on how we live. The oceans feed us, we travel on them, and they influence our climate in ways we still do not completely understand. This enormous eco-system, part of the global commons, is essentially a free zone, owned by no one but traversed by thousands of ships. These ships, whose ownership is murky but who are ultimately under the authority of large corporations, travel over the oceans under the flags of various nations that have limited control over their operations.[70]

The system was designed by the United States during the defense of the UK in the early days of World War II. The United States wanted to avoid violating neutrality laws and upsetting Germany but also wanted to support the UK's conflict with Germany. American-owned ships were re-flagged as Panamanian vessels and were able to deliver materials to the UK. After the war, ship owners realized the system allowed them to avoid paying the high wages required by U.S. law and limited the regulatory requirements imposed on all U.S. flagships under U.S. law. The oil companies, who owned most of these ships, created a Liberian registry for their ships that was sanctioned by the U.S. government; at this point, two registries—Panama and Liberia—were used by ship owners to send their ships around the world. The system proliferated in the 1980s, with an increasing number of countries becoming registration harbors for ship owners. Possibly as a result of this system, there have been growing problems in the maritime region involving pollution, overfishing, and destruction of habitat. This has now been exacerbated by the warming of the climate and the resultant acidification of the ocean. In effect, the non-ocean world is slowly destroying its ocean sibling.[71]

The United Nations, through its specialized London-based agency, the International Maritime Organization (IMO), has issued regulations believed necessary to keep order in the system and provide standards for the maintenance and operation of ships at sea. The IMO's laws and regulations, termed conventions, govern only the member states of the United Nations that adopt them. The IMO also has no enforcement powers. The modern practice of piracy has taken advantage of today's freedom of the seas as it has always done throughout history. The high seas used to begin over the horizon. Today, by convention, the high seas begin 12 miles from the shore of bordering nations, with some exceptions linked to the territorial and riverine systems of the nations that border the maritime region.[72]

There are international conventions concerning piracy and terrorism in the maritime environment. Piracy under the United Nations Convention on the Law of the Sea (UNCLOS) does not cover all acts of armed robbery against ships:

Article 101. Definition of piracy. Piracy consists of any of the following acts:

(a) any illegal acts of violence or detention, or any act of depredation, committed for private ends by the crew or the passengers of a private ship or a private aircraft, and directed:

  (i) on the high seas, against another ship or aircraft, or against persons or property on board such ship or aircraft;

  (ii) against a ship, aircraft, persons or property in a place outside the jurisdiction of any State;

(b) any act of voluntary participation in the operation of a ship or of an aircraft with knowledge of facts making it a pirate ship or aircraft;

(c) any act of inciting or of intentionally facilitating an act described in subparagraph (a) or (b).[73]

The piracy convention requires that the act take place on the high seas, although most acts of ship robbery take place in territorial waters or in port. The perpetrators must also be members of the crew or passengers on another ship. The UNCLOS does not apply to acts of terrorism, as it specifically restricts its jurisdiction to acts "committed for private ends." The hijacking of the *Achille Lauro* by Palestinian terrorists was treated legally as an act of piracy rather than terrorism. This led to the subsequent international law designed to furnish jurisdiction over acts of piracy that are committed for political purposes: the Convention for the Suppression of Unlawful Acts against the Safety of Maritime Navigation.[74]

The potentially critical issue involving the maritime region is the development of terrorist pirate hybrid groups that intend to inflict damage to people and the natural environment by (1) hijacking a petroleum tanker, converting it to what seems to be a legitimate vessel, loading it with explosives, and then detonating it in a port; (2) hijacking a very large crude carrier (VLCC) and destroying it in a critical strait or off a valuable coastline where the oil would leak from the ship and create an environmental disaster and, if in a strait, shut down the transit of vital goods to the nations of the world; and (3) using a small, explosives-packed vessel in a suicide attack, steering it into an oil or chemical tanker in order to cause a loss of lives and an environmental catastrophe.

Pirates have already successfully taken large oil and chemical tankers, which are very valuable targets. In April 1998, pirates hijacked a petroleum tanker, *Petro Ranger*, in the South China Sea between Singapore and Vietnam. They took the ship to China, where they sold the fuel.[75] In 1985, pirate terrorists hijacked the *Achille Lauro*, which was discussed in chapter 6. Between 1992 and 1994, terrorists of the Al-Gama'a Al-Islamiyya targeted cruise ships on the Nile River in order to destroy Egypt's tourist trade as a tactical approach to destroying the economic well-being of that country.[76] In 1996, Chechen rebels hijacked a Turkish passenger ferry in the Black Sea for four days, holding the passengers hostage and threatening to blow up the ship as part of a strategy to bring attention to the Chechen cause.[77] In 2000, al Qaeda attacked the USS *Cole* with a bombing attack. Al Qaeda used 600 pounds of C4 explosives packed into a small attack vessel. The attack happened while the ship was refueling at the port of Aden in Yemen. It resulted in the deaths of 17 U.S. sailors and injuries to 39 sailors, along with severe structural damage to the ship.[78] In 2002, al Qaeda claimed credit for another suicide bombing attack, this time an oil tanker, the M/V *Limburg*, attacked off the coast of Yemen.[79] In 2003, the Gerakan Aceh Merdeka hijacked a fully loaded oil tanker, M/V *Penrider*, while the ship was en route to Penang from Singapore. The group of hostages was released upon payment of a ransom.[80] In 2004, Abu Sayyaf was responsible for bombing the Philippine SuperFerry 14, causing the deaths of 116 people—probably the most destructive act of maritime terrorism to date.[81] In November of 2008, Somalian pirates hijacked a 1,000-foot super tanker, the *Sirius Star*, a Liberian flag vessel owned by Aramco (Saudi Arabia's national oil company.) The ship was carrying over $100 million worth of oil and was taken, along with its 25 crew members, to the Somali coast by the pirates.[82]

The latest troubling incident occurred in August 2010, when Somali pirates hijacked the M/V *Suez*, a Panamanian-flagged cargo ship, along with its 23 crew members. The pirates used small arms fire against the ship and took command of it. The ship was only carrying cement, but the attack took place in the internationally recommended transit corridor, which is considered relatively safe as it is regularly patrolled by a coalition of navy ships.[83] Even worse, during the last week of July 2010, the 333-meter-long oil tanker M *Star* was attacked in the Persian Gulf near the Strait of Hormuz by what was believed to have been a small boat containing explosives that was steered into the ship and exploded. The details are sketchy, but, after the incident, the Abdullah Azzam brigades, a group linked to al Qaeda, claimed it had carried out a suicide attack on the ship. The Japanese-owned ship was docked at the United Arab Emirates's (UAE) main port, and the UAE took charge of investigating the event. According to Reuters, on August 6, the Emerati state news agency WAM said the ship was struck by a boat filled with explosives. If the incident was a terrorist attack, it demonstrates the continued interest and capability of terrorist pirate hybrid or terrorist groups in attacking large ships, thus operating as a serious threat to our maritime regions.[84]

The worst site for an attack utilizing an explosives-packed fuel tanker would be in one the world's major ports. Ports are attractive targets as they often contain chemical and petroleum facilities. Terrorists know how lethal this type of attack would be and realize it would engender an enormous amount of publicity and fear on the part of the public.[85]

The critical ocean straits, particularly the straits of Hormuz and Malacca, are a hot spot. If the terrorist attack on the M *Star*, which occurred near the Strait of Hormuz, had been successful in disabling and destroying the ship, it could have affected not only the ecology of that region, but also the transit of sea-borne petroleum through the strait, which currently sees 40 percent of the traffic in that region.[86] To view the straits of Hormuz and Malacca, see the maps of the Middle East and Southeast Asia, respectively, in appendix B.

Large and very large tankers are attractive targets to terrorists. However, tankers are not easy to destroy as the modern ships have double hulls and watertight compartments built to sustain extremely heavy collisions without excessive damage. But, pirates have hijacked these ships in the past, and terrorists can do so in the future. A difficult target is like any other target: given enough time and thought, it can be successfully attacked.[87]

Cruise ships are also attractive and vulnerable targets because of the large numbers of persons on board. Terrorists have already hijacked cruise ships and have successfully attacked them. Terrorist attacks on these targets will occur again.[88]

COUNTERMEASURES

The selection and application of countermeasures is the signature skill of the security expert. All countermeasures can be defeated, but they can be employed to defeat most attackers. A complete review and analysis of countermeasure methodology is beyond the scope of this book and would entail presenting information that can also be obtained from many other sources. This chapter presents some general concepts of the use of countermeasures relevant to environmentally linked terrorism, and analyzes the tactics most likely to be used by ecoterrorists and nihilistic terrorists. It then focuses on three proactive, detection-oriented countermeasures designed to stop a potential terrorist attack during the planning stage: covert social network analysis to identify and determine the scope of a terrorist threat, surveillance and countersurveillance techniques to identify potential threats and determine the locations of the residences and meeting places of terrorist group members, and personnel protection tactics to stymie one of the easiest terrorist attacks for small nihilistic cells to accomplish—kidnapping key corporate or government employees.

General Concepts

There are varying levels of facility security. The first level—level one, or minimum security—is designed for low-threat environments, such as a home in a low-crime area that can be protected by locks on doors and windows. The highest level—level five, or maximum security—has redundant security in depth, involving several layers and including sophisticated intrusion detection systems and an on-site, armed response force. In some dangerous areas of the world or in certain industries (e.g., nuclear power plants), maximum security is required.[89]

For ecoterrorists who adhere to the guideline of not harming any animal or human, medium security (level three) or enhanced level-two security is sufficient for the prevention of an attack. Enhancement of a level-two security system necessitates the addition of an intrusion detection system that annunciates at a separate location staffed with a response group or a nearby police department. If the system only annunciates locally, it is necessary to also have an unarmed security officer capable of communicating with a local police department. For nihilistic terrorist threats, medium- or high-level security is necessary, with the decision between specific levels based upon the threat assessment. Some elements of a security system should not be concealed. The idea is to display your strength as a capable guardian to decrease the motivation of potential attackers. This concept, at the core of situational crime prevention, deters criminals and will deter ecoterrorists and some nihilistic groups depending upon their degree of capability.

Tactical Choices of Terrorists

The range of possible attacks against facilities is fairly extensive. The U.S. Army, in their *Physical Security Manual*, identifies 15 tactics that terrorists have used to achieve their objectives. The choice of tactic is dependent upon the capabilities of the terrorist group and the defenses of the target.[90]

The choices of ecoterrorist and nihilistic groups will differ in some aspects, particularly in regard to the more lethal tactics. The behavioral characteristics of the two types of terrorists will also influence their choice of tactics and are one of the main reasons for the emphasis in this book on knowing the enemy.

Ecoterrorist Tactics

- **Exterior attack:** The ecoterrorist often attacks the exterior of structures with firebombs or tools. The goal is to destroy the facility by arson or damage it by what is seemingly an attack by vandals.
- **Forced entry:** The ecoterrorist uses tools to enter a facility. Once within, the release of caged animals is effectuated and property maintained within the facility can be destroyed or sabotaged.

- **Covert entry:** The ecoterrorist may enter a facility by using false credentials or stealth. The goals are the same as for forced entry.

- **Insider compromise:** This tactic has been used by the ALF. The terrorist gains authorized access to a facility and has several options: (1) compromise the security of the facility by taking photographs and stealing or copying confidential records, (2) smuggle incendiary devices into the facility for later use, or (3) use monkeywrenching to disrupt the operations of the facility.

- **Visual surveillance:** The ecoterrorist uses ocular and photographic equipment to develop intelligence about the operations of the facility. This tactic can be used as the primary tactic for some facilities or as a pre-attack tactic when the goal is to attack the facility.[91]

Ecoterrorists, such as ELF or ALF and their franchisees, use arson as their most violent primary tactic. They believe it is an effective and efficient tactic for their capabilities and that it causes as much economic damage as high explosives.[92] Their other primary tactics are sabotage (severe damage to vehicles and property) and vandalism (low-level damage to property, graffiti, or breaking windows). ALF and ELF cells have utilized preoperational video and photographic surveillance and have obtained intelligence from open sources. The ALF Web site contains a link to Bruce Schneier's security blog. These groups target low-security targets and use social engineering and develop company insiders or place sympathizers in low-level positions as aids to carrying out attacks. Their valued targets include the facilities and property of companies involved in logging; genetic engineering; home building; automobile dealerships, if SUVs are sold; energy production and distribution; and the hospitality industry, if operating within or near ecologically vulnerable areas. They have recently targeted new construction, if considered urban sprawl, and continue to target facilities that hold animals for use in experiments or to obtain their fur for commercial purposes.[93]

Nihilistic terrorists, whose behavioral characteristics entail extreme acts of violence, including suicide attacks, have a wider choice of tactics that also include the tactics used by ecoterrorists.

Nihilistic Terrorist Tactics

- **Vehicle bombs:** The terrorist may use both stationary and moving (suicide attack) vehicles packed with explosives to ensure a powerful explosion that can be effective even if it is an exterior attack.

- **Standoff weapons:** The terrorist can use military weapons or improvised versions of those weapons to attack a facility from a distance. This is an indiscriminate tactic used to kill and destroy.

- **Ballistics:** The terrorist uses small arms (e.g., pistols, rifles, and submachine guns) from a distance or at close range in an assault on a facility.

- **Mail-bomb delivery:** Theodore Kaczynski is an example of a nihilistic terrorist who used this tactic. Small bombs are delivered to a target in letters or packages. The goal is to kill or injure people.

- **Supplies-bomb delivery:** The terrorist conceals powerful bombs in containers and inserts them into shipments to be delivered to a facility.

- **Airborne contamination:** The terrorist gains access to a facility's air supply and contaminates it with chemical or biological agents.

- **Waterborne contamination:** The terrorist contaminates a facility's water supply at a point in the water distribution system past the decontamination point. The terrorist will use biological or chemical agents with varying effects based upon the quantity of water and the chemical or biological agent employed.[94]

Specific Defenses

The basic countermeasure for most ecoterrorist attacks is the perimeter fence in conjunction with a human response capability. The fence often used is a chain-link fence, seven or eight feet in height and topped by strands of barbed wire six inches apart and angled outward 30 to 45 degrees from the vertical. The standard perimeter fence, however, should not be overrated as a defense. It can be climbed without aids, with the assistance of one person who does not cross over, within 3½ to 5 seconds. For maximum security, the perimeter fence has to be combined with an intrusion detection method. Remember, if sufficient time is taken for study, all fences can be climbed.[95]

Nihilistic terrorists, individuals and cells, demand a higher level of security than ecoterrorists, and the possibility of their attacks on an international basis is also much greater. The belief that a corporation is harming the environment in a developing area of the world will only be part of a litany of reasons for the use of terrorism by these groups. But resource scarcity, made worse by climate change, will amplify any existing antagonism, possibly generating an attack. In regard to resource scarcity caused by global warming, the Pew Center on Global Climate Change offers this warning: "As is the case today, America will not be able to help everyone. Those most affected by climate change could come to resent the imposition of climate change. As the world's largest historical emitter of heat-trapping greenhouse gases, the United States is likely to be the chosen target of resentment. . . . Al Qaeda leaders have cited global warming repeatedly in propaganda intended to foment anti-American sentiment."[96]

Michael Harvey's 1993 study of how multinational corporations manage their risk of terrorism concluded that most corporations focus too much on the hardware component of security countermeasures. Harvey believes their defensive emphasis on the protection of physical assets was matched by a lack of environmental scanning. The corporation, in effect, became a target waiting to be attacked but without any idea of the plans and movements being made by potential attackers. This lack of proactive intelligence gathering meant the attackers' capabilities and methods of attack could over-match the corporations' security measures because the hardware was no longer a useful defense. Harvey believes that adaptable terrorists can bypass or eliminate hardware countermeasures and that "more attention needs to be directed at early warning systems to detect possible attacks."[97] To support his position that current security practices should be changed to a more proactive model, Harvey used data from the ITERATE Database, a database on international terrorism, to determine the type and success rate of terrorist attacks. Harvey's analysis showed that terrorists were successful 87 percent of the time with bombing attacks, 76 percent of the time with hostage-taking missions, and 75 percent of the time with assassinations.[98]

Proactive Detection

The first step in a proactive strategy of detection countermeasures is to identify the threat—the terrorist groups that are likely attackers. This entails not just the name of a group and its capabilities and motivations but the names and other identifying information of the individual members. In a foreign environment, the ease of obtaining this information will depend partially on the relationship between the corporation and relevant law enforcement agencies. Law enforcement agencies include U.S. law enforcement and intelligence agencies that participate in the partnership relationship between multinational corporations and the U.S. government. After the initial identifying data is obtained, it can be enhanced by the utilization of social network analysis and physical surveillance.

Social Network Analysis

Social network analysis, introduced in chapter 7, may be problematic as to its feasibility and effectiveness, but, for a sophisticated security program of a multinational company charged with the security of work sites in urban or suburban locations, SNA can be a valuable tool that should be examined as a countermeasure.

Traditionally, SNA uses all available information to determine the membership and association of overt social groups, not terrorist groups. Historically, law enforcement investigators have always tried to determine the membership of criminal organizations. This approach became systemized by the 1970s with the development of a logical analytical method referred to as link analysis.[99] SNA developed from a variety of academic disciplines. In the field of social science, Stanley Milgram's experiments, which examined relationship links between people who were not aware of one another, resulted in the finding that most people in a society are linked by six individuals—thus the phrase "six degrees of separation."[100]

Researchers in the fields of social and cognitive psychology and anthropology were instrumental in the development of SNA through their work on information flow in groups and through anthropological field studies on various methods used to examine interpersonal relationships within subgroups. Currently, SNA has two orientations. In one, SNA is used to capture and describe social network data for the purpose of understanding individual behavior. This perspective on human behavior sees social relationships as the major contributor to human behavior because behavior is based upon the processes of socialization. The second orientation is to use relational data between nodes (i.e., links among individuals, groups, or objects) for the purpose of describing a specific network of individuals. One result of this application of SNA is the socio-gram, a picture using points and links to show relationships between individuals. Sociograms are a staple of organized crime, gang, and terrorism investigations today.[101]

In their overview of SNA theory, criminal justice researchers Jean McGloin and David Kirk state that SNA has three mathematical foundations and three types of analyses. The mathematical foundations are (1) graph theory, (2) algebraic models, and (3) statistical/probability theory. The analyses are (1) description graphs, (2) network measures, and (3) network modeling techniques.[102]

For terrorist groups that are loosely coupled organizations, their mode of operation is usually a network system. In utilizing SNA, the basic assumption has to be accepted that individual behavior is affected, negatively or positively, by a person's position in a social network, such as a gang.[103] The most advanced methodology for studying social network dynamics is network modeling, which uses computation tools to predict how people in a network will react to certain designated situations.[104]

Valdis Krebs, a prominent expert in SNA, applied SNA to a covert group—in this case, the 9/11 hijackers. According to Krebs, traditional SNA was used for identifying overt, known members of social groups. Terrorist groups, however, because of their members' general disinclination to identify themselves as terrorists, may be hard to identify prior to an attack. Krebs, in analyzing and mapping the 9/11 cell, used open-source data, predominantly newspaper information, public documents (e.g., court documents), and the search engine Google.[105]

Krebs discovered that the 9/11 terrorist network was diffusely spread with minimal centrality. Krebs saw this as evidence of organizational methods to prevent the total compromise of the network if an individual member was captured or cooperating with the government. Krebs determined that the problem in analyzing covert networks is that they just do not behave like normal networks. The strongest ties in covert networks will be hard to detect or may masquerade as weak ties by only infrequently demonstrating activity with the network. Krebs points out, however, that "the covert network must be active at times" and "it is during these periods of activity that they may be most vulnerable to discovery."[106]

Security planners with knowledge of the mathematical and statistical tools of SNA could employ SNA methodology to map terrorist groups located in their areas of responsibility. The available research, discussed in chapter 7, on the spatial characteristics of international and domestic terrorist groups is definitive in regard to the relatively short distances between the residences of terrorists and their targets. Once the network is mapped, descriptive information (i.e., photographs and public source descriptions of network members) can be obtained. Krebs describes the process of attacking the mapped terrorist network: "The best solution for network disruption may be to discover possible suspects and then, via snowball sampling, map their ego networks—see whom else they lead to, and where they overlap."[107]

Once the network is mapped, all available information concerning suspected terrorists should be collected, analyzed, furnished to trusted law enforcement partners, and to the external-threat component of the organization's security group. As Krebs recommends, the background investigation of suspected members should include the skill sets possessed by those members.[108] By identifying the skills that are essential to feasible attacks, emphasis can be given to removing those individuals from the network. The network analysis will rely upon, and in turn will aid, the organization's external-threat component responsible for surveillance and countersurveillance operations.

Surveillance/Countersurveillance

The security planning and operational structure of a multinational corporation will need to move beyond a static defense strategy and incorporate an external-threat unit that includes a strong surveillance/countersurveillance operational capability. Terrorists need to obtain information about their target. This necessity offers the best opportunity to identify previously unknown members of a terrorist group.

As previously explained, ecoterrorist and nihilistic groups engage in pre-attack surveillance of their targets. In addition, lone wolves are prone to being identified through countersurveillance. Lone wolves are vulnerable when surveilling their targets because of the absence of partners who normally enable members of a surveillance team to break off the surveillance either at predetermined intervals or when needed to prevent being compromised by the target's countersurveillance operation. A solo surveillance conducted by the same person more than once will give a surveillance team the opportunity to identify a potential attacker. It is a rare and highly skilled individual who can conduct a one-person surveillance on an aware target for any significant period of time.[109]

Unlike larger terrorist groups, small ecoterrorist and nihilistic cells have difficulty in utilizing separate intelligence/surveillance subcells. However, they may possess the information and training necessary to discover or avoid a subpar level of proficiency in surveillance operations directed against them. Some specific guidelines for surveillance of their enemies' locations is contained in the al Qaeda manual discovered in Britain titled "Military Studies in the Jihad against the Tyrants." This manual stresses the value of photography to an effective surveillance: "It is preferable to photograph the area as a whole first, then the street of the location. If possible, panoramic pictures should be taken. . . . The brother/photographer should use a modern camera that can photograph at night or from a distance, and only the lens of the camera should be visible."[110]

Information on countermeasure techniques is covered in a well-known manual for ecoterrorism titled *Ecodefense: A Field Guide to Strategic Monkeywrenching*, which presents the following observations concerning law enforcement surveillance techniques:

Don't look around in an obvious manner. The trick is to spot the surveillance without the bad guys knowing it. . . . Most cautious people only check for surveillance shortly after leaving home, work, or school. Most professional surveillance picks up after this to avoid being 'made.' Make your checks random. . . . If you live in a remote area, concealed video cameras may monitor your home. Take walks in the area and be alert to new boxes on power poles, unexplained cables, or monitoring vehicles parked at some distance. . . . Be suspicious of night-flying aircraft when you're out driving. They'll usually maintain a healthy distance to avoid tipping you off. . . . The FBI will commonly use six vehicles when tailing a suspect. One vehicle will follow within sight for awhile, and then drop out as another takes over. The tailing vehicles will be in radio contact so all know where the suspect vehicle is at all times.[111]

The Brazilian revolutionary Carlos Marighella, in his manual on urban guerilla tactics, stressed that "North American firms and properties in the country for their part must become such frequent targets of sabotage that the volume of actions directed against them surpasses the total of all other actions against vital enemy points."[112] In explaining the techniques of attacking targets, Marighella stressed the importance of surprise to make up for what could be a disadvantage in capabilities between the urban guerilla and government forces. He based the technique of surprise on four requisites, the first being the importance of intelligence gathering and surveillance activities: "To compensate for his general weakness and shortage of arms compared to the enemy, the urban guerilla uses surprise. . . . Surprise is based on four essential requisites of which the first is to know the situation of the enemy we are going to attack, usually by means of precise information and meticulous observation."[113] The *Encyclopedia of Afghan Jihad* offers an example of how a jihadi checks to see if he or she has been under observation while surveilling a target by "casually dropping something out of your pocket and observing who will pick it up."[114]

For a countersurveillance unit to be successful, it has to be staffed so it is capable of operating on a 24-hour basis. The number of personnel is dependent on the scope of the program, the scale of the facilities at risk, and the personnel under protection. If it is limited to a countersurveillance program at the physical sites of facilities, it is easier to staff, less risky, and less expensive. If the program involves active surveillance of individuals who have been identified as terrorist suspects through countersurveillance at the corporation's facilities or through network analysis, the cost of personnel and the risk go up with the increase in targets. One of the most important surveillance-related activities for foreign corporations is personnel protection.

Personnel Protection

Multinational corporations have long recognized the risk that employees could be victims of kidnappings in both foreign and domestic locations. These kidnappings can happen on land or on the open seas and can be carried out by terrorist groups, criminals, or hybrid groups. Major insurance brokerages routinely arrange kidnap-and-ransom insurance policies for corporations. These policies should include provisions for assistance in the negotiation and recovery of kidnap victims by a team of recognized professionals. One problem with evaluating the threat of kidnapping is the lack of reliable data. Ann Hagedorn Auerbach, in her examination of international kidnappings that occurred over a two-year period from 1997 to 1999, states that statistics concerning kidnappings are problematical. She found that many incidents of kidnapping were not reported and that the incidents that were reported may not have been accurately reported due to political reasons. One obvious reason is the impact a rash of kidnappings could have on the economies of countries that rely on the tourist industry or foreign corporation investments for a large part of their national income. She believes that only 30 percent of kidnappings on a worldwide basis are reported and that "in some countries, the reporting rate is as low as 10 percent."[115]

In the United States, kidnapping is a rare crime. Foreign locations have significantly higher numbers even when corporations have active anti-kidnapping procedures and personnel protection plans in place. Identifying whether a kidnapping is committed by a terrorist group or by common criminals is difficult. Terrorists sometimes employ criminals to act on their behalf by kidnapping individuals and holding them for ransom even though the ultimate beneficiary of the act is the terrorist organization, which takes the bulk of the ransom money and gives the criminal kidnappers a set fee or percentage of the ransom. Today, kidnapping operations are sometimes even more complicated. Terrorists with criminal accomplices often work in separate cell structures, with each cell responsible for a different part of the kidnapping. For example, one cell will snatch the subject, another cell will guard and take care of the subject, and a third cell will handle the ransom negotiation and turnover of the victim. One important characteristic of kidnapping is that it can happen to corporate employees at all job levels of

the corporation; thus, corporations should have personnel protection programs that are not limited to only executive-level employees.[116]

According to Auerbach, "One five-year study, beginning in 1992, showed
that of the foreign nationals kidnapped, 66 percent were eventually released after some sort of negotiation, 20 percent were rescued, 9 percent
were killed or died in captivity, and 5 percent escaped."[117] Protection procedures for a kidnap attempt have to include the possibility that the kidnap is
actually an assassination attempt. The basic procedures for the two crimes
are essentially the same.[118]

Kidnapping a protected employee with a full-time security detail is a
complex operation. As part of the operation, the kidnap team will surveil
the target to gather information about her routine and determine the best
venue for the attack. Then, the kidnappers initiate the operation by an attack on the victim's home, vehicle, or out-of-office location. The specific actions and training a security detail must undergo are outside the scope of
this book, but there are four tactical issues that are so important but often
neglected that they need to be covered:

- Unless the protectee is armed and has the ability to protect herself and intends
  to assume that responsibility, there should be a minimum of two security personnel with the protectee any time the protectee is at an unsecured location,
  which includes the vehicle and most residences.

- The most dangerous time is when the protectee is in transit, as over 70 percent of all successful kidnappings take place under these conditions. During
  movement by vehicle, the protectee is most vulnerable entering and leaving the
  vehicle.[119] The locations of entry and exit from the transport vehicle should be
  closely examined during protection planning. Ideally, entrance and exit from a
  vehicle should occur at a protected location with no one, except cleared personnel, within 50 feet of the vehicle.

- Routes of travel should be varied on a random basis. Periodically, several
  surveillance-detection checks should be made. This procedure will necessitate
  long-range optical viewing devices and cameras with telephoto lenses. The surveillance-detection sites should be established at vehicle choke points, where
  a suspect's vehicle during the surveillance of the protectee's vehicle has to
  pass by the surveillance-detection site. All vehicles passing through the choke
  point detection site should be photographed and described by the surveillance
  team manning that site. This should be done for several minutes after the protectee's vehicle passes the choke point. This same procedure should be implemented at two additional locations during the same surveillance-detection
  check on the protectee's route of travel. At the conclusion of the detection check,
  the vehicle photos and descriptions from the three locations should be compared to detect similarities. If the same vehicle passed two of the choke point
  detection sites after the protectee's car, it is almost certain the protectee is being
  surveilled, possibly as a preliminary step to a kidnap attempt. This same tactic
  can be employed if an employee of the company reports possible hostile surveillance or has other reasons to fear she could be the target of a prospective
  kidnap attempt.

- Company employees involved in ocean-shipping activities in certain areas of the maritime region are at risk of being taken hostage by pirates or terrorists and held for ransom. Historically, pirates have often taken hostages and held them for ransom. The pirates of the Barbary Coast took so many Americans hostage in the early 19th century that it led to the formation of an international coalition, including the United States, to control the actions of the Barbary pirates.[120]

In today's world, security planning for terrorism will involve both private industry and the government working together as partners in the long, possibly never-ending battle against terrorism. Successful terrorist attacks in most countries not involved in a national insurgency are rare. But as the climate changes, environmental conditions will become worse in those countries that cannot mitigate destructive changes. Striking out against foreign multinational corporations occurred in a variety of countries during the 1970s, 1980s, 1990s, and it is occurring today. Attacks with linkages to environmental conditions, such as resource scarcity, could significantly increase in the next decade as the effects of climate change worsen. To protect an organization against terrorist attacks, active countermeasures designed to both detect and prevent deadly actions should be the goal of security planning on behalf of both the government and private industry.

CHAPTER 9

Conclusion

On September 1, 2010, at the headquarters building of Discovery Communications in Silver Spring, Maryland, James J. Lee, a known environmental extremist, entered the first-floor lobby of the building and forcibly took two Discovery Communications employees and a security guard hostage, thus beginning a four-hour siege. Lee was armed with what were believed to be pistols, had at least one explosive device strapped to his body, and was carrying boxes and backpacks. Lee had previously protested at the building over Discovery's television programming. He wanted new shows designed to save the planet and reduce the human population, which Lee saw as the main threat to the planet.[1]

During negotiations with the police, Lee told them he was prepared to die. The police response team, monitoring Lee on the building's security cameras, entered the building after Lee was observed pointing what appeared to be a pistol at a hostage; the team shot Lee, killing him and causing an explosive device on his body to go off. Prior to the police assault, Lee had told an NBC news producer, who had called the building, that he was armed with a gun and bombs, one of which would go off if he dropped it. After their successful assault, the police determined that Lee's weapons were actually starter pistols designed to make noise but incapable of harming anyone.[2]

Arguably, the nature of Lee's actions—the use of violence to obtain a political or social goal—meets most statutory definitions of terrorism. If he had planned to detonate the explosives, it would also be the "first recorded incident of environmentally motivated suicide terrorism in the United States, and likely the first worldwide."[3]

Although Lee was unsuccessful in that he did not obtain his goal, he did succeed in capturing the attention of television and Internet viewers for several hours. If his plan had been better executed and he had possessed better weapons and greater expertise in bomb making, the situation would probably have involved a mass murder before Lee was shot by police or took his own life. Lee's irrational decision to take human hostages to resolve an environmentally linked dispute illustrates the difficulty in predicting a terrorist attack. However, we can now reach some important conclusions about the current status and future of environmentally linked terrorism.

THE WORSENING ENVIRONMENT

On August 15, 2010, *New York Times* reporter Justin Gillis, in an article titled "Extreme Weather Raising Global Warming Questions," reviewed the climate-caused disasters that occurred in 2010: heat waves in the United States; flooding in the United States and Pakistan; and heat waves, wildfires, and drought in Africa, Eastern Asia, and Russia. In reviewing information gleaned from a variety of sources on the hottest year on record so far, Gillis wrote the following: "Certain recent weather events were so extreme that a few scientists are shedding their traditional reluctance to ascribe specific disasters to global warming."[4]

Terrible weather in 2010 has caused famines and contagious disease outbreaks in some of the endangered areas of the world. It seems apparent that global warming is causing or contributing to serious weather problems on a worldwide basis. In May 2010, the National Academy of Sciences issued three reports outlining the problems caused by global warming and recommending that world governments take responsive actions. The prestigious scientific body also called for a drastic, 80 percent reduction of U.S. carbon emissions from 2012 to 2050.[5] According to Susan Solomon, a respected climate scientist, the current physical climate changes caused by anthropogenic carbon dioxide in the atmosphere are essentially irreversible. This means that the warming of the planet that has already occurred will continue to cause environmental damage in different regions and sectors of the world, specifically related to the patterns and amount of precipitation and rising sea levels. These changes can have a negative impact on current populations in affected regions, including "heavy rainfall and flooding."[6]

During the summer of 2010, the results of climate change have already had catastrophic results in many regions of the world. In Russia, a record-breaking heat wave and the resultant drought caused numerous wildfires that inundated Moscow with smog. The death rate in Moscow doubled, at one point rising to 700 deaths a day. The 2007 IPCC report had predicted droughts and fires for Russia, along with future crop losses. The 2007 IPCC report had also predicted an increase in rain and flooding in Pakistan, China, and the United States. In China, flooding in the summer of

2010 resulted in 1,100 deaths. All the IPCC's predictions occurred in the identified nations.[7]

The current strategy for reducing global warming does not seem effective. Both the UN 2009 Climate Conference in Copenhagen and the UN 2010 Climate Conference in Cancun reached uncertain results. In 2009, the major industrial nations would not agree to definitive cuts in carbon emissions but did reach a political agreement (Copenhagen Accord) in which the nations with the largest economies offered specific pledges to reduce emissions. In 2010, the world's nations again failed to produce a treaty but did reach agreement (Cancun Agreements) on several issues. Essentially, the results could be characterized as "hopeful."[8] In the U.S. Congress, it seems unlikely that any type of effective climate control legislation, which would require deep cuts in carbon emissions, will become law. The transportation industry, in particular, is united in opposing climate change legislation and will probably win.[9] Climate change will never be addressed from an international perspective until the current environmental crisis becomes a disaster affecting such a large number of countries that the nations of the world will have to unite in bringing down GHG emissions. Unfortunately, that may be too late. The warming natural environment will increasingly serve as a nexus for terrorism in the years to come.

TERRORISM

Protests, civil disobedience, minor acts of sabotage, and vandalism by individuals and small groups of eco-warriors will continue to occur in the United States and Europe, with likely increases in the future. The potential for extremely consequential attacks is not predictable, but this group of activists, who adamantly oppose both violence directed against people and arson attacks against property, has never committed consequential attacks. For U.S. ecoterrorists, who since 2000 have committed 37 percent of all terrorist attacks in the United States, pressure by law enforcement organizations and the federal government's successful prosecutions of the few significant groups should deter most individuals and small cells from escalating their direct actions to major attacks on property and sectors of the national infrastructure. These groups have, over a 30-year period, rarely used bombs or explosives. The majority of their attacks have utilized improvised incendiary devices. Prior to James Lee's armed hostage taking, none of these groups or individuals had used firearms or taken a hostage.[10] Ecoterrorists remain a major threat to commit serious acts of environmentally linked property damage, but only outliers—lone wolves and small groups with nihilistic motivations—will pose a threat capable of causing serious death or injury to human beings.

Nihilistic terrorists, particularly lone wolves, are always a threat to commit deadly acts of terrorism. Their professed motivation may be to protect the environment, as James Lee demonstrated, or they could seemingly be motivated by religion, such as homegrown jihadi terrorists, but their real impetus for attacks will be nihilistic alienation and anger. These individuals have observed the extreme harm that can be caused by wildfires and damage to petroleum infrastructure. They can see the advantages of using the environment as a weapon or attacking the nexus of the natural environment with the built environment. These individuals and small groups could become a threat to U.S. interests and multinational corporations operating in dangerous regions of the developing world, particularly to industries related to the extraction of natural resources for profit.[11]

The culmination of environmental change and resource depletion in certain nations of the world, such as Nigeria and the Democratic Republic of the Congo, will increase the amount of diffuse, subnational conflict. The interests of the United States could be bound up in these conflicts and U.S. government personnel and facilities could become terrorist targets for environmentally linked reasons.

It is also likely that ecoterrorists, nihilistic terrorists, and hybrid groups will perceive elements of the petroleum infrastructure in the maritime regions of the world as attractive and vulnerable targets. The targets are numerous: manned and unmanned oil-well drilling platforms, petroleum tankers, and various hazardous facilities in the world's seaports.[12] The oil-well blowout in the Gulf of Mexico focused the world on the dangers the petroleum infrastructure poses to the most critical regions of our environment. This will motivate ecoterrorists to take actions to protect these regions by dissuading oil-well drilling through attacks on selected parts of the infrastructure that do not pose a risk of damaging the environment. Nihilistic groups will see this infrastructure as vulnerable to attack and the presence of multinational companies operating in developing regions as posing a threat to the environment, thus offering a justification for deadly attacks on Western companies.

The increasing degradation of the natural environment will continue to serve as a catalyst for environmentally linked terrorism in many regions of the world, including the United States, for years to come.

APPENDIX A

Attack Tree: Destruction of Urban Fixed Facility

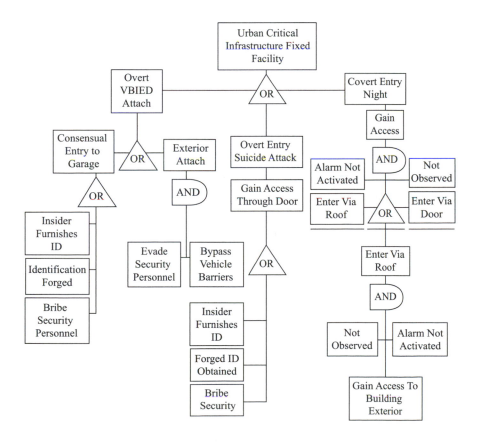

APPENDIX B

Maps

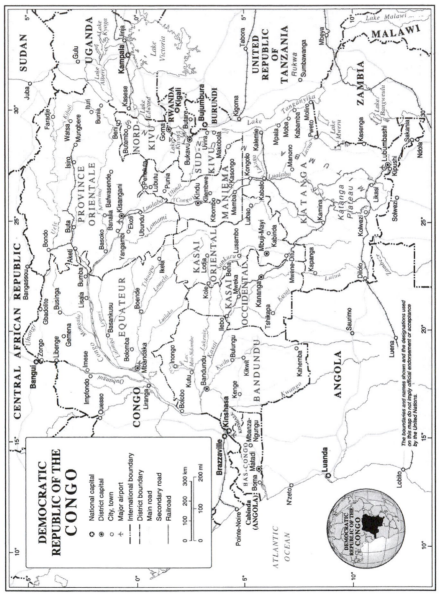

Democratic Republic of the Congo, Map No. 4007 Rev. 8, January 2004, United Nations.

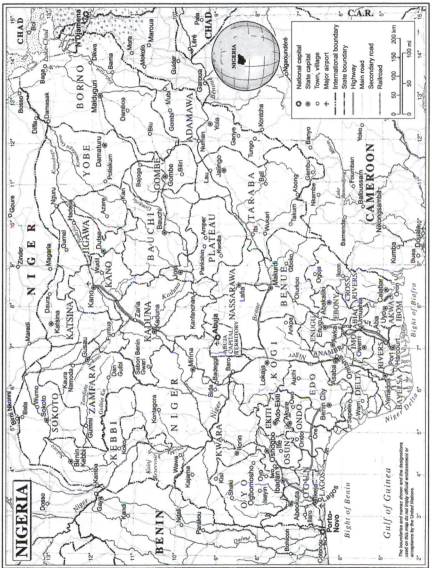

Nigeria, Map No. 4228, October 2004, United Nations.

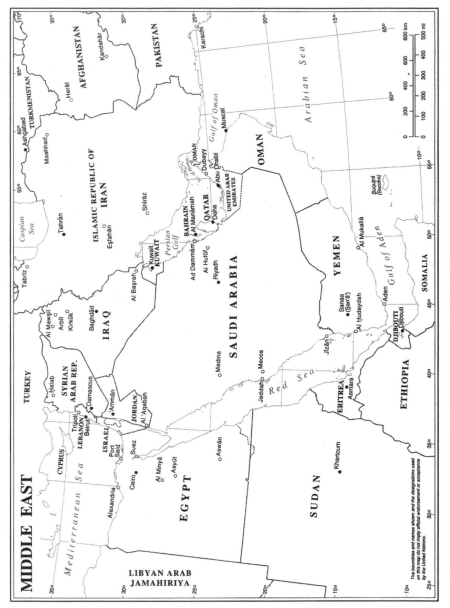

Middle East Region, Map No. 4102 Rev. 3, August 2004, United Nations.

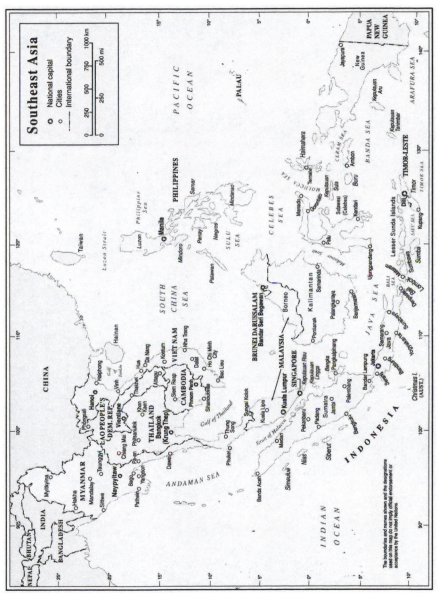

Southeast Asia

- ⊙ National capital
- ○ Cities
- --- International boundary

0 250 500 750 1000 km
0 250 500 750 1000 mi

Southeast Asia, Map No. 4365, May 2009, United Nations.

The boundaries and names shown and the designations
used on this map do not imply official endorsement or
acceptance by the United Nations.

Notes

PREFACE

1. Jacques Barzun and Henry F. Graff, *The Modern Researcher*, 6th ed. (Belmont, CA: Wadsworth Thompson Learning, 2004), 132.

CHAPTER 1: INTRODUCTION

1. Sergey Nechaev, "Catechism of the Revolutionist (1869)," in *Voices of Terror: Manifestos, Writings and Manuals of Al Qaeda, Hamas, and other Terrorists from around the World and Throughout the Ages*, ed. Walter Laqueur (New York: Reed Press, 2004), 71–75.

2. Sun Tzu, *The Art of War*, trans. Ralph D. Sawyer (New York: Barnes and Noble, 1994), 227–28.

3. For a discussion of the various stages of a crisis, see Steven Fink, *Crisis Management: Planning for the Inevitable* (Lincoln, NE: iUniverse, 2002), 20–28.

4. Thomas L. Friedman, *Hot, Flat, and Crowded* (New York: Farrar, Straus, and Giroux, 2008), 5.

5. See McGraw-Hill, *Encyclopedia of Science and Technology*, 9th ed. (New York: McGraw-Hill, 2002), 56.

6. The built environment is often the target of attacks by both ecoterrorists and environmental terrorists.

7. Carolyn Merchant, *American Environmental History: An Introduction* (New York: Columbia University Press, 2007), 247.

8. McGraw-Hill, *Encyclopedia of Science and Technology*, 57.

9. McGraw-Hill, *Encyclopedia of Science and Technology*, 57; Thomas F. Homer-Dixon, *Environment, Scarcity, and Violence* (Princeton, NJ: Princeton University Press, 1999), 40–41.

10. National Academies, *Understanding and Responding to Climate Change*, Highlights of National Academies Reports 2008 Edition, 7, http://www.nationalacad emies.org/morenews/20080519.html.

11. For an overview of society's major environmental problems, see Jared Diamond, *Collapse: How Societies Choose to Fail or Succeed* (New York: Penguin Books, 2005), 486; Intergovernmental Panel on Climate Change, *Climate Change 2007: Synthesis Report, 2007*, 30, http://www.ipcc.ch/pdf/assessment-report/ar4/syr/ar4_ syr_spm.pdf.

12. Diamond, *Collapse*, 479–92.

13. "Foreseeing a showdown over climate change, the energy industry had been busy packing Capitol Hill with lobbyists." Jeffrey Goodell, "As the World Burns," *Rolling Stone*, January 21, 2010, 32–33.

14. Diamond, *Collapse*, 491–92.

15. Intergovernmental Panel on Climate Change, *Climate Change 2007*, 30; see Tim Dickinson, "The Climate Killers," *Rolling Stone*, January 21, 2010, 35.

16. Intergovernmental Panel on Climate Change, *Climate Change 2007*, 53.

17. Anti-Defamation League, "Ecoterrorism: Extremism in the Animal Rights and Environmentalist Movements: 2007," http://www.adl.org/learn/extremism. For a classic and still perceptive explanation of why some individuals become fanatical members of revolutionary movements, see Eric Hoffer, *The True Believer* (New York: Perennial, 2007), 117–68.

18. *America's Most Wanted*, "Daniel Andreas San Diego," http://www.amw. com/fugitives/brief.cfm?id=25800.

19. Jeffrey F. Addicott, *Terrorism Law: The Rule of Law and the War on Terror*, 2nd ed. (Tucson, AZ: Lawyers and Judges, 2004), 1.

20. Gérard Chaliand and Arnaud Blin, eds., "Preface," in *The History of Terrorism: From Antiquity to Al Qaeda*, trans. Edward Schneider, Kathryn Pulver, and Jesse Browner (Berkeley: University of California Press, 2007), vii.

21. David Andress, *The Terror: The Merciless War for Freedom in Revolutionary France* (New York: Farrar, Straus, and Giroux, 2005), 178–82. "It is time that equality bore its scythe above all heads. It is time to horrify all the conspirators. So legislators, place Terror on the order of the day! Let us be in revolution, because everywhere counter-revolution is being woven by our enemies." Archives parlementaires de 1787 à 1860, première sèrie, M.J. Mavidal et al., eds., Paris, 1868, vol. 73, p. 420, quoted in Andress, *The Terror*, 179; Bruce Hoffman, *Inside Terrorism* (New York: Columbia University Press, 1998), 17.

22. Ariel Merari, "Terrorism as a Strategy of Insurgency," in *The History of Terrorism* (see note 20), 14.

23. House Committee on Resources, *Ecoterrorism and Lawlessness on the National Forests*, Oversight Hearing before the Subcommittee on Forests and Forest Health, 107th Cong., 2nd sess., 2002, 48–49 (statement and testimony of James F. Jarboe, Domestic Terrorism section chief, Counterterrorism Division, FBI Headquarters), http://frwebgate.access.gpo.gov/cgi-bin/getdoc.cgi?dbname=107_ house_hearings&docid=f:77615.pdf.

24. Chrystal Mancuso-Smith, *From Monkeywrenching to Mass Destruction: Eco-Sabotage and the American West*, 26 Journal of Land, Resources, and Environmental Law (2006): 319, 321–23.

25. The radical environmental movement includes many disparate groups and individuals who engage in environmental activism that sometimes includes illegal acts. See Christopher Manes, *Green Rage: Radical Environmentalism and the*

Unmaking of Civilization (Boston: Little, Brown, 1990), 7, where Manes describes the movement as "motivated by a vision of the world that rejected the premise held by government, industry, and mainstream environmental groups alike that mankind should control and manage the natural world."

26. For an analysis of the connection between water resources and terrorism that includes the distinction between tool and target, see Pacific Institute, "Water Conflict Chronology, November 2009," http://worldwater.org/conflict/index.html.

27. "FBI: Eco-Terrorism Remains No. 1 Domestic Terror Threat," FOX News, March 31, 2008, http://www.foxnews.com/printer_friendly_story/0,3566,343768,00.html.

28. Walter Laqueur, *No End to War: Terrorism in the Twenty-First Century* (New York: Continuum International, 2003), 209.

29. The insurance industry has developed a probabilistic model to assess terrorism risk. See Air Worldwide Corporation, "The Air Loss Estimation Model," http://www.air-worldwide.com/publicationsitem.aspx?id=15854; Henry H. Willis et al., *Estimating Terrorism Risk*, MG-388 (Santa Monica, CA: RAND Corporation, 2005), 25, http://www.rand.org/pubs/monographs/MG388.html.

30. Melinda L. Reynolds, Student Author, *Landowner Liability for Terrorist Acts*, 47 Case W. Res. L. Rev. 155, 184 (1996).

31. Joseph T. McCann, *Terrorism on American Soil: A Concise History of Plots and Perpetrators from the Famous to the Forgotten* (Boulder, CO: Sentient Publications, 2006), 231.

32. NEFA Foundation, "United States v. Shnewer et al—Fort Dix Trial," http://www1.nefafoundation.org/ftdixdocs.html.

33. Sun Tzu, *Art of War*, 179.

CHAPTER 2: THE ENVIRONMENTAL NEXUS TO TERRORISM

1. Gérard Chaliand and Arnaud Blin, eds., "Preface," in *The History of Terrorism: From Antiquity to Al Qaeda*, trans. Edward Schneider, Kathryn Pulver, and Jesse Browner (Berkeley: University of California Press, 2007), 6–7; National Academies, *Understanding and Responding to Climate Change*, Highlights of National Academies Reports 2008 Edition; Pew Center on Global Climate Change and the Pew Center on the States, *Climate Change 101: Understanding and Responding to Global Climate Change*, January 2009, 1, which discusses various reports concerning climate change.

2. Carolyn Merchant, *American Environmental History: An Introduction* (New York: Columbia University Press, 2007), 194–209.

3. Intergovernmental Panel on Climate Change, *Climate Change 2007: Synthesis Report, 2007*, 56, http://www.ipcc.ch/pdf/assessment-report/ar4/syr/ar4_syr_spm.pdf.

4. Paul R. Ehrlich and Anne H. Ehrlich, *The Dominant Animal: Human Evolution and the Environment* (Washington, DC: Island Press, 2008), 258–63.

5. Intergovernmental Panel on Climate Change, *Climate Change 2007*, 30.

6. Ibid., 31.

7. Ibid., 37.

8. Ibid., 41.

9. Ibid., 41.

10. Ibid., 53.

11. National Academies, "Understanding and Responding to Climate Change," 4–17, http://americasclimatechoices.org/climate_change_2008_final.pdf.

12. Ibid.

13. National Research Council of the National Academies, *Ecological Impacts of Climate Change* (Washington, DC: National Academies Press, 2008), 4–8, http://www.nap.edu/catalog.php?record_id=12491.

14. Jared Diamond, *Collapse: How Societies Choose to Fail or Succeed* (New York: Penguin Books), 479–83.

15. Thomas F. Homer-Dixon, "Environmental Scarcities and Violent Conflict: Evidence from Cases," *International Security* 19, no. 1 (Summer 1994): 6; Ehrlich and Ehrlich, *Dominant Animal*, 236–46; Diamond, *Collapse*, 486–96.

16. Diamond, *Collapse*, 491–92; Ronald G. Burns, Michael J. Lynch, and Paul Stretesky, *Environmental Law, Crime, and Justice* (New York: LFB Scholarly Publishing, 2008), 9–22.

17. James Inhofe, "Consensus Is No Such Thing," *U.S. News and World Report*, April 2010, 20.

18. George F. Will, "Everyone Out of the Water!" *Newsweek*, November 16, 2009, 32.

19. Merchant, *American Environmental History*, 221.

20. Jeff Goodell, "As the World Burns," *Rolling Stone*, January 21, 2010, 31–34. "They pointed to a study by the Heritage Foundation, long a purveyor of junk science favored by the energy industry. . . . Not surprisingly, the Heritage study predicted economic disaster if the climate bill were signed into law." Ibid., 33.

21. Ehrlich and Ehrlich, *Dominant Animal*, 339; Thomas L. Friedman, *Hot, Flat, and Crowded* (New York: Farrar, Straus, and Giroux, 2008), 137–39; James Hansen, *Storms of My Grandchildren: The Truth about the Coming Climate Catastrophe and Our Last Chance to Save Humanity* (New York: Bloomsbury, 2009), 167–68; Jeff Goodell, "As the World Burns"; Tim Dickinson, "The Climate Killers: Meet the 17 Polluters and Deniers Who Are Derailing Efforts to Curb Global Warming," *Rolling Stone*, January 21, 2010, 35–41; John M. Broder, "Modest Deal on Emissions Concludes Climate Talks," *New York Times International*, December 12, 2010.

22. Pew Center on Global Climate Change, *Summary: Copenhagen Climate Summit*, http://www.pewclimate.org/docUploads/copenhagen-cop15-summary.pdf. See Nick Sundt, "Texas Congressman in Copenhagen Dismisses Climate Science: 'We Don't Have an Icecap in Texas,'" WWF Climate Blog, December 23, 2009, http://www.climatesciencewatch.org/index.php/csw/details/barton-sensenbrenner-copenhagen.

23. Brett Pelham, "Awareness, Opinions about Global Warming Vary Worldwide," Gallup, April 22, 2009, http://www.gallup.com/poll/117772/awareness-opinions-global-warming-vary-worldwide.aspx.

24. Jeffrey Jones, "In U.S., Outlook for Environmental Quality Improving," Gallup, April 21, 2009, http://www.gallup.com/poll/117769/outlook-environmental-quality-improving.aspx.

25. Geoffrey D. Dabelko, "Environmental Security Heats Up," *Environmental Change and Security Program Report* 13 (2008–9): viii; Center for Naval Analysis, *Naval Security and the Threat of Climate Change* (Alexandria, VA: CNA Corporation, 2007), http://securityandclimate.cna.org/report/SecurityandClimate_Final.pdf; Robert M. Gates, *National Defense Strategy*, U.S. Department of Defense, June

2008, http://www.defenselink.mil/news/2008%20national%20defense%20strat egy.pdf.

26. Thucydides, *The Peloponnesian War*, ed. Martin Hammond (New York: Oxford University Press, 2009), 209.

27. Exodus 14:21–28.

28. Sun Tzu, *The Art of War*, ed. Ralph D. Sawyer (New York: Barnes and Nobel, 1994), 227 and note 215.

29. Peter H. Gleick, "Water and Conflict: Freshwater Resources and International Security," *International Security* 18, no. 1 (Summer 1993): 85–87, citing M. S. Drower, "Water-Supply, Irrigation, and Agriculture," in *A History of Technology*, ed. C. Singer, E. J. Holmyard, and A. R. Hall (New York: Oxford University Press, 1954); Nelson Marmiroli, Marta Marmiroli, and Elena Maestri, "Monitoring of Environmental Resources against Intentional Threats," in *Threats to Food and Water Chain Infrastructure*, ed. V. Koukouliou et al. (Dordrecht, Netherlands: Springer, 2010), 51, http://www.springerlink.com/content/g6703763h113p407.

30. Alexis de Tocqueville, *Democracy in America*, trans. and ed. Harvey C. Mansfield and Delba Winthrop (Chicago: University of Chicago Press, 2000), 307–11; David D. Smits, "The Frontier Army and the Destruction of the Buffalo: 1865–1883," *Western Historical Quarterly* 25, no. 3 (Autumn 1994): 313–38.

31. Richard A. Matthew and Bryan McDonald, "Environmental Security: Academic and Policy Debates in North America," in *Facing Global Environmental Change: Environmental, Human, Energy, Food, Health, and Water Security Concepts*, ed. Hans Gunter Brauch et al. (Berlin, Germany: Springer, 2009), 792, http://www.springerlink.com/content/h52t18631j1363j5.

32. Daniel M. Schwartz, "Environmental Terrorism: Analyzing the Concept," *Journal of Peace Research* 35, no. 4 (July 1988): 483–96, http://www.jstor.org/pss/425754.

33. Ibid., 484.

34. Ibid., 485–91.

35. See Robert Arthur Baird, "Pyro-Terrorism—The Threat of Arson-Induced Forest Fires as a Future Terrorist Weapon of Mass Destruction," *Studies in Conflict and Terrorism* 29, no. 5 (2006): 419–23.

36. Schwartz, "Environmental Terrorism," 484 and note 3.

37. See Elizabeth L. Chalecki, "A New Vigilance: Identifying and Reducing the Risks of Environmental Terrorism," *Global Environmental Politics* 2, no. 1 (February 2002): 50–55, http://www.mitpressjournals.org/toc/glep/2/1. Chalecki explains the use of the environment as a tool and as a target of terrorism: "The former occurs when environmental resources such as crops, livestock, or water supplies are used as a delivery vehicle to carry a destructive agent to a human population."

38. Jessica Tuchman-Mathews, "Redefining Security," *Foreign Affairs* 68, no. 2 (Spring 1979): 162–77; Environmental Protection Agency, "National Security Implications of Global Climate Change," http://www.epa.gov/climatechange/effects/forests.html.

39. Matthew and McDonald, "Environmental Security: Academic and Policy Debates," 792–96.

40. Ibid., 793.

41. Tuchman-Mathews, "Redefining Security," 162.

42. Robert Kaplan, "The Coming Anarchy," *Atlantic*, February 1994.

43. Matthew and McDonald, "Environmental Security: Academic and Policy Debates," 793–94.

44. Matthew and McDonald, "Environmental Security: Academic and Policy Debates," 795; Richard A. Matthew, Ted Gaulin, and Bryan McDonald, "The Elusive Quest: Linking Environmental Change and Conflict," *Canadian Journal of Political Science* 36, no. 4 (September 2003): 857–78; Thomas F. Homer-Dixon and Marc A. Levy, "Correspondence: Environment and Security," *International Security* 20, no. 3 (Winter 1995/96): 189–98; Marc A. Levy, "Is the Environment a National Security Issue," *International Security* 20, no. 2 (Fall 1995): 35–62.

45. George H. W. Bush, *A National Security Strategy for the United States* (Washington, DC: White House, 1991), http://www.fas.org/man/docs/918015-nss.htm.

46. Ehrlich and Ehrlich, *The Dominant Animal*, 355–56; Al Gore, "Introduction," in *An Inconvenient Truth: The Planetary Emergency of Global Warming and What We Can Do about It* (New York: Rodale, 2006).

47. Gleick, "Water and Conflict," 79–83.

48. Homer-Dixon and Levy, "Correspondence," 56; Thomas F. Homer-Dixon, "Environmental Scarcities and Violent Conflict," *International Security* 19, no. 1 (Summer 1994): 189–98.

49. Center for Naval Analysis, "National Security and the Threat of Climate Change," 9–10, http://securityandclimate.cna.org/report; United Nations Environment Program, *From Conflict to Peacebuilding: The Role of Natural Resources and the Environment* (Nairobi, Kenya: United Nations Environment Program, 2009), 6–11, http://www.unep.org/pdf/pcdmb_policy_01.pdf.

50. United Nations Environment Program, *From Conflict to Peacebuilding*, 6–11.

51. Center for Naval Analysis, "National Security and the Threat," 9–10.

52. United Nations Environment Program, *From Conflict to Peacebuilding*, 6–11. A 2009 report on climate change, prepared by the United Nations General Assembly, states that "the nature and full degree of the security implications of climate change are still largely untested." United Nations General Assembly, *Climate Change and Its Possible Security Implications: Report of the Secretary-General*, September 2009, 4, http://www.unhcr.org/refworld/docid/4ad5e6380.html.

53. *Goldwater-Nichols Department of Defense Reorganization Act of 1986*, U.S. *Code* 50, sec. 404a.

54. Bush, *A National Security Strategy*.

55. Bush, "The Environment," in *A National Security Strategy* (see note 45).

56. Barack Obama, "Introduction," in *National Security Strategy* (Washington, DC: White House, 2010), http://www.whitehouse.gov/sites/default/files/rss_viewer/national_security_strategy.pdf.

57. Ibid., 1.

58. Zbigniew Brzezinski and Brent Scowcroft, *America and the World: Conversations on the Future of American Foreign Policy* (New York: Basic Books, 2008), 241–43.

59. Obama, *National Security Strategy*, 5.

60. Ibid., 8.

61. Ibid., 30.

62. Ibid., 47.

63. Ibid.

64. Ibid.

65. Ibid., 49–50.

66. Ibid., 50.

67. Ibid., 51.

68. United Nations Environment Program, *From Conflict to Peacebuilding* (New York: United Nations Security Council, 2008) 9; Ban Ki Moon, "A Climate Culprit in Darfur," *Washington Post,* June 16, 2007.

69. United Nations Environment Program, *From Conflict to Peacebuilding*; Ban Ki Moon, "A Climate Culprit in Darfur," *Washington Post,* June 16, 2007.

70. United Nations General Assembly, *Climate Change and Its Possible Security Implications: Report of the Secretary-General,* September 11, 2009, A/64/350, 6–7, http://www.unhcr.org/refworld/docid/4ad5e6380.html.

71. Ibid., 9–20.

72. Ibid., 7–26.

73. Jonathan B. Tucker, ed., *Toxic Terror: Assessing Terrorist Use of Chemical and Biological Weapons* (Cambridge, MA: MIT Press, 2000), 6–14.

74. Jonathan Fighel, "The 'Forest Jihad,'" International Institute for Counter-Terrorism, October 28, 2008, 1–7, http://www.ict.org.il/Articles/tabid/66/Articlsid/506/currentpage/1/Default.aspx.

75. Ibid.

76. United States Fire Administration, "Wildland Fires: A Historical Perspective," *U.S. Fire Administration Topical Fire Research Series* 1, no. 3 (October 2000, Rev. December 2001), http://www.usfa.dhs.gov/downloads/pdf/tfrs/v1i3-508.pdf.

77. Joshua Rhett Miller, "Australian Wildfires Could Fuel 'Forest Jihad' Terrorists, Experts Say," FOX News, February 9, 2009, http://www.foxnews.com/story/0,2933,490306,00.html.

78. Baird, "Pyro-Terrorism," 415–28.

79. Federal Bureau of Investigation, "Terrorism: 2002–2005," *Terrorism in the United States,* 13, http://www.fbi.gov/stats-services/publications/terrorism-2002-2005/terror02_05.pdf.

80. Choe Sang-Hun, "South Korea Demands Apology from North over Dam Incident," *New York Times,* September 9, 2009, http://www.nytimes.com/2009/09/09/world/asia/09korea.html.

81. "Sri Lanka Rebels 'Lose Last Town,'" *Al Jazeera,* January 26, 2009, http://english.aljazeera.net/news/asia/2009/01/2009125133055917676.html.

82. Jane Perlez and Pir Zubair Shah, "Confronting Taliban, Pakistan Finds Itself at War," *New York Times (Asia Pacific),* October 2, 2008, http://www.nytimes.com/2008/10/03/world/asia/03pstan.html.

83. Tucker, *Toxic Terror,* 154.

84. Michael T. Osterholm and John Schwartz, *Living Terrors: What America Needs to Know to Survive the Coming Bioterrorist Catastrophe* (New York: Delacorte Press, 2000), 87–90.

85. Marmiroli, Marmiroli, and Maestri, "Monitoring of Environmental Resources," 51–67.

86. United States Department of Health and Human Services, Centers for Disease Control and Prevention, "Botulism," http://www.cdc.gov/nczved/dfbmd/disease_listing/botulism_gi.html.

87. Judith Miller, Stephen Engelberg, and William Broad, *Germs: Biological Weapons and America's Secret War* (New York: Simon and Schuster, 2001), 15–33.

88. Al Qaeda's 11-volume *Encyclopedia of Afghan Jihad* contains a section on conducting assassinations with poisons: "Poisoning from eating spoiled food. Since 0.000028 gram will kill a person, this poison is absolutely lethal. How to prepare spoiled food. Fill a pot with corn and green beans. Put in a small piece of meat and about two spoonfuls of excrement." Al Qaeda, "Examples of Training Manuals for Terrorism and Guerilla Warfare," appendix to *The Making of a Terrorist*, vol. 2, *Training*, ed. James J. F. Forest (Westport, CT: Praeger Security International, 2006), 319.

89. Thomas F. Homer-Dixon, *Environment, Scarcity, and Violence* (Princeton, NJ: Princeton University Press, 1999), 12–18.

90. National Commission on Terrorist Attacks upon the United States, *The 9/11 Commission Report* (New York: W. W. Norton, n.d.), 380.

91. Federal Bureau of Investigation, "Anthrax Investigation: Closing a Chapter," *Headline Archives*, August 6, 2008, http://www.fbi.gov/page2/august08/amerithrax080608a.html.

92. Osterholm and Schwartz, *Living Terrors*, 78–90.

93. Ibid., 85.

94. Ibid., 49–51.

95. United States Fire Administration, "Wildland Fires: A Historical Perspective."

96. Herman Shugart, Roger Sedjo, and Brent Sohngen, *Forest and Global Climate Change: Potential Impacts on U.S. Forest Resources*, Pew Center on Global Climate Change, 2003, 1–64, http://www.pewclimate.org/docUploads/forestry.pdf.

97. United States Fire Administration, "Fires in the Wildland/Urban Interface," *U.S. Fire Administration Topical Fire Research Series* 2, no. 16 (March 2002), 1–4, http://www.usfa.dhs.gov/downloads/pdf/tfrs/v2i16-508.pdf.

98. Ibid.

99. Nick Wadhams, "Endangered Gorillas Held Hostage by Rebels in African Park," *National Geographic News*, May 23, 2007, http://news.nationalgeographic.com/news/2007/05/070523-gorillas-hostage.html; International Union for Conservation of Nature, "Gorilla beringei ssp. beringei," *The IUCN Red List of Threatened Species*, 2008, http://www.iucnredlist.org/apps/redlist/details/39999/0.

100. Dennis Cauchon, "Invasive Carp Threatens Great Lakes," *USA Today*, December 12, 2009, http://www.usatoday.com/news/nation/2009-11-30-asian-carp_N.htm.

101. Stefan Lovgren, "Huge, Freed Pet Pythons Invade Florida Everglades," *National Geographic News*, June 3, 2004, http://news.nationalgeographic.com/news/2004/06/0603_040603_invasivespecies.html.

102. See Lizzy Davies, "French Transport Workers Threaten to Pollute River Seine," *Guardian News and Media*, August 20, 2009, http://www.guardian.co.uk/environment/2009/aug/20/france-transport-river-seine-pollution. Ms. Davies is one of many sources for Antoine Faucher's comments concerning the threatened poisoning of the River Seine.

103. John Lichfield, "First They Poisoned the River. Now the Desperate Workers of Givet Threaten to Blow Up Their Town," *Independent*, July 19, 2000, http://www.independent.co.uk/news/world/europe/first-they-poisoned-the-river-now-the-desperate-workers-of-givet-threaten-to-blow-up-their-town-707736.html.

104. Middle East Media Research Institute (MEMRI), "Islamist Forum Member Proposes Poisoning Water Systems of Major American Cities," *The Jihad and*

Terrorism Threat Monitor 2021, August 12, 2008, http://www.memrijttm.org/content/en/report.htm?report=2829.

105.   See Stephanie Berrong, "The Golden Rule," *Security Management*, May 2010, 84–90. Berrong describes the vulnerabilities and security issues involved in the operation of Latin America's largest gold mine. The mine, called Yanacocha, is located in Peru in the Andes Mountains but is owned by a U.S. company.

106.   See Robert Elliott, "Crude Oil and Corruption," *Security Management*, June 2007, 67–74. Elliott examines the problems facing multinational oil companies operating in Nigeria. Security issues involve an insurgent movement that uses the terrorist tactics of kidnappings, bombings, and sabotage.

107.   Doron Elhanani, "Environmental Protection vs. Eco and Environmental Terrorism: Threats, Impact, and Contingency Plans," in *GeoSpatial Visual Analytics: Geographical Information Processing and Visual Analytics for Environmental Security*, ed. R. De Amicis et al. (Dordrecht, Netherlands: Springer, 2008), 483–86, which claims high priority should be given to protection of water- and oil-related targets; for an environmental activist's perspective on the bombings of EnCana's pipelines, see "Targeting EnCana," *Resistance: Journal of the Earth Liberation Movement* (Fall 2009): 32–34.

108.   Elhanani, "Environmental Protection vs. Eco and Environmental Terrorism."

CHAPTER 3: THE BASIC CONCEPTS OF TERRORISM

1.   NBC News, "Gunman Kills 12, Wounds 31 at Fort Hood," November 5, 2009, http://www.msnbc.msn.com/id/33678801; KWTX News, "Hasan Trial Date Moved," June 1, 2010, http://www.kbtx.com/home/headlines/95329534.html.

2.   Federal Bureau of Investigation, "In Focus: 30 Years of Terrorism," *Terrorism in the United States 1999*, 15.

3.   Caleb Carr, *The Lessons of Terror: A History of Warfare Against Civilians*, rev. ed. (New York: Random House Trade Paperback, 2003), 31–32.

4.   Ibid., 6.

5.   Albert Parry, *Terrorism: From Robespierre to Arafat* (New York: Vanguard Press, 1976), 40–54.

6.   Nikolai Morozov, "The Terrorist Struggle," in *Voices of Terror: Manifestos, Writings, and Manuals of Al Qaeda, Hamas, and Other Terrorists from Around the World and Throughout the Ages*, ed. Walter Laqueur (New York: Reed Press, 2004), 76.

7.   See Bruce Hoffman, *Inside Terrorism* (New York: Columbia University Press, 1998), 24–37, for an excellent description of this ongoing debate.

8.   Hoffman, *Inside Terrorism*, 43.

9.   Jeffrey F. Addicott, *Terrorism Law: The Rule of Law and the War on Terror*, 2nd ed. (Tucson, AZ: Lawyers and Judges, 2004), 11.

10.   Richard A. Falk, "A Duel Reality: Terrorism against the State and Terrorism by the State," in *New Global Terrorism: Characteristics, Causes, Controls*, ed. Charles W. Kegley (Upper Saddle River, NJ: Prentice Hall, 2003), 53–59.

11.   Addicott, *Terrorism Law*, 4.

12.   Mark Juergensmeyer, *Terror in the Mind of God: The Global Rise of Religious Violence*, 3rd ed. (Berkeley and Los Angeles: University of California Press, 2003), 9.

13. Walter Laqueur, *No End to War: Terrorism in the Twenty-First Century* (New York: Continuum International, 2003), 139; Steven Best and Anthony J. Nocella II, "Defining Terrorism," appendix 3 in *Terrorists or Freedom Fighters? Reflections on the Liberation of Animals* (New York: Lantern Books, 2004), 361–77.

14. Nicholas J. Perry, "The Numerous Federal Legal Definitions of Terrorism: The Problem of Too Many Grails," *Journal of Legislation* 30 (2004): 249–55; for the international community's approach to this issue, cf. John Norton Moore and Robert F. Turner, eds., *National Security Law*, 2nd ed. (Durham, NC: Carolina Academic Press, 2005), 462–63.

15. M. E. Bowman, "Domestic Terrorism," in *National Security Law* (see note 14), 971–72 and note 19 on page 971.

16. M. E. Bowman, "Domestic Terrorism," 972.

17. *U.S. Code* 50, sec. 1801 (c) (2006).

18. *U.S. Code* 18, sec. 2331 (1) (2006).

19. M. E. Bowman, "Domestic Terrorism," 977.

20. Perry, "Numerous Federal Legal Definitions of Terrorism," 257.

21. Hoffman, *Inside Terrorism*, 25; Laqueur, *No End to War*, 140. cf. Richard Falk, "A Duel Reality," in *New Global Terrorism* (see note 10), 54. Falk defines terrorism as "any type of political violence that lacks an adequate moral and legal justification, regardless of whether the actor is a revolutionary group or the government."

22. Walter Laqueur, ed., "Introduction," in *Voices of Terror* (see note 6), 8–9.

23. Walter Laqueur, *Terrorism: A Study of National and International Political Violence* (Boston: Little, Brown, 1977), 7–9; Andrew Sinclair, *An Anatomy of Terror: A History of Terrorism* (London: Macmillan, 2003), 5–30.

24. Susan Sorek, *Jews against Rome: War in Palestine AD 66-73* (London: Continuum, 2008), 34–35; Bernard Lewis, *The Assassins: A Radical Sect in Islam* (New York: Basic Books, 1968), 125–40; Andrew Sinclair, *An Anatomy of Terror: A History of Terrorism* (London: Macmillan, 2003), 5–30.

25. Max Nomad, *Apostles of Revolution* (Boston: Little, Brown, 1939), 146–200; Jonathan R. White, *Terrorism and Homeland Security*, 6th ed. (Belmont, CA: Wadsworth Cengage Learning, 2009), 126–30; Parry, *Terrorism: From Robespierre to Arafat*, 82–90.

26. Sinclaire, *An Anatomy of Terror*, 130–34; David C. Rapoport, "The Four Waves of Rebel Terror and September 11," in *New Global Terrorism* (see note 10), 36–40.

27. Rapoport, "The Four Waves of Rebel Terror and September 11," 36–40.

28. Sanford J. Ungar, *FBI: An Uncensored Look Behind the Walls* (Boston and Toronto: Little, Brown, 1976), 42–45; James Lardner and Thomas Reppetto, *NYPD: A City and Its Police* (New York: Henry Holt, 2000), 186–89.

29. For a thorough examination of the influence of Crna ruka on Gavrilo Princip's actions, see Hoffman, *Inside Terrorism*, 22–23.

30. John Weinzierl, "Terrorism: Its Origin and History," in *Understanding Terrorism: Threats in an Uncertain World*, ed. Akorlie A. Nyatepe-Coo and Dorothy Zeisler-Vralsted (Upper Saddle River, NJ: Prentice Hall, 2004), 34–35; Gérard Chaliand and Arnaud Blin, "Terrorism in Time of War," in *The History of Terrorism: From Antiquity to Al Qaeda*, ed. Gérard Chaliand and Arnaud Blin, trans. Edward Schneider, Kathryn Pulver, and Jesse Browner (Berkeley: University of California Press, 2007), 211–13.

31. Tim Pat Coogan, *The IRA: A History* (Niwot, CO: Roberts Rinehart, 1994), 3–4.

32. White, *Terrorism and Homeland Security*, 152; Coogan, *The IRA: A History*, 290–93.

33. Chaliand and Blin, "Terrorism in Time of War," 208–17; White, *Terrorism and Homeland Security*, 166–68.

34. Rapoport, "The Four Waves of Rebel Terror," 41–43.

35. Leonard Zeskind, *Blood and Politics: The History of the White Nationalist Movement from the Margins to the Mainstream* (New York: Farrar, Straus, and Giroux, 2009), 540–42; Coogan, *The IRA: A History*, 341–43.

36. Philip Lamy, *Millennium Rage: Survivalists, White Supremacists, and the Doomsday Prophecy* (New York: Plenum Press, 1996), 115–34.

37. Carr, *The Lessons of Terror*, 73–77; Juergensmeyer, *Terror in the Mind of God*, 6–7.

38. White, *Terrorism and Homeland Security*, 262–64.

39. Juergensmeyer, *Terror in the Mind of God*, 21–22.

40. Lamy, *Millennium Rage*, 132–34.

41. Federal Bureau of Investigation, *In Focus*, 40–41.

42. Lou Michel and Dan Herbeck, *American Terrorist: Timothy McVeigh and the Tragedy at Oklahoma City* (New York: Avon Books, 2002), 1; Joseph T. McCann, *Terrorism on American Soil: A Concise History of Plots and Perpetrators from the Famous to the Forgotten* (Boulder, CO: Sentient Publications, 2006), 221 (Theodore Kaczynski).

43. For a complete treatment of this subject, see James Adams, *The Financing of Terror: How the Groups That Are Terrorizing the World Get the Money to Do It* (New York: Simon and Schuster, 1986), 179–218.

44. Letizia Paoli, *Mafia Brotherhoods: Organized Crime, Italian Style* (New York: Oxford University Press, 2003), 207.

45. Bernard Lewis, *The Assassins: A Radical Sect in Islam* (New York: Basic Books, 1968), 130–34.

46. Sergey Nechaev, "Catechism of the Revolutionist (1869)," in *Voices of Terror* (see note 6), 71–75.

47. Laqueur, *Terrorism*, 34–38.

48. Yves Ternon, "Russian Terrorism, 1878–1908," in *History of Terrorism* (see note 30), 156–57.

49. Olivier Hubac-Occhipinti, "Anarchist Terrorists of the 19th Century," in *History of Terrorism* (see note 30), 116–23.

50. White, *Terrorism and Homeland Security*, 51–52.

51. Louis Beam, "Leaderless Resistance," in *The Seditionist* 12 (February 1992): 2–4, http://www.louisbeam.com/leaderless.htm; Federal Bureau of Investigation, "In Focus," 18.

52. Andrew H. Kydd and Barbara F. Walter, "The Strategies of Terrorism," *International Security* 31, no. 1 (Summer 2006): 52.

53. Ariel Merari, "Terrorism as a Strategy of Insurgency," in *History of Terrorism* (see note 30), 31.

54. Terrorists, both group and individual, can employ conventional squad and individual military tactics against most civilian police forces. However, if they become successful with actions directed at the police, the military will be brought in, and the terrorists will either have to adapt their tactics or be eliminated. See Parry,

Terrorism: From Robespierre to Arafat, 278–80, for an explication of this principle as applied to the Uruguayan Tupamaro terrorist organization.

55. Merari, "Terrorism as a Strategy of Insurgency," in *History of Terrorism* (see note 30), 33; Gregory A. Raymond, "The Evolving Strategies of Political Terrorism," in *New Global Terrorism* (see note 10), 72–74.

56. Brigitte L. Nacos, *Terrorism and Counterterrorism: Understanding Threats and Responses in the Post 9/11 World,* 3rd ed. (Boston: Pearson-Longman, 2010), 37.

57. Carlos Marighella, *Minimanual of the Urban Guerrilla,* 30, http://ballistichel met.org/school/urban_warfare.pdf.

58. Martha Crenshaw, "The Effectiveness of Terrorism in the Algerian War," in *Terrorism in Context,* ed. Martha Crenshaw (University Park: Pennsylvania State University Press, 2001), 474.

59. Merari, "Terrorism as a Strategy," 34.

60. Ibid., 35–36.

61. Ibid., 36–37.

62. Raymond, "The Evolving Strategies of Political Terrorism," in *New Global Terrorism* (see note 10), 72–74.

63. Martha Crenshaw, "The Causes of Terrorism," in *New Global Terrorism* (see note 10), 96–99.

64. Brian M. Jenkins, "International Terrorism: The Other World War," in *New Global Terrorism* (see note 10), 23.

65. Laqueur, *Terrorism,* 93; Sinclair, *An Anatomy of Terror,* 360.

66. Marighella, *Minimanual of the Urban Guerrilla,* 6–7.

67. Chaliand and Blin, *History of Terrorism,* 179–80.

68. Isaac Cronin, *Confronting Fear: A History of Terrorism* (New York: Thunder's Mouth Press, 2002), 17–21.

69. Simon Reeve, *The New Jackals: Ramzi Yousef, Osama bin Laden, and the Future of Terrorism* (Boston: Northeastern University Press, 1999), 154; James M. Poland, *Understanding Terrorism: Groups, Strategies, and Responses* (Upper Saddle River, NJ: Prentice Hall, 2011), 171–74.

70. A variety of media sources have recounted the travails of the "hot foot" and "hot crotch" bombers. See, e.g., Mark Hosenball, Michael Isikoff, and Evan Thomas, "The Radicalization of Umar Farouk Abdulmutallab," *Newsweek,* January 11, 2010, 37.

71. Poland, *Understanding Terrorism,* 176.

72. Ibid., 185.

73. Ibid., 200–201.

74. Ibid., 181–83.

75. Nathan I. Yungher, *Terrorism: The Bottom Line* (Upper Saddle River, NJ: Prentice Hall, 2008), 221–23.

76. Ibid.

77. Nacos, *Terrorism and Counterterrorism,* 40.

78. National Consortium for the Study of Terrorism and Responses to Terrorism (START), data from "Global Terrorism Database," GTD ID#200408240001, http://www.start.umd.edu/gtd (accessed August 27, 2010).

79. Margaret G. Hermann and Charles F. Hermann, "Hostage Taking, the Presidency, and Stress," in *Origins of Terrorism: Psychologies, Ideologies, Theologies, States of Mind,* ed. Walter Reich (Washington, DC: Woodrow Wilson Center Press, 1998), 211–13; Poland, *Understanding Terrorism,* 142–43.

80. National Consortium for the Study of Terrorism and Responses to Terrorism (START), data from "Global Terrorism Database," http://www.start.umd.edu/gtd (accessed February 28, 2010).

81. Ibid.

82. Ibid.

83. United States Department of Justice, *Amerithrax Investigative Summary*, February 19, 2010, 1–3, http://www.justice.gov/amerithrax/docs/amx-investigative-summary.pdf.

84. National Consortium for the Study of Terrorism and Responses to Terrorism (START), data from "Global Terrorism Database," GTD ID#200402020010, 200310150003, and 200311120005, http://www.start.umd.edu/gtd (accessed February 28, 2010).

85. National Consortium for the Study of Terrorism and Responses to Terrorism (START), data from "Global Terrorism Database," GTD ID#199810250005, http://www.start.umd.edu/gtd (accessed February 28, 2010); Jessica Stern, *The Ultimate Terrorists* (Cambridge, MA: Harvard University Press, 1999), 60.

86. See Stern, *The Ultimate Terrorists*, 77–86. "Two kinds of groups are of particular concern: millenarian groups, including Christian Patriots, and radical Islamic fundamentalists organized as ad hoc groups." Ibid., 85–86.

87. See Nacos, *Terrorism and Counterterrorism*, 281.

CHAPTER 4: THE TERRORIST MINDSET

1. United States Department of Justice, "Nine Members of a Militia Group Charged with Seditious Conspiracy and Related Charges," March 29, 2010, http://www.justice.gov/opa/pr/2010/March/10-ag-334.html.

2. *United States v. Stone*, 2:10-cr-20123, indictment at 1–5 (E.D. Mich., filed Mar. 23, 2010).

3. Claudia Boyd-Barrett and Mark Reiter, "Prosecutor: Militia Plotted against U.S.," *Pittsburgh Post-Gazette*, April 1, 2010, final edition.

4. Ibid.

5. Rex A. Hudson, *Who Becomes a Terrorist and Why: The 1999 Government Report on Profiling Terrorists* (Guilford, CT: Lyons Press, 2002), 97–100.

6. Randy Borum, "Understanding the Terrorist Mindset," *FBI Law Enforcement Bulletin*, July 2003, 1–2, http://works.bepress.com/randy_borum/7.

7. Mont Judd Harmon, *Political Thought: From Plato to the Present* (New York: McGraw Hill, 1964), 154–57.

8. Niccolò Machiavelli, *The Prince*, trans. Ninian Hill Thompson (Norwalk, CT: Easton Press, 1980), 122–31.

9. Harmon, *Political Thought*, 215–20; Peter Brimacombe, *Guy Fawkes Gunpowder Plot*, Pitkin Guides (Norwich, UK: Jarrold Publishing, 2005), 1–19; Guy Fawkes's first name, Guy, became a term that was applied to all young, adventurous males who still make up the overwhelming percentage of terrorists; Mark Juergensmeyer, *Terror in the Mind of God: The Global Rise of Religious Violence*, 3rd ed. (Berkeley and Los Angeles: University of California Press, 2003), 201.

10. Thomas Hobbes, *The Leviathan*, ed. Francis B. Randall (New York: Washington Square Press, 1964), 84.

11. Ibid., 118–22.

12. Alexander Hamilton, James Madison, and John Jay, *The Federalist*, ed. Benjamin Fletcher Wright (New York: Metro Books, 1961), 26–29.

13. Steven Pinker, *The Blank Slate: The Modern Denial of Human Nature* (New York: Penguin Group, 2002), 315–29; impulsiveness in children often begins a path that results in those children becoming violent criminals by early adulthood. Daniel Goleman, *Emotional Intelligence: Why It Can Matter More Than IQ* (New York: Bantam Books, 1995), 278.

14. Paul R. Ehrlich and Anne H. Ehrlich, *Dominant Animal: Human Evolution and the Environment* (Washington, DC: Island Press, 2008), 55–96.

15. Ibid., 102.

16. Ibid., 89–103.

17. Ibid., 104.

18. Irenäus Eibl-Eibesfeldt, *The Biology of Peace and War: Men, Animals, and Aggression*, trans. Eric Mosbacher (New York: Viking Press, 1979), 86–96.

19. Ibid., 240.

20. Carlos Marighella, *Minimanual of the Urban Guerrilla*, 8, http://ballistichel met.org/school/urban_warfare.pdf.

21. Morton Hunt, *The Story of Psychology* (New York: Doubleday, 1993), 200–207; John Horgan, *The Psychology of Terrorism* (New York: Routledge, 2005), 60–62.

22. Horgan, *The Psychology of Terrorism*, 331–49.

23. Jerrold M. Post, "Terrorist Psycho-Logic: Terrorist Behavior as a Product of Psychological Forces," in *Origins of Terrorism: Psychologies, Ideologies, Theologies, States of Mind*, ed. Walter Reich (Washington, DC: Woodrow Wilson Center Press, 1998), 27–38; "Explanations of terrorism at the level of individual psychology are insufficient in trying to understand why people become involved in terrorism." Jerrold M. Post, *The Mind of the Terrorist: The Psychology of Terrorism from the IRA to Al-Qaeda* (New York: Palgrave MacMillan, 2007), 7.

24. Post, "Terrorist Psycho-Logic," 28–31.

25. Horgan, *The Psychology of Terrorism*, 76.

26. Eric Hoffer, *The True Believer: Thoughts on the Nature of Mass Movements* (New York: Perennial Classics, 2002), xii.

27. Ibid., 58–125.

28. Ibid., 107.

29. Ted Robert Gurr, *Why Men Rebel* (Princeton, NJ: Princeton University Press, 1970), 13.

30. Bruce Hoffman, *Inside Terrorism* (New York: Columbia University Press, 1998), 183.

31. Ibid., 168–69.

32. John E. Douglas et al., *Crime Classification Manual: A Standard System for Investigating and Classifying Violent Crimes* (New York: Lexington Books/Macmillan, 1992), 21; Pinker, *The Blank Slate*, 315; Hoffman, *Inside Terrorism*, 169.

33. Donatella della Porta, "Left-Wing Terrorism in Italy," in *Terrorism in Context*, ed. Martha Crenshaw (University Park: Pennsylvania State University Press, 2001), 139–41.

34. Ibid., 144.

35. Frederick J. Hacker, *Crusaders, Criminals, Crazies: Terror and Terrorism in Our Time* (New York: W. W. Norton, 1976), 8.

36. Ibid., 12.

37. Horgan, *The Psychology of Terrorism*, 50–53.

38. Robert D. Hare, *Without Conscience: The Disturbing World of Psychopaths Among Us* (New York: Pocket Books, 1993), 83–104. "Many psychopaths never go to prison or any other facility. They appear to function reasonably well—as lawyers, doctors, psychiatrists, academics, mercenaries, police officers, cult leaders, military personnel . . . and so forth—without breaking the law, or at least without being caught and convicted." Ibid., 113.

39. Ibid., 108–15.

40. Michael Burleigh, *Blood and Rage: A Cultural History of Terrorism* (New York: HarperCollins, 2009), 304–9; Burleigh is definitive in his description of Murphy: "Not all terrorists are psychopaths but Lenny Murphy of the Shankill Butchers undoubtedly was." Ibid., 592. See Tim Pat Coogan, *The IRA: A History* (Niwot, CO: Roberts Rinehart, 1994), for a description of the downfall of the Shankill Butchers.

41. Hacker, *Crusaders, Criminals, Crazies*, 8–9.

42. Ibid., 9.

43. Gurr, *Why Men Rebel*, 194.

44. Ibid., 196.

45. Albert Bandura, "Mechanisms of Moral Disengagement," in *Origins of Terrorism* (see note 23), 161–63.

46. Ibid., 171–72.

47. Ibid., 170–81.

48. David C. Rapoport, "Sacred Terror: A Contemporary Example from Islam," in *Origins of Terrorism* (see note 23), 119; a member of the Phineas Priesthood would poison the water supply of a major city and justify the act as necessary because he was at war with elements of our secular society. Mark Juergensmeyer, *Terror in the Mind of God*, 158.

49. Post, "Terrorist Psycho-Logic," 31–32.

50. Martha Crenshaw, "Logic of Terrorism: Terrorist Behavior as a Product of Strategic Choice," in *Origins of Terrorism* (see note 23), 8–9; Post, "Terrorist Psycho-Logic," 31–38.

51. Post, "Terrorist Psycho-Logic," 36.

52. Hoffman, *Inside Terrorism*, 168.

53. Bandura, "Mechanisms of Moral Disengagement," 176.

54. Walter Laqueur, *No End to War: Terrorism in the Twenty-First Century* (New York: Continuum International, 2003), 209–23; "The mindset of a terrorist group reflects the personality and ideology of its top leader and other circumstantial traits . . . as well as group dynamics." Hudson, *Who Becomes a Terrorist and Why*, 98.

55. Mitchell D. Silber and Arvin Bhatt, *Radicalization in the West: The Homegrown Threat* (New York: New York City Police Department, 2007), 16.

56. Todd C. Helmus, "Why and How Some People Become Terrorists," in *Social Science for Counterterrorism: Putting the Pieces Together*, ed. Paul K. Davis and Kim Cragin (Santa Monica, CA: RAND Corporation, 2009), 74–79, http://www.rand.org/pubs/monographs/MG849.html; Silber and Bhatt, *Radicalization in the West*, 5–7.

57. Helmus, "Why and How Some People Become Terrorists," 74–79; Silber and Bhatt, *Radicalization in the West*, 13–18.

58. Silber and Bhatt, *Radicalization in the West*, 16–20.

59. Tinka Veldhuis and Jørgen Staun, *Islamist Radicalisation: A Root Cause Model* (The Hague: Netherlands Institute of International Relations Clingendael, 2009), 2, http://www.clingendael.nl.

60. Marc Sageman, *Understanding Terror Networks* (Philadelphia: University of Pennsylvania Press, 2004), 1.

61. Hudson, *Who Becomes a Terrorist and Why*, 104–5.

62. See Veldhuis and Staun, *Islamist Radicalisation*, 4. "When people are ripe for a mass movement, they are usually ripe for any effective movement, and not solely for one with a particular doctrine or program." Hoffer, *The True Believer*, 16.

63. Carol Dyer, Ryan E. McCoy, Joel Rodriguez, and Donald N. Van Duyn, "Countering Violent Islamic Extremism: A Community Responsibility," *FBI Law Enforcement Bulletin* 76, no. 12 (December 2007): 4–7, http://www.fbi.gov/publi cations/leb/2007/dec2007/december2007leb.htm.

64. Helmus, "Why and How Some People Become Terrorists," 77–80; For an historical and current treatment of prisons as an incubator for radicalization, see J. Michael Waller, "Prisons as Terrorist Breeding Grounds," in *The Making of a Terrorist: Recruitment, Training, and Root Causes*, vol. 1, *Recruitment*, ed. James J. F. Forest (Westport, CT: Praeger Security International, 2006), 23.

65. Sageman, *Understanding Terror Networks*, 108–13.

66. See Brian Michael Jenkins, "Going Jihad: The Fort Hood Slayings and Home-Grown Terrorism," testimony presented before the Senate Homeland Security and Governmental Affairs Committee, CT 336, November 19, 2009 (Santa Monica, CA: RAND Corporation, November 2009), 1–5, http://www.rand.org/pubs/testimonies/CT336.html.

CHAPTER 5: THE RADICAL ENVIRONMENTAL MOVEMENT: ECO-WARRIORS OR TERRORISTS?

1. Marlise Simons, "Dutch Suspect in Slaying Championed Animal Rights," *New York Times*, May 9, 2002, late edition—final.

2. Ibid.

3. Marlise Simons, "Dutch Court Sentences Killer of Politician to 18-Year Term," *New York Times*, April 16, 2003.

4. Rik Scarce, *Eco-Warriors: Understanding the Radical Environmental Movement* (Walnut Creek, CA: Left Coast Press, 2006), 284–85; North American Earth Liberation Front Press Office (NAELFPO), "Frequently Asked Questions," 8, http://www.animalliberationfront.com/ALFront/ELF/elf_faq.pdf.

5. Federal Bureau of Investigation, "In Focus: 30 Years of Terrorism," *Terrorism in the United States 1999*, 15–27; Bard E. O'Neill, *Insurgency and Terrorism from Revolution to Apocalypse* (Washington, DC: Potomac Books, 2005), 26.

6. Scarce, *Eco-Warriors*, 31.

7. Donald R. Liddick, *Eco-Terrorism: Radical Environmental and Animal Liberation Movements* (Westport, CT: Praeger, 2006), 19; Sean Parson, "Understanding the Ideology of the Earth Liberation Front," *Green Theory and Praxis: The Journal of Ecopedagogy* 4, no. 2 (2008): 54–55, http://greentheoryandpraxis.org/journal/index.php/journal/issue/view/7.

8. Carolyn Merchant, *American Environmental History: An Introduction* (New York: Columbia University Press, 2007), 74.

9. Lewis Hyde, ed., *The Essays of Henry D. Thoreau* (New York: North Point Press, 2002), xxvii–xxviii.

10. Ibid., xxi.

11. Henry D. Thoreau, *A Week on the Concord and Merrimack Rivers* (New York: Penguin Group, 1998), 37.

12. Hyde, *The Essays of Henry D. Thoreau*, 128.

13. Ibid., 189.

14. Ibid., 276.

15. Animal Liberation Front, "ALF and Civil Disobedience," http://www. animalliberationfront.com/ALFront/ALFandCivilDis.htm.

16. Merchant, *American Environmental History*, 241–42; Roderick Frazier Nash, *Wilderness and the American Mind*, 4th ed. (New Haven, CT: Yale University Press, 2001), 104–5.

17. Nash, *Wilderness and the American Mind*, 122–40; Merchant, *American Environmental History*, 150–51.

18. Nash, *Wilderness and the American Mind*, 169–79; Merchant, *American Environmental History*, 193.

19. Nash, *Wilderness and the American Mind*, 182–99; Merchant, *American Environmental History*, 240–41.

20. Douglas Brinkley, "Introduction," in *The Monkey Wrench Gang*, by Edward Abbey (New York: Harper Collins, Harper Perennial Modern Classics, 2006), xviii–xxi.

21. Ibid.

22. Ibid., xxii.

23. Merchant, *American Environmental History*, 234; David Foreman, *Confessions of an Eco-Warrior* (New York: Crown Publishers, 1991), 25–35.

24. Foreman, *Confessions of an Eco-Warrior*, 25–35; Liddick, *Eco-Terrorism*, 60, note 20.

25. Sean Egan, "From Spikes to Bombs," *Studies in Conflict and Terrorism* 19, no. 1 (1996): 7.

26. Paul Watson, *Sea Shepherd: My Fight for Whales and Seals* (New York: W. W. Norton, 1982), 152–59.

27. Egan, "From Spikes to Bombs," 5.

28. Watson, *Sea Shepherd*, 152.

29. "On the Frontlines: With Captain Paul Watson and the Sea Shepherd Conservation Society," *Resistance: Journal of the Earth Liberation Movement* (Fall 2009): 15–17; Watson, *Sea Shepherd*, 154.

30. Eagan, "From Spikes to Bombs," 3–4; Liddick, *Eco-Terrorism*, 19–20.

31. Bill Devall and George Sessions, *Deep Ecology: Living As If Nature Mattered* (Salt Lake City, UT: Gibbs Smith, 1985), 70.

32. Sean Parson, "Understanding the Ideology of the Earth Liberation Front," 55.

33. Martha Crenshaw, "The Causes of Terrorism," in *New Global Terrorism: Characteristics, Causes, Controls*, ed. Charles W. Kegley (Upper Saddle River, NJ: Prentice Hall), 93–96.

34. Liddick, *Eco-Terrorism*, 74–75.

35. Crenshaw, "The Causes of Terrorism," 93–96.

36. Liddick, *Eco-Terrorism*, 74–75; Scarce, *Eco-Warriors*, 12.

37. Anti-Defamation League, "Ecoterrorism: Extremism in the Animal Rights and Environmental Movements," *Extremism in America*, 9–10, http://adl.org/learn/ext_us/Ecoterrorism.asp?LEARN_Cat=Extremism&LEARN_Su. Today's terrorists are using the Internet as more than a communication device and repository for information: "They are using the Internet to raise funds, recruit, incite violence, and provide training. They are also using it to plan, network, and coordinate attacks." Gabriel Weimann, *Terror on the Internet: The New Arena, the New Challenges* (Washington, DC: United States Institute of Peace Press, 2006), 144–45.

38. Crenshaw, "The Causes of Terrorism," 94; Dave Foreman and Bill Haywood, eds., *Ecodefense: A Field Guide to Monkeywrenching* (Chico, CA: Abbzug Press, 2003), 13–14.

39. Crenshaw, "The Causes of Terrorism," 94; James Long and Bryan Denson, "Crimes in the Name of the Environment: Can Sabotage Have a Place in a Democratic Community?" *Oregonian*, September 29, 1999, 207, http://www.landrights. org/ALRA.oregon.eco-terrorism.htm.

40. Crenshaw, "The Causes of Terrorism," 94; Christopher Manes, *Green Rage: Radical Environmentalism and the Unmaking of Civilization* (Boston: Little, Brown, 1999), 166–74.

41. Ibid.

42. Crenshaw, "The Causes of Terrorism," 95.

43. Richard Kahn, "From Herbert Marcuse to the Earth Liberation Front: Considerations for Revolutionary Ecopedagogy," *Green Theory and Praxis: The Journal of Ecopedagogy* 1, no. 1 (2005): 5–8, http://greentheoryandpraxis.org/journal/index. php/journal/issue/view/5.

44. Crenshaw, "The Causes of Terrorism," 95.

45. Animal rights' activist Volkert van der Graaf's murder of Dutch politician Pim Fortuyn caused a backlash against environmental groups by an angry public who had previously been supportive of the REM. Simons, "Dutch Suspect in Slaying."

46. O'Neill, *Insurgency and Terrorism*, 106–8. Historically, using terrorism to garner popular support for a movement has had very little success. Ibid., 103.

47. Ibid., 104–5.

48. Crenshaw, "The Causes of Terrorism," 98.

49. John Horgan, *The Psychology of Terrorism* (New York: Routledge, 2005), 62.

50. Ibid., 45.

51. Liddick, *Eco-Terrorism*, 79.

52. Liddick, *Eco-Terrorism*, 82–83. Age is a constitutional factor that strongly affects the incidence of all criminal acts. No other variable is as robust and independent in analyzing crime rates and predicting individual criminal behavior. James Q. Wilson and Richard J. Herrnstein, *Crime and Human Nature* (New York: Simon and Schuster, 1985), 126–36.

53. Daniel Goleman, *Emotional Intelligence: Why It Can Matter More Than IQ* (New York: Bantam Books, 1995), 226–27.

54. Jack Katz, *Seductions of Crime: Moral and Sensual Attractions in Doing Evil* (New York: Basic Books, 1988), 53–54. Katz's perspective on crime is contrary to commonly held instrumental theories of criminality: "Dominant political and sociological understanding that crime is motivated by materialism is poorly grounded empirically." Ibid., 10.

55. Jeffrey "Free" Luers, "How I Became an Ecowarrior," *Earth First! Journal*, 4, http://www.earthfirstjournal.org/article.php?id=186.

56. Katz, *Seductions of Crime*, 79. Repetition of the same type of crime may diminish the "thrill" of committing the crime.

57. Rod Coronado, "Direct Actions Speak Louder Than Words," in *Terrorists or Freedom Fighters? Reflections on the Liberation of Animals*, ed. Steven Best and Anthony J. Nocella II (New York: Lantern Books, 2004), 178–84; Rod Coronado, "My Experience with Government Harassment," appendix to *Terrorists or Freedom Fighters?*, ed. Best and Nocella, 345–54.

58. Coronado, "Direct Actions Speak Louder Than Words," 178–84; Coronado, "My Experience with Government Harassment," 345–54.

59. Luers, "How I Became an Ecowarrior," 2.

60. Ibid.

61. Ibid., 5.

62. Ibid., 5.

63. Ibid., 6–7.

64. Civil Liberties Defense Center, "Eco-Prisoner Jeff 'Free' Luers Released from Prison," December 16, 2009, http://freefreenow.org/assets/pdfs/JeffReleased.pdf.

65. "Letters from the Underground," appendix to *Terrorists or Freedom Fighters?* (see note 57), 355.

66. Ibid.

67. Ibid., 360.

68. Horgan, *The Psychology of Terrorism*, 136–37.

69. Scarce, *Eco-Warriors*, 31.

70. Unlike the REM, the mainstream environmental movement is comprised of 10 well-known organizations that are structured like any other large, nonprofit organizations that conduct lobbying activities. Egan, "From Spikes to Bombs," 4.

71. Egan, "From Spikes to Bombs," 5; Scarce, *Eco-Warriors*, 51–55; Watson, *Sea Shepherd*, 151–54.

72. Sea Shepherd Conservation Society, "Who We Are," http://www.seashepherd.org/who-we-are.

73. Joseph Elliott Roeschke, *Eco-Terrorism and Piracy on the High Seas: Japanese Whaling and the Rights of Private Groups to Enforce International Conservation Law in Neutral Waters*, 20 Villanova Environmental Law Journal, no. 1 (2009): 125–30.

74. The Sea Shepherd Conservation Society's mission statement, written mandate, and the UN World Charter for Nature are located on its Web site, http://www.seashepherd.org. To understand Captain Watson's viewpoint on strategy and tactics, see "On the Frontlines: With Captain Paul Watson and the Sea Shepherd Conservation Society," *Resistance: Journal of the Earth Liberation Movement* (Fall 2009): 15–16.

75. Louis Beam, "Leaderless Resistance," in *The Seditionist* 12 (February 1992): 2–4, http://www.louisbeam.com/leaderless.htm. An argument can be made that the 19th-century anarchist movement was the forerunner of the autonomous cell concept; see Jean Marc Flükiger, "The Radical Animal Liberation Movement: Some Reflections on Its Future," *Journal for the Study of Radicalism* 2, no. 2 (June 2009): 111–32.

76. Animal Liberation Front, "The ALF Credo and Guidelines," http://www.animalliberationfront.com/ALFront/alf_credo.htm.

77. Flükiger, "The Radical Animal Liberation Movement," 118–19.

78. Animal Liberation Front, "The ALF Credo and Guidelines," http://www.animalliberationfront.com/ALFront/alf_credo.htm.

79. Pattrice Jones, "Mothers with Monkeywrenches: Feminist Imperatives and the ELF," in *Terrorists or Freedom Fighters?* (see note 57), 144.

80. "No Compromise in Defense of Mother Earth," *Earth First! Journal*, http://www.earthfirstjournal.org/section.php?id=1; Manes, *Green Rage*, 66–75; Scarce, *Eco-Warriors*, 57–67.

81. Scarce, *Eco-Warriors*, 57–63; Foreman, *Confessions of an Eco-Warrior*, 216–17.

82. Scarce, *Eco-Warriors*, 57–74.

83. Earth First! Worldwide, "About Earth First!" http://www.earthfirst.org/about.htm.

84. Foreman, *Confessions of an Eco-Warrior,* 216–18.

85. NAELFPO, "Frequently Asked Questions," is the source for all historical and background information on the ELF.

86. Ibid., 2.

87. Anthony J. Nocella II and Matthew J. Walton, "Standing up to Corporate Greed," *Green Theory and Praxis: The Journal of Ecopedagogy* 1, no. 1 (2005): 11–14, http://greentheoryandpraxis.org/journal/index.php/journal/issue/view/5; Parson, "Understanding the Ideology of the Earth Liberation Front," 62–63.

88. Parson, "Understanding the Ideology of the Earth Liberation Front," 51. ELF's first, 1997 communiqué titled "Beltane" stated that ELF believes in both social and deep ecology, that the end goal of ELF is to undermine the foundations of the state, and that the capitalist system will be ruined by causing economic damage to corporations. Nocella II and Walton, "Standing up to Corporate Greed," 6–7.

89. NAELFPO, "Frequently Asked Questions."

90. Ibid.

91. Kahn, "From Herbert Marcuse," 1–4.

92. Peter Chalk et al., *Trends in Terrorism: Threats to the United States and the Future of the Terrorism Risk Insurance Act* (Santa Monica, CA: RAND Corporation, 2005), 50–52, http://www.rand.org/pubs/monographs/MG393.html.

93. Liddick, *Eco-Terrorism,* 19–21.

94. Flükiger, *The Radical Animal Liberation Movement,* 125–28.

95. NAELFPO, "NIO's First Annual Animal Liberation/Militant Direct Action (MDA) Awards, Best ELF Action: November 23, 2009, Santiago, Chile, ELF Torches Slaughterhouse," http://www.animalliberationfront.com/News/2010_0 1/2010MilitantDirectActionAwards.htm.

96. Horacio R. Trujillo, "The Radical Environmentalist Movement," in *Aptitude for Destruction,* vol. 2, *Case Studies of Organizational Learning in Five Terrorist Groups,* MG-332-NIJ (Santa Monica, CA: RAND Corporation, 2005), 163, http://www.rand.org/pubs/monographs/MG332.html.

97. Brian A. Jackson, "Groups, Networks, or Movements: A Command-and-Control-Driven Approach to Classifying Terrorist Organizations and Its Application to Al Qaeda," *Studies in Conflict and Terrorism* 29, no. 3 (2006), 248.

98. Ibid.

99. Ibid., 252–54.

100. Ibid.

101. Federal Bureau of Investigation, "Eco-Terror Indictments," *Headline Archives,* January 20, 2006, http://www.fbi.gov/page2/jan06/elf012006.htm; Anti-Defamation League, "Two Women Plead Guilty in Seattle Ecoterror Arson," *Extremism in America: Updates,* October 10, 2006, http://www.adl.org/learn/extremism_in_america_updates/movements/ecoterrorism/operation_backfire.htm.

102. Anti-Defamation League, "Two Women Plead Guilty in Seattle Ecoterror Arson," *Extremism in America: Updates,* October 10, 2006, http://www.adl.org/learn/extremism_in_america_updates/movements/ecoterrorism/operation_backfire.htm.

103. Animal Liberation Front, "Revolutionary Cells—Animal Liberation Brigade," 2–3, http://www.animalliberationfront.com/ALFront/Premise_History/RevolutionaryCells.htm.

104. Ibid.

105. America's Most Wanted, "Daniel Andreas San Diego," http://www.amw.com/fugitives/brief.cfm?id=25800.

106. Anti-Defamation League, "Ecoterrorism," 7–8, http://www.adl.org/learn/ext_us/ecoterrorism.asp?learn_cat=extremism&learn_subcat=extremism_in_america&xpicked=4&item=eco.

107. Ibid., 7–9.

108. For a comprehensive typology and analysis of the types and frequency of REM actions, see Liddick, *Eco-Terrorism*, 71–76.

109. Foreman and Haywood, *Ecodefense*, 9–11.

110. *U.S. Code* 18, sec. 1864 (a) (2) (2006). For a complete explanation of anti–tree spiking legislation, see Rebecca K. Smith, Student Author, *Ecoterrorism: A Critical Analysis of the Vilification of Radical Environmental Activists as Terrorists*, 38, Environmental Law 537-48 (Spring 2008), http://legacy.lclark.edu/org/envtl/objects/38-2_Smith.pdf.

111. Foreman and Haywood, *Ecodefense*, 61.

112. Ibid., 62–63.

113. Ibid.

114. Ibid.

115. Ibid.

116. Leslie James Pickering, "A Brief Look at 40 Years of Guerrilla Sabotage in Defense of the Earth," *Resistance: Journal of the Earth Liberation Movement* (Spring 2010): 52.

117. Federal Bureau of Investigation, "Seattle Eco-Terrorism Investigation," *Headline Archives*, March 4, 2008, http://www.fbi.gov/page2/march08/seattle arson_030408.html.

118. Sara Jean Green, "Environmental Radicals: We Toppled Radio Towers," *Seattle Times*, September 5, 2009, http://seattletimes.nwsource.com/html/localnews/2009809764_radiotowers05m.html; NAELFPO, "ELF Topples Radio Station Towers in Washington," September 4, 2009, http://www.indybay.org/newsitems/2009/09/04/18620846.php.

119. Bootlyg, "Insurrectionary Mexico Celebrates Black Christmas," *Earth First! Journal*, http://chipuco.co.tv/earthfirstjournal.

120. Federal Bureau of Investigation, "Putting Intel to Work against ELF and ALF Terrorists," *Headline Archives*, June 30, 2008, http://www.fbi.gov/page2/june08/ecoterror_063008.html.

121. "Earth Day: 40 Years and Still Fucked. So Where Do We Go from Here?" *Resistance: Journal of the Earth Liberation Movement* (Spring 2010): 54–55.

CHAPTER 6: NIHILISTIC TERRORISTS: FANATICAL CELLS, LONE WOLVES, AND HYBRID GROUPS

1. The term *jihadi* comes from the Arabic word *jihad*, which means "striving or effort." In "Muslim history jihad was most commonly interpreted to mean armed struggle for the defense or advancement of Muslim power." Bernard Lewis, *The Crisis of Islam: Holy War and Unholy Terror* (New York: Random House, 2004), 31. All references to *jihadi* in this book mean an individual who professes to follow the dictates of the Islamic faith but has self-designated himself as a "holy warrior"

who engages in an armed struggle (the jihad) against Islam's enemies. The traditional enemies are apostates and nonbelievers. Today, the enemies are the Western world and those secular governments in the Islamic world whose leaders are considered apostates.

2. The facts concerning the murder of Theo van Gogh by Mohammad Bouyeri were drawn from the following sources: Albert Benschop, "Chronicle of a Political Murder Foretold: Jihad in the Netherlands," trans. Connie Menting, http://www.sociosite.org/jihad_nl_en.php; Mitchell Silber and Arvin Bhatt, *Radicalization in the West: The Homegrown Threat* (New York: New York City Police Department, 2007), 47–48; Lorenzo Vidino, "The Hofstad Group: The New Face of Terrorist Networks in Europe," *Studies in Conflict and Terrorism* 30, no. 7 (2007): 581–84.

3. Bill Durodié, "Home-Grown Nihilism: The Clash within Civilizations," *Journal of Homeland Security* (May 2007): 5, http://www.homelandsecurity.org/journal/Default.aspx?oid=156&ocat=1; Durodié believes it is our "cultural malaise and pessimistic outlook that forms the backdrop, and inevitably shapes, contemporary terrorism." This cultural environment is "sustained . . . by the radical nihilists who are prepared to lose their lives . . . in their misguided determination to leave their mark upon a world that they reject, and the nihilist intellectuals who help frame a public discourse and culture of apocalyptic failure and rejection." Ibid., 12–13.

4. Albert Parry, *Terrorism: From Robespierre to Arafat* (New York: Vanguard Press, 1976), 107.

5. Michael Burleigh, *Blood and Rage: A Cultural History of Terrorism* (New York: HarperCollins, 2009), 32.

6. Ted Honderich, ed., *The Oxford Guide to Philosophy* (New York: Oxford University Press: 1995), 659.

7. Burleigh, *Blood and Rage*, 36–39; Max Nomad, *Apostles of Revolution* (Boston: Little, Brown, 1939), 247–53.

8. Burleigh, *Blood and Rage*, 36–39; Yves Ternon, "Russian Terrorism, 1878–1908," in *The History of Terrorism: From Antiquity to Al Qaeda*, ed. Gérard Chaliand and Arnaud Blin, trans. Edward Schneider, Kathryn Pulver, and Jesse Browner (Berkeley: University of California Press, 2007), 137–38.

9. For definitions and a comprehensive discussion of cells, social movements, and loosely coupled movements, see Brian A. Jackson, "Groups, Networks, or Movements: A Command-and-Control-Driven Approach to Classifying Terrorist Organizations and Its Application to Al Qaeda," *Studies in Conflict and Terrorism* 29, no. 3 (2006): 241–62.

10. The FBI's guidelines specifically restrict investigating U.S. persons "solely for the purpose of monitoring activities protected by the First Amendment." John Ashcroft, *The Attorney General's Guidelines for FBI National Security Investigations and Foreign Intelligence Collection*, October 31, 2003, I.B.3., http://www.fas.org/irp/agency/doj/fbi/nsiguidelines.pdf.

11. Vidino, "The Hofstad Group," 588.

12. See Walter Laqueur, *No End to War: Terrorism in the Twenty-First Century* (New York: Continuum International, 2003), 212–23, who although not using the term *nihilistic* discusses the increasing threat of individuals and groups who meet this book's description of nihilistic terrorists.

13. Ibid., 33–34.

14. Jarret Brachman and William McCants, "Stealing Al Qaeda's Playbook," (West Point, NY: Combating Terrorism Center at West Point, 2006), 15–17, www. ctc.usma.edu.

15. Marc Sageman, *Understanding Terror Networks* (Philadelphia: University of Pennsylvania Press, 2004), 1–9; Brachman and McCants, "Stealing Al Qaeda's Playbook," 17.

16. Marc Sageman, *Leaderless Jihad: Terror Networks in the Twenty-First Century* (Philadelphia: University of Pennsylvania Press, 2008), 33–35.

17. National Commission on Terrorist Attacks upon the United States, *The 9/11 Commission Report* (New York: W. W. Norton, n.d.), 50–51.

18. Silber and Bhatt, *Radicalization in the West*, 6.

19. Ibid., 6.

20. Ibid., 7.

21. Kim Cragin, *Understanding Terrorist Motivations* (Santa Monica, CA: RAND Corporation, December 2009), 3–4, http://www.rand.org/pubs/testimonies/ CT338.html.

22. Sageman, *Leaderless Jihad*, 84.

23. Robert S. Mueller, "Congressional Testimony before the Senate Committee on Homeland Security and Government Affairs," September 2009, 3, www.fbi. gov/congress/congress09/mueller093009.htm.

24. Steve Ressler, "Social Networks Analysis as an Approach to Combat Terrorism: Past, Present, and Future Research," *Homeland Security Affairs* 2, no. 2 (July 2006): 1–3, http://www.hsaj.org/?fullarticle=2.2.8; Valdis E. Krebs, "Mapping Networks of Terrorist Cells," *International Network for Social Network Analysis: Connections* 24, no. 3 (2002): 43–49.

25. The case example of the Hofstad group is based on information from several sources. See note 2.

26. Vidino, "The Hofstad Group," 585–87.

27. Ibid. The strategic objectives of jihadi groups are "always the same—to punish the West, overthrow the democratic order, re-establish the Caliphate, and institute sharia." Silber and Bhatt, *Radicalization in the West*, 43.

28. Vidino, "The Hofstad Group," 587–89.

29. Bill Devall and George Sessions, *Deep Ecology: Living As If Nature Mattered* (Salt Lake City, UT: Gibbs Smith, 1985), 70.

30. Mohammad Akef Jamal, "Exorcizing the Demon of Terrorism," *Gulfnews. com*, January 2010, 2, http://gulfnews.com/opinions/columnists/exorcising-the-demon-of-terrorism-1.566180. Jamal links nihilism with rapid societal change: "It is also an element which enhances the spirit of despair in human beings, thus making them easy targets for others to lead toward terrorism in order to fulfill their own selfish objectives."

31. Devall and Sessions, *Deep Ecology*, 42–49.

32. Ibid., 70.

33. Philip Lamy, *Millennium Rage: Survivalists, White Supremacists, and the Doomsday Prophecy* (New York: Plenum Press, 1996), 98–103; Laqueur, *No End to War*, 212–16.

34. Horacio Trujillo, "The Radical Environmentalist Movement," in *Case Studies of Organizational Learning in Five Terrorist Groups*, vol. 2, *Aptitude for Destruction* (Santa Monica, CA: RAND Corporation, 2005), 159–61, http://www.rand.org/ pubs/monographs/MG332.html.

35. Leslie James Pickering, "A Brief Look at 40 Years of Guerrilla Sabotage in Defense of the Earth," *Resistance: Journal of the Earth Liberation Movement* (Spring 2010): 52.

36. Ibid., 47–50.

37. Laqueur, *No End to War*, 223.

38. Silber and Bhatt, *Radicalization in the West*, 50.

39. Jean Marc Flükiger, "The Radical Animal Liberation Movement: Some Reflections on Its Future," *Journal for the Study of Radicalism* 2, no. 2 (2009): 117–19. In referring to leaderless resistance movements, Flükiger states, "A common general outlook and a common philosophy are decisive and necessary for the determination of actions and for the very existence of the movement." Ibid., 118.

40. This chapter's case example of a putative ecoterrorist cell, identified by the acronym RISE and also referred to in other sources as the Rising Sun, is a summary of an excellent, comprehensive case study by W. Seth Carus and Ron Purver's summary of other published accounts in the academic literature. See W. Seth Carus, "R.I.S.E. (1972)," in *Toxic Terror: Assessing Terrorist Use of Chemical and Biological Weapons*, ed. Jonathan B. Tucker (Cambridge, MA: MIT Press, 2000), 54–70; Ron Purver, *Chemical and Biological Terrorism: The Threat According to the Open Literature* (Ottawa: Canadian Security Intelligence Service, June 1995), 37.

41. Brian Michael Jenkins, *Going Jihad: The Fort Hood Slayings and Home-Grown Terrorism*, testimony presented before the Senate Homeland Security and Governmental Affairs Committee on November 19, 2009 (Santa Monica, CA: RAND Corporation, 2009), 2, http://www.rand.org/pubs/testimonies/CT338.html

42. Ibid.

43. FBI, "Domestic Terrorism in the Post-9/11 Era," *Headline Archives*, September 7, 2009, 2, http://www.fbi.gov/page2/sept09/domesticterrorism090709.html.

44. Ibid.

45. Lou Michel and Dan Herbeck, *American Terrorist: Timothy McVeigh and the Tragedy at Oklahoma City* (New York: Avon Books, 2002), 361.

46. William Pierce [Andrew MacDonald, pseud.], *Hunter* (Hillsboro, WV: Vanguard Books: 1989), 12, 258.

47. Michel and Herbeck, *American Terrorist*, 361–62.

48. The case example of Joseph Paul Franklin is based on information from the following sources: John Douglas et al., *Crime Classification Manual* (New York: Lexington Books/Macmillan, 1992), 106–11; John Douglas and Mark Olshaker, *The Anatomy of Motive: The FBI's Legendary Mindhunter Explores the Key to Understanding and Catching Violent Criminals* (New York: Pocket Books, 1999), 205–314; Kris Hollington, *Wolves, Jackals, and Foxes: The Assassins Who Changed History* (New York: St. Martin's Press, 2007), 211–19.

49. Douglas and Olshaker, *The Anatomy of Motive*, 309.

50. Douglas et al., *Crime Classification Manual*, 106–11.

51. R. T. Naylor, *Wages of Crime: Black Markets, Illegal Finance, and the Underworld Economy* (New York: Cornell University Press, 2002), 53–57.

52. Ibid., 57.

53. Ibid.

54. See Frederick J. Hacker, *Crusaders, Criminals, Crazies: Terror and Terrorism in Our Time* (New York: W. W. Norton), 8–9.

55. The case example of the Aryan Republican Army is based on information from several sources. See Mark S. Hamm, *In Bad Company: America's Terrorist*

Underground (Boston: Northeast University Press, 2002); National Consortium for the Study of Terrorism and Responses to Terrorism (START), "Terrorist Organization Profile: Aryan Republican Army (ARA)," http://www.start.umd.edu/start/data_collections/tops/terrorist_organization_profile.asp?id=3412; Mark Hamm, "Crimes Committed by Terrorist Groups: Theory, Research, and Prevention," final report, U.S. Department of Justice, National Criminal Justice Reference Service, NCJ211203, September 2005, 187–216, http://www.ncjrs.gov/pdffiles1/nij/grants/211203.pdf.

56. Mark Hamm, "Crimes Committed by Terrorist Groups: Theory, Research, and Prevention," *Trends in Organized Crime* 9, no. 2 (2005): 187–200.

57. James Adams, *The Financing of Terror* (New York: Simon and Schuster, 1986), 216–19.

58. Naylor, *Wages of Crime*, 68.

59. The facts concerning the taking of the *Achille Lauro* are based on the following sources: Hoffman, *Inside Terrorism*, 144–45; Oliver Revell and Dwight Williams, *A G-Man's Journal: A Legendary Career inside the FBI—From the Kennedy Assassination to the Oklahoma City Bombing* (New York: Pocket Books, 1998), 268–72.

60. Peter Chalk, "Contemporary Maritime Piracy in Southeast Asia," *Studies in Conflict and Terrorism* 21, no. 1 (1998): 91.

61. Richard Platt, "Corsairs of the Mediterranean," in *Pirates: Terror on the High Seas—From the Caribbean to the South China Sea*, ed. David Cordingly (East Bridgewater, MA: World Publications, 2007), 77–98.

62. Dian H. Murray, "Chinese Pirates," in *Pirates: Terror on the High Seas* (see note 61), 222–23.

63. Ibid., 229–35.

64. Ibid., 235.

65. Jenifer G. Marx, "Pirate Round," in *Pirates: Terror on the High Seas* (see note 61), 144.

66. Ibid., 146–52.

67. James Kraska and Brian Wilson, "Fighting Pirates: The Pen and the Sword," *World Policy Journal* 25, no. 4 (2008): 44.

68. Michael Buky, "Terrorism, Piracy, and Climate Change: Challenges to International Maritime Governance," *Social Alternatives* 28, no. 2 (2009), 14.

69. International Maritime Organization, "Piracy in Waters off the Coast of Somalia," http://www.imo.org/home.asp?topic_id=1178; "Combating Piracy off Somalia: Swift Naval Response Is Only Part of the Solution," *Strategic Comments* 15, no. 1 (February 2009): 1–2.

70. J. Peter Pham, "Anti-Piracy, Adrift," *Journal of International Security Affairs*, no. 18 (Spring 2010): 81, http://www.securityaffairs.org/issues/2010/18/pham.php.

71. "Combating Piracy off Somalia," *Strategic Comments*.

72. Kraska and Wilson, "Fighting Pirates," 41.

73. Brian A. Jackson, "Organizational Decisionmaking by Terrorist Groups," in *Social Science for Counterterrorism: Putting the Pieces Together*, ed. Paul K. Davis and Kim Cragin (Santa Monica, CA: RAND Corporation, 2009), 216–29, http://www.rand.org/pubs/monographs/2009/RAND_MG849.pdf; Andrew H. Kydd and Barbara F. Walter, "The Strategies of Terrorism," *International Security* 31, no. 1 (Summer 2006): 51–56.

74. Douglas et al., *Crime Classification Manual*, 184.

75. Nick Deshpande, "Pyro-Terrorism: Recent Cases and the Potential for Proliferation," *Studies in Conflict and Terrorism* 32, no. 1 (2009): 38.

76. Ibid., 39; James Kirkhope of the Terrorism Studies Group has furnished a cogent analysis of the "forest jihad" threat to Australia: "Despite the unlikelihood that the February 2009 Australian wildfires mark al Qaeda's first operation of a 'Forest Jihad,' it is critical for Responders and Analysts to understand that militant jihadi's [sic] have considered setting fires both strategically as a form of economic warfare and operationally identifying targets and discussing appropriate manpower for over a decade." James Kirkhope, "Australia 2009 Arson Wildfires: Possible Wildfire Jihad Tactic?" Terrorism Studies Group, February 9, 2009, http://www.terrorism-studies.com/Australia_2009_Arson_Wildfires.pdf.

77. "FBI: Al-Qaeda Detainee Spoke of Fire Plot," *USA Today*, July 11, 2003, http://www.usatoday.com/news/washington/2003-07-11-alqaeda-fire_x.htm.

78. Joseph T. McCann, *Terrorism on American Soil: A Concise History of Plots and Perpetrators from the Famous to the Forgotten* (Boulder, CO: Sentient Publications, 2006), 282–87. Letters containing anthrax threats but determined by testing to be a variety of benign powders were received by a variety of individuals and organizations prior to the 9/11 attacks. Ibid., 283.

79. See United States Department of Justice, *Amerithrax Investigative Summary*, February 19, 2010, http://www.justice.gov/amerithrax/docs/amx-investigative-summary.pdf, for a complete description of the successful investigation.

80. Gregory D. Koblent and Jonathan B. Tucker, "Tracing an Attack: The Promise and Pitfalls of Microbial Forensics," *Survival* 52, no. 1 (February–March 2010): 162.

81. Judith Miller, Stephen Engelberg, and William Broad, *Germs: Biological Weapons and America's Secret War* (New York: Simon and Schuster, 2001), 317; Jessica Stern, *The Ultimate Terrorists* (Cambridge, MA: Harvard University Press, 1999), 79; Rocco Casagrande, "Biological Terrorism Targeted at Agriculture: The Threat to U.S. National Security," *Nonproliferation Review* 7, no. 3 (2000): 100, note 61.

82. Federal Bureau of Investigation, *Amerithrax: Linguist/Behavioral Analysis*, November 9, 2001, http://www.fbi.gov/anthrax/amerithrax.htm.

83. Stern, *The Ultimate Terrorists*, 70.

84. Tucker, *Toxic Terror*, 6–9.

85. Tucker, *Toxic Terror*, 242, note 68.

86. Ibid., 244, note 81.

87. Ibid., 8–9.

88. Ibid., 8.

89. Michael T. Osterholm and John Schwartz, *Living Terrors: What America Needs to Know to Survive the Coming Bioterrorist Catastrophe* (New York: Delacorte Press/Random House, 2000), 113; Stern, *The Ultimate Terrorists*, 53, note 13.

90. Tucker, *Toxic Terror*, 6–9.

91. For a listing of U.S. domestic terrorists' use or attempted use of biological weapons and a chronological listing of reports concerning al Qaeda's involvement with biological weapons, see Tucker, *Toxic Terror*, 250–51; Center for Nonproliferation Studies, "Chart: Al-Qa'ida's WMD Activities," http://cns.miis.edu/other/sjm_cht.htm.

92. Audrey Kurth Cronin, *Terrorist Motivations for Chemical and Biological Weapons Use: Placing the Threat in Context*, Congressional Research Service Report for

Congress, Order Code RL31831, March 28, 2003, 5, http://www.fas.org/irp/crs/RL31831.pdf.

93. Ibid., 5–6.

94. For a complete examination of Ivins's motivations, see U.S. Department of Justice, *Amerithrax Investigative Summary*, 38–41.

95. Casagrande, "Biological Terrorism Targeted at Agriculture," 93.

96. Ibid., 94–95.

97. Ibid., 96–100.

98. Jeremy Sobel, Ali Khan, and David Swerdlow, "Threat of a Biological Terrorist Attack on the U.S. Food Supply: The CDC Perspective," *Lancet* 359 (March 2002): 874–80.

99. Tucker, *Toxic Terror*, 154, notes 83 and 84.

100. Stern, *The Ultimate Terrorists*, 53–55.

101. W. Seth Carus "The Rajneeshees (1984)," in Tucker, *Toxic Terror*, 133. The Rajneeshees used either *Salmonella* or a mixture of raw sewage and dead rats to contaminate the water supply. Ibid., 132–33.

102. Phillipe Migaux, "The Future of the Islamist Movement," in *The History of Terrorism* (see note 8), 354–55; "A Synopsis of the Terrorist Threat Facing the O&G Industry," *Oil and Gas Industry Terrorism Monitor*, http://www.ogi-tm.com/ogi_threats_st.php.

103. Paul W. Parfomak, *Pipeline Security: An Overview of Federal Activities and Current Policy Issues*, Congressional Research Service Report for Congress, Order Code RL31990, updated February 5, 2004, http://www.fas.org/sgp/crs/RL31990.pdf.

104. Ibid.

105. "A Synopsis of the Terrorist Threat Facing the O&G Industry."

106. Parfomak, *Pipeline Safety and Security: Federal Programs*, Congressional Research Service Report for Congress, Order Code RL33347, updated February 29, 2008, http://www.fas.org/sgp/crs/homesec/RL33347.pdf, citing David S. Cloud, "A Former Green Beret's Plot to Make Millions through Terrorism," *Ottawa Citizen*, December 24, 1999, E15.

107. Parfomak, *Pipeline Safety and Security*, citing Yereth Rosen, "Alaska Critics Take Potshots at Line Security," *Houston Chronicle*, February 17, 2002, 8.

108. "Targeting Encana in British Columbia," *Resistance: Journal of the Earth Liberation Movement* (Fall 209): 33–34.

109. Gal Luft, "Pipeline Sabotage Is Terrorist's Weapon of Choice," *Energy Security*, March 28, 2005, http://www.iags.org/n0328051.htm. The Saudi Arabian branch of al Qaeda has referred to the world's energy system as "the provision line and the feeding to the artery of the life of the crusader nation." Ibid.

CHAPTER 7: THE RISK OF TERRORISM

1. Paul Schneider, "The Well from Hell," *Men's Journal*, August 2010, 80–87.

2. Sam Friedman, "BP Oil Spill a Stain on Risk Management," *National Underwriter*, May 31, 2010, 5.

3. Eric H. May, "Rush Is Right about a BP Horizon Terror Attack," *Lone Star Iconoclast*, May 3, 2010, http://lonestaricon.com/index.php?option=com_content&view=article&id=622:rush-is-right-about-a-bp-horizon-terror-attack&

catid=46:military-analysis&Itemid=95; John Myers, "A Crude Coincidence—
The Gulf Oil Spill Works Out Well for the Greens," *Personal Liberty Digest*, May 5,
2010, http://www.personalliberty.com/personal-liberty-articles/a-crude-coinci
dence%e2%80%94the-gulf-oil-spill-works-out-well-for-the-greens.

4. Friedman, "BP Oil Spill," 5.

5. National Commission on Terrorist Attacks upon the United States, *The 9/11
Commission Report*, (New York: W. W. Norton, n.d.), 339–44.

6. Ibid., 428.

7. Christopher M. Blanchard, *Al Qaeda: Statements and Evolving Ideology*, Congressional Research Service Report for Congress, Order Code RL32759, February 4, 2005, 3, http://www.fas.org/irp/crs/RL32759.pdf.

8. Melanie C. Cummings, David C. McGarvey, and Peter M. Vinch, *Homeland Security Risk Assessment*, vol. 1, *Setting* (Arlington, VA: Homeland Security
Institute, 2006), 2, http://www.homelandsecurity.org/hsireports/Risk%20Assess
ment%20Volume%201%20Setting.pdf.

9. Peter L. Bernstein, *Against the Gods* (New York: John Wiley and Sons,
1996), 8.

10. Ibid., 16.

11. Ibid., 13.

12. Ibid., 57.

13. James F. Broder, *Risk Analysis and the Security Survey*, 3rd ed. (Burlington,
MA: Butterworth-Heinemann, 2006), 3.

14. Randall Nichols, Daniel J. Ryan, and Julie J.C.H. Ryan, *Defending Your Digital Assets against Hackers, Crackers, Spies, and Thieves* (New York: McGraw-Hill,
2000), 70.

15. Bernstein, *Against the Gods*, 197.

16. Broder, *Risk Analysis*, 27.

17. Joseph Straw, "How Vulnerable Are We," *Security Management*, August
2008, 103.

18. ASIS International Guidelines Commission, *The General Security Risk Assessment Guideline* (Alexandria, VA: ASIS International, 2003), 16, http://www.
asisonline.org/guidelines/published.htm.

19. Nichols, Ryan, and Ryan, *Defending Your Digital Assets*, 70.

20. Joel Leson, *Assessing and Managing the Terrorism Threat*, NCJ 210680 (Washington, DC: U.S. Department of Justice, Bureau of Justice Assistance, 2005), 9,
http://www.ncjrs.gov/pdffiles1/bja/210680.pdf.

21. D. Anthony Nichter, "Betting on Enterprise Risk Management," *Security
Management*, September 2008, 113.

22. Broder, *Risk Analysis*, 4.

23. The Society for Risk Analysis, http://www.sra.org.

24. John Baker et al., *Risk Analysis and Intelligence Communities Collaborative
Framework*, final report (Arlington, VA: Homeland Security Institute, April 23,
2009), 19, http://www.homelandsecurity.org/Content.aspx?mid=278.

25. Ibid., 20.

26. Broder, *Risk Analysis*, 4.

27. Brian A. Jackson et al., *Aptitude for Destruction*, vol. 2, *Case Studies of Organizational Learning in Five Terrorist Groups*, MG-332-NIJ (Santa Monica, CA: RAND
Corporation, 2005), 1–2, http://www.rand.org/pubs/monographs/MG332.

28. Baker et al., *Risk Analysis and Intelligence Communities*, 21.

29. G. A. Ackerman, "It's Hard to Predict the Future: The Evolving Nature of Threats and Vulnerabilities," *Scientific and Technical Review* 25, no. 1 (2006): 354.

30. Cummings, McGarvey, and Vinch, *Homeland Security Risk Assessment*, viii; Broder, *Risk Analysis*, 27.

31. Richard Platt, "Corsairs of the Mediterranean," in *Pirates: Terror on the High Seas—From the Caribbean to the South China Sea*, ed. David Cordingly (East Bridgewater, MA: World Publications, 2007), 76.

32. For a comprehensive treatment of the value of historical analysis as a tool to predict terrorism trends, see Christopher Andrew, "Intelligence Analysis Needs to Look Backwards before Looking Forward: Why Lessons of the Past Can Help Fight Terror of the Future," Centre for Counterterrorism Studies, June 2, 2004, http://www.historyandpolicy.org/papers/policy-paper-23.html.

33. Brian A. Jackson and David R. Frelinger, *Understanding Why Terrorist Operations Succeed or Fail* (Santa Monica, CA: RAND Corporation, 2009), 5–6 , http://www.rand.org/pubs/occasional_papers/OP257.html.

34. Ibid., 10.

35. *United States v. Stone*, Case no. 2:10-cr-20123, indictment at 1–5 (E.D. Mich., filed March 23, 2010).

36. Joseph T. McCann, *Terrorism on American Soil: A Concise History of Plots and Perpetrators from the Famous to the Forgotten* (Boulder, CO: Sentient Publications, 2006), 242; Edward McCleskey et al., *Underlying Reasons for Success and Failure of Terrorist Attacks: Selected Case Studies*, Final Report (Arlington, VA: Homeland Security Institute, June 4, 2007), 25–31, http://www.homelandsecurity.org/Content.aspx?mid=278.

37. Horace R. Trujillo, "The Radical Environmentalist Movement," in *Aptitude for Destruction*, vol. 2 (see note 27), 171.

38. Ibid., 155–56.

39. Ibid., 153–54.

40. Ibid., 157.

41. Ibid., 156.

42. Ibid., 155

43. Ibid., 169–70.

44. Ibid., 169.

45. David J. Kilcullen, "Countering Global Insurgency," *Journal of Strategic Studies* 28, no. 4 (August 2005): 601–3; Max Abrahms, "What Terrorist Really Want," *International Security* 32, no. 4 (Spring 2008): 84.

46. Ruth Margolies-Beitler, "The Complex Relationship between Global Terrorism and U.S. Support for Israel," in *The Making of a Terrorist: Recruitment, Training, and Root Causes*, vol. 3, *Root Causes*, ed. James J. F. Forest (Westport, CT: Praeger Security International, 2006), 71.

47. Eugenia K. Guilmartin, "Rejection of Political Institutions by Right Wing Extremists in the United States," in *The Making of a Terrorist*, vol. 3 (see note 46), 98.

48. Kilcullen, "Countering Global Insurgency," 598.

49. Ibid., 601–3.

50. Ibid., 608–9.

51. Ibid., 602.

52. Ibid.

53. *The 9/11 Commission Report*, 56.

54. Abrahms, "What Terrorists Really Want," 80.

55. Ibid., 87.

56. Ibid., 89–91.

57. Ibid., 96.

58. Ibid., 98.

59. Jerrold M. Post, *The Mind of the Terrorist: The Psychology of Terrorism from the IRA to Al-Qaeda* (New York: Palgrave MacMillan, 2007), 6.

60. Abrahms, "What Terrorists Really Want," 80.

61. Fred Burton, "'Direct Action' Attacks: Terrorism by Another Name?" STRATFOR Global Intelligence, May 23, 2007, 1–4, http://www.stratfor.com/direct_action_attacks_terrorism_another_name.

62. Mark Hamm, "Crimes Committed by Terrorist Groups: Theory, Research, and Prevention," final report, U.S. Department of Justice, National Criminal Justice Reference Service, NCJ211203, September 2005, 187–216, http://www.ncjrs.gov/pdffiles1/nij/grants/211203.pdf.

63. Ibid., 7.

64. Brent Smith, "A Look at Terrorist Behavior: How They Prepare, Where They Strike," *NIJ Journal*, no. 260 (July 2008): 3, http://www.ncjrs.gov/pdffiles1/nij/222900.pdf.

65. Ibid.

66. Ibid.

67. Ibid.

68. Ibid., 4.

69. Ibid.

70. Ibid.

71. Ibid.

72. Ibid.

73. Ibid., 5.

74. Robert A. Fein and Bryan Vossekuil, "Assassination in the United States: An Operational Study of Recent Assassins, Attackers, and Near-Lethal Approachers, *Journal of Forensic Science* 44, no. 2 (March 1999): 324, http://www.secretservice.gov/ntac/ntac_jfs.pdf.

75. Ibid., 325–26.

76. Ibid.

77. Ibid., 328; Charles Montaldo, "About.com Guide to Historical Crimes," http://crime.about.com/od/murder/p/squeaky.htm.

78. Fein and Vossekuil, "Assassination in the United States," 329.

79. Ibid., 330.

80. Ibid.

81. Ibid.

82. Ibid., 333.

83. Jonathan B. Tucker, ed., *Toxic Terror: Assessing Terrorist Use of Chemical and Biological Weapons* (Cambridge, MA: MIT Press, 2000), 254.

84. See, e.g., *United States v. Tankersley*, CR No. 06-60071-1-AA, Information (D. Oregon, filed July 20, 2005).

85. Cummings, McGarvey, and Vinch, *Homeland Security Risk Assessment*, 12.

86. Nichols, Ryan, and Ryan, *Defending Your Digital Assets*, 71.

87. Cummings, McGarvey, and Vinch, *Homeland Security Risk Assessment*, 8.

88. ASIS International, *Protection of Assets Manual*, vol. 1 (Alexandria, VA: ASIS, 2004), 2-I-5.

89. Leson, *Assessing and Managing the Terrorism Threat*, 8.

90. Cummings, McGarvey, and Vinch, *Homeland Security Risk Assessment*, 12.

91. Ibid., 12–13; See ASIS International, *Protection of Assets Manual*, 2-I-1–2-I-25, for a more in-depth presentation of the vulnerability assessment process.

92. ASIS International, *Emergency Planning Handbook*, 2nd ed. (Alexandria, VA: ASIS International, 2003), 105; Tracy Knippenburg Gillis, *Emergency Exercise Handbook: Evaluate and Integrate Your Company's Plan* (Tulsa, OK: Penn Well Books, 1996), 112.

93. ASIS International, *Protection of Assets Manual*, 2-I-22.

94. Ibid., 2-I-21.

95. Ted Almay, "Seeing the Risk through the Trees," *Security Management*, September 2006, 101–11.

96. ASIS International, *Protection of Assets Manual*, 2-I-22.

97. See *9/11 Commission Report*, 339.

98. Nassim Nicholas Taleb, *The Black Swan: The Impact of the Highly Improbable* (New York: Random House, 2007), 42.

99. Ibid., 147.

100. Ibid., 152.

101. Bernstein, *Against the Gods*, 335.

102. Taleb, *The Black Swan*, 42.

103. Bernstein, *Against the Gods*, 245.

104. Bernstein cites a large body of literature on the theories of Daniel Kahneman and Amos Tversky in *Against the Gods*, 270–72.

105. Bernstein, *Against the Gods*, 281.

106. Richards J. Heuer Jr., *Psychology of Intelligence Analysis* (Langley, VA: CIA Center for the Study of Intelligence, 1999), 127–38, https://www.cia.gov/library/center-for-the-study-of-intelligence/csi-publications/books-and-monographs/psychology-of-intelligence-analysis/PsychofIntelNew.pdf.

107. Andrew Curry, "Mathematics of Terror," *Discover*, July/August 2010, 43.

108. Taleb, *The Black Swan*, 136.

109. G. K. Chesterton, *Orthodoxy* (New York: Lane Press, 1909), 149–50 (repr. Westport, CT: Greenwood Press, 1974), cited in Bernstein, *Against the Gods*, 331.

CHAPTER 8: SECURITY PLANNING FOR ENVIRONMENTALLY LINKED TERRORISM

1. David Johnston, "Vail Fires Were Probably Arson, U.S. Agents Say," *New York Times*, October 23, 1998.

2. James Brooke, "Group Claims Responsibility for Blazes at Vail Resort," *New York Times*, October 22, 1998.

3. Joseph T. McCann, *Terrorism on American Soil: A Concise History of Plots and Perpetrators from the Famous to the Forgotten* (Boulder, CO: Sentient Publications, 2006), 258–60 and note 19 on 260.

4. Federal Bureau of Investigation, "Eco-Terror Indictments: 'Operation Backfire' Nets 11," *Headline Archives*, January 20, 2006; a second federal indictment was issued on May 19, 2006, in Denver, Colorado, charging four of the same individuals who had been indicted in Oregon with arson of Vail Resorts's property on

Vail Mountain. Kirk Johnson, "Four Are Indicted on Arson Charges in 1998 Fires at a Resort in Vail," *New York Times,* May 20, 2006.

5. Steven Fink, *Crisis Management: Planning for the Inevitable* (Lincoln, NE: iUniverse, 2002), 168–69; Margaret E. Kosal, "Terrorism Targeting Industrial Chemical Facilities: Strategic Motivations and the Implications for U.S. Security," *Studies in Conflict and Terrorism* 29, no. 7 (2006): 724.

6. Fink, *Crisis Management,* 174.

7. Kosal, "Terrorism Targeting Industrial Chemical Facilities," 724.

8. Ibid., 725.

9. Ann Hagedorn Auerbach, *Ransom: The Untold Story of International Kidnapping* (New York: Henry Holt, 1998), 380–83.

10. Ibid., 23.

11. National Commission on Terrorist Attacks upon the United States, *The 9/11 Commission Report* (New York: W. W. Norton, n.d.), 397–98.

12. Bruce Schneier, *Schneier on Security* (Indianapolis, IN: Wiley, 2008), 185.

13. Leonard Goodstein, Timothy Nolan, and J. William Pfeiffer, *Applied Strategic Planning: A Comprehensive Guide* (New York: McGraw-Hill, 1993), 3.

14. Ibid., 3.

15. Ibid., 6–7.

16. Ibid., 3.

17. Ibid., 4.

18. Ibid., 221.

19. "Venezuela's Hugo Chavez Targets Major Foreign Oil Companies in Nationalization Fight," FOX News, January 16, 2007,
http://www.foxnews.com/printer_friendly_story/0,3566,243901,00.html.

20. Lynn Berry, "Co-Pilot Putin Helps Put out Russia's Wildfires," Associated Press, August 10, 2010.

21. Goodstein, Nolan, and Pfeiffer, *Applied Strategic Planning,* 309–12.

22. Ibid., 309.

23. Bruce Schneier, *Beyond Fear: Thinking Sensibly about Security in an Uncertain World* (New York: Copernicus Books, 2003), 13.

24. Ibid., 233.

25. Ibid., 103–6.

26. Ibid., 123.

27. United States Department of Homeland Security, *National Infrastructure Protection Plan: Partnering to Enhance Protection and Resiliency,* 2009, 7–8, http://www.fas.org/irp/agency/dhs/nipp2009.pdf. Chemical facilities that present high levels of risk can be regulated by the Department of Homeland Security under Chemical Facility Anti-Terrorism Standards. Ibid., 109.

28. The President's Commission on Critical Infrastructure Protection, *Critical Foundations: Protecting America's Infrastructures,* October 13, 1997, http://www.fas.org/sgp/library/pccip.pdf.

29. William J. Clinton, "Protecting America's Critical Infrastructure," Presidential Decision Directive NSC 63, May 22, 1998, http://www.fas.org/irp/offdocs/pdd/pdd-63.htm.

30. United States Homeland Security Council, *National Strategy for Homeland Security,* October 2007, 4, http://www.dhs.gov/xlibrary/assets/nat_strat_homelandsecurity_2007.pdf.

31. Ibid., 27.

32. Ibid., 42.

33. United States Department of Homeland Security, *National Infrastructure Protection Plan*, 9.

34. Ibid., 11.

35. Ibid. The focus of the National Strategy in regard to terrorism is on al Qaeda but also includes homegrown Islamic extremism and other domestic threats, which the National Strategy refers to as single-issue groups, including white supremacist groups, animal rights extremists, and ecoterrorist groups, among others. United States Homeland Security Council, *National Strategy for Homeland Security*, 9–10.

36. United States Department of Homeland Security, *National Infrastructure Protection Plan*, 11.

37. Ibid.

38. United States Department of Homeland Security, *National Response Framework*, January 2008, 1.

39. Ibid., 3.

40. Ibid., 2.

41. Ibid., 71.

42. Ibid., 74.

43. Ibid., 75.

44. Ibid.

45. Ibid., 74.

46. Goodstein, Nolan, and Pfeiffer, *Applied Strategic Planning*, 102.

47. Schneier, *Beyond Fear*, 133.

48. Ibid., 139–40.

49. National Intelligence Council, "Global Trends 2025: A Transformed World," *Global Trends 2025: The National Intelligence Council's 2025 Project*, NIC2008-003, November 2008, 66–67, http://www.dni.gov/nic/NIC_2025_project.html.

50. Thomas F. Homer-Dixon, *Environment, Scarcity, and Violence* (Princeton, NJ: Princeton University Press, 1999), 179.

51. An example of this premise was the Bougainville Island Rebellion in 1990, as described in Michael T. Klare, *Resource Wars: The New Landscape of Global Conflict* (New York: Henry Holt, 2001), 195–98.

52. National Counterterrorism Center, *2009 Report on Terrorism* (Washington, DC: National Counterterrorism Center, 2010), 4, http://www.nctc.gov/witsbanner/docs/2009_report_on_terrorism.pdf.

53. Ibid.

54. Ibid., 9–10.

55. Ibid., 18.

56. Klare, *Resource Wars*, 217–21.

57. Ibid.; Barack Obama, *National Security Strategy* (Washington, DC: White House, May 2010), 4–5, http://www.whitehouse.gov/sites/default/files/rss_viewer/national_security_strategy.pdf.

58. Klare, *Resource Wars*, 217–21.

59. Ibid.

60. Robert Young Pelton, *The World's Most Dangerous Places*, 4th ed. (New York: Harper Resource/HarperCollins, 2000), 474.

61. Adam Hochschild, "Blood and Treasure: Why One of the World's Richest Countries Is Also One of Its Poorest," *Mother Jones* 35, no. 2 (April 2010): 52–65.

62. Ibid., 57–62.

63. Pelton, *The World's Most Dangerous Places*, 916–17; National Consortium for the Study of Terrorism and Responses to Terrorism (START), "Terrorist Organization Profile: Lord's Resistance Army (LRA)," http://www.start.umd.edu/start/data_collections/tops/terrorist_organization_profile.asp?id=3513.

64. Robert Elliott, "Crude Oil and Corruption," *Security Management*, June 2007, 68.

65. National Consortium for the Study of Terrorism and Responses to Terrorism (START), "Terrorist Organization Profile: Movement for the Emancipation of the Niger Delta (MEND)," http://www.start.umd.edu/start/data_collections/tops/terrorist_organization_profile.asp?id=4692.

66. "Ecoterrorist of the Season: Shell," *Resistance: Journal of the Earth Liberation Movement* (Fall 2009): 25.

67. National Consortium for the Study of Terrorism and Responses to Terrorism, "Terrorist Organization Profile: Movement for the Emancipation of the Niger Delta."

68. Julia Baird, "Oil Shame in Africa: In Nigeria, Spills are Weekly Events," *Newsweek*, July 26, 2010, 27.

69. John Barham, "Fueling Nigeria's Conflict," *Security Management*, August 2008, 50.

70. William Langewiesche, *The Outlaw Sea: A World of Freedom, Chaos, and Crime* (New York: North Point Press, 2004), 1–5.

71. Ibid.

72. Langewiesche, *The Outlaw Sea*, 32–38.

73. United Nations, *Convention on the Law of the Sea, Article 101*, December 10, 1982, UNTS 3, entered into force on November 16, 1994, http://www.un.org/Depts/los/convention_agreements/texts/unclos/unclos_e.pdf.

74. United Nations, *Convention for the Suppression of Unlawful Acts against the Safety of Maritime Navigation*, adopted March 10, 1988, UNTS, entered into force March 1, 1992, http://treaties.un.org/doc/db/Terrorism/Conv8-english.pdf.

75. John S. Burnett, *Dangerous Waters: Modern Piracy and Terror on the High Seas* (New York: Penguin Group), 227. According to Burnett, the pirates were operating under the control of a crime syndicate with bosses in Singapore, Hong Kong, and China.

76. Peter Chalk, *The Maritime Dimension of International Security: Terrorism, Piracy, and Challenges for the United States* (Santa Monica, CA: RAND Corporation, 2008), 48, hhttp://www.rand.org/pubs/monographs/MG697.html.

77. Ibid., 49.

78. Ibid.

79. Ibid., 49.

80. Ibid., 50.

81. Ibid., 51.

82. James Kraska and Brian Wilson, "Fighting Pirates: The Pen and the Sword," *World Policy Journal* 25, no. 4 (Winter 2008/9): 41.

83. Katharine Houreld, "Somali Pirates Hijack Cargo Ship with 23 Crew," ABC News, August 2, 2010, http://abcnews.go.com/International/wireStory?id=11302800.

84. "Japanese Tanker Attack Highlights Shipping Risks: Report," *Business Insurance.com*, August 6, 2010, http://www.businessinsurance.com/article/20100806/NEWS01/100809947.

85. Chalk, *Maritime Dimension of International Security*, 22–23.

86. Burnett, *Dangerous Waters*, 286–87.

87. Ibid., 287–92.

88. Chalk, *Maritime Dimension of International Security*, 37–38.

89. Richard Gigliotti and Ronald Jason, "Approaches to Physical Security," in *Handbook of Loss Prevention and Crime Prevention*, ed. Lawrence J. Fennelly (Boston: Butterworth-Heinemann, 1999), 169–71.

90. Headquarters, Department of the Army, *Physical Security Manual*, FM 3–19.30, January 18, 2001, 2-8–2-10.

91. Ibid.

92. Horacio R. Trujillo, "The Radical Environmentalist Movement," in *Aptitude for Destruction*, vol. 2, *Case Studies of Organizational Learning in Five Terrorist Groups* (Santa Monica, CA: RAND Corporation, 2005), 155, http://www.rand.org/pubs/monographs/MG332.html.

93. Stefan H. Leader and Peter Probst, "The Earth Liberation Front and Environmental Terrorism," *Terrorism and Political Violence* 15, no. 4 (Winter 2003): 37–58.

94. Headquarters, Department of the Army, *Physical Security Manual*, FM 3-19.30, January 18, 2001, 2-8–2-10.

95. Gigliotti and Jason, "Approaches to Physical Security," 194.

96. Pew Center on Global Climate Change, *National Security Implications of Global Climate Change*, August 2009, http://www.pewclimate.org/docUploads/national-security-implications-memo-august2009.pdf.

97. Michael G. Harvey, "A Survey of Corporate Programs for Managing Terrorist Threats," *Journal of International Business Studies* 24, no. 3 (1993): 465–78.

98. Ibid.

99. Steve Ressler, "Social Network Analyses as an Approach to Combat Terrorism: Past, Present, and Future Research," *Homeland Security Affairs* 2, no. 2 (July 2006), http://www.hsaj.org/?fullarticle=2.2.8.

100. Ibid.

101. Jean Marie McGloin and David S. Kirk, "An Overview of Social Network Analysis," *Journal of Criminal Justice Education* 21, no. 2 (June 2010): 171.

102. Ibid.

103. Ibid.

104. Ressler, "Social Network Analysis," 5.

105. Valdis E. Krebs, "Mapping Networks of Terrorist Cells," *International Network for Social Network Analysis: Connections* 24, no. 3 (2002): 43–52.

106. Ibid., 49.

107. Ibid., 51.

108. Ibid., 50–51.

109. Fred Burton, "The Challenge of the Lone Wolf," STRATFOR, May 30, 2007, 5–6, http://www.stratfor.com/challenge_lone_wolf.

110. "Military Studies in the Jihad against the Tyrants," 31–32, http://feastofhateandfear.com/archives/al_qaeda.html.

111. Dave Foreman and Bill Haywood, eds., *Ecodefense: A Field Guide to Monkeywrenching* (Chico, CA: Abbzug Press, 2003), 281–82.

112. Carlos Marighella, *Minimanual of the Urban Guerrilla*, 24, http://ballistichel met.org/school/urban_warfare.pdf.

113. Ibid., 10.

114. Al Qaeda, "Examples of Training Manuals for Terrorism and Guerilla Warfare," appendix to *The Making of a Terrorist*, vol. 2, *Training*, ed. James J. F. Forest (Westport, CT: Praeger Security International, 2006), 319.

115. Auerbach, *Ransom*, 435.

116. Ibid., 24–34.

117. Ibid., 35.

118. See Gavin de Becker, Tom Taylor, and Jeff Marquart, *Just Two Seconds: Using Time and Space to Defeat Assassins* (Studio City, CA: Gavin de Becker Center for the Study and Reduction of Violence, 2008), 378.

119. Ibid., 8.

120. David A. Soskis and Clinton R. Van Zandt, "Hostage Negotiation: Law Enforcement's Most Effective Non-Lethal Weapon," *FBI Management Quarterly* 6, no. 4 (Autumn 1986): 1.

CHAPTER 9: CONCLUSION

1. Sarah Brumfield, "Police Kill Suspect in Discovery Channel Siege," *Pittsburgh Post Gazette*, September 2, 2010, A-6.

2. Alex Johnson, Elizabeth Chuck, Bob Sullivan, Thomas Roberts, and Peter Alexander, "Sources: Discovery Suspect Had Starter Guns," NBC News, September 2, 2010, 1–6, http://www.msnbc.msn.com/id/38968317/ns/us_news_ crime_and_courts.

3. National Consortium for the Study of Terrorism and Responses to Terrorism (START), "Background Report: Discovery Communications Building Hostage-Taking," September 1, 2010, 3, http://www.start.umd.edu/start/announcements/ announcement.asp?id=205.

4. Justin Gillis, "Extreme Weather Raising Global Warming Questions," *New York Times*, reprinted in *Pittsburgh Post Gazette* 84, no. 15 (August 15, 2010), A-1–A-2.

5. Thomas H. Maugh II, "Science Society Urges Strong Action to Battle Warming," *Pittsburgh Post Gazette* 83, no. 293 (May 20, 2010), A-2.

6. Susan Solomon, Gian-Kasper Plattner, Reto Knutti, and Pierre Friedling-stein, "Irreversible Climate Change Due to Carbon Dioxide Emissions," *Proceedings of the National Academy of Sciences of the United States of America* 106, no. 6 (February 10, 2009), 1704, http://www.pnas.org/cgi/doi/10.1073/pnas.0812721106.

7. Charles J. Hanley, "Long, Hot Summer: Catastrophic Fires, Floods Fit Scientists' Predictions," *Pittsburgh Post Gazette*, August 13, 2010, A-4.

8. Pew Center on Global Climate Change, *Summary: Copenhagen Climate Summit*, http://www.pewclimate.org/international/copenhagen-climate-summit-summary; John M. Broder, "Modest Deal on Emissions Concludes Climate Talks," *New York Times International*, December 12, 2010.

9. Jon Schmitz, "Coalition Lines Up against Climate Bill," *Pittsburgh Post Gazette* 83, no. 293 (May 20, 2010), A-2.

10. National Consortium for the Study of Terrorism and Responses to Terrorism, "Background Report," 2.

11.   Cf. National Intelligence Council, *Global Trends 2025: A Transformed World* (Washington, DC: U.S. Government Printing Office, August 2008), 95–96, http://www.dni.gov/nic/NIC_2025_project.html.

12.   See Brynjar Lia and Åshild Kjøk, "Energy Supply as Terrorist Targets? Patterns of 'Petroleum Terrorism' 1968–99," in *Oil in the Gulf: Obstacles to Democracy and Development*, ed. Daniel Heradstveit and Helge Hveem (Burlington, VT: Ashgate, 2004), 121–22.

Bibliography

Abrahms, Max. "What Terrorist Really Want." *International Security* 32, no. 4 (Spring 2008): 78–105.

Ackerman, G. A. "It's Hard to Predict the Future: The Evolving Nature of Threats and Vulnerabilities." *Scientific and Technical Review* 25, no. 1 (2006): 353–60.

Adams, James. *The Financing of Terror: How the Groups That Are Terrorizing the World Get the Money to Do It.* New York: Simon and Schuster, 1986.

Addicott, Jeffrey F. *Terrorism Law: The Rule of Law and the War on Terror.* 2nd ed. Tucson, AZ: Lawyers and Judges, 2004.

Air Worldwide Corporation. "The Air Loss Estimation Model." http://www.airworldwide.com/publicationsitem.aspx?id=15854.

Akef Jamal, Mohammad. "Exorcizing the Demon of Terrorism." *Gulfnews.com*, January 2010. http://gulfnews.com/opinions/columnists/exorcising-the-demon-of-terrorism-1.566180.

Al Qaeda. "Examples of Training Manuals for Terrorism and Guerilla Warfare." Appendix to *The Making of a Terrorist: Recruitment, Training, and Root Causes.* Vol. 2, *Training*, edited by James J. F. Forest, 311–33. Westport, CT: Praeger Security International, 2006.

Almay, Ted. "Seeing the Risk through the Trees." *Security Management*, September 2006.

America's Most Wanted. "Daniel Andreas San Diego." http://www.amw.com/fugitives/brief.cfm?id=25800.

Andress, David. *The Terror: The Merciless War for Freedom in Revolutionary France.* New York: Farrar, Straus, and Giroux, 2005.

Andrew, Christopher. "Intelligence Analysis Needs to Look Backwards before Looking Forward: Why Lessons of the Past Can Help Fight Terror of the Future." Centre for Counter Terrorism Studies, June 2, 2004. http://www.historyandpolicy.org/papers/policy-paper-23.html.

Animal Liberation Front. "ALF and Civil Disobedience." http://www.animallib
    erationfront.com/ALFront/ALFandCivilDis.htm.
Animal Liberation Front. "The ALF Credo and Guidelines." http://www.animal
    liberationfront.com/ALFront/alf_credo.htm.
Animal Liberation Front. "Revolutionary Cells—Animal Liberation Brigade."
    http://www.animalliberationfront.com/ALFront/Premise_History/Rev
    olutionaryCells.htm.
Anti-Defamation League. "Ecoterrorism: Extremism in the Animal Rights and En-
    vironmentalist Movements." *Extremism in America.* http://adl.org/learn/
    ext_us/Ecoterrorism.asp?LEARN_Cat=Extremism&LEARN_Su.
Anti-Defamation League. "Two Women Plead Guilty in Seattle Ecoterror Arson."
    Extremism in America: Updates, October 10, 2006. http://www.adl.org/learn/
    extremism_in_america_updates/movements/ecoterrorism/operation_
    backfire.htm.
Ashcroft, John. *The Attorney General's Guidelines for FBI National Security Investiga-
    tions and Foreign Intelligence Collection.* October 31, 2003. http://www.fas.
    org/irp/agency/doj/fbi/nsiguidelines.pdf.
ASIS International. *Emergency Planning Handbook.* Alexandria, VA: ASIS Interna-
    tional, 2003.
ASIS International. *Protection of Assets Manual.* Vol. 1. Alexandria, VA: ASIS Inter-
    national, 2004.
ASIS International Guidelines Commission. *The General Security Risk Assessment
    Guideline.* Alexandria, VA: ASIS International, 2003. http://www.asison
    line.org/guidelines/published.htm.
Auerbach, Ann Hagedorn. *Ransom: The Untold Story of International Kidnapping.*
    New York: Henry Holt, 1998.
Baird, Julia. "Oil Shame in Africa: In Nigeria, Spills Are Weekly Events." *Newsweek,*
    July 26, 2010.
Baird, Robert Arthur. "Pyro-Terrorism—The Threat of Arson-Induced Forest Fires
    as a Future Terrorist Weapon of Mass Destruction." *Studies in Conflict and
    Terrorism* 29, no. 5 (2006): 415–28.
Baker, John, Meghan Wool, Adrian Smith, Jerome Kahan, Clarke Ansel, Philip
    Hammar, David McGarvey, Matthew Phillips, and Rosemary Lark. *Risk
    Analysis and Intelligence Communities Collaborative Framework.* Final Report.
    Arlington, VA: Homeland Security Institute, April 23, 2009. http://www.
    homelandsecurity.org/Content.aspx?mid=278.
Bandura, Albert. "Mechanisms of Moral Disengagement." In *Origins of Terrorism:
    Psychologies, Ideologies, Theologies, States of Mind,* edited by Walter Reich,
    161–91. Washington, DC: Woodrow Wilson Center Press, 1998.
Barham, John. "Fueling Nigeria's Conflict." *Security Management,* August 2008.
Barzun, Jacques, and Henry F. Graff. *The Modern Researcher.* 6th ed. Belmont, CA:
    Wadsworth Thompson Learning, 2004.
Beam, Louis. "Leaderless Resistance." In *The Seditionist* 12 (February 1992): 2–4.
    http://www.louisbeam.com/leaderless.htm.
Benschop, Albert. *Chronicle of a Political Murder Foretold: Jihad in the Netherlands.* Trans-
    lated by Connie Menting. http://www.sociosite.org/jihad_nl_en.php.
Bernstein, Peter L. *Against the Gods.* New York: John Wiley and Sons, 1996.
Berrong, Stephanie. "The Golden Rule." *Security Management,* May 2010.

Berry, Lynn. "Co-Pilot Putin Helps Put out Russia's Wildfires." Associated Press, August 10, 2010.

Best, Steven, and Anthony J. Nocella II, eds. *Terrorists or Freedom Fighters? Reflections on the Liberation of Animals*. New York: Lantern Books, 2004.

Best, Steven, and Anthony J. Nocella II. "Defining Terrorism." Appendix 3 in *Terrorists or Freedom Fighters? Reflections on the Liberation of Animals*, edited by Steven Best and Anthony J. Nocella II, 361–78. New York: Lantern Books, 2004.

Blanchard, Christopher M. *Al Qaeda: Statements and Evolving Ideology*. Congressional Research Service Report for Congress, Order Code RL32759, February 4, 2005. http://www.fas.org/irp/crs/RL32759.pdf.

Bootlyg. "Insurrectionary Mexico Celebrates Black Christmas." *Earth First! Journal*. http://chipuco.co.tv/earthfirstjournal.

Borum, Randy. "Understanding the Terrorist Mindset." *FBI Law Enforcement Bulletin*, July 2003. http://works.bepress.com/randy_borum/7.

Bowman, M. E. "Domestic Terrorism." In *National Security Law*, edited by John Norton Moore and Robert F. Turner, 967–73. Durham, NC: Carolina Academic Press, 2005.

Brachman, Jarret, and William F. McCants. "Stealing Al Qaeda's Playbook." West Point, NY: Combating Terrorism Center at West Point, 2006.

Brimacombe, Peter. *Guy Fawkes Gunpowder Plot*. Pitkin Guides. Norwich, Great Britain: Jarrold, 2005.

Brinkley, Douglas. "Introduction." In *The Monkey Wrench Gang*, by Edward Abbey. New York: HarperCollins, Harper Perennial Modern Classics, 2006.

Broad, William, Stephen Engelberg, and Judith Miller. *Germs: Biological Weapons and America's Secret War*. New York: Simon and Schuster, 2001.

Broder, James F. *Risk Analysis and the Security Survey*. Burlington, MA: Butterworth-Heinemann, 2006.

Brzezinski, Zbigniew, and Brent Scowcroft. *America and the World: Conversations on the Future of American Foreign Policy*. New York: Basic Books, 2008.

Buky, Michael. "Terrorism, Piracy, and Climate Change: Challenges to International Maritime Governance." *Social Alternatives* 28, no. 2 (2009): 13–17.

Burleigh, Michael. *Blood and Rage: A Cultural History of Terrorism*. New York: HarperCollins, 2009.

Burnett, John S. *Dangerous Waters: Modern Piracy and Terror on the High Seas*. New York: Penguin Group, 2003.

Burns, Ronald G., Michael J. Lynch, and Paul Stretesky. *Environmental Law, Crime, and Justice*. New York: LFB Scholarly, 2008.

Burton, Fred. "The Challenge of the Lone Wolf." STRATFOR Global Intelligence, May 30, 2007. http://www.stratfor.com/challenge_lone_wolf.

Burton, Fred. "'Direct Action' Attacks: Terrorism by Another Name?" STRATFOR Global Intelligence, May 23, 2007. http://www.stratfor.com/direct_action_attacks_terrorism_another_name.

Bush, George H. W. *A National Security Strategy for the United States*. Washington, DC: White House, 1991. http://www.fas.org/man/docs/918015-nss.htm.

Carr, Caleb. *The Lessons of Terror: A History of Warfare against Civilians*. Rev. ed. New York: Random House, 2003.

Casagrande, Rocco. "Biological Terrorism Targeted at Agriculture: The Threat to US National Security." *The Nonproliferation Review* 7, no. 3 (2000): 92–105.

Center for Nonproliferation Studies. "Chart: Al-Qa'ida's WMD Activities." http://
cns.miis.edu/other/sjm_cht.htm.

Chalecki, Elizabeth L. "A New Vigilance: Identifying and Reducing the Risks of
Environmental Terrorism." *Global Environmental Politics* 2, no. 1 (February
2002). http://www.mitpressjournals.org/toc/glep/2/1.

Chaliand, Gérard, and Arnaud Blin, eds. "Preface." In *The History of Terrorism: From
Antiquity to Al Qaeda*, vii–viii. Translated by Edward Schneider, Kathryn
Pulver, and Jesse Browner. Berkeley: University of California Press, 2007.

Chaliand, Gérard, and Arnaud Blin. "Terrorism in Time of War: From World War II
to the Wars of National Liberation." In *The History of Terrorism: From Antiquity to Al Qaeda*, 208–220. Translated by Edward Schneider, Kathryn Pulver,
and Jesse Browner. Berkeley: University of California Press, 2007.

Chalk, Peter. "Contemporary Maritime Piracy in Southeast Asia." *Studies in Conflict and Terrorism* 21, no. 1 (1998): 87–112.

Chalk, Peter. *The Maritime Dimension of International Security: Terrorism, Piracy, and
Challenges for the United States*. Santa Monica, CA: RAND Corporation, 2008.
http://www.rand.org/pubs/monographs/MG697.html.

Chalk, Peter, Bruce Hoffman, Robert Reville, and Anna-Britt Kasupski. *Trends in
Terrorism: Threats to the United States and the Future of the Terrorism Risk Insurance Act*. Santa Monica, CA: RAND Corporation, 2005. http://www.rand.
org/pubs/monographs/MG393.html.

Clinton, William J. "Protecting America's Critical Infrastructure." Presidential Decision Directive/NSC 63, May 22, 1998. http://www.fas.org/irp/offdocs/
pdd/pdd-63.htm.

CNA Corporation. *National Security and the Threat of Climate Change*. Alexandria,
VA: CNA Corporation, 2007. http://securityandclimate.cna.org/report/
SecurityandClimate_Final.pdf.

"Combating Piracy off Somalia: Swift Naval Response Is Only Part of the Solution." *Strategic Comments* 15, no. 1 (February 2009): 1–2.

Coogan, Tim Pat. *The IRA: A History*. Niwot, CO: Roberts Rinehart, 1994.

Coronado, Rod. "Direct Actions Speak Louder Than Words." In *Terrorists or Freedom Fighters?: Reflections on the Liberation of Animals*, edited by Steven Best
and Anthony J. Nocella II, 178–84. New York: Lantern Books, 2004.

Coronado, Rod. "My Experience with Government Harassment." Appendix to
Terrorists or Freedom Fighters? Reflections on the Liberation of Animals, ed-
ited by Steven Best and Anthony J. Nocella II, 345–54. New York: Lantern
Books, 2004.

Cragin, Kim. *Understanding Terrorist Motivations*. Santa Monica, CA: RAND Corporation, December 2009. http://www.rand.org/pubs/testimonies/CT338.
html.

Crenshaw, Martha. "The Causes of Terrorism." In *New Global Terrorism: Characteristics, Causes, Controls*, edited by Charles W. Kegley, 92–105. Upper Saddle
River, NJ: Prentice Hall, 2003.

Crenshaw, Martha. "The Effectiveness of Terrorism in the Algerian War." In *Terrorism
in Context*, 475–513. University Park: Pennsylvania State University Press, 2001.

Crenshaw, Martha. "The Logic of Terrorism: Terrorist Behavior as a Product of
Strategic Choice." In *Origins of Terrorism: Psychologies, Ideologies, Theologies,
States of Mind*, edited by Walter Reich, 7–24. Washington, DC: Woodrow
Wilson Center Press, 1998.

Cronin, Audrey Kurth. *Terrorist Motivations for Chemical and Biological Weapons Use: Placing the Threat In Context.* Congressional Research Service Report for Congress, Order Code RL31831, March 28, 2003. http://www.fas.org/irp/crs/RL31831.pdf.

Cronin, Isaac. *Confronting Fear: A History of Terrorism.* New York: Thunder's Mouth Press, 2002.

Cummings Melanie C., David C. McGarvey, and Peter M. Vinch. *Homeland Security Risk Assessment.* Vol. 1, *Setting.* Arlington, VA: Homeland Security Institute, 2006. http://www.homelandsecurity.org/hsireports/Risk%20Assessment%20Volume%201%20Setting.pdf.

Curry, Andrew. "Mathematics of Terror." *Discover,* July/August 2010.

Dabelko, Geoffrey D. "Environmental Security Heats Up." *Environmental Change and Security Program Report* 13 (2008–9): viii–x.

de Becker, Gavin, Tom Taylor, and Jeff Marquart. *Just Two Seconds: Using Time and Space to Defeat Assassins.* Studio City, CA: Gavin de Becker Center for the Study and Reduction of Violence, 2008.

della Porta, Donatella. "Left-Wing Terrorism in Italy." In *Terrorism in Context,* edited by Martha Crenshaw, 105–59. University Park: Pennsylvania State University Press, 2001.

Deshpande, Nick. "Pyro-Terrorism: Recent Cases and the Potential for Proliferation." *Studies in Conflict and Terrorism* 32, no. 1 (2009): 36–44.

Devall, Bill, and George Sessions. *Deep Ecology: Living As If Nature Mattered.* Salt Lake City, UT: Gibbs Smith, 1985.

Diamond, Jared. *Collapse: How Societies Choose to Fail or Succeed.* New York: Penguin Books, 2005.

Dickinson, Tim. "The Climate Killers: Meet the 17 Polluters and Deniers Who Are Derailing Efforts to Curb Global Warming." *Rolling Stone,* January 21, 2010.

Douglas, John, and Mark Olshaker. *The Anatomy of Motive: The FBI's Legendary Mindhunter Explores the Key to Understanding and Catching Violent Criminals.* New York: Pocket Books, 1999.

Douglas, John E., Ann W. Burgess, Allen G. Burgess, and Robert K. Ressler. *Crime Classification Manual: A Standard System for Investigating and Classifying Violent Crimes.* New York: Lexington Books/Macmillan, 1992.

Durodié, Bill. "Home-Grown Nihilism: The Clash within Civilizations." *Journal of Homeland Security,* May 2007. http://www.homelandsecurity.org/journal/Default.aspx?oid=156&ocat=1.

Dyer, Carol, Ryan E. McCoy, Joel Rodriguez, and Donald N. Van Duyn. "Countering Violent Islamic Extremism: A Community Responsibility." *FBI Law Enforcement Bulletin* 76, no. 12 (December 2007). http://www.fbi.gov/publications/leb/2007/dec2007/december2007leb.htm.

"Earth Day: 40 Years and Still Fucked. So Where Do We Go from Here?" *Resistance: Journal of the Earth Liberation Movement* (Spring 2010): 53–55.

Earth First! Worldwide. "About Earth First!" http://www.earthfirst.org/about.htm.

"Ecoterrorist of the Season: Shell." *Resistance: Journal of the Earth Liberation Movement* (Fall 2009): 24–26.

Egan, Sean. "From Spikes to Bombs." *Studies in Conflict and Terrorism* 19, no. 1 (1996): 1–18.

Ehrlich, Paul R., and Anne H. Ehrlich. *The Dominant Animal: Human Evolution and the Environment.* Washington, DC: Island Press, 2008.

Eibl-Eibesfeldt, Irenäus. *The Biology of Peace and War: Men, Animals, and Aggression.* Translated by Eric Mosbacher. New York: Viking Press, 1979.

Elhanani, Doron. "Environmental Protection vs. Eco and Environmental Terrorism: Threats, Impact and Contingency Plans." In *GeoSpatial Visual Analytics: Geographical Information Processing and Visual Analytics for Environmental Security,* edited by Raffaele de Amicis, Radovan Stojanovic, and Giuseppe Conti, 479–90. Dordrecht, Netherlands: Springer, 2008.

Elliott, Robert. "Crude Oil and Corruption." *Security Management,* June 2007.

Encyclopedia of Science and Technology. 9th ed. New York: McGraw-Hill, 2002.

Environmental Protection Agency. "National Security Implications of Global Climate Change." http://www.epa.gov/climatechange/effects/forests.html.

Falk, Richard A. "A Duel Reality: Terrorism against the State and Terrorism by the State." In *New Global Terrorism: Characteristics, Causes, Controls,* edited by Charles W. Kegley, 53–59. Upper Saddle River, NJ: Prentice Hall, 2003.

"FBI: Al-Qaeda Detainee Spoke of Fire Plot." *USA Today,* July 11, 2003. http://www.usatoday.com/news/washington/2003-07-11-alqaeda-fire_x.htm.

"FBI: Eco-Terrorism Remains No. 1 Domestic Terror Threat." FOX News, March 31, 2008. http://www.foxnews.com/printer_friendly_story/0,3566,343768,00.html.

Federal Bureau of Investigation. "Amerithrax: Linguist/Behavioral Analysis." November 9, 2001. http://www.fbi.gov/anthrax/amerithrax.htm.

Federal Bureau of Investigation. "Anthrax Investigation: Closing a Chapter." *Headline Archives,* August 6, 2008. http://www.fbi.gov/page2/august08/amerithrax080608a.html.

Federal Bureau of Investigation. "Domestic Terrorism in the Post-9/11 Era." *Headline Archives,* September 7, 2009. http://www.fbi.gov/page2/sept09/domesticterrorism090709.html.

Federal Bureau of Investigation. "Eco-Terror Indictments." *Headline Archives,* January 20, 2006. http://www.fbi.gov/page2/jan06/elf012006.htm.

Federal Bureau of Investigation. "In Focus: 30 Years of Terrorism." *Terrorism in the United States 1999.* http://www.fbi.gov/stats-services/publications/terror_99.pdf.

Federal Bureau of Investigation. "Putting Intel to Work against ELF and ALF Terrorists." *Headline Archives,* June 30, 2008. http://www.fbi.gov/page2/june08/ecoterror_063008.html.

Federal Bureau of Investigation. "Seattle Eco-Terrorism Investigation." *Headline Archives,* March 4, 2008. http://www.fbi.gov/page2/march08/seattlearson_030408.html.

Federal Bureau of Investigation. "Terrorism 2002–2005." *Terrorism in the United States.* http://www.fbi.gov/stats-services/publications/terrorism-2002-2005/terror02_05.pdf.

Fein, Robert A., and Bryan Vossekuil. "Assassination in the United States: An Operational Study of Recent Assassins, Attackers, and Near-Lethal Approachers." *Journal of Forensic Science* 44, no. 2 (March 1999): 321–33. http://www.secretservice.gov/ntac/ntac_jfs.pdf.

Fighel, Jonathan. "The Forest Jihad." International Institute for Counter-Terrorism, October 28, 2008, 1–7. http://www.ict.org.il/Articles/tabid/66/Articlsid/506/currentpage/1/Default.aspx.

Fink, Steven. *Crisis Management: Planning for the Inevitable.* Lincoln, NE: iUniverse, 2002.

Flükiger, Jean Marc. "The Radical Animal Liberation Movement: Some Reflections on Its Future." *Journal for the Study of Radicalism* 2, no. 2 (2009): 111–32.

Foreman, Dave, and Bill Haywood, eds. *Ecodefense: A Field Guide to Monkeywrenching.* Chico, CA: Abbzug Press, 2003.

Foreman, David. *Confessions of an Eco-Warrior.* New York: Crown Publishers, 1991.

Freidman, Sam. "BP Oil Spill a Stain on Risk Management." *National Underwriter,* May 31, 2010.

Friedman, Thomas L. *Hot, Flat, and Crowded.* New York: Farrar, Straus, and Giroux, 2008.

Gates, Robert M. *National Defense Strategy.* U.S. Department of Defense, June 2008. http://www.defenselink.mil/news/2008%20national%20defense%20strategy.pdf.

Gigliotti, Richard, and Ronald Jason. "Approaches to Physical Security." In *Handbook of Loss Prevention and Crime Prevention,* edited by Lawrence J. Fennelly, 135–47. Boston: Butterworth-Heinemann, 1999.

Gillis, Tracy Knippenburg. *Emergency Exercise Handbook: Evaluate and Integrate Your Company's Plan.* Tulsa, OK: Penn Well Books, 1996.

Gleick, Peter H. "Water and Conflict: Freshwater Resources and International Security." *International Security* 18, no. 1 (Summer 1993): 79–112.

Goldwater-Nichols Department of Defense Reorganization Act of 1986, *U.S. Code* 50, Sec. 404a.

Goleman, Daniel. *Emotional Intelligence: Why It Can Matter More Than IQ.* New York: Bantam Books, 1995.

Goodell, Jeffrey. "As the World Burns." *Rolling Stone,* January 21, 2010.

Goodstein, Leonard, Timothy Nolan, and J. William Pfeiffer. *Applied Strategic Planning: A Comprehensive Guide.* New York: McGraw-Hill, 1993.

Gore, Al. *An Inconvenient Truth: The Planetary Emergency of Global Warming and What We Can Do about It.* New York: Rodale, 2006.

Guilmartin, Eugenia K. "Rejection of Political Institutions by Right Wing Extremists in the United States." In *The Making of a Terrorist: Recruitment, Training, and Root Causes.* Vol. 3, *Root Causes,* edited by James J. F. Forest, 92–106. Westport, CT: Praeger Security International, 2006.

"Gunman Kills 12, Wounds 31 at Fort Hood." NBC News, November 5, 2009. http://www.msnbc.msn.com/id/33678801.

Gurr, Ted Robert. *Why Men Rebel.* Princeton, NJ: Princeton University Press, 1970.

Hacker, Frederick J. *Crusaders, Criminals, Crazies: Terror and Terrorism in Our Time.* New York: W. W. Norton, 1976.

Hamilton, Alexander, James Madison, and John Jay. *The Federalist,* edited by Benjamin Fletcher Wright. New York: Metro Books, 1961.

Hamm, Mark. "Crimes Committed by Terrorist Groups: Theory, Research, and Prevention." Final Report. U.S. Department of Justice, National Criminal Justice Reference Service, NCJ211203, September 2005, 187–216. http://www.ncjrs.gov/pdffiles1/nij/grants/211203.pdf.

Hamm, Mark S. *In Bad Company: America's Terrorist Underground.* Boston: Northeast University Press, 2002.

Hansen, James. *Storms of My Grandchildren: The Truth about the Coming Climate Catastrophe and Our Last Chance to Save Humanity.* New York: Bloomsbury, 2009.

Hare, Robert D. *Without Conscience: The Disturbing World of Psychopaths among Us.* New York: Pocket Books, 1993.

Harmon, Mont Judd. *Political Thought: From Plato to the Present.* New York: McGraw-Hill, 1964.

Harvey, Michael G. "A Survey of Corporate Programs for Managing Terrorist Threats." *Journal of International Business Studies* 24, no. 3 (1993): 465–78.

"Hasan Trial Date Moved." KWTX News, June 1, 2010. http://www.kbtx.com/home/headlines/95329534.html.

Headquarters, Department of the Army. *Physical Security.* FM 3–19.30, January 18, 2001, 2-8–2-9.

Helmus, Todd C. "Why and How Some People Become Terrorists." In *Social Science for Counterterrorism: Putting the Pieces Together,* edited by Paul K. Davis and Kim Cragin, 71–109. Santa Monica, CA: RAND Corporation, 2009. http://www.rand.org/pubs/monographs/MG849.html.

Hermann, Margaret G., and Charles F. Hermann. "Hostage Taking, the Presidency, and Stress." In *Origins of Terrorism: Psychologies, Ideologies, Theologies, States of Mind,* edited by Walter Reich, 211–29. Washington, DC: Woodrow Wilson Center Press, 1998.

Heuer, Richards J., Jr. *Psychology of Intelligence Analysis.* Langley, VA: Center for the Study of Intelligence, Central Intelligence Agency, 1999. https://www.cia.gov/library/center-for-the-study-of-intelligence/csi-publications/books-and-monographs/psychology-of-intelligence-analysis/PsychofIntel New.pdf.

Hobbes, Thomas. *The Leviathan.* Edited by Francis B. Randall. New York: Washington Square Press, 1964.

Hochschild, Adam. "Blood and Treasure: Why One of the World's Richest Countries Is Also One of Its Poorest." *Mother Jones* 35, no. 2 (April 2010): 52–65.

Hoffer, Eric. *The True Believer.* New York: Perennial Classics, 2007.

Hoffman, Bruce. *Inside Terrorism.* New York: Columbia University Press, 1998.

Hollington, Kris. *Wolves, Jackals, and Foxes: The Assassins Who Changed History.* New York: St. Martin's Press, 2007.

Homer-Dixon, Thomas F. *Environment, Scarcity, and Violence.* Princeton, NJ: Princeton University Press, 1999.

Homer-Dixon, Thomas F. "Environmental Scarcities and Violent Conflict: Evidence from Cases." *International Security* 19, no. 1 (Summer 1994): 5–40.

Homer-Dixon, Thomas, and Jessica Blitt, eds. *Ecoviolence: Links among Environment, Population, and Security.* Lanham, MD: Rowman and Littlefield, 1998.

Homer-Dixon, Thomas F., and Marc A. Levy. "Correspondence: Environment and Security." *International Security* 20, no. 3 (Winter 1995/96): 189–98.

Honderich, Ted, ed. *The Oxford Guide to Philosophy.* New York: Oxford University Press, 1995.

Horgan, John. *The Psychology of Terrorism.* New York: Routledge, 2005.

Hosenball, Mark, Michael Isikoff, and Evan Thomas. "The Radicalization of Umar Farouk Abdulmutallab." *Newsweek,* January 11, 2010.

Houreld, Katharine. "Somali Pirates Hijack Cargo Ship with 23 Crew." ABC News, August 2, 2010. http://abcnews.go.com/International/wireStory?id=11302800.

Hubac-Occhipinti, Olivier. "Anarchist Terrorists of the Nineteenth Century." In *The History of Terrorism: From Antiquity to Al Qaeda*, edited by Gérard Chaliand and Arnaud Blin, 113–31. Translated by Edward Schneider, Kathryn Pulver, and Jesse Browner. Berkeley: University of California Press, 2007.

Hudson, Rex A. *Who Becomes a Terrorist and Why: The 1999 Government Report on Profiling Terrorists*. Guilford, CT: Lyons Press, 2002.

Hunt, Morton. *The Story of Psychology*. New York: Doubleday, 1993.

Inhofe, James. "Consensus is No Such Thing." *U.S. News and World Report*, April 2010.

Intergovernmental Panel on Climate Change. *Climate Change 2007: Synthesis Report*, 2007. http://www.ipcc.ch/pdf/assessment-report/ar4/syr/ar4_syr_spm.pdf.

International Maritime Organization. "Piracy in Waters off the Coast of Somalia." http://www.imo.org/home.asp?topic_id=1178.

International Maritime Organization. *Reports on Acts of Piracy and Armed Robbery against Ships*. MSC. 4/Circ. 154, May 5, 2010, 1. http://www.imo.org/includes/blastDataOnly.asp/data_id%3D28862/154.pdf.

International Union for Conservation of Nature. "Gorilla beringei ssp. Beringei." *The IUCN Red List of Threatened Species*, 2008. http://www.iucnredlist.org/apps/redlist/details/39999/0.

Jackson, Brian A. "Groups, Networks, or Movements: A Command-and-Control-Driven Approach to Classifying Terrorist Organizations and Its Application to Al Qaeda." *Studies in Conflict and Terrorism* 29, no. 3 (2006): 241–62.

Jackson, Brian A. "Organizational Decisionmaking by Terrorist Groups." In *Social Science for Counterterrorism: Putting the Pieces Together*, edited by Paul K. Davis and Kim Cragin, 209–56. Santa Monica, CA: RAND Corporation, 2009.

Jackson, Brian A., John C. Baker, Peter Chalk, Kim Cragin, John V. Parachini, and Horacio R. Trujillo. *Aptitude for Destruction*. Vol. 2, *Case Studies of Organizational Learning in Five Terrorist Groups*. MG-332-NIJ. Santa Monica, CA: RAND Corporation, 2005. http://www.rand.org/pubs/monographs/MG332.html.

Jackson, Brian A., and David R. Frelinger. *Understanding Why Terrorist Operations Succeed or Fail*. Santa Monica, CA: RAND Corporation, 2009.

"Japanese Tanker Attack Highlights Shipping Risks: Report." Business Insurance. com, August 6, 2010. http://www.businessinsurance.com/article/2010 0806/NEWS01/100809947.

Jenkins, Brian M. "International Terrorism: The Other World War." In *New Global Terrorism: Characteristics, Causes, Controls*, edited by Charles W. Kegley, 15–26. Upper Saddle River, NJ: Prentice Hall, 2003.

Jenkins, Brian Michael. *Going Jihad: The Fort Hood Slayings and Home-Grown Terrorism*. Santa Monica, CA: RAND Corporation, November 2009. http://www.rand.org/pubs/testimonies/CT336.html.

Johnson, Alex, Elizabeth Chuck, Bob Sullivan, Thomas Roberts, and Peter Alexander. "Sources: Discovery Suspect Had Starter Guns." NBC News, September 2, 2010. http://www.msnbc.msn.com/id/38968317/ns/us_news_crime_and_courts.

Jones, Jeffrey. "In U.S., Outlook for Environmental Quality Improving." Gallup, April 21, 2009. http://www.gallup.com/poll/117769/outlook-environmental-quality-improving.aspx.

Jones, Pattrice. "Mothers with Monkeywrenches: Feminist Imperatives and the ELF." In *Terrorists or Freedom Fighters?: Reflections on the Liberation of Animals*, edited by Steven Best and Anthony J. Nocella II, 137–56. New York: Lantern Books, 2004.

Juergensmeyer, Mark. *Terror in the Mind of God: The Global Rise of Religious Violence*. 3rd ed. Berkeley and Los Angeles: University of California Press, 2003.

Kahn, Richard. "From Herbert Marcuse to the Earth Liberation Front: Considerations for Revolutionary Ecopedagogy." *Green Theory and Praxis: The Journal of Ecopedagogy* 1, no. 1 (2005): 1–29. http://greentheoryandpraxis.org/journal/index.php/journal/issue/view/5.

Kaplan, Robert D. "The Coming Anarchy." *Atlantic*, February 1994.

Kaplan, Robert D. *The Ends of the Earth: From Togo to Turkmenistan, from Iran to Cambodia—A Journey to the Frontiers of Anarchy*. New York: Random House/Vintage Departures, 1996.

Katz, Jack. *Seductions of Crime: Moral and Sensual Attractions in Doing Evil*. New York: Basic Books, 1988.

Kilcullen, David J. "Countering Global Insurgency." *Journal of Strategic Studies* 28, no. 4 (August 2005): 597–617.

Kirkhope, James. "Australia 2009 Arson Wildfires: Possible Wildfire Jihad Tactic?" Terrorism Studies Group, February 9, 2009. http://www.terrorism-studies.com/Australia_2009_Arson_Wildfires.pdf.

Klare, Michael T. *Resource Wars: The New Landscape of Global Conflict*. New York: Henry Holt, 2001.

Koblent, Gregory D., and Jonathan B. Tucker. "Tracing an Attack: The Promise and Pitfalls of Microbial Forensics." *Survival: Global Politics and Strategy* 52, no. 1 (February–March 2010): 159–86.

Kosal, Margaret E. "Terrorism Targeting Industrial Chemical Facilities: Strategic Motivations and the Implications for U.S. Security." *Studies in Conflict and Terrorism* 29, no. 7 (2006): 719–51.

Kraska, James, and Brian Wilson. "Fighting Pirates: The Pen and the Sword." *World Policy Journal* 25, no. 4 (Winter 2008/9): 41–52.

Krebs, Valdis E. "Mapping Networks of Terrorist Cells." *International Network for Social Network Analysis: Connections* 24, no. 3 (2002): 43–52.

Kydd, Andrew H., and Barbara F. Walter. "The Strategies of Terrorism." *International Security* 31, no. 1 (Summer 2006): 51–56.

Lamy, Philip. *Millennium Rage: Survivalists, White Supremacists, and the Doomsday Prophecy*. New York: Plenum Press, 1996.

Langewiesche, William. *The Outlaw Sea: A World of Freedom, Chaos, and Crime*. New York: North Point Press, 2004.

Laqueur, Walter, ed. "Introduction." In *Voices of Terror: Manifestos, Writings, and Manuals of Al Qaeda, Hamas, and Other Terrorists from Around the World and Throughout the Ages*. New York: Reed Press, 2004.

Laqueur, Walter. *No End to War: Terrorism in the Twenty-First Century*. New York: Continuum International, 2003.

Laqueur, Walter. *Terrorism: A Study of National and International Political Violence*. Boston: Little, Brown, 1977.

Lardner, James, and Thomas Reppetto. *NYPD: A City and Its Police*. New York: Henry Holt, 2000.

Leader, Stefan H., and Peter Probst. "The Earth Liberation Front and Environmental Terrorism." *Terrorism and Political Violence* 15, no. 4 (Winter 2003): 37–58.

Leson, Joel. *Assessing and Managing the Terrorism Threat.* NCJ 210680. Washington, DC: U.S. Department of Justice, Bureau of Justice Assistance, 2005. http://www.ncjrs.gov/pdffiles1/bja/210680.pdf.

"Letters from the Underground: Parts I and II." Appendix to *Terrorists or Freedom Fighters?: Reflections on the Liberation of Animals,* edited by Steven Best and Anthony J. Nocella II, 354–60. New York: Lantern Books, 2004.

Levy, Marc A. "Is the Environment a National Security Issue." *International Security* 20, no. 2 (Fall 1995): 35–62.

Lewis, Bernard. *The Assassins: A Radical Sect in Islam.* New York: Basic Books, 1968.

Lewis, Bernard. *The Crisis of Islam: Holy War and Unholy Terror.* New York: Random House, 2004.

Lia, Brynjar, and Åshild Kjøk. "Energy Supply as Terrorist Targets? Patterns of 'Petroleum Terrorism' 1968–99." In *Oil in the Gulf: Obstacles to Democracy and Development,* edited by Daniel Heradstveit and Helge Hveem, 100–24. Burlington, VT: Ashgate, 2004.

Lichfield, John. "First They Poisoned the River. Now the Desperate Workers of Givet Threaten to Blow up Their Town." *Independent,* July 19, 2000. http://www.independent.co.uk/news/world/europe/first-they-poisoned-the-river-now-the-desperate-workers-of-givet-threaten-to-blow-up-their-town-707736.html.

Liddick, Donald R. *Eco-Terrorism: Radical Environmental and Animal Liberation Movements.* Westport, CT: Praeger, 2006.

Long, James, and Bryan Denson. "Crimes in the Name of the Environment." *Oregonian,* September 29, 1999. http://www.landrights.org/ALRA.oregon.eco-terrorism.htm.

Lovgren, Stefan. "Huge, Freed Pet Pythons Invade Florida Everglades." *National Geographic News,* June 3, 2004. http://news.nationalgeographic.com/news/2004/06/0603_040603_invasivespecies.html.

Luers, Jeffrey "Free." "How I Became an Ecowarrior." *Earth First! Journal,* http://www.earthfirstjournal.org/article.php?id=186.

Luft, Gal. "Pipeline Sabotage Is Terrorist's Weapon of Choice." *Energy Security,* March 28, 2005. http://www.iags.org/n0328051.htm.

Machiavelli, Niccoló. *The Prince.* Translated by Ninian Hill Thompson. Norwalk, CT: Easton Press, 1980.

Mancuso-Smith, Chrystal. *From Monkeywrenching to Mass Destruction: Eco-Sabotage and the American West.* 26 Journal of Land, Resources, and Environmental Law (2006): 319–31.

Manes, Christopher. *Green Rage: Radical Environmentalism and the Unmaking of Civilization.* Boston: Little, Brown, 1990.

Margolies-Beitler, Ruth. "The Complex Relationship between Global Terrorism and U.S. Support for Israel." In *The Making of a Terrorist: Recruitment, Training, and Root Causes.* Vol. 3, *Root Causes,* edited by James J.F. Forest, 62–73. Westport, CT: Praeger Security International, 2006.

Marighella, Carlos. *Minimanual of the Urban Guerrilla.* http://ballistichelmet.org/school/urban_warfare.pdf.

Marmiroli, Nelson, Marta Marmiroli, and Elena Maestri. "Monitoring of Environmental Resources against Intentional Threats." In *Threats to Food and Water Chain Infrastructure*, edited by Virginia Koukouliou, Magdalena Ujevic, and Otto Premstaller, 51–74. Dordrecht, Netherlands: Springer, 2010.

Marx, Jenifer G. "Pirate Round." In *Pirates: Terror on the High Seas—From the Caribbean to the South China Sea*, edited by David Cordingly, 140–63. East Bridgewater, MA: World Publications Group, 1998.

Matthew, Richard A., Ted Gaulin, and Bryan McDonald. "The Elusive Quest: Linking Environmental Change and Conflict." *Canadian Journal of Political Science* 36, no. 4 (September 2003): 857–78.

Matthew, Richard A., and Bryan McDonald. "Environmental Security: Academic and Policy Debates in North America." In *Facing Global Environmental Change: Environmental, Human, Energy, Food, Health, and Water Security Concepts*. Berlin, Germany: Springer, 2009. http://www.springerlink.com/content/h52t18631j1363j5.

May, Eric H. "Rush is Right about a BP Horizon Terror Attack." *Lone Star Iconoclast*, May 3, 2010. http://lonestaricon.com/index.php?option-com_content&view=article&id=622.

McCann, Joseph T. *Terrorism on American Soil: A Concise History of Plots and Perpetrators from the Famous to the Forgotten*. Boulder, CO: Sentient Publications, 2006.

McCleskey, Edward, Diana McCord, Jennifer Leetz, and John Markey. *Underlying Reasons for Success and Failure of Terrorist Attacks: Selected Case Studies*. Final Report. Arlington, VA: Homeland Security Institute, 2007. http://www.homelandsecurity.org/Content.aspx?mid=278.

McGloin, Jean Marie, and David S. Kirk. "An Overview of Social Network Analysis." *Journal of Criminal Justice Education* 21, no. 2 (June 2010): 169–81.

Merari, Ariel. "Terrorism as a Strategy of Insurgency." In *The History of Terrorism: From Antiquity to Al Qaeda*, edited by Gérard Chaliand and Arnaud Blin, 12–54. Translated by Edward Schneider, Kathryn Pulver, and Jesse Browner. Berkeley: University of California Press, 2007.

Merchant, Carolyn. *American Environmental History: An Introduction*. New York: Columbia University Press, 2007.

Michel, Lou, and Dan Herbeck. *American Terrorist: Timothy McVeigh and the Tragedy at Oklahoma City*. New York: Avon Books, 2002.

Middle East Media Research Institute (MEMRI). "Islamist Forum Member Proposes Poisoning Water Systems of Major American Cities." *Jihad and Terrorism Threat Monitor* 2021, August 12, 2008. http://www.memrijttm.org/content/en/report.htm?report=2829.

Migaux, Phillipe. "The Future of the Islamist Movement." In *The History of Terrorism: From Antiquity to Al Qaeda*, edited by Gérard Chaliand and Arnaud Blin, 349–62. Translated by Edward Schneider, Kathryn Pulver, and Jesse Browner. Berkeley: University of California Press, 2007.

Military Studies in the Jihad against the Tyrants. http://feastofhateandfear.com/archives/al_qaeda.html.

Miller, Joshua Rhett. "Australian Wildfires Could Fuel 'Forest Jihad' Terrorists, Experts Say." FOX News, February 9, 2009. http://www.foxnews.com/story/0,2933,490306,00.html.

Montaldo, Charles. "About.com Guide to Historical Crimes." http://crime.about.com/od/murder/p/squeaky.htm.

Moore, John Norton, and Robert F. Turner, eds. *National Security Law*. Durham, NC: Carolina Academic Press, 2005.

Morozov, Nikolai. "The Terrorist Struggle." In *Voices of Terror: Manifestos, Writings, and Manuals of Al Qaeda, Hamas, and Other Terrorists from Around the World and Throughout the Ages*, edited by Walter Laqueur, 76–82. New York: Reed Press, 2004.

Mueller, Robert S. "Congressional Testimony before the Senate Committee on Homeland Security and Government Affairs," September 2009. http://www.fbi.gov/congress/congress09/mueller093009.htm.

Murray, Dian H. "Chinese Pirates." In *Pirates: Terror on the High Seas—From the Caribbean to the South China Sea*, edited by David Cordingly, 212–35. East Bridgewater, MA: World Publications Group, 2007.

Myers, John. "A Crude Coincidence—The Gulf Oil Spill Works Out Well for the Greens." *Personal Liberty Digest*, May 5, 2010. http://www.personalliberty.com/personal-liberty-articles/a-crude-coincidence%e2%80%94the-gulf-oil-spill-works-out-well-for-the-greens.

Nacos, Brigitte L. *Terrorism and Counterterrorism: Understanding Threats and Responses in the Post 9/11 World*. 3rd ed. Boston: Pearson-Longman, 2010.

Nash, Roderick Frazier. *Wilderness and the American Mind*. 4th ed. New Haven, CT: Yale University Press, 2001.

National Academies. "Understanding and Responding to Climate Change." Highlights of National Academies Reports 2008 Edition. http://www.nationalacademies.org/morenews/20080519.html.

National Commission on Terrorist Attacks upon the United States. *The 9/11 Commission Report*. New York: W. W. Norton, n.d.

National Consortium for the Study of Terrorism and Responses to Terrorism (START). "Background Report: Discovery Communications Building Hostage-Taking." September 1, 2010. http://www.start.umd.edu/start/announcements/announcement.asp?id=205.

National Consortium for the Study of Terrorism and Responses to Terrorism. "Terrorist Organization Profile: Aryan Republican Army (ARA)." http://www.start.umd.edu/start/data_collections/tops/terrorist_organization_profile.asp?id=3412.

National Consortium for the Study of Terrorism and Responses to Terrorism. "Terrorist Organization Profile: Lord's Resistance Army (LRA)." http://www.start.umd.edu/start/data_collections/tops/terrorist_organization_profile.asp?id=3513.

National Consortium for the Study of Terrorism and Responses to Terrorism. "Terrorist Organization Profile: Movement for the Emancipation of the Niger Delta (MEND)." http://www.start.umd.edu/start/data_collections/tops/terrorist_organization_profile.asp?id=4692.

National Consortium for the Study of Terrorism and Responses to Terrorism. "Global Terrorism Database." http://www.start.umd.edu/gtd (accessed February 28, 2010).

National Consortium for the Study of Terrorism and Responses to Terrorism. "Global Terrorism Database." GTD ID#200402020010, 200310150003, and 200311120005. http://www.start.umd.edu/gtd (accessed February 28, 2010).

National Consortium for the Study of Terrorism and Responses to Terrorism. "Global Terrorism Database." GTD ID#199810250005. http://www.start.umd.edu/gtd (accessed February 28, 2010).

National Counterterrorism Center. *2009 Report on Terrorism*. Washington, DC: National Counterterrorism Center, 2010. http://www.nctc.gov/witsbanner/docs/2009_report_on_terrorism.pdf.

National Intelligence Council. *Global Trends 2025: A Transformed World*. Washington, DC: U.S. Government Printing Office, August 2008. http://www.dni.gov/nic/NIC_2025_project.html.

National Research Council of the National Academies. *Ecological Impacts of Climate Change*. Washington, DC: The National Academies Press, 2008. http://www.nap.edu/catalog.php?record_id=12491.

Naylor, R. T. *Wages of Crime: Black Markets, Illegal Finance, and the Underworld Economy*. New York: Cornell University Press, 2002.

Nechaev, Sergey. "Catechism of the Revolutionist (1869)." In *Voices of Terror: Manifestos, Writings, and Manuals of Al Qaeda, Hamas, and Other Terrorists from Around the World and Throughout the Ages*, edited by Walter Laqueur, 71–75. New York: Reed Press, 2004.

NEFA Foundation. "United States v. Shnewer et al—Fort Dix Trial." http://www1.nefafoundation.org/ftdixdocs.html.

Nichols, Randall, Daniel J. Ryan, and Julie J.C.H. Ryan. *Defending Your Digital Assets against Hackers, Crackers, Spies, and Thieves*. New York: McGraw-Hill, 2000.

Nichter, D. Anthony. "Betting on Enterprise Risk Management." *Security Management*, September 2008.

"No Compromise in Defense of Mother Earth." *Earth First! Journal*. http://www.earthfirstjournal.org/section.php?id=1.

Nocella II, Anthony J., and Matthew J. Walton. "Standing up to Corporate Greed." *Green Theory and Praxis: The Journal of Ecopedagogy* 1, no. 1 (2005): 1–17. http://greentheoryandpraxis.org/journal/index.php/journal/issue/view/5.

Nomad, Max. *Apostles of Revolution*. Boston: Little, Brown and Company, 1939.

North American Earth Liberation Front Press Office (NAELFPO). "NIO's First Annual Animal Liberation/Militant Direct Action (MDA) Awards" http://www.animalliberationfront.com/News/2010_01/2010MilitantDirectActionAwards.htm.

North American Earth Liberation Front Press Office. "ELF Topples Radio Station Towers in Washington." September 4, 2009. http://www.indybay.org/newsitems/2009/09/04/18620846.php.

North American Earth Liberation Front Press Office. "Frequently Asked Questions." http://www.animalliberationfront.com/ALFront/ELF/elf_faq.pdf.

Obama, Barack. *National Security Strategy*. Washington, DC: White House, May 2010. http://www.whitehouse.gov/sites/default/files/rss_viewer/national_security_strategy.pdf.

O'Neill, Bard E. *Insurgency and Terrorism: From Revolution to Apocalypse*. Washington, DC: Potomac Books, 2005.

Osterholm, Michael T., and John Schwartz. *Living Terrors: What America Needs to Know to Survive the Coming Bioterrorist Catastrophe*. New York: Delacorte Press/Random House, 2000.

U.S. Congress. Committee on Resources. *Ecoterrorism and Lawlessness on the National Forests*. Oversight Hearing before the Subcommittee on Forests and Forest Health. 107th Cong., 2nd sess., 2002, 48–49. Statement and testimony of James F. Jarboe, domestic terrorism section chief, Counterterrorism Division, FBI Headquarters.http://frwebgate.access.gpo.gov/cgi-bin/getdoc.cgi?dbname=107_house_hearings&docid=f:77615.pdf.

Pacific Institute. "Water Conflict Chronology, November 2009." http://world water.org/conflict/index.html.

Paoli, Letizia. *Mafia Brotherhoods: Organized Crime, Italian Style*. New York: Oxford University Press, 2003.

Parfomak, Paul W. *Pipeline Safety and Security: Federal Programs*. Congressional Research Service Report for Congress, Order Code RL33347. Updated February 29, 2008. http://www.fas.org/sgp/crs/homesec/RL33347.pdf, citing David S. Cloud, "A Former Green Beret's Plot to Make Millions through Terrorism." *Ottawa Citizen*, December 24, 1999.

Parfomak, Paul W. *Pipeline Security: An Overview of Federal Activities and Current Policy Issues*. Congressional Research Service Report for Congress, Order Code RL31990. Updated February 5, 2004. http://www.fas.org/sgp/crs/RL31990.pdf.

Parry, Albert. *Terrorism: From Robespierre to Arafat*. New York: Vanguard Press, 1976.

Parson, Sean. "Understanding the Ideology of the Earth Liberation Front." *Green Theory and Praxis: The Journal of Ecopedagogy* 4, no. 2 (2008): 50–66. http://greentheoryandpraxis.org/journal/index.php/journal/issue/view/7.

Pelham, Brett. "Awareness, Opinions about Global Warming Vary Worldwide." Gallup, April 22, 2009. http://www.gallup.com/poll/117772/awareness-opinions-global-warming-vary-worldwide.aspx.

Pelton, Robert Young. *The World's Most Dangerous Places*. New York: Harper Resource/Harper Collins, 2000.

Perry, Nicholas J. "The Numerous Federal Legal Definitions of Terrorism: The Problem of Too Many Grails." *Journal of Legislation* 30 (2004): 249–74.

Pew Center on Global Climate Change. *National Security Implications of Global Climate Change*. August 2009. http://www.pewclimate.org/docUploads/national-security-implications-memo-august2009.pdf.

Pew Center on Global Climate Change. *Summary: Copenhagen Climate Summit*. http://www.pewclimate.org/international/copenhagen-climate-summit-summary.

Pew Center on Global Climate Change and the Pew Center on the States. *Climate Change 101: Understanding and Responding to Global Climate Change*. January 2009. http://www.pewclimate.org/docUploads/Climate101-Complete-Jan09.pdf.

Pham, J. Peter. "Anti-Piracy, Adrift." *Journal of International Security Affairs* 18 (Spring 2010): 81–88. http://www.securityaffairs.org/issues/2010/18/pham.php.

Pickering, Leslie James. "A Brief Look at 40 Years of Guerrilla Sabotage in Defense of the Earth." *Resistance: Journal of the Earth Liberation Movement* (Spring 2010): 47–52.

Pierce, William. [Andrew MacDonald, pseud.]. *Hunter*. Hillsboro, WV: Vanguard Books, 1989.

Pinker, Steven. *The Blank Slate: The Modern Denial of Human Nature*. New York: Penguin Group, 2002.

Platt, Richard. "Corsairs of the Mediterranean." In *Pirates: Terror on the High Seas—From the Caribbean to the South China Sea*, edited by David Cordingly, 76–99. East Bridgewater, MA: World Publications Group, 2007.

Poland, James M. *Understanding Terrorism: Groups, Strategies, and Responses*. Upper Saddle River, NJ: Prentice Hall, 2011.

Post, Jerrold M. *The Mind of the Terrorist: The Psychology of Terrorism from the IRA to Al-Qaeda*. New York: Palgrave MacMillan, 2007.

Post, Jerrold M. "Terrorist Psycho-Logic: Terrorist Behavior as a Product of Psychological Forces." In *Origins of Terrorism: Psychologies, Ideologies, Theologies, States of Mind*, edited by Walter Reich, 25–42. Washington, DC: Woodrow Wilson Center Press, 1998.

President's Commission on Critical Infrastructure. *Critical Foundations: Protecting America's Infrastructures*. October 13, 1997. http://www.fas.org/sgp/library/pccip.pdf.

Purver, Ron. *Chemical and Biological Terrorism: The Threat According to the Open Literature*. Ottawa: Canadian Security Intelligence Service, 1995.

Rapoport, David C. "The Four Waves of Rebel Terror and September 11." In *New Global Terrorism: Characteristics, Causes, Controls*, edited by Charles W. Kegley, 36–52. Upper Saddle River, NJ: Prentice Hall, 2003.

Rapoport, David C. "Sacred Terror: A Contemporary Example from Islam." In *Origins of Terrorism: Psychologies, Ideologies, Theologies, States of Mind*, edited by Walter Reich, 103–30. Washington, DC: Woodrow Wilson Center Press, 1998.

Raymond, Gregory A. "The Evolving Strategies of Political Terrorism." In *New Global Terrorism: Characteristics, Causes, Controls*, edited by Charles W. Kegley, 71–83. Upper Saddle River, NJ: Prentice Hall, 2003.

Reeve, Simon. *The New Jackals: Ramzi Yousef, Osama bin Laden, and the Future of Terrorism*. Boston: Northeastern University Press, 1999.

Reich, Walter, ed. "Introduction." In *Origins of Terrorism: Psychologies, Ideologies, Theologies, States of Mind*, 1–6. Washington, DC: Woodrow Wilson Center Press, 1998.

Ressler, Steve. "Social Network Analyses as an Approach to Combat Terrorism: Past, Present, and Future Research." *Homeland Security Affairs* 2, no. 2 (July 2006). http://www.hsaj.org/?fullarticle=2.2.8.

Revell, Oliver, and Dwight Williams. *A G-Man's Journal: A Legendary Career inside the FBI—From the Kennedy Assassination to the Oklahoma City Bombing*. New York: Pocket Books, 1998.

Reynolds, Melinda L. *Landowner Liability for Terrorist Acts*, 47 Case W. Res. L. Rev. 155, 184 (1996).

Roeschke, Joseph Elliott. *Eco-Terrorism and Piracy on the High Seas: Japanese Whaling and the Rights of Private Groups to Enforce International Conservation Law in Neutral Waters*, 20 Villanova Environmental Law Journal, no. 1 (2009): 99–136.

Sageman, Marc. *Leaderless Jihad: Terror Networks in the Twenty-First Century*. Philadelphia: University of Pennsylvania Press, 2008.

Sageman, Marc. *Understanding Terror Networks*. Philadelphia: University of Pennsylvania Press, 2004.

Scarce, Rik. *Eco-Warriors: Understanding the Radical Environmental Movement*. Walnut Creek, CA: Left Coast Press, 2006.

Schneider, Paul. "The Well From Hell." *Men's Journal*, August 2010, 80–87.

Schneier, Bruce. *Beyond Fear: Thinking Sensibly about Security in an Uncertain World*. New York: Copernicus Books, 2003.

Schneier, Bruce. *Schneier on Security*. Indianapolis, IN: Wiley, 2008.

Schwartz, Daniel M. "Environmental Terrorism: Analyzing the Concept." *Journal of Peace Research* 35, no. 4 (July 1988): 483–96. http://www.jstor.org/pss/425754.

Sea Shepherd Conservation Society. "Who We Are." http://www.seashepherd.org/who-we-are.

Shugart, Herman, Roger Sedjo, and Brent Sohngen. *Forest and Global Climate Change: Potential Impacts on U.S. Forest Resources*. Pew Center on Global Climate Change, 2003. http://www.pewclimate.org/docUploads/forestry.pdf.

Silber, Mitchell D., and Arvin Bhatt. *Radicalization in the West: The Homegrown Threat*. New York: New York City Police Department, 2007.

Sinclair, Andrew. *An Anatomy of Terror: A History of Terrorism*. London: Macmillan, 2003.

Smith, Brent. "A Look at Terrorist Behavior: How They Prepare, Where They Strike." *NIJ Journal* 260 (July 2008): 2–6. http://www.ncjrs.gov/pdffiles1/nij/222900.pdf.

Smith, Rebecca K. *Ecoterrorism: A Critical Analysis of the Vilification of Radical Environmental Activists as Terrorists*. 38 Environmental Law 537-48 (Spring 2008). http://legacy.lclark.edu/org/envtl/objects/38-2_Smith.pdf.

Smits, David D. "The Frontier Army and the Destruction of the Buffalo: 1865–1883." *Western Historical Quarterly* 25, no. 3 (Autumn 1994): 313–38.

Sobel, Jeremy, Ali Khan, and David Swerdlow. "Threat of a Biological Terrorist Attack on the US Food Supply: The CDC Perspective." *Lancet* 359 (March 2002): 874-880.

Solomon, Susan, Gian-Kasper Plattner, Reto Knutti, and Pierre Friedlingstein. "Irreversible Climate Change Due to Carbon Dioxide Emissions." *Proceedings of the National Academy of Sciences of the United States of America* 106, no. 6 (February 10, 2009): 1704–9. http://www.pnas.org/cgi/doi/10.1073/pnas.0812721106.

Sorek, Susan. *Jews against Rome: War in Palestine AD 66–73*. London: Continuum, 2008.

Soskis, David A., and Clinton R. Van Zandt. "Hostage Negotiation: Law Enforcement's Most Effective Non-Lethal Weapon." *FBI Management Quarterly* 6, no. 4 (Autumn 1986): 1–9.

"Sri Lanka Rebels 'Lose Last Town.'" *Al Jazeera*, January 26, 2009. http://english.aljazeera.net/news/asia/2009/01/2009125133055917676.html.

Stern, Jessica. *The Ultimate Terrorists*. Cambridge, MA: Harvard University Press, 1999.

Straw, Joseph. "How Vulnerable Are We." *Security Management*, August 2008.

Sun Tzu. *The Art of War*. Translated by Ralph D. Sawyer. New York: Barnes and Noble, 1994.

Sundt, Nick. "Texas Congressman in Copenhagen Dismisses Climate Science: 'We Don't Have an Icecap in Texas.'" WWF Climate Blog, December 23, 2009. http://www.climatesciencewatch.org/index.php/csw/details/barton-sensenbrenner-copenhagen.

"A Synopsis of the Terrorist Threat Facing the O&G Industry." *Oil and Gas Industry Terrorism Monitor*. http://www.ogi-tm.com/ogi_threats_st.php.

Taleb, Nassim Nicholas. *The Black Swan: The Impact of the Highly Improbable.* New York: Random House, 2007.

"Targeting EnCana." *Resistance: Journal of the Earth Liberation Movement* (Fall 2009): 32–35.

Ternon, Yves. "Russian Terrorism, 1878–1908." In *The History of Terrorism: From Antiquity to Al Qaeda,* edited by Gérard Chaliand and Arnaud Blin, 132–74. Translated by Edward Schneider, Kathryn Pulver, and Jesse Browner. Berkeley: University of California Press, 2007.

Thoreau, Henry D. *The Essays of Henry D. Thoreau.* Edited by Lewis Hyde. New York: North Point Press, 2002.

Thoreau, Henry D. *A Week on the Concord and Merrimack Rivers.* New York: Penguin Group, 1998.

Thucydides. *The Peloponnesian War.* Translated by Martin Hammond. New York: Oxford University Press, 2009.

Tocqueville, Alexis de. *Democracy in America.* Translated and edited by Harvey C. Mansfield and Delba Winthrop. Chicago: University of Chicago Press, 2000.

Trujillo, Horacio R. "The Radical Environmentalist Movement." In Brian A. Jackson, John C. Baker, Kim Cragin, John Parachini, Horacio R. Trujillo, and Peter Chalk, *Aptitude for Destruction.* Vol. 2, *Case Studies of Organizational Learning in Five Terrorist Groups,* 141–72. Santa Monica, CA: RAND Corporation, 2005.

Tuchman-Mathews, Jessica. "Redefining Security." *Foreign Affairs* 68, no. 2 (Spring 1979): 162–77.

Tucker, Jonathan B. ed. *Toxic Terror: Assessing Terrorist Use of Chemical and Biological Weapons.* Cambridge, MA: MIT Press, 2000.

Ungar, Sanford J. *FBI: An Uncensored Look behind the Walls.* Boston and Toronto: Little, Brown, 1976.

United Nations. *Convention on the Law of the Sea.* Article 101, December 10, 1982. UNTS 3, entered into force on November 16, 1994. http://www.un.org/Depts/los/convention_agreements/texts/unclos/unclos_e.pdf.

United Nations. *Convention for the Suppression of Unlawful Acts against the Safety of Maritime Navigation.* Adopted March 10, 1988; UNTS, entered into force March 1, 1992. http://treaties.un.org/doc/db/Terrorism/Conv8-english.pdf.

United Nations Environment Program. *From Conflict to Peacebuilding: The Role of Natural Resources and the Environment.* Nairobi, Kenya: United Nations Environment Program, 2009. http://www.unep.org/pdf/pcdmb_policy_01.pdf.

United Nations General Assembly. *Climate Change and Its Possible Security Implications: Report of the Secretary-General.* September 2009, 4. http://www.unhcr.org/refworld/docid/4ad5e6380.html.

United States v. Stone. Case No. 2:10-cr-20123. Indictment at 1–5. E.D. Mich., filed March 23, 2010.

United States v. Tankersley. CR No. 06-60071-1-AA. Information D. Oregon, filed July 20, 2005.

United States Department of Health and Human Services. Centers for Disease Control and Prevention. "Botulism." http://www.cdc.gov/nczved/dfbmd/disease_listing/botulism_gi.html.

United States Department of Homeland Security. Office of Intelligence and Analysis. *National Infrastructure Protection Plan: Partnering to Enhance Protection and Resiliency.* 2009. http://www.fas.org/irp/agency/dhs/nipp2009.pdf.

United States Department of Homeland Security. Office of Intelligence and Analysis. *National Response Framework.* January 2008. http://www.fema.gov/pdf/emergency/nrf/nrf-core.pdf.

United States Department of Justice. *Amerithrax Investigative Summary.* February 19, 2010. http://www.justice.gov/amerithrax/docs/amx-investigative-summary.pdf.

United States Fire Administration. "Fires in the Wildland/Urban Interface." *U.S. Fire Administration Topical Fire Research Series* 2, no. 16 (March 2002). http://www.usfa.dhs.gov/downloads/pdf/tfrs/v2i16-508.pdf.

United States Fire Administration. "Wildland Fires: A Historical Perspective." *U.S. Fire Administration Topical Fire Research Series* 1, no. 3 (October 2000, Rev. December 2001). http://www.usfa.dhs.gov/downloads/pdf/tfrs/v1i3-508.pdf.

United States Homeland Security Council. *National Strategy for Homeland Security.* October 2007. http://www.dhs.gov/xlibrary/assets/nat_strat_homelandsecurity_2007.pdf.

U.S. Code 18, Sec. 1864 (a) (2) (2006).

U.S. Code 18, Sec. 2331 (1) (2006).

U.S. Code 50, Sec. 1801 (c) (2006).

Veldhuis, Tinka, and Jørgen Staun. *Islamist Radicalisation: A Root Cause Model.* The Hague: Netherlands Institute of International Relations Clingendael, 2009. http://www.clingendael.nl.

"Venezuela's Hugo Chavez Targets Major Foreign Oil Companies in Nationalization Fight." FOX News, January 16, 2007. http://www.foxnews.com/printer_friendly_story/0,3566,243901,00.html.

Vidino, Lorenzo. "The Hofstad Group: The New Face of Terrorist Networks in Europe." *Studies in Conflict and Terrorism* 30, no. 7 (2007): 579–92.

Wadhams, Nick. "Endangered Gorillas Held Hostage by Rebels in African Park." *National Geographic News,* May 23, 2007. http://news.nationalgeographic.com/news/2007/05/070523-gorillas-hostage.html.

Waller, J. Michael. "Prisons as Terrorist Breeding Grounds." In *The Making of a Terrorist: Recruitment, Training, and Root Causes.* Vol. 1, *Recruitment,* edited by James J. F. Forest, 23–40. Westport, CT: Praeger Security International, 2006.

Watson, Paul. "On the Frontlines: With Captain Paul Watson and the Sea Shepherd Conservation Society." *Resistance: Journal of the Earth Liberation Movement* (Fall 2009): 14–19.

Watson, Paul. *Sea Shepherd: My Fight for Whales and Seals.* New York: W. W. Norton, 1982.

Weimann, Gabriel. *Terror on the Internet: The New Arena, the New Challenges.* Washington, DC: United States Institute of Peace Press, 2006.

Weinzierl, John. "Terrorism: Its Origin and History." In *Understanding Terrorism: Threats in an Uncertain World,* edited by Akorlie A. Nyatepe-Coo and Dorothy Zeisler-Vralsted, 34–35. Upper Saddle River, NJ: Prentice Hall, 2004.

White, Jonathan R. *Terrorism and Homeland Security.* 6th ed. Belmont, CA: Wadsworth Cengage Learning, 2009.

Will, George F. "Everyone Out of the Water!" *Newsweek,* November 16, 2009.

Willis, Henry H., Andrew R. Morral, Terrence K. Kelly, and Jamison Jo Medby. *Estimating Terrorism Risk.* MG-388. Santa Monica, CA: RAND Corporation, 2005. http://www.rand.org/pubs/monographs/MG388.html.

Wilson, James Q., and Richard J. Herrnstein. *Crimes and Human Nature*. New York: Simon and Schuster, 1985.

Yungher, Nathan I. *Terrorism: The Bottom Line*. Upper Saddle River, NJ: Prentice Hall, 2008.

Zeskind, Leonard. *Blood and Politics: The History of the White Nationalist Movement from the Margins to the Mainstream*. New York: Farrar, Straus, and Giroux, 2009.

Index

Abbey, Edward, 80, 85, 96
Abdulmutallab, Umar Farouk, 51
Abrahms, Max, 150–51
Addicott, Jeffrey, 35
Aden-Abyan Islamic Army, 134–35
Ael Fatmi, Nouredine, 114
Africa, 176–80
Air pollution, 14, 27–28
Aleatoric uncertainty principle, 140
Alexander II (Czar), 109–10
Algemene Inlichtingen-en Veiligheids-
    dienst (AIVD), 108, 115
Ali, Hirsi, 107–8
Al Issar, Riduan, 108
Al Qaeda terrorists: arson attacks by,
    130; and bioweapons, 132; oil/gas
    industry attacks by, 135–36; orga-
    nizational structure of, 110, 112;
    radicalization process of, 72–73;
    religious nature of, 43; risk of, 138,
    162; security planning for, 186, 190;
    strategy of, 24, 127, 148–50; tactics
    of, 51–52, 53; and U.S. interests, 139.
    See also Jihadism
Al Suri, Abu Musab, 111–12
Amerithrax case, 27
Amory, Cleveland, 94

Anarchist-terrorism, 38–40, 45, 48,
    80, 99
ANFO bomb, 51
Animal Liberation Front (ALF):
    autonomous cell structure of, 95–96,
    98–99; direct actions by, 101, 102–4;
    founding of, 78, 95–96; and radical
    environmental movement, 4, 35–36,
    104; tactics of, 185
Anthrax. See *Bacillus anthracis*
    (anthrax)
Antiabortion terrorists, 6
Anticapitalism groups, 99, 102, 116
Antiglobalization groups, 99, 102,
    115–17
Anti-Semitism, 120
Antiterrorism statutes, 114
Antithetical terrorists, 4
Applied Strategic Planning (Goodstein,
    Nolan, Pfeiffer), 169–70, 174
Army of God, 43
Arson attacks: and ELF, 98; on envi-
    ronment, 25–26, 28–29, 31, 74; fire-
    fighting concerns, 28–29; by Islamic
    terrorists, 23; by lone wolf terror-
    ists, 24–25; overview, 53–54; and
    radical environmental movement,

90–92, 91; Vail Mountain fires,
    165–66; on wildlands, 129–30
Art of War, The (Sun Tzu), 1, 7
Aryan Nations, 42, 122
Aryan Republican Army (ARA),
    122–23
Asian carp concerns, 30
Assassins, 38, 44–45
Attack tree model, 161–62
Attrition principle, 49–50
Auerbach, Hagedorn, 168, 191–92
Aum Shinrikyo cult, 28, 55
Autonomous cell structure, 95–96,
    98–99, 110
Azzan, Abudallah, 150
Azzouz, Samir, 113–14

Bacillus anthracis (anthrax), 27, 54,
    130–31
Baird, Julia, 179–80
Ban Ki-moon, 21
Barbary corsairs, 125, 193
Barnard, Chester, 150
Basque Fatherland and Liberty Move-
    ment, 64
Beam, Louis, 46, 95
Berg, Alan, 156
Bernstein, Peter, 140
Bhopal incident, 167
Bin Laden, Osama, 3–4, 132, 150
Biocentrism principle, 81, 82, 91, 96
Biological warfare, 15, 26, 118–19, 121,
    130–34
*Biology of Peace and War: Men, Ani-
    mals, and Aggression, The* (Eibl-
    Eibesfeldt), 62
Blank Slate, The (Pinker), 61
Bombs/bombings, 28, 31, 50–53,
    92, 102, 185. *See also* Suicide
    bombers
Bottom-up radicalization, 72–73
Bouyeri, Mohammed, 107–8, 114
British Petroleum (BP), 137–39
Broder, James, 140, 142
Brown, John, 78
Built environments, 2, 28–29, 31–32,
    134–36
Bureau of Land Management, 98
Bush, George H.W., 15, 18, 19

Cancun Agreement, 13
Cap and trade legislation, 13
Carbon dioxide (CO2) emissions, 2,
    10–11, 13
Carson, Rachel, 12, 16, 86
Carter, Jimmy, 17
Castro, Fidel, 41
Catechism of the Revolutionist
    (Nechaev), 1, 45, 109
Catell, Raymond, 64
Cell terrorist structure: and anarchy,
    80; autonomous, 95–96, 98–99,
    110; bottom-up process, 73; of
    Catholic revolutionaries, 59; con-
    trol of, 100–101; methods of, 45–47;
    mindset of, 71; motivations of, 88;
    of radical environmental move-
    ment, 84, 89, 92–93; of Sunni Islam,
    44–45; vulnerability of, 101–2,
    127–28
Center for Nonproliferation Studies,
    132
Center for Terrorism Law, 35
Centers for Disease Control and
    Prevention (CDC), 133–34
Central Intelligence Agency (CIA),
    162
Chalk, Peter, 99
Chaos principle, 49, 131–32, 137
Chavez, Hugo, 170
Chechen suicide bombers, 53
Chemical, biological, nuclear, and
    radiological weapons (CBNR), 54
Cheng I and Cheng I Sao, 125–26
Chernobyl nuclear facility, 17
Chesterton, G. K., 164
Chinese pirates, 125–26
Chiron Life Science Center, 102
Chlorofluorocarbons (CFCs), 9
Christian corsairs, 125, 144
Civil Disobedience (Thoreau), 78
Civil War terrorism, 40–41, 62
Climate change: deniers, 12–13; fire
    risks with, 24; GHG emissions, 99;
    global warming, 1–2, 13–14; impact
    of, 9–11, 18. *See also* Greenhouse
    gases (GHG)
*Climate Change and Its Possible Security
    Implications* (UN report), 22

Climate Conference in Copenhagen, 196
Clinton, Bill (administration), 16, 18, 172
Clostridium botulinum, 26, 133–34
Collins, Michael, 41
Column terrorist structure, 45–46
Combat Organization (CO), 45
Conference of Parties (COP), 9
Contagion effect, 87–88
Convention on the Law of the Seas, 94
Convention on the Prohibition of Military or Any Other Hostile Use of Environmental Modification Techniques, 15
Copenhagen Accord, 21, 196
Coronado, Ron, 90–91
Corporate terrorism, 166–68
Countermeasures for security planning, 183–93
Counterterrorism strategies, 37, 44, 149–51, 176
Cragin, Kim, 113
Craig, Jean, 156
Crazy terrorist, 67
Crenshaw, Martha, 49–50, 83–84
Criminal-terrorists, 43–44, 67, 93, 121–24. *See also* Organized crime; Robbery crimes
Critical infrastructure and key resources (CIKR), 171, 173
Cromwell, Oliver, 60
Crusader terrorist, 67, 68
Cuban revolution, 41–42
Czolgosz, Leon, 39

Darfur, Sudan, 21–22
Deep Ecology: Living As If Nature Mattered (Sessions, Devall), 82–83
Deep ecology principle, 82–83, 96, 116
Deepwater Horizon disaster, 137
Defending Your Digital Assets (Nichols), 140–42
Defensive security planning, 6
Della Porta, Donatella, 66
Democratic Republic of the Congo (DRC), 176–78, 197

Department of Homeland Security, 138, 142–43, 169, 174
Devall, Bill, 82–83
Direct actions: by Animal Liberation Front, 101, 102–4; by Earth Liberation Front, 98, 101, 103–4
Disengagement technique of demonization, 69–70
Domestic terrorism, 36
Dostoevsky, Fyodor, 109
Douglas, John, 121

Earth Day, 8
Earth First! group, 80–81, 84–85, 91, 96–97
Earth Liberation Front (ELF): and antiglobalism, 117; direct actions by, 98, 101, 103–4; founding of, 97–99; ideology of, 98, 99–100; Operation Bite Back, 91; and radical environmental movement, 4, 85, 92; tactics of, 185; Vail Mountain fires by, 165–66
Ecodefense: A Field Guide to Monkeywrenching (Foreman), 80–81, 104–5
Ecological Society of America, 79
Economic jihad concept, 24
Ecosystem, 2, 11, 29–30. *See also* Environment
Ecoterrorism: capabilities of, 145; case analysis of, 157–58; deep ecology principle, 82–83, 96; goal of, 16; groups, 4; and invasive species, 30; by nihilistic terrorists, 26, 74, 133; species killing, 29; tactics of, 183, 184–85; targets of, 93. *See also* Environmental terrorism; Radical environmental movement (REM)
Eco-warriors, 76, 87, 89, 93, 96, 196. *See also* Ecoterrorism; Environmental terrorism; Radical environmental movement (REM); Terrorist(s)
Eco-Warriors: Understanding the Radical Environmental Movement (Scarce), 93
Ehrlich, Paul and Anne, 61–62
Eibl-Eibesfeldt, Irenäus, 62–63
Emerson, Ralph Waldo, 77
Environment: controversy surrounding, 12–13; defined, 2; and human

conflicts, 14–16, 18; pollution in, 8–9, 11; and public opinion polls, 13–14; security of, 16–19. *See also* Climate change; Greenhouse gases (GHG)

Environment Program (UNEP), 9, 18–19

Environmental Protection Agency (EPA), 8

Environmental terrorism: on corporations, 166–68; defined, 4; growth of, 8–9; history of, 14–16; by Iraq, 15; and National Security Strategy, 19–21; targets of, 15–16, 26–32; UN's position on, 21–23; weapons of, 23–26. *See also* Ecoterrorism; Radical environmental movement (REM); Security planning

Epistemic uncertainty, 140

Escherichia coli (E-coli), 26, 134

European terrorism, 38–39

Euskadi Ta Askatasuna (ETA), 64

Evan Mecham Eco-Terrorist International Conspiracy (EMETIC), 117

Exceptional Case Study Project (ECSP), 154–56

Explosively formed projectiles (EFPs), 56

External environment security planning, 175–83

Falk, Richard, 35

Family terrorist group, 101–2, 105, 151–52, 157–58

FARC. *See* Revolutionary Armed Forces of Colombia (FARC)

Fathers and Sons (Turgenev), 109

Fawkes, Guy, 59–60

Federal Bureau of Investigation (FBI): criminal terrorist groups, 123; failure of, 162; and the Internet, 113; investigations by, 7, 36–37, 101–2, 151–52; Joint Terrorism Task Forces, 5, 87; and loan wolf terrorists, 119; Most Wanted Terrorists list, 4, 103; Operation Backfire, 101–2, 105, 166; and radical environmental movement, 86; security tactics of, 190; and trait trilogy, 66

Ferdinand, Franz, 40

Field desertification, 11

Firefighting concerns, 28–29

Flynt, Larry, 121

Food chain attacks, 25–26

Forces for Liberation of Rwanda (FLR), 177

Ford, Gerald, 155–56

Foreign Intelligence Surveillance Act (FISA), 36–37

Foreman, Dave, 80–81, 91

Fortuyn, Pim, 75–76

Framework Convention on Climate Change (UNFCCC), 9, 18

Franklin, Benjamin, 121

Franklin, Joseph Paul, 120–21

Freedom fighters, 35

Frelinger, David, 144–45

Freud, Sigmund, 63–64

Friedman, Thomas, 1

Fromme, Lynette "Squeaky," 155–56

Front de Libération Nationale (FLN), 48

Fund for Animals, 94

German Red Army Faction (RAF), 47, 64

Gillis, Justin, 195

Glacier melt, 22–23

Gleick, Peter, 18

Glen Canyon Dam, 80, 97

Global warming, 1–2, 13–14

Goebbels, Joseph, 121

Goldwater, Barry, 80

Goodstein, Leonard, 169–71, 174

Gore, Al, 18

Great Terror, 34

Greenhouse gases (GHG): carbon dioxide (CO2) emissions, 2, 10–11, 13; and climate change, 99; effects of, 9–11; halocarbons, 2; methane (CH4), 2; nitrous oxide (N2O), 2; reduction of, 21; standards for, 13; and terrorism, 2

Greenpeace, 81–82, 94

Group terrorists. *See* Terrorist(s), groups

Gulf War, 15

Gurr, Ted, 65–66

Guthrie, Richard, 122

Hacker, Frederick, 67–69
Halocarbons, 2
Hamas terrorists, 23–24
Hare, Robert, 67
Harvey, Michael, 186–87
Hasan, Nidal Malik, 33, 119
Hasan-i Sabbah, 44–45
Heuer, Richards, 163
Hezbollah terrorists, 23–24, 73
Hijacking tactics, 52–53
Himalayan glacier melt, 22–23
Hobbes, Thomas, 58–61, 63
Hoffer, Eric, 65
Hoffman, Bruce, 35, 66
Hofstad group, 108, 110–11, 113–15
Horgan, John, 64–65
Hoskins, Richard, 128
Human cognitive problems, 162–63
Human conflicts, 14–16, 18
Hunter (Pierce), 120, 128
Huntingdon Life Science (HLS), 102
Hutaree militant group, 56–57, 145–46
Hybrid terrorist groups, 44

Ideology: of Earth Liberation Front,
   99–100; of jihadism, 70–71; of lone
   wolf terrorists, 66, 70; of nihilistic
   terrorists, 5, 46, 111–13; of radical
   environmental movement, 99–100
Improvised explosive devices (IEDs),
   56, 135, 146
Improvised incendiary devices (IIDs),
   157
Individual motivation violence, 88–93
Infrastructure importance, 171–72
Inhofe, James, 12
Intergovernmental Panel on Climate
   Change (IPCC), 3, 9–10, 22, 195–96
International Maritime Organization
   (IMO), 126
International People's Court of Retri-
   bution, 155–56
International terrorism, 36–37
Internet for terrorism, 84, 113–14
Intimidation principle, 48–49
Iraq, 15, 72
Irish nationalism, 41
Irish Republican Army (IRA), 41, 44,
   45–46

Ishutin, Nikolai, 110
Islamic terrorists, 43, 73, 107–8. *See
   also* Jihadism; Sharia (Islamic Law)
Israel, 23–24
ITERATE Database, 187
Ivins, Bruce, 27, 53, 121, 131, 133

Jackson, Brian, 100, 144–45
Japan, 94
J-curve theory, 170
Jenkins, Brian, 50, 119
Jihadism: arson attacks by, 130; economic jihad concept, 24; ideology
   of, 70–71; and nihilistic terrorists,
   107–8, 118; oil/gas industry attacks
   by, 135–36; organizational structure
   of, 44; radicalization, 72–73; as religious terrorism, 43; Salafist
   jihadism, 73, 112–13, 118, 148–49;
   security planning for, 190; tactics
   of, 48. *See also* Al Qaeda terrorists
Joint Terrorism Task Forces, 5, 87
Jonathan Troy (Abbey), 80
Jones, James, 20
Jordan, Vernon, 121
Juergensmeyer, Mark, 35

Kabila, Laurent, 178
Kaczynski, Theodore, 44, 51, 121, 148
Kahneman, Daniel, 163
Kaplan, Robert, 17
Karakozov, Dmitry, 110
Karen National Liberation Army
   (KNLA), 124
Katz, Jack, 89
Khalil, Lafi, 146
Kidnappings, 53, 168, 183, 191–92
Kilcullen, David, 149
Kirk, David, 188
Klare, Michael, 177–78
Krebs, Valdis, 188–89
Ku Klux Klan (KKK), 42, 46, 95, 121
Kyoto Protocol, 9, 13, 18

Lane, David, 156
Langan, Peter, 122
Leaderless Jihad (Sageman), 112
Leaderless resistance, 46–47
Lee, James, 194–96

Leopold, Aldo, 79
Leviathan, The (Hobbes), 60
Liddick, Donald R., 99
Living Terrorism (Osterholm, Schwartz), 132
Lone wolf terrorists: and anarchism, 45; arson tactics by, 24–25; crazy terrorist as, 67; and environment, 5–7; ideology of, 66, 70; and the Internet, 84; mindset of, 55, 61, 63; as nihilistic, 119–21, 128, 196–97; and radical environmental movement, 93; violence by, 66, 74, 90
Lord's Resistance Army (LRA), 177–79
Ludwig, Wiebo, 32
Luers, Jeff "Free," 89, 91–92

Machiavelli, Niccolò, 58–61
Maltese (Christian) corsairs, 125, 144
Man and Nature (Marsh), 78
Manson, Charles, 155–56
Marighella, Carlos, 48, 63, 190
Maritime region concerns, 180–83
Marsh, George Perkins, 78
Marx, Karl, 39
Mathematical models for risk prediction, 163–64
Mathews, Robert Jay, 156
McGloin, Jean, 188
McKinley, William, 39
McVeigh, Timothy, 44, 51, 73, 120
Medical Research Institute of Infectious Diseases (USAMRIID), 131
Medici family, 58
Methane (CH4), 2
Methyl isocyanate (MIC), 167
Mezer, Gazi Abu, 146
Middle Eastern terrorists groups, 23–24
Milestones (Qutb), 111
Mind of the Terrorist, The (Post), 151
Mindset of terrorists, 57–58, 63, 88
Mining facility targets, 31
Mobuto Sese Seko, 178
Mobutu, Joseph, 178
Monkey Wrench Gang, The (Abbey), 80, 85, 96
Monkeywrenching, 80, 81, 85, 96, 104–5

Most, Johann, 51
Most Wanted Terrorists list, 103
Motivation of terrorist groups, 67–69, 88–93, 148–52, 196–97
Movement for the Emancipation of the Niger Delta (MEND), 179
Movement for the Survival of the Ogoni People (MOSOP), 179
Muir, John, 78–79
Mumbai terrorists, 50
Murphy, Hugh Leonard, 68
Muslim corsairs, 144

Narcotics trade, 124
Nasar, Mustafa Setmarian, 111–12
Nasser, Gamal Abdel, 111
National Academy of Sciences, 195
National Center for the Analysis of Violent Crime, 121
National Infrastructure Protection Plan (NIPP), 173
National Institute of Justice (NIJ), 153
Nationalist-terrorism, 40–41
National Liberation Army (ELN), 31–32
National Park System, 79
National Response Framework (NRF), 173–74
National Security Council, 20
National Security Strategy (NSS), 19–21, 32, 177
National Strategy for Homeland Security, 172–73
Native Americans, 14–15
Nazism, 121
Nechaev, Sergey, 1, 45, 109
Nechaev's edict, 5
New York Police Department (NYPD), 72–73, 112–13, 118
Nichols, Randall, 140–42
Nietzsche, Friedrich, 109
Nigeria, 179–80
Nihilistic terrorists: and anarchism, 48; Aryan Republican Army, 122–23; capabilities of, 145–47, 172; cell structure of, 110, 127–28; criminal hybrid groups, 43–44, 121–24; deep ecology principle, 116; ecoterrorism by, 26, 74, 133;

Hofstad group, 108, 110–11, 113–15; ideology of, 5, 46, 111–13; and jihadism, 107–8, 118; lone wolf terrorists as, 119–21, 128, 196–97; motivation of, 148, 196–97; organizations, 110–13; overview, 109–10; pirates as, 124–27; pre-attack threats of, 154–55; religion in, 111; RISE (Rising Sun) group, 118–19; security planning for, 184, 186, 189; strategy of, 127–28; tactics of, 24, 128–36, 152, 183, 185–86; targets of, 31–32; weapons of, 55
9/11 attack. *See* September 11, 2001
9/11 Commission, 138, 168–69
Nitrous oxide (N2O), 2
Nobel, Alfred, 50
Nolan, Timothy, 169, 174
Nongovernment organizations (NGOs), 6, 176
Nonviolent civil disobedience, 104

Obama, Barack (administration), 20
Oil/gas industry attacks, 31–32, 135–36, 137–39
Oklahoma City bombing, 44, 51, 73, 120
Olympic Games, 6
Operational security, 146–47
Operation Backfire (FBI), 101–2, 105, 166
Operation Bite Back, 91
Organization of Petroleum Exporting Countries (OPEC), 16
Organized crime, 43, 52, 60, 67, 127, 149, 152, 188
Oromo Liberation Front, 54–55
Oso Complex Fire, 24
Osterholm, Michael, 132

Palestine, 40
Palestine Liberation Organization (PLO), 42
Palmer, A. Mitchell, 39
Patriot Act, 37
Peace Conquerors, 167
Pelton, Robert Young, 178
Pera, Steven J., 118–19
Personality profiling, 64, 66, 100, 131

Personal protection, 191–93
Pesticide concerns, 12, 167
Pew Center on Global Climate Change, 186
Pfeiffer, William, 169, 174
Phantom cell structure, 95
Pickering, Leslie James, 117
Pierce, Bruce, 156
Pierce, William, 120, 128
Pinchot, Gifford, 79
Pinker, Stephen, 61
Piracy, 124–27, 144
Poisoning concerns, 25–27, 30–31
Political terrorism, 88, 120–21
Pollution concerns, 8–9, 11, 14, 27–28
Popular Front for the Liberation of Palestine (PFLP), 52
Post, Jerrold, 64, 70–71, 151
Pre-attack threats, 152–56
Prediction problems, 162–64
Prince, The (Machiavelli), 58–59
Princip, Gavrilo, 40
Private enterprise perspective, 168–71
"Propaganda by deed," 48
Proudhon, Pierre-Joseph, 39
Provocation violence, 48, 87
Psychodynamic theories, 63–64
Psychology of Intelligence Analysis (Heuer), 163
Psychopathic terrorists, 67–69
Publicity violence, 86–87
Public-private partnership, 171–75
Pyro-terrorism. *See* Arson attacks

Qutb, Sayyid, 111

Racist terrorism, 121
Radical environmental movement (REM): causation process in, 83–86; cell structure of, 100–102; deep ecology principle, 82–83, 96, 116; enabling preconditions with, 85–86; ideology of, 99–100; learning ability of, 147–48; and lone wolf terrorists, 93; organizations in, 93–102; overview, 4, 75–76; philosophical foundation of, 76–83; pre-attack indicators of, 154; tactics by, 102–6; tolerance of, 84–85; and violence,

86–93. *See also specific terrorist groups*
Radicalization process, 72–74, 113
Rajneeshees cult, 26, 27
RAND Corporation, 99, 113, 119, 144, 147
Rapoport, David, 70
Raymond, Gregory, 49
Reactionary-terrorism, 42
Reagan, Ronald (administration), 8–9, 96
Red Army Faction (RAF), 122
Red Scare raids, 39–40
Reed, Richard, 51
Religious-terrorism, 43, 66, 69, 70, 111
REM. *See* Radical environmental movement (REM)
Revolutionary Armed Forces of Colombia (FARC), 31–32, 44, 123–24
Revolutionary Cells—Liberation Brigade, 4
Revolutionary Force 9, 117
Revolutionary ideology, 99–100
Revolutionary-terrorism, 42
Ricin poison, 54
RISE (Rising Sun) group, 118–19
Risk assessment, 5–6, 136, 138–64, 170
Risk assessments, 143–45
Robbery crimes, 49, 122, 152, 181
Rock python concerns, 30
Roosevelt, Theodore, 39, 79
Ross, John, 120
Rudolph, Eric, 6, 121
Russian Socialist Revolutionary Party, 45
Rwanda, 178

Sagebrush Rebellion, 96
Sageman, Marc, 73–74, 112
Salafist jihadism, 73, 112–13, 118, 148–49
Salmonella enterica (serovar Typhi), 26, 27, 134
San Diego, Daniel Andreas, 3–4, 103
Sand Country Almanac, A (Leopold), 79
Sandoval, Raymond Anthony, 24
Sarin gas, 28, 55
Scarce, Rik, 93

Schneier, Bruce, 171, 175
Schwander, Allen, 118–19
Schwartz, Daniel, 15
Schwartz, John, 132
Scutari, Richard, 156
Sea Shepherd Conservation Society (SSCS), 81–82, 90, 94–95, 100
Secret Service (U.S.), 154–56
Security Council (UN), 126
Security planning: countermeasures for, 183–93; and external environment, 175–83; general concepts of, 184; overview, 5–7, 165–68; personal protection, 191–93; private enterprise perspective, 168–71; proactive detection, 187–93; process of, 168–75; social network analysis, 113, 187–89; specific defenses for, 186–87; surveillance/counter-surveillance, 189–91; and tactical choices, 184–86
Seductions of Crime, The (Katz), 89
Self-radicalized terrorists, 72, 74
September 11, 2001, 51–52, 73, 119, 138, 168–69
Serbian Nationalist Society, 40
Sessions, George, 82–83
Shankill Butchers, 68
Sharia (Islamic law), 43, 112, 115
Shigella dysenteriae, 26, 134
Shiite Muslims, 44–45
Shnewer, Mohamed, 7
Sicarii sect, 38, 48
Sierra Club, 79, 94
Silent Spring (Carson), 12, 16, 86
Single-issue terrorism, 43
Sirius Star hijack, 127
Smith, Brent, 153–54
Social network analysis (SNA), 113, 187–89
Solomon, Susan, 195
Standard risk management (SRM), 142
"State terror," 38
Sterns, Jessica, 131–32
Stop Huntingdon Animal Cruelty (SHAC), 102–3
Strait of Hormuz, 183
Strait of Malacca, 183
Suicide bombers, 51–53, 121, 141, 145

Sun Tzu, 1, 7
Sunni Muslims, 44, 111
Surveillance/countersurveillance, 189–91

Takfiri Islam, 108
Taleb, Nicholas, 162
Taliban terrorists, 25
Tamil Tigers terrorists, 25
Targets: of ecoterrorism, 93; of environmental terrorism, 15–16, 26–32; mining facilities as, 31; vulnerability of, 158–60
Terror in the Mind of God (Juergensmeyer), 35
Terrorism: age variable in, 88–89; counterterrorism strategies, 37, 44, 149–51, 176; defined, 4, 34–36; the Internet for, 113; oil/gas industry attacks, 135–36, 137–39; organization structure of, 44–47; organized crime as, 43, 52, 60, 67, 127, 149, 152, 188; overview, 196–97; piracy as, 124–27, 144; radicalization process of, 72–74; revolutionary, 42; security planning against, 5–7; statistics on, 176–77; statutory definitions, 36–37; tactics, 50–55; typology of, 37–44; during World War II, 41, 51, 62. *See also* Ecoterrorism; Environmental terrorism
Terrorism, risks: analysis of, 141–42; assessment of, 5–6, 136, 138–64, 170; kidnappings, 53, 168, 183, 191–92; management of, 140–41; mathematical models for, 163–64; and methodology, 160–62; overview, 139–40; prediction problems with, 162–64; and prediction strategies, 143–44; tactical choices of, 184–86; threat assessments, 143–45
Terrorist(s): arson tactics by, 53–54, 92, 98, 105; vs. freedom fighters, 35; groups, 7, 44, 70–72; mindset, 57–58, 63, 88; motivations of, 67–69; nihilistic, 26, 32; strategy of, 47–50; suicide bombers, 51–53, 121, 141, 145; traits of, 65–66; urban guerrillas as, 50; weapons of, 26–27. *See*

also Cell terrorist structure; Lone wolf terrorists; Nihilistic terrorists; *and individual terrorists; specific terrorist groups*
Terrorist(s), groups: capabilities and resources, 145–47; learning ability of, 147–48; motivation of, 148–52; pre-attack indicators, 152–53; and target vulnerability, 158–60. *See also* Radical environmental movement (REM)
Thoreau, Henry David, 77–78
Threat scenario analysis, 160–61
Thurber, Mark, 168
Top-down radicalization, 72–74
Toxic Terror (Tucker), 156–57
Toxic waste, 14
Trait theory, 64–66
Trans-Alaska Pipeline, 135
Transcendentalism, 77–78
Trinitrotoluene (TNT), 51
True Believer, The (Hoffer), 65
"True believer" terrorist, 65
Trujillo, Horace, 147
Tuchman-Mathews, Jessica, 17
Tucker, Jonathan, 132, 156–57
Turgenev, Ivan, 109
Turner Diaries, The (Pierce), 120, 128
Tversky, Amos, 163
Tyrannicide, 38

Uganda, 178–79
Ulster Defense Association, 42, 122
Ulster Volunteer Force (UVF), 68
Ultimate Terrorists, The (Sterns), 131–32
Unintended Consequences (Ross), 120
Union Carbide, 167
Union of Soviet Socialist Republics (USSR), 17
Union Oil Company disaster, 86
United Nations (UN): Convention on the Law of the Seas, 94; Convention on the Prohibition of Military or Any Other Hostile Use of Environmental Modification Techniques, 15; defining terrorism, 35; Environment Program, 9, 18–19; environmental position of, 21–23;

Framework Convention on Climate
  Change, 9, 18; Intergovernmental
  Panel on Climate Change, 3, 9–10,
  22; Security Council, 126; World
  Charter for Nature, 95
United States v. Keith, 36
Unmanned aerial vehicle (UAV), 135
Urban guerrillas, 50
UVB radiation, 9

Vail Mountain fires, 165–66
Van der Graaf, Volkert, 75–76
Van Gogh, Theo, 107–8, 114
Vehicle bombs, 52, 185
Vietnam War, 15, 16, 62
Vigilantes of Christendom (Hoskins),
  128
Violence: aptitude for, 61–65; direct
  actions of, 103–4; justification for,
  69–70; by lone wolf terrorists, 66,
  74, 90; philosophy of, 58–61; against
  property, 84–85; provocation for, 48,
  87; for publicity, 86–87; reasons for,
  86–93; as terrorist trait, 66
Virunga Mountain gorillas, 29

Volya, Narodnaya, 45
Vulnerability assessment methodology, 159–60

Walters, Jason, 113–14
Water concerns, 2, 25, 27, 30–32
Watson, Paul, 81–82, 94
Weapons of mass destruction (WMD),
  23, 27, 53, 54–55
*Week on the Concord and Merrimack
  Rivers, A* (Thoreau), 77
White supremacy, 44
Why Men Rebel (Gurr), 65
Wilderness preservation efforts, 97
Wildlands attacks, 28–29, 129–30
Will, George, 12
Wilson, Woodrow, 39
World Charter for Nature, 95
World Meteorological Organization
  (WMO), 9
World War II terrorism, 41, 51, 62
World's Most Dangerous Places, The
  (Pelton), 178

Zubair, Abu, 107–8

About the Author

LAWRENCE E. LIKAR is an associate professor and chair of the Department of Justice, Law, and Security at La Roche College. Over the last 10 years he has taught courses involving terrorism, security planning, criminal deviance, law, and the environment. From 2006 to 2008, he was a security consultant and senior risk advisor on crime and terrorism to the Hilb Rogal and Hobbs Company. Prior to his academic career, Lawrence E. Likar spent 23 years with the FBI. During his FBI career, he served at various times as a senior SWAT leader, crisis negotiator, and field office coordinator for the National Center for the Analysis of Violent Crime. In 1985, he was the operational planner for the FBI's arrests of members of the Machetero terrorist organization. He ended his FBI career as the supervisory special agent of the Violent Crimes and Major Offenders Squad in the Pittsburgh Division. He is also a former A-Team member in the U.S. Army's Special Forces. He has appeared as a commentator and guest expert on the CNN and FOX news networks.